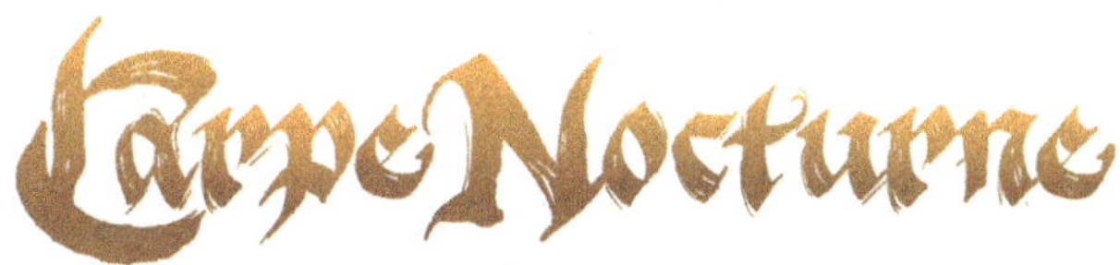

ARTS

ENTERTAINMENT

FASHION

FILM AND LITERATURE

INTERVIEWS

LIFE AND STYLE

MUSIC

REVIEWS

TECHNOLOGY

Carpe Nocturne Magazine
Volume X • Spring 2015
is a publication of Visual Adjectives, LLC and published four times a year.
All reviews and coverage expressed in this publication are the opinions of the writer and/or
those being interviewed and may not be shared by Visual Adjectives.
Copyright © 2015 by Visual Adjectives, LLC. All rights reserved. April 2015.
14280 Military Trail, #7501, Delray Beach, FL 33482, USA.
No work may be copied or reproduced without the express permission of the editor or publisher.
Correspondence should be addressed to:
Visual Adjectives
ATTN: Publisher, Carpe Nocturne Magazine
14280 Military Trail, #7501, Delray Beach, FL 33482, USA.
E-mail: editor@carpenocturnemagazine.com
www.carpenocturnemagazine.com
561-809-3834.

SUBSCRIBE AND SAVE

Name *(Print)*

Address 1 *(Print)*

Address 2 *(Print)*

City/State/Zip *(Print)*

Phone *(Print)*

❑ Digital $10.00
❑ Print $30.00
❑ Print and Digital $36.00

❑ Bill me!
❑ Check/money order enclosed.

Charge: ❑MC ❑Visa ❑Amex ❑Disc

Card# *(Print)*

Exp. Date *(Print)*

Signature
You will be contacted before processing.

SAVE NOW ON Digital and Print Edition!

❑ **Yes, I would like to sign up for your monthly newletter.**

Email *(Print)*

Mail to:
Carpe Nocturne Magazine
ATTN: Subscribe
14280 Military Trail, #7501
Delray Beach, FL 33482

Carpe Nocturne is published 4 times a year. The cover price is $12.95. Canada add $9 per year, all other countries $15 per year. Must be paid in U.S. funds.

Carpe Nocturne

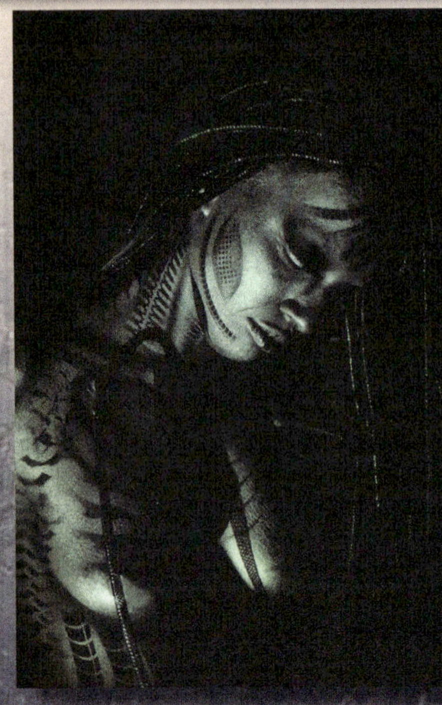

ON OUR COVER
*Model: Luna Minuit,
Read more on page 44.
'Giger' page 72.*

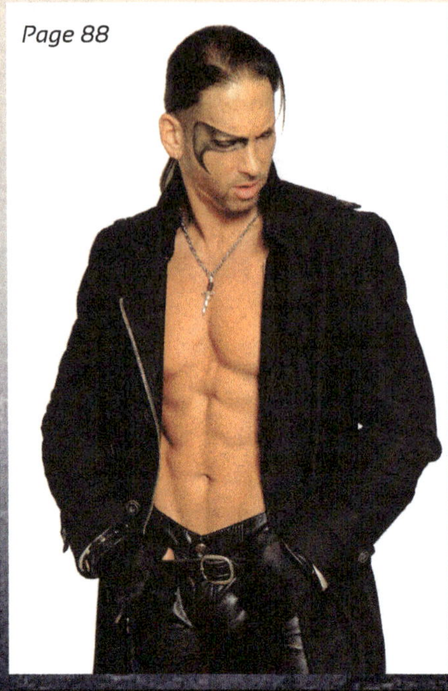

Page 88

FEATURES

INTERVIEWS

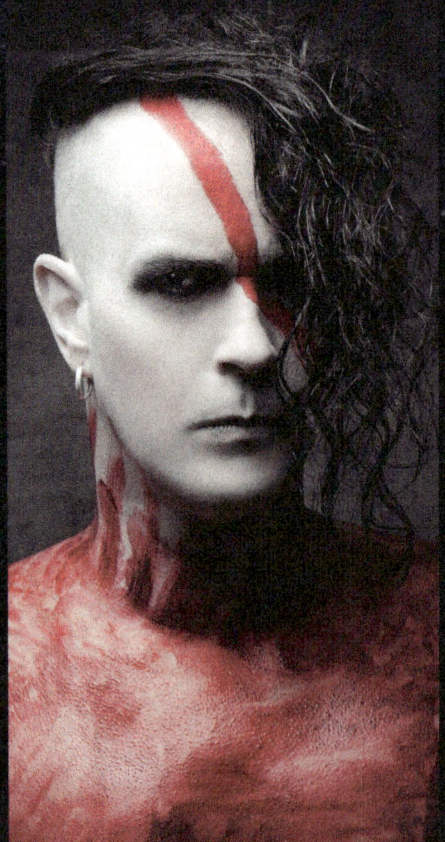

Page 110

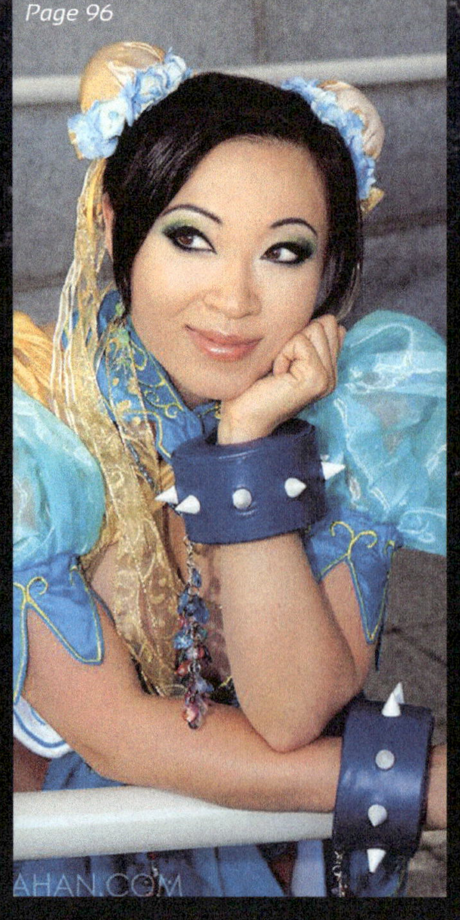

Page 96

OTHER THAN THE NORM

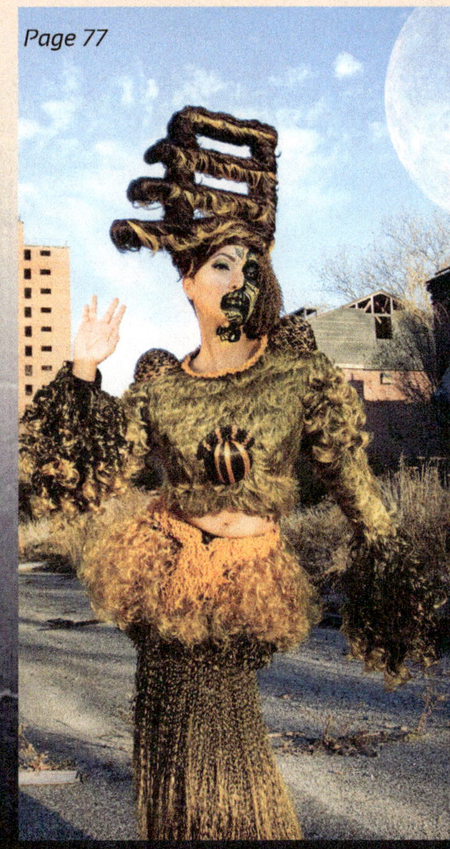

Page 77

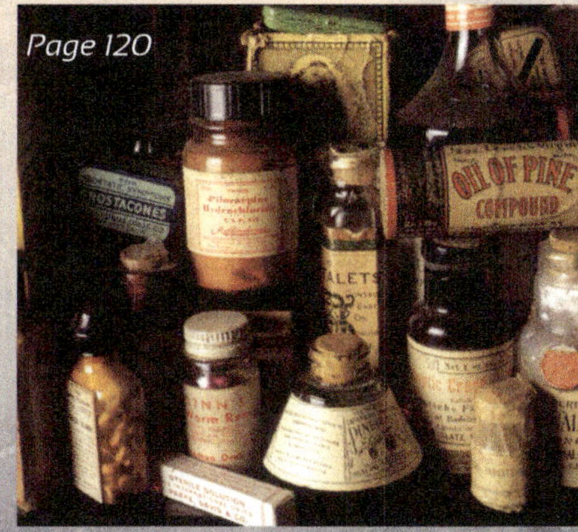

Page 120

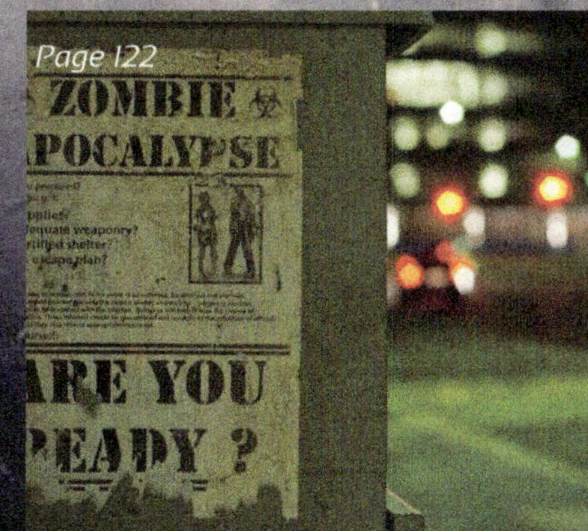

Page 122

REGULARS

REVIEWS

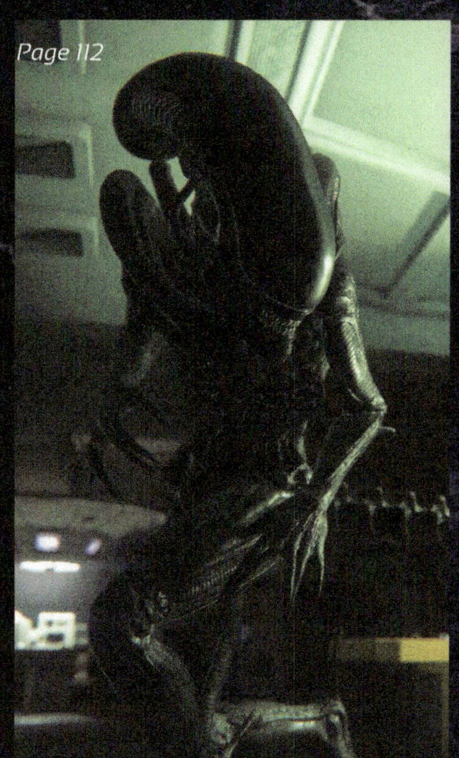

Page 112

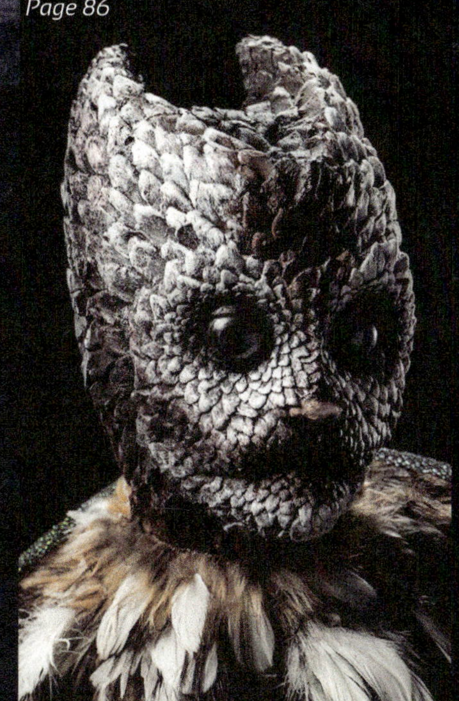

Page 86

FROM THE EDITOR

Open your mind to the vastness that is the universe and the depth that is consciousness.

Welcome to the Sci-Fi issue of Carpe Nocturne.

In this issue, we focus on the expanse that is the science fiction segment of the Creative Culture. Whether it is from the edgy depth of the techno funk, groove, and rhythm from the plethora of music in the genre, or even the costumes imagined from the minds of people with ideas that go beyond our world, we will strive to always provide unique experiences with Carpe Nocturne Magazine and its contents.

With the release of our first Sci-Fi issue, we are proud to show the contributions with many old and new fans of the magazine. The staff has worked hard to produce this magazine and furnish it with articles, spotlights, reviews, interviews, and galleries of many different parts of the Sci-Fi Creative Culture.

We are always grateful for the support that our community has been giving us. The immense amount of work that the writers and editors of the magazine put into it will continue to represent our own artistic values and quality in relation to the magazine.

Please, feel free to contact us about any questions, comments, concerns, suggestions, or complaints you may have with the magazine so that we can make it better and better and even better still.

We are honored to have you read our work of art, and we thank you for your support!

Michelle Lawrence,
Publisher
mlawrence@carpenocturne.net

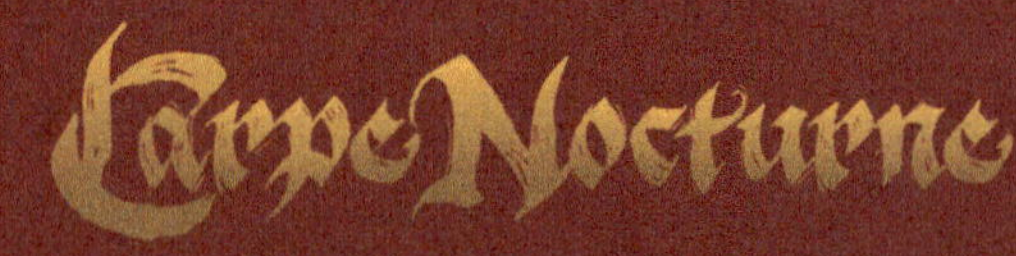

CREDITS

Publisher
Michelle Lawrence

Managing Editor
Michael Jack

Layout and Design
Annabella Rios

FEATURE EDITORS

Art
Zahara

Entertainment
Fairlyinnocent

Fashion
Kathleen Sharkey

Film and Literature
LinnieSarah Helpern

Life and Style
XXX Zombieboy XXX

Music
Michael Jack

CONTRIBUTORS

Asylum Attendant
Chirality
Dawn Wood
Isolde de Mortimer
Jezibell Anat
K.A. Morris
Katie Mckensie
River Gareth
Sergio Manghina
Sonnett57
Yasaman Vrd'dhi

Bob Donovan
Founder

Corporate Goth

By Chirality

I will start this off by saying I am VERY lucky. I work full time. We are allowed to display tattoos and piercings, tastefully of course. Since we have this freedom, there is no need to go overboard. We also have a uniform, so there is no question on what to wear. I am also lucky because I have a boss who is gothic. We will sit and talk about things she cannot talk to others about. I took the polite approach when I started working there. I asked what was acceptable and what wasn't. I even went so far as to let them know I would take out what they did not approve of, or wear long sleeves. I myself have 16+ tattoos and 6 piercings.

I know people are not so lucky. I have not gotten many jobs due to my appearance. My resume was pristine, but it did not matter. They took one look at my snakebite piercings, and that was that. Needless to say, they are gone. I am not saying you cannot be yourself, but in order for us to get where we want, the sad truth is, we must compromise, especially when you want to work more corporate or high end positions. I know we all want to be the artist, musician, etc. but we all know the sad truth.

I read the term "Corporate Goth" once before, and thought it was great. The person who Monday through Friday is suit and tie, yet when the weekend hits, watch out. It is a little sad we have had to "hide" ourselves due to what the public deems acceptable. I for one think that bleach blond hair and hot pink lipstick should be a felony, but that is just me.

It's NOT fair. I know some people reading are thinking "Fuck this. I will do what I want!" They say this now, but when there is no money to not only to pay bills, but to buy that corset you want... trust me, sometimes doing what you want is no longer valid. Now I am not saying you should drive a minivan and throw everything you like into the wind. I am just saying sometimes you have to do what you have to do. There is good news though! There are ways to not lose yourself while kicking ass at the same time!

Clothes do not fully make us Goth, so we need to address how we survive. How do we deal with those whose conversations are about little Johnny's soccer practice or The Real Housewives? It's quite easy, but I know sometimes it can be tough. Just remember to never take yourself too seriously. If someone pokes fun, poke back gently, or laugh with them. In time, when they know you, the stereotypes will be shattered. Remember to always be professional. Your behavior will outweigh your attire. There is no reason to try and scare people at work. Don't do it! As funny as it would be, it's not worth that pink slip.

The long and short of this is: You can still be you and work at a corporate place. Do not let anyone tell you that you are a sell out! Goths have bills to pay as well!!

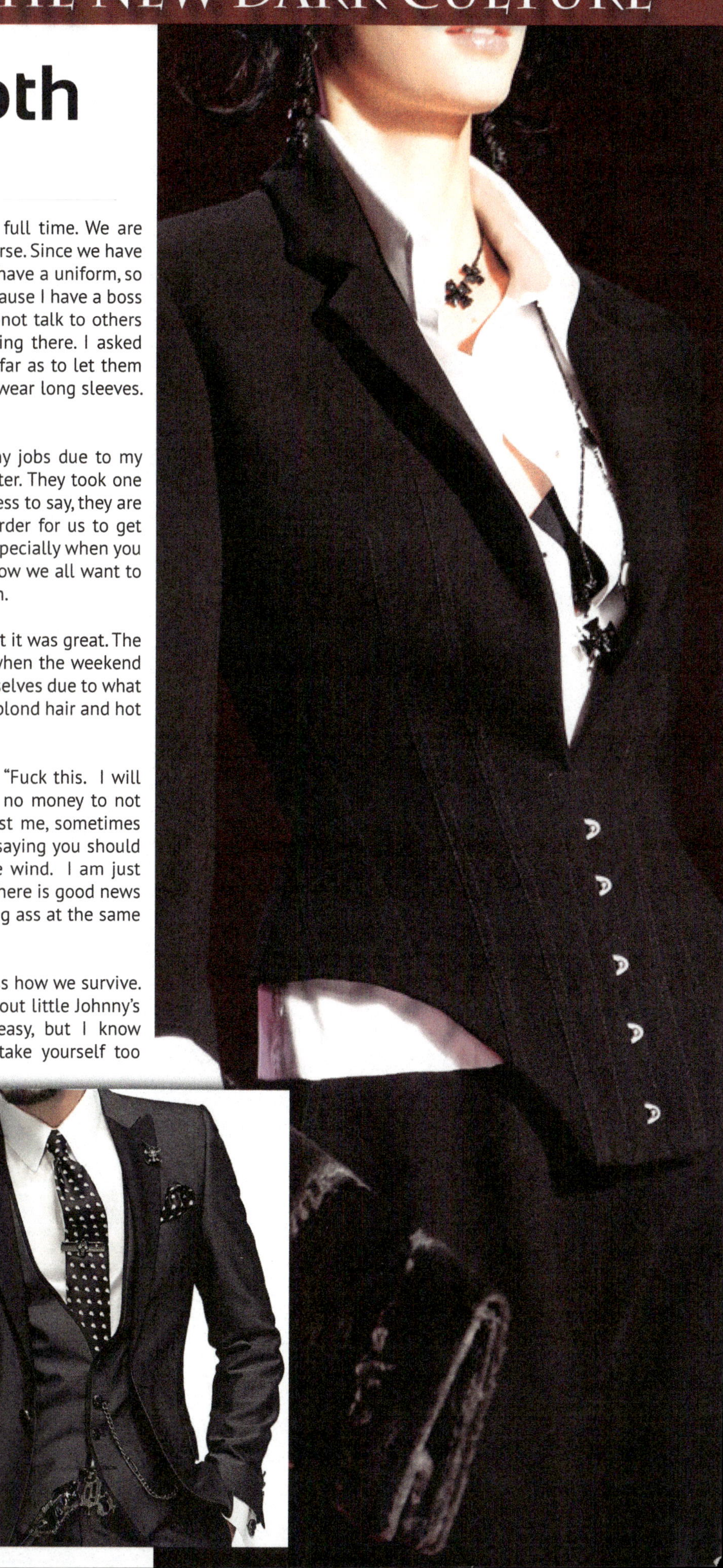

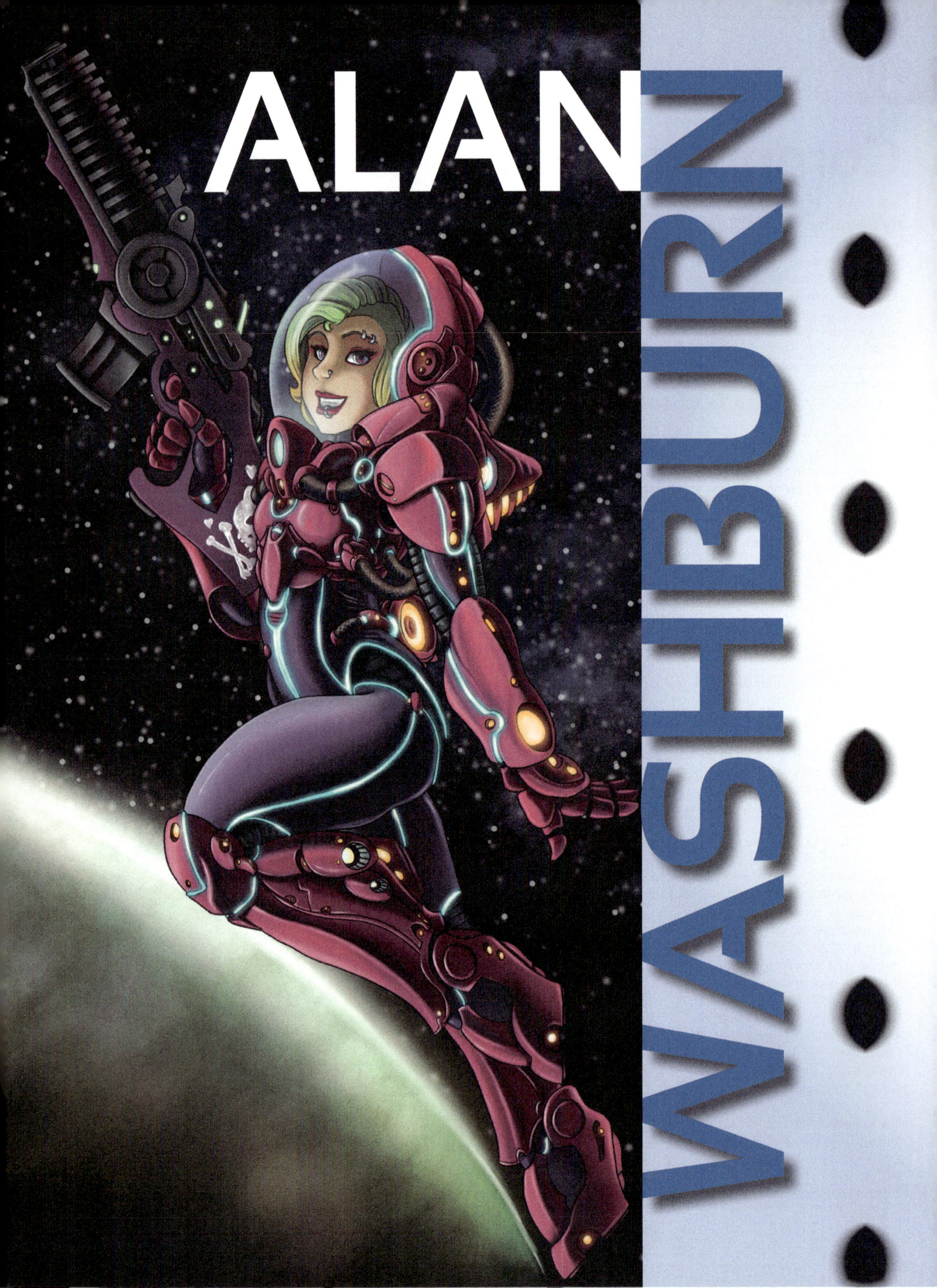

ALAN
WASHBURN

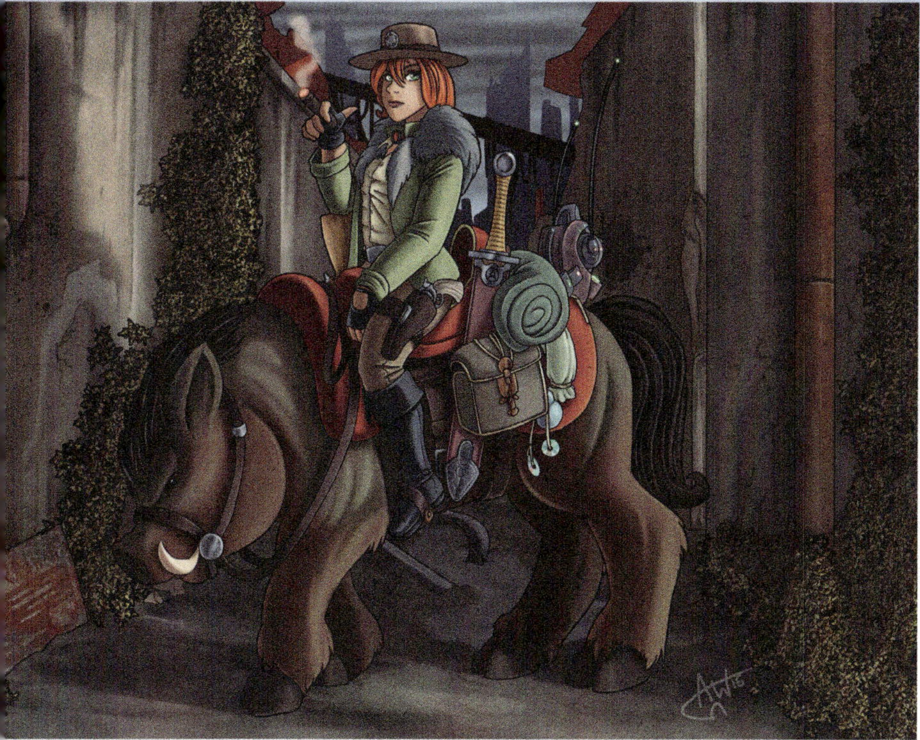

By Kathleen Sharkey

[Carpe Nocturne] *First could you introduce yourself to our readers?*

[Alan Washburn] My name is Alan Washburn. I am a freelance graphic designer and digital artist working in Reno, Nevada, though I serve clients from all around the country. I don't have any formal education experience in the form of art school or college, though I have been drawing for most of my life.

[CN] *When did you start doing artwork?*

[Alan] As far back as I can remember, I've been drawing. I started when I was four, I believe, with drawing some artwork for my mom and dad.

[CN] *How has your artwork developed with the addition of computer art tools?*

[Alan] For the most part, my interests have always been with figure drawing. Up until expanding into digital work, I had briefly toyed with painting, but most of my work was plain gray scale pencil work. About a year ago, I decided to expand into using a Wacom tablet for the first time, and I haven't really looked back since. It has allowed me to bring a level of color and depth to my work that it previously didn't have.

[CN] *Do you prefer one medium over the other?*

[Alan] I would say currently I prefer the digital medium to others I've tried, but I am always interested in exploring new artistic methods.

[CN] *Where do you find your inspiration for your artwork?*

[Alan] Most often I find inspiration for my artwork in movies and video games, since I tend to work with primarily fantasy and sci-fi themes. I look to artwork from the past as well, with some of my favorite sources of inspiration being old pinups and Art Deco-styled works.

[CN] *Do you have a structure that you follow when creating your pieces of art or do you free form your work and then work from what comes naturally?*

[Alan] Since I primarily do figure drawing, most of my work will start with me laying down the foundation for the figure, getting it posted, and then filling in the details from there. Once I have the basic figure in place, though, I will often free form design elements off of concepts in my head, letting things change as I go. I try not to get too stuck in creating the exact image I have in my mind, but rather just let things come together while I work.

[CN] *Your art covers a myriad of different genres, do you have a favorite genre?*

[Alan] I would say that my favorite genre is science fiction, though most of the color work I've done up to this point has been fantasy-oriented. I find myself often commissioned for fantasy pieces over sci-fi.

[CN] *What do you find is the easiest genre to create for?*

[Alan] Following from the previous question, I find that fantasy is one of the easier genres to create for. There is a wide range of material for the genre to draw inspiration from and so many different elements can be encompassed under that umbrella.

[CN] *Do you have a favorite piece?*

[Alan] I wouldn't say so. I think that I am very happy with the outcome of all of my pieces, liking elements of each one more than others. I wouldn't say I've created something yet that I would consider my masterpiece.

[CN] *Do you have a genre you would like to do art for that you have never done before?*

[Alan] I would like to do more work with Art Deco-inspired pieces.

[CN] *Do you take requests?*

[Alan] I don't often take requests because of the time commitments my work often entails, but I do take commissions.

[CN] *What advice would you give to other artists just starting out?*

[Alan] If you are interested in drawing and art in general, you need to actually do it. Work on your forms, practice your art, and never be afraid to show your work to others. If you are creating any kind of art completely alone, then you only have your own thoughts an opinions on it to work with. Exposure means feedback, and while it won't all be positive, it absolutely will all be useful. Creativity and mastery do not happen in a vacuum.

That being said, practice is also key. If you are practicing, you will get better, no matter what you are working at. Any professional can tell you that you have to start somewhere, but more than that, you have to keep going. Passion is important, but nothing happens without action.

See more of Alan's artwork:

jackwrench.deviantart.com
jackwrench.tumblr.com

FILM

By **LinnieSarah** (@linnieloowho)

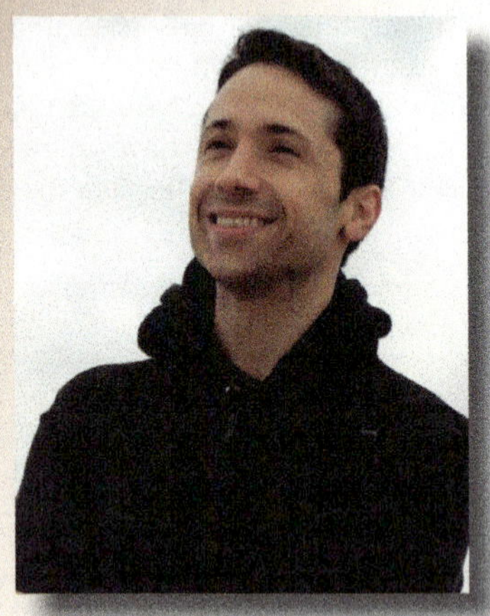

If you live and breathe horror movies (as many of us do), you know that many of the best fright films are coming from the world of independent filmmaking. On shoe-string budgets and limited time frames, indie directors and writers work at a breakneck pace to deliver original stories to the horror-loving masses. Actor/writer/director Dave Campfield is one of these intrepid visionaries and if you don't know about him (or Caesar and Otto) yet, it's time you learned…

[LinnieSarah] *For those who haven't had the pleasure of meeting Caesar and Otto, can you give us a little bio?*

[Dave] I was one of those kids who never fit in. Not good at sports, awkward, and uncomfortable in my own skin. Therein lie the beauty of the movies for me as a kid. It was my retreat. I could sit in darkness, and gaze up at the majestic images of people I wished I could be and places I longed to visit. As far as I see, it's the children that are the square pegs in the round hole of society that gravitate to the arts. I loved nothing more than cinema, and it was a world I yearned to be part of.

Armed with a script and demo reel, I managed to get an impromptu meeting at New Line Cinema at age twenty one. And to my chagrin, they were interested! But after a year of rewrites, I knew the writing was on the wall. My production was in limbo.

So, I took matters into my own hands and self produced the script on a microbudget. That first movie, Dark Chamber, was released in 2008, and began my venture into the world of uber-indie filmmaking.

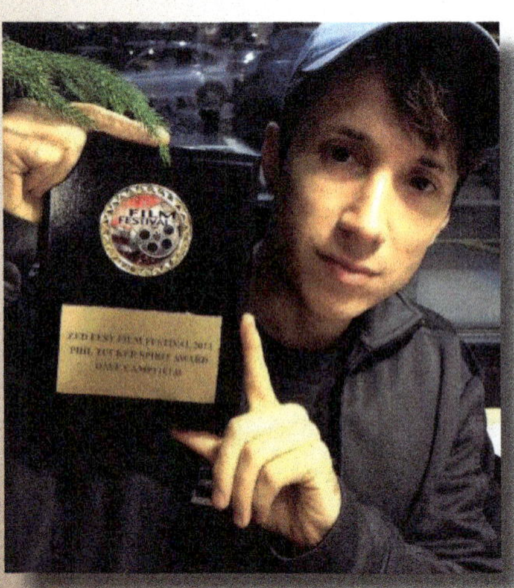

2011 saw the release of Caesar & Otto's Summer Camp Massacre. It was my first comedy-horror and a movie that introduced Trai Byers to the film-going public. He's now co-starring on Fox's Empire, and appeared in this year's Best Picture nominee Selma. Caesar & Otto's Deadly Xmas followed in 2013 and now Caesar & Otto's Paranormal Halloween in 2015.

[L] *How did you come to invent these characters?*

[D] Paul Chomicki (Otto) and I are friends from way back. We're both cinema junkies of the highest order. I'd always invite him over for on camera acting exercises (don't get the wrong idea you perv!). One night I came up with the characters of Caesar & Otto. The characters took root, and a couple of years later we made a $707 feature simply titled CAESAR & OTTO. Years later, a producer asked me for a comedy horror, and I pitched those same Caesar & Otto characters in a slasher film setting. Boom. Done. The comedy horror series began.

[L] *Your films are more loving homage than spoofs of the horror genre. What inspired you to make these movies?*

[D] I love comedy horror. Love it, damn it! Whether it's Abbott and Costello Meets Frankenstein, Ghostbusters, Shaun of the Dead, or any of the Simpsons Treehouse of Terror installments, it's a genre that I love to death. No pun intended. And since comedy duo/horror movies really aren't done in this day and age, I feel I'm delving into a niche that's underrepresented.

[L] *Your next movie is Caesar & Otto's Paranormal Halloween. What can you tell us about?*

[D] It's the Caesar & Otto take on the Haunted House genre. You know what that means: meta comedy, slapstick, lots of horror movie icon star cameos, and a dose of satire. Let's just say you'll see some of Caesar's dark side in this one.

[L] *Independent film seems to be where horror film is thriving these days. Can you ever imagine yourself working on a big budget film?*

[D] Absolutely. But until that day comes, I'm happy making movies on an ace rent a car budget.

[L] *What are your plans beyond Paranormal Halloween?*

[D] A new podcast named Production Hell, that delves into the horror show that is indie filmmaking, a new dramatic feature named FEAR THE REAPER (almost ten years in the making now), while doing any number of odd jobs for my favorite indie label, Wild Eye Releasing. Plus I have plans for at least one more Caesar & Otto feature.

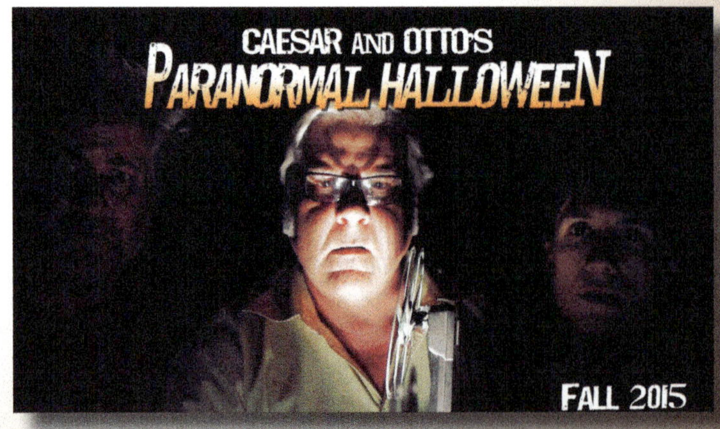

THE NEW ALBUM
BRAINDANCE
MASTER OF DISGUISE

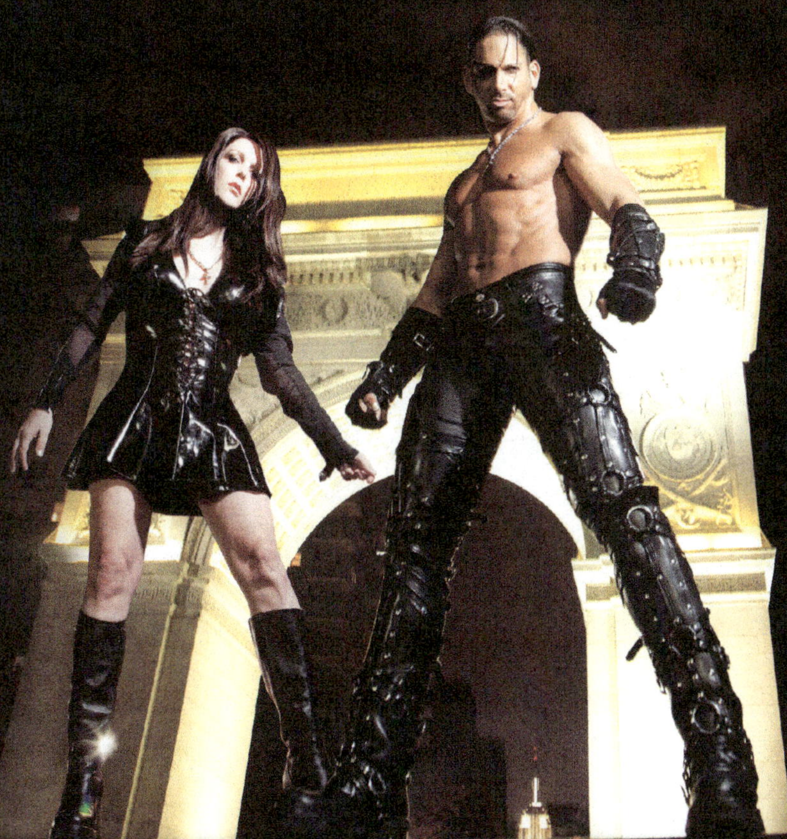

"TAKING THE DARK STYLE
IN NEW DIRECTIONS."
-BILLBOARD

"MAJOR LABEL MATERIAL
FROM THE UNDERGROUND."
-QUINTESSENCE

"THE FUSION OF PAST
AND FUTURE -
ABSOLUTELY UNIQUE."
-URANIUM

"PASSIONATE DELIVERY
WITHOUT COMPARISON."
-BW&BK

"A REMARKABLE ACHIEVEMENT
THAT'S LIGHT YEARS AHEAD."
-SEA OF TRANQUILITY

"A NEW RUNG ON THE
EVOLUTIONARY LADDER
OF MODERN MUSIC."
-PROGRESSION

"UNLIKE EVERYTHING
I'VE EVER HEARD THAT LEFT ME
BEGGING FOR MORE."
- PROGPOWER.COM

"A NEW PERSPECTIVE
ON THE MEANING OF
ORIGINALITY AND INNOVATION."
-MUSICIAN'S EXCHANGE

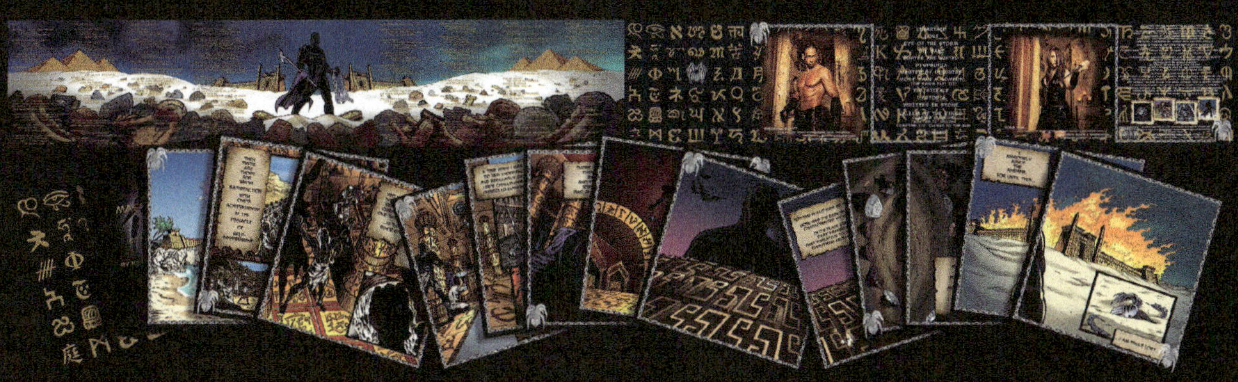

THE LONG-AWAITED RELEASE CONTAINING FIVE SINGLES,
AN EPIC TRILOGY AND GRAPHIC NOVELETTE - AVAILABLE NOW

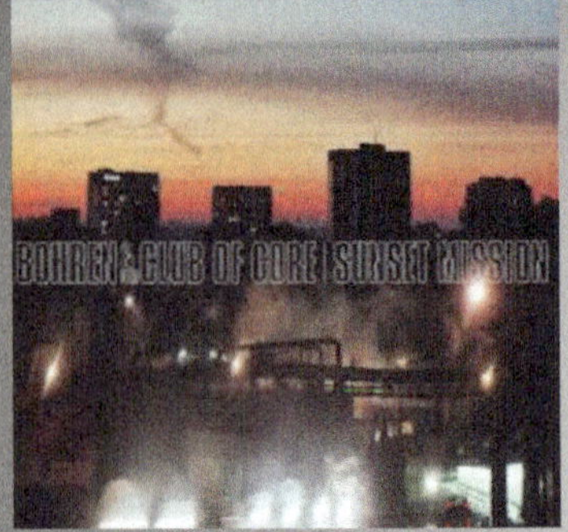

BOHREN & DER CLUB OF GORE
"SUNSET MISSION"
Label: WONDER
Year: 2000

There is an apparent quiet, something immaterial, trapped inside this ambient-jazz by Bohren & Der Club of Gore. If Lounge Lizards, John Zorn and Clock DVA, each in its own way, drew the soundtrack for imaginary urban-noir movies, with their sound oblique and neurotic, these skilled Germans have realized an introverted version of it, slow, shady and terribly nostalgic, ecstatic in its own alienated condition.

"Prowler", the first track, already contains into its kernel, all the remaining pieces and - together - the desire of this album to be loved or hated until the last beat. Soft touches of piano, almost imperceptibles brushes that swish on the drums, feeble and smoky rings of saxophone, vanishing like a sigh into the night air of a desert street, with evanescent neon lights immersed in the fog and then diluted in the pelting rain..Something like a dark symphony for lost souls.

CHAINED SHADOWS

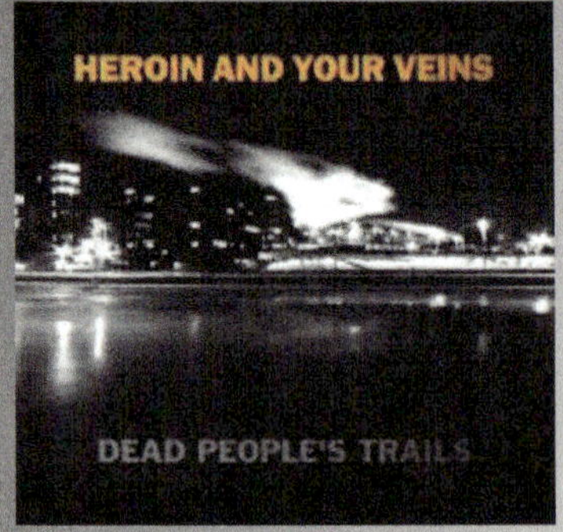

HEROIN AND YOUR VEIN
"DEAD PEOPLE'S TRAILS"
Label: Solina Records
Year: 2007

Heroin and Your Vein is the solo project of Janne Perttula who we already knew in an eclectic band called UltraNoir, and also author of some pretty interesting works, between post-rock and ambient jazz. This guy comes from Finland and always shows a formidable ability to dash catchy and dark-tinged melodies worthy of some comparison with Angelo Badalementi.

For example, it's very hard to resist the charm of a song like "Bad Luck", a quasi-waltz that seems to emerge from a plumbeous night of Twin Peaks and may induces an obsessive need for repeated listening, again and again. The scratchy twangy guitar carves impervious paths over a percussive and solemn beat in the background. And it is just the tip of the iceberg, the best track of an album marked by some absolutely fine musical arrangements, including the always incantatory reverb and vibrato effects, typical of the vintage surf guitar sound.

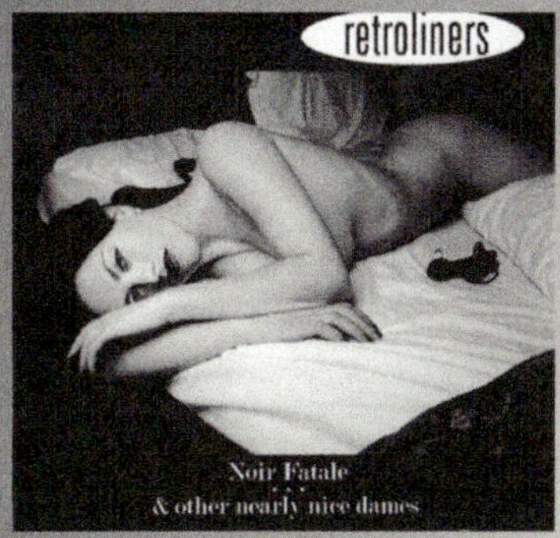

THE RETROLINERS
"NOIR FATALE"
Label: HOUSEHOLDER
Year: 2013

An irresistible mix of instrumental surf, rock, pop, punk, coloured in pure spy-cocktail style, between serious and funny. The Retroliners displace the incautious listener with their metronomic drumming, vintage Hammond & Wurlitzer keyboards and - above all - a savage assault of guitar twang. Perhaps less exotica respect to similar bands such as Aqua Velvets but absolutely 'noirish' in pieces like "Hotel Calibre", "Darkness Doubled", "Ms. St.", "Detour From The Usual", each title recalls a noir movie or a noir icon, as in the case of "Stalked By Stanwyck", dedicated to the immense actress Barbara Stanwyck.

A Gathering of Things in Noir Style

by SERGIO MANGHINA

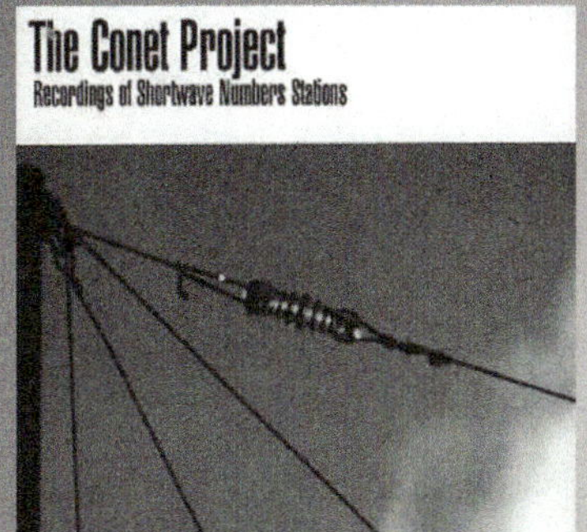

THE CONET PROJECT
Recordings of Shortwave Numbers Stations
Label: IRDIAL RECORDS
Year: 1997, 2013

This is more a spy thriller than a noir story. Endless sequences of numbers, letters of the alphabet with no apparent meaning, in English, French, German, Spanish, and then female voices or childish, mesmerizing jingles, next to electronic impulses. This is the door to another (parallel) dimension, a drug-free trip across the obsolete shortwaves.

It is only necessary to have a good transcontinental receiver, a lot of patience into a sleepless night, to discover the so-called numbers stations and their enigmatic signals, maybe communications between spies and several secret services. Otherwise, Irdial Records, a London based label devoted to avantgarde sounds, provides this fabulous five-disc edition, a mammoth collection of ethereal strangeness for passionate listeners and researchers as well as all the conspiracy theory lovers around the world.

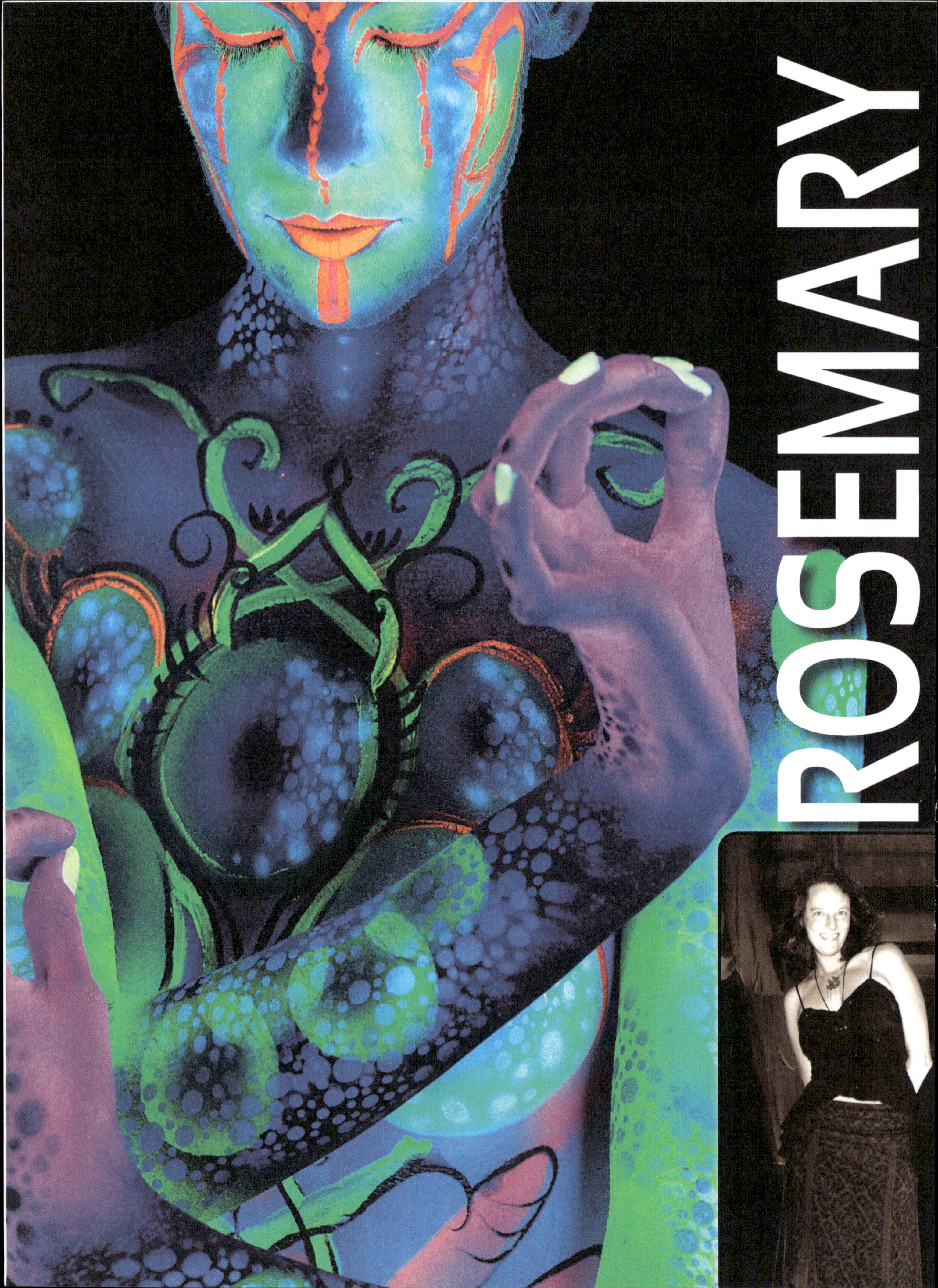

ROSEMARY

KIMBLE

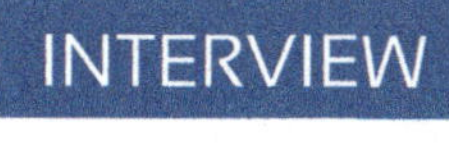

By Fairlyinnocent

[Carpe Nocturne] Tell us, *what type of art do you enjoy being involved in?*

[Rosemary Kimble] I love being a director of theatrical body art events. It brings me great joy to connect people, watch them create art together and form friendships. But on a personal level, my favorite art form is making costumes. I create the costume headdresses for all of my productions.

[CN] *Can you tell us about your head pieces and how the feathers are obtained as well as if there are any dangers to the birds?*

[Rosemary] Many of my head pieces include cruelty free feathers. It is rare to find cruelty free feathers for sale and so all of mine are donated by bird pet owners. The birds naturally molt so it's easy to collect them. In the feather industry they are plucked causing undue harm and when I learned about that, after years of being naive to it, I had to stop using manufactured feathers in my work. Most of the feathers I use and get are from macaws, cockatoos and peacocks. Other feathers include many varieties of parrots, turkey and rooster. All feathers from native birds are actually illegal to own, since many birds were nearly wiped out 100 years ago by the fashion industry and laws had to be made to protect them from going extinct including owls, eagles, and song birds.

[CN] *How long have you been involved in the arts?*

[Rosemary] I was born an artist. I knew in grade school that I would grow doing art for a living.

[CN] *Who/what inspired you to get into body art?*

[Rosemary] I was inspired to get into body art because I had been making costumes for a while and wanted to add another element to my characters.

[CN] *Are there any artists who inspire you today?*

[Rosemary] The artists that especially inspire me are mostly deceased and include actresses, painters, musicians and performers such as Salvador Dali, Audrey Hepburn, the Velvet Underground under Warhol's influence, and Jim Morrison. I also love Lady Gaga, as she seems to be one of the few using performance art and costumes in her work these days and has some pretty brilliant concepts. Of a very different genre I love Andy Goldsworthy and aspire to be a nature artist like him some day.

[CN] *Do you have any schooling/training in body art?*

[Rosemary] None, I am a completely self-taught artist of henna, face painting and body painting. When I started in 1992, there were no schools for these things.

[CN] *What/who are your favorite subjects?*

[Rosemary] Costume and Body Art, Healthy Lifestyles, Shamanism, Indigenous Cultures, Interspecies relationships

[CN] *Is your work compared to the work of anyone else?*

[Rosemary] I hope not! Not that I have heard of. I am kind of a diverse costume artist. None of my headdresses really are like the rest of my pieces in my opinion.

[CN] *Do you sell/show your work at any galleries?*

[Rosemary] I have had my masks in a New Orleans shop called the Maskarade in the French Quarter since 1998. Mostly I make custom pieces or create the headdresses for the performers in the shows that I direct.

[CN] *Was your family supportive in your choice of career?*

[Rosemary] Mostly, my dad has always been an artist too, a jeweler and metal smith and when he had a hard time making a living at it in his early years, he kind of freaked that I would want to do such a thing. Now days they all look at my body art as just another of Rosemary's unique traits.

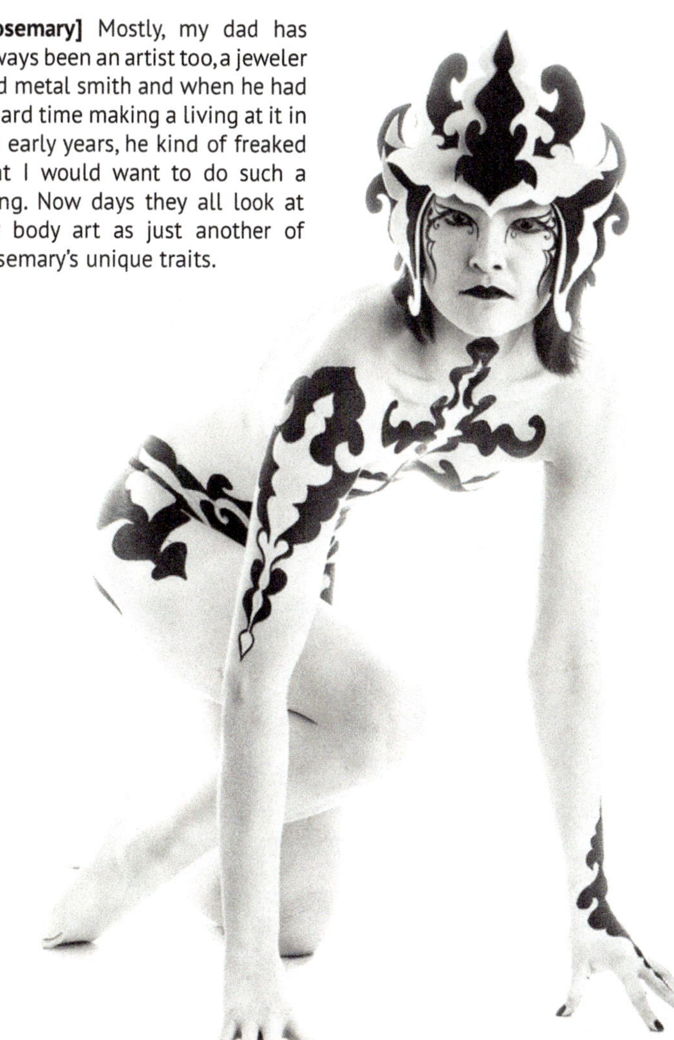

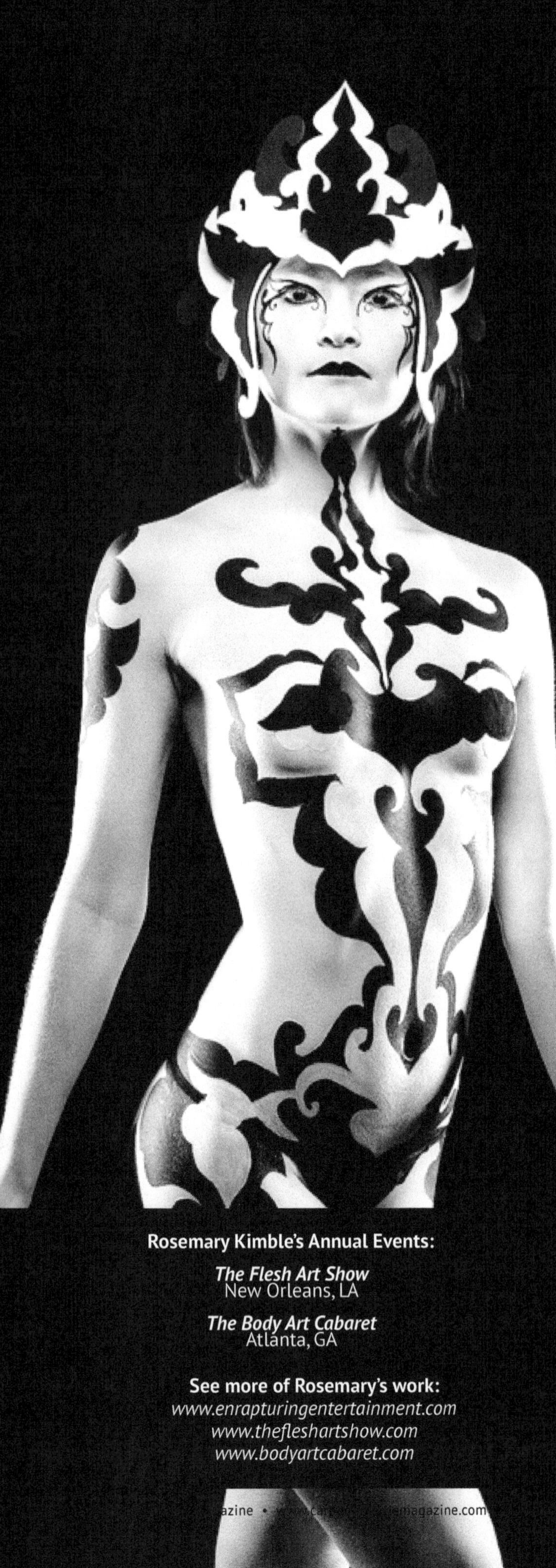

[CN] *Was this your original career vision?*

[Rosemary] My original career vision was always to be an artist but as a teenager I was an actress and absolutely fascinated with film. I wanted to be a film director and act in my films. My room was plastered from floor to ceiling with photos of my favorite actresses and directors. That dream has never gone away. Don't be surprised if you see me on set behind a film camera someday.

[CN] *What do you feel has been your biggest accomplishment/s?*

[Rosemary] I think to date my biggest accomplishments have been creating, directing and producing two fine art body painting shows, the Body Art Cabaret and the New Orleans Flesh Art Show.

[CN] *Could you tell us what fundraising/foundation/organizations you are affiliated with?*

[Rosemary] I work with Living Art America, the US Body Painting Championships to produce the Body Art Cabaret in Atlanta. My New Orleans event, the Flesh Art Show, benefits Art Docs, providing affordable medical care for artists. I also started an organization in 2005 called the Feather Drop, for the collection and reuse of cruelty-free feathers for use in art. Any head pieces I make that use feathers in them are created from donations through the Feather Drop. We have a Facebook page with over 1,200 followers.

[CN] *Could you tell us what events you have produced/participated in?*

[Rosemary] Besides the aforementioned, I used to put on a huge costume exhibition, before Hurricane Katrina, of my work in New Orleans in celebration of the opening of Mardi Gras season called a 12th Night Celebration. I have curated art shows, and run variety shows since the late 90's.

[CN] *Is there any artist that you would absolutely love to work with?*

[Rosemary] Lady Gaga

[CN] *Do you offer any type of workshops to help other aspiring artists?*

[Rosemary] Not at this time. I just have not found the time for such.

[CN] *Please elaborate on anything you would like the readers to know about body art that they may not know.*

[Rosemary] My favorite quote I ever heard about body art is that "body art is a 4 dimensional art form; it's about working with the spirit of your canvas, a human being that interacts and has fluid energy. The artist is just one half. The model brings the art to life."

[CN] *What are your future goals and endeavors?*

[Rosemary] To buy all of the rainforests and remaining wilderness of the world, in order to keep them safe and intact for future generations, to clean all of the oceans and to direct film's that inspire and bring joy to humanity.

THE BODY ART CABARET

By Fairlyinnocent

The Body Art Cabaret is an annual cabaret style variety show held in the fall featuring amazing body artists from around the world. The artists "canvases" are live performers who present their talents such as acrobats, pole dancers, burlesque, and belly dancers who showcase the artist's work on stage and around the theater to music while interacting with the attendees.

The event was held at an absolutely beautiful location steeped in history called the Georgia Railroad Freight Depot in Atlanta, GA and it really fit the theme. They had vendors selling their wares at the venue as well as body painting for the patrons. There was one area of the venue that had a wonderful art gallery to enjoy including painted living statues outside posing and a band with a belly dancer prior to the show beginning. This event encourages guests to dress in period clothing so they are more involved in the whole experience. They also have the opportunity to have photos taken with the painted models/performers as well as a fantastic after party.

Bodies as a Work of Art and Living Art America benefit The Chelko Foundation with a portion of its proceeds going towards their scholarship and grant foundation. "The proceeds help to end gender bias and violence against women and girls through art, education and partnership by awarding scholarships in the arts as well as presenting special humanitarian grants". This is the main platform for artists to combine their vision, techniques, and media in order to create phenomenal one of a kind art on live models. The Body Art Cabaret is one of three events during that weekend. The other two are the US Body Painting Championships, and the US Body Painting Festival. This year's lineup, starting with the Body Art Cabaret, will be Friday, October 2, 2015 from 9pm-12am.

This is an eyegasm of vibrant colors, beauty, and talent with performances that are not to be matched anywhere else. The body artist responsible for the Body Art Cabaret is Rosemary Kimble of EnRapturing Entertainment. She specializes in body art, face painting, and henna. She does all her own non-feather and feather head pieces and started a foundation called The Feather Drop using cruelty free feathers in her work. "Since I was a child I have had a strong will to make a career for myself as a successful and self-taught artist. By revising new and used materials I create fabulous works of art designed to enrapture the eye. You can see from the intensity of detail and the quality of my work that this art form is the way that I enjoy expressing myself the most in life. Each piece is a symbol of my true essence and of the greatest gift I have ever been given…to create.

Each of my pieces are one of a kind works of art, handcrafted and adorned with imported trims, feathers and glass Swarovski crystals. They are most often used for masquerading, pageantry, stage shows and weddings and are considered collectables".

Photography provided for this review by Fairlyinnocent Photography at www.fairlyinnocentphotography.weebly.com

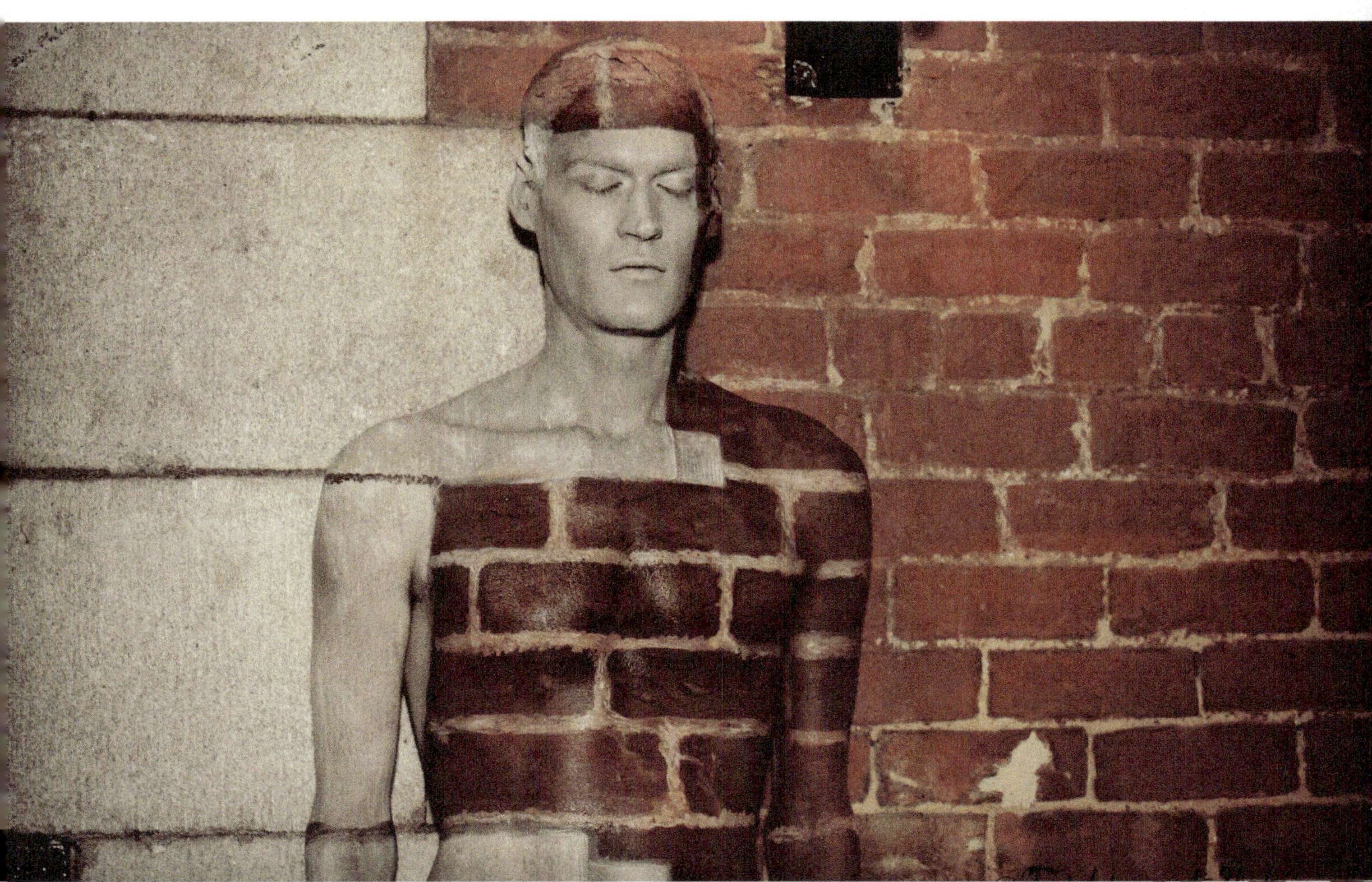

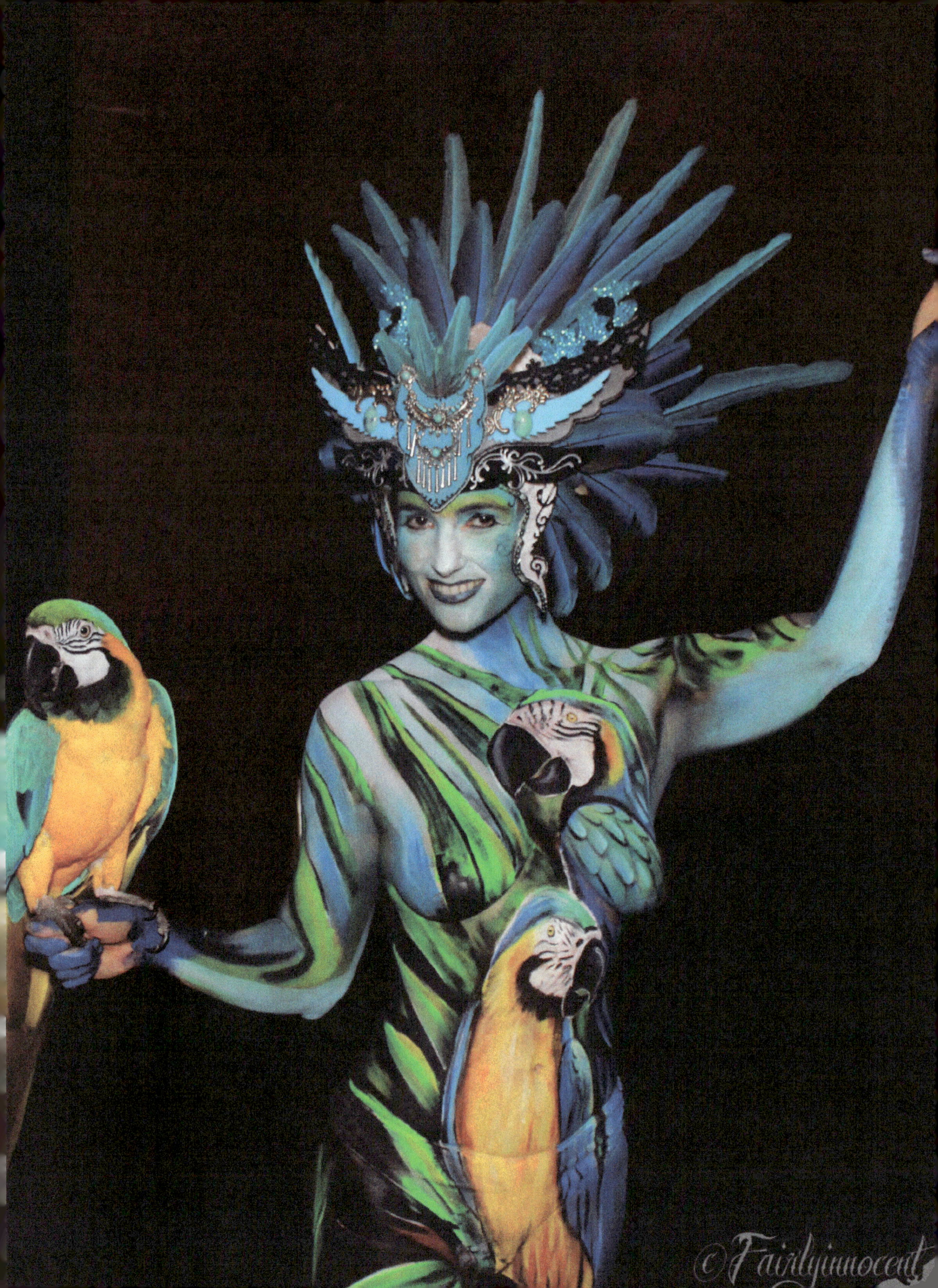
©Fairlyinnocent

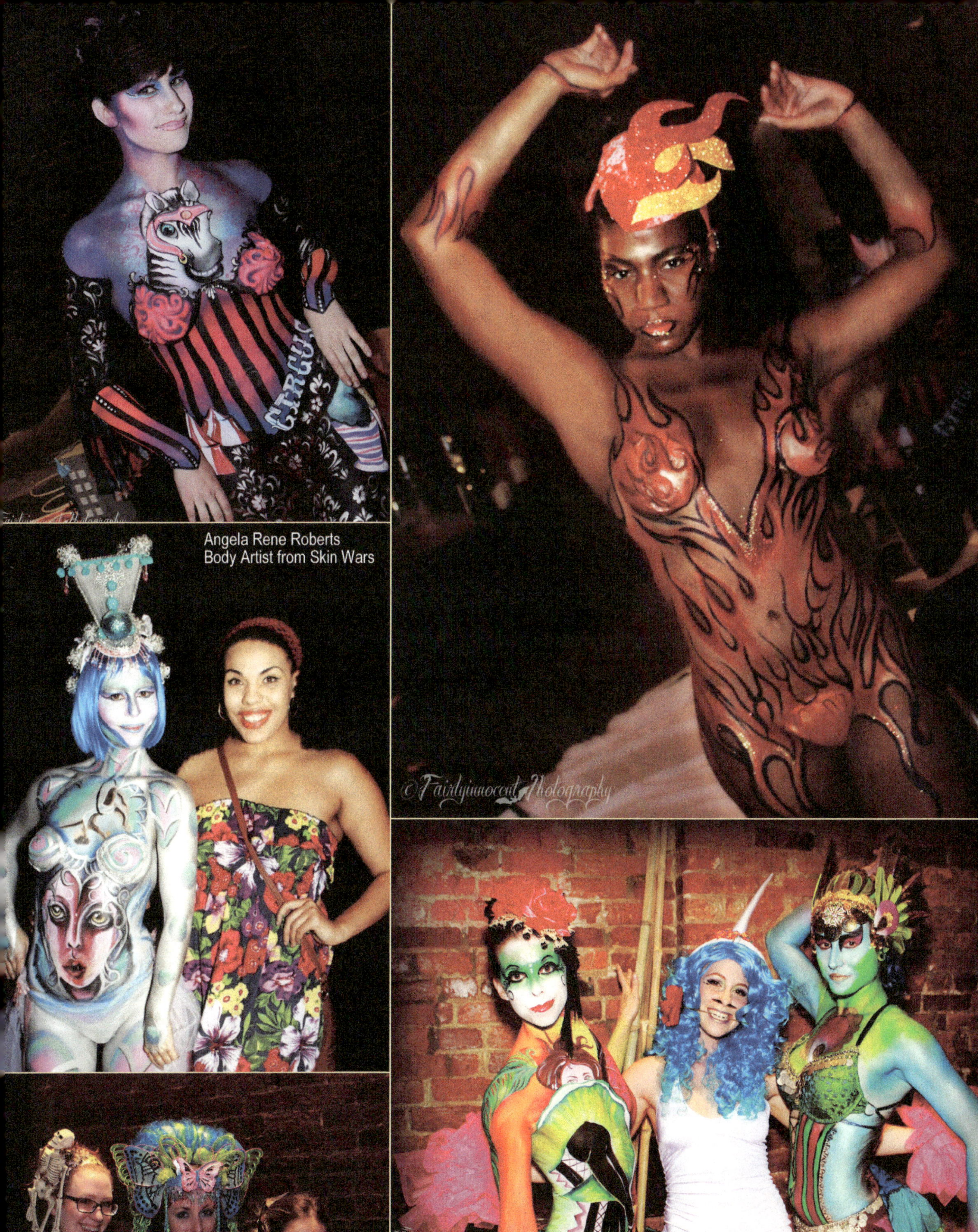

Angela Rene Roberts
Body Artist from Skin Wars

ANTHONY GRANATO

By Sonnett57

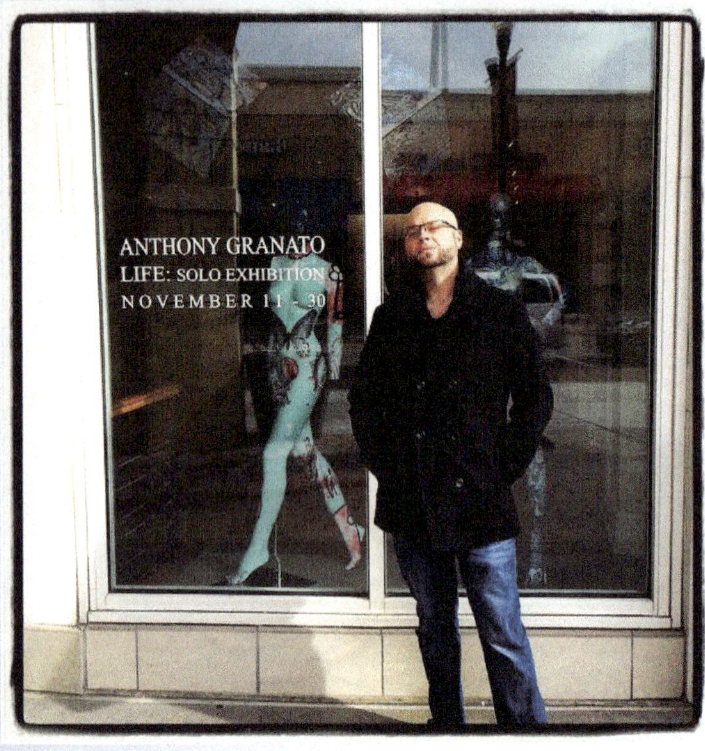

Creating art began for Anthony Granato at the tender age of five. It was a simple matter of instinct for him, and he has turned that instinct into a multi-award winning career. Anthony's art is featured in many venues and bars across the Salt Lake Valley, as well as in multiple publications over the past several years. He normally holds anywhere from 12 to 18 showings per year, which include galleries, festivals, and events like Comic Con. His mediums are fine art, giclee prints, illustrations, Polaroids, and sketches. Besides the creative, Anthony has a keen business sense when it comes to his artwork. He believes in keeping a fresh stylistic inventory, and turning over what is out of date.

When approaching art, Anthony has his own unique style. His favorite things to draw are figures, birds, and rhinoceroses. The latter he considers to be the one of the last living dinosaurs. Anthony also favors the use of skulls in his artwork, because he finds they are likely to evoke reactions and morality issues. Many find them either frightening or exciting, and sometimes even both. Anthony often uses Victorian flourishes and filigree for ornamentation because he loves the detail. This practice began 10 years ago when he started paying attention to stylistic designs and patterns. Anthony was captivated by their intricacy and visual movement.

Anthony Granato also has a penchant for antique frames, and a unique style of combining fresh art with them. His love began a decade ago while visiting a friend in Portland who did framing. Inspired, he envisioned a large antique frame that was given to him once as a gift. Immediately, his mind exploded with ideas. He began rearranging artwork in his head. When he actually touched the frame, he knew it was the direction he needed to take. Anthony still has that frame, and has recently contemplated using it in his work.

Anthony considers himself to be a geek. He is inspired by the Star Wars franchise, and if he is inspired by it, he paints it. In fact, his work has even been featured in the Star Wars Gamer Magazine. Anthony is also fascinated with gas masks. He finds they are visually dynamic and are great for social commentary. The gas mask is a way to protect yourself, a barrier between you and the toxicity around you. They give a sense of security, while adding a certain creepiness to his work. Anthony is also one of the many drawn to the number 23. He, as well as the others, consider it to be the "answer to the Universe." This theory resonates with him on many levels. Anthony finds the number 23 visually beautiful, and when he puts it in a painting, that piece will sell faster.

Photography is another avenue of art Anthony pursues. He is known for his Polaroids, and has his own distinct style of holding up 35mm lens in front of the camera. When it comes to choosing a model, there are no set rules. Usually, Anthony chooses someone with a distinctive feature unique to only themselves. Sometimes that uniqueness can be their personality. Anthony has even approached people in the grocery store and asked them to model.

As with many artists, creativity strikes at various times. For Anthony, it is the moments right before sleep or upon waking he is most inspired, and sometimes even when brushing his teeth. Tight deadlines and the pressure to perform also influence his creativity. The work must get done at all costs. When signing a piece, Anthony has found his signature was not aesthetically pleasing. Adding the year only made it more complex. Therefore, he chooses to use a wax seal. This practice came about when his mother gave him a T stamp and he used it to correspond with her. Anthony finds the wax seal adds to the creativity of the piece, and he changes it every year, thus dating the work. Therefore, if you do not see the wax seal, it is not an original Anthony Granato.

In His Own Words:

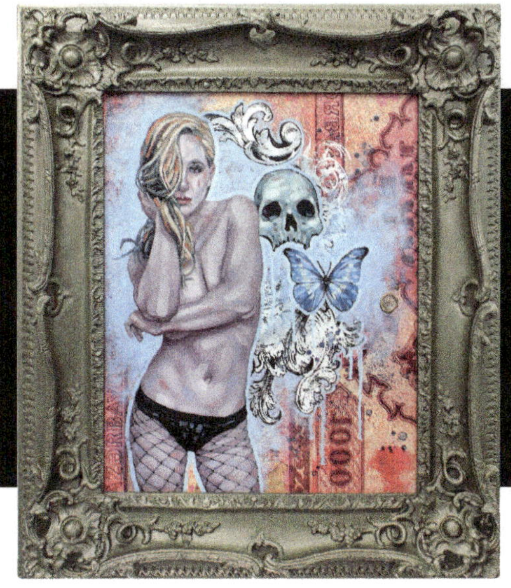

Black Rainbow

As always, I love dichotomies. Conceptually, the idea of a black rainbow is a contradiction, which is why it makes to so intriguing. Bringing together a beautiful woman, a skull, and a butterfly evokes a similar contradiction of beauty and death.

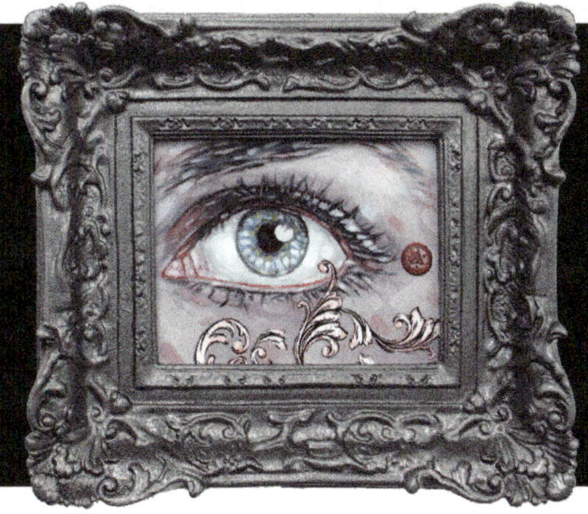

Clemency

There are so many telling aspects of the eye. We have so much going on within ourselves that are reflected through them. This eye in specific spoke to me in a merciful way. There is such an enormous range of emotions that our eyes can express that it's possible this painting could be the beginning of a series.

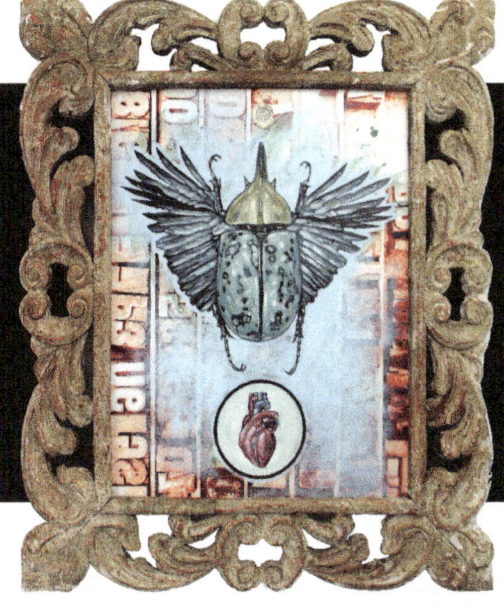

Dystopia

I am constantly interested in duality. I wanted to explore the utopian/dystopian concept. Because we all fantasize about our own utopias, I thought it'd be more challenging to find a way to visually represent it's opposite. With the diseased color palate of the beetle, the degradation of the frame and background, the colorless wings and the hemophiliac red tones, I felt like this was a good first attempt at describing this unpleasant land.

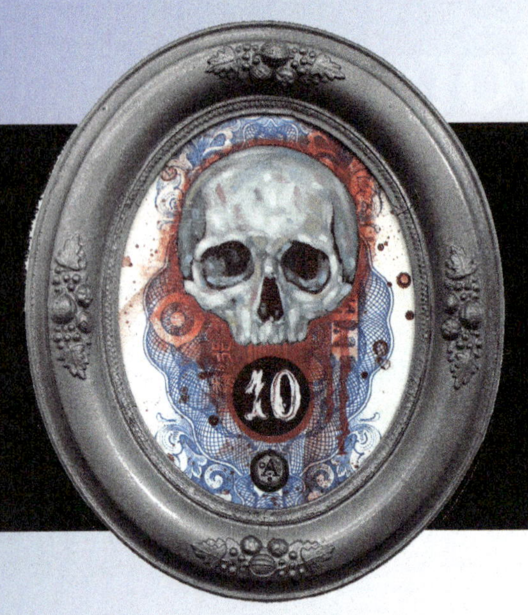

Happy Face 10

This is part of a series called Happy Faces 1 through 13. I thought it would be funny to call them happy faces because most people equate skulls with death, destruction, disease and other morbid associations. I guess it's my sick sense of humor that wants to give people a different perspective.

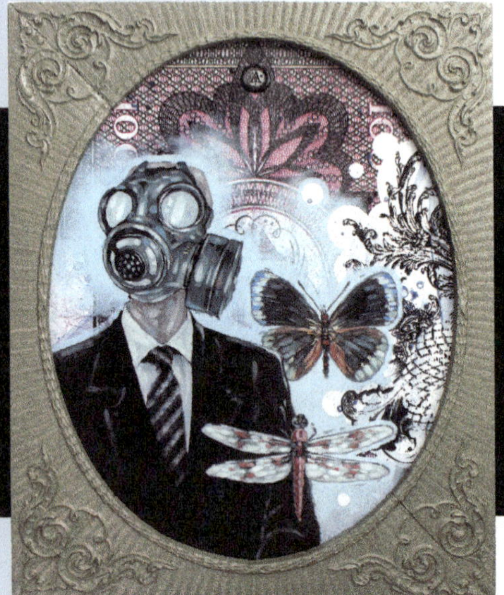

Nuclear Daydream

I'm a huge Bowie fan, and I took a departure from one of his songs: Moonage Daydream. I thought of a post apocalyptic version of the idea with some social commentary sprinkled on top. Then, to make it even more serendipitous, Joseph Arthur (another musician I enjoy) titled his album Nuclear Daydream. Crazy.

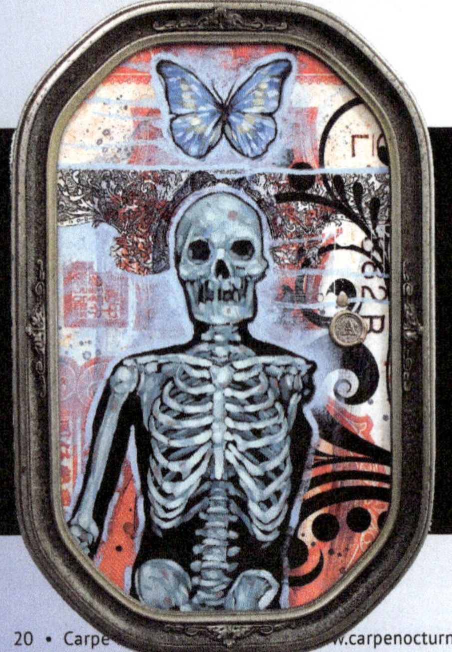

Triage

I've always been fascinated with the idea that anyone in the medical field who is attending to a large group of sick or wounded people has to prioritize who gets treated first. They need to base this on many different variables, but the I couldn't imagine being in the position to make those absolute life or death choices for other people. There is something wonderful about men and women that can do this successfully. Hence, the beauty of the butterfly over a diseased carcass.

LIGHTS

By Asylum Attendant

I can't recall whether I heard the song "Drive My Soul" or "February Air" first in an Old Navy commercial years ago, but I do recall the urge to discover the breathy voiced artist behind the catchy snippet of indie electropop. Once I learned her name was Lights (and that's her legal name, too), I've followed her bright career ever since.

Canadian Lights got her start as a songwriter for Sony/ATV Music Publishing and wrote music for the teen TV show Instant Star, which my friends and I totally watched. Not quite as good as the drama on Degrassi, but definitely entertaining. Soon after, Lights decided to focus on a music career of her own. She released her debut single "Drive My Soul" in 2008, which made it to No. 18 on the Canadian Hot 100 chart. The airy synthpop track is about staying out of the darkness through the presence of someone or something meaningful. The equally poppy and sweet second single "February Air" was released later that year. The campy space themed music videos for both songs tell the love story of Lights and an astronaut. Super adorable.

Lights' intergalactic first album The Listening was released in 2009. The light electropop sound is similar to electronica artist Owl City, who Lights later toured and collaborated with. Her third single "Ice" displayed the stronger side of this bubbly artist. The song features a fast-moving new wave synth line and lyrics about an emotionally distant boyfriend. Airy vocals are replaced with frenetic articulations. Lights may come off innocent, but treat her wrong and watch out. She played on the male rock band dominated Vans Warped Tour, so she can hold her own.

The experimental second album Siberia was released in 2011 and featured bitpop, dubstep and even hip hop. The album was delayed because Lights' label Last Gang Records feared the new sound was too different. The promotional single "Everybody Breaks a Glass" featured a rap verse from hip hop artist Shad and glitchy keyboards. There is heavier percussion on the single "Toes", but the song still retains Lights' signature pop melodies and spacey synths. She sings about a relationship in which the other person surprises and excites her. Perhaps she wrote this song for Beau Bokan of the metalcore band Blessthefall, her future husband. Siberia (Acoustic) was released in 2013.

Light's latest cheerful album Little Machines is reminiscent of her first album. The instrumentation is lusher than The Listening, but the themes aren't so introspective. Lights took inspiration for this album from her favorite female artists such as Bjork, Kate Bush and Cyndi Lauper. The infectious and elevating "Up We Go" is sing-a-long electropop with guitars to add some depth. The music video includes crazy antics in an elevator, including argumentative wrestlers and a couple in lust. "Running with the Boys" takes the listener right back to childhood and fun afternoons playing with neighborhood friends. The sound is really fresh and youthful, but timeless, too.

I hope that Lights continues to craft breezy synthpop music for many years to come. Her playful spirit really illuminates the music industry.

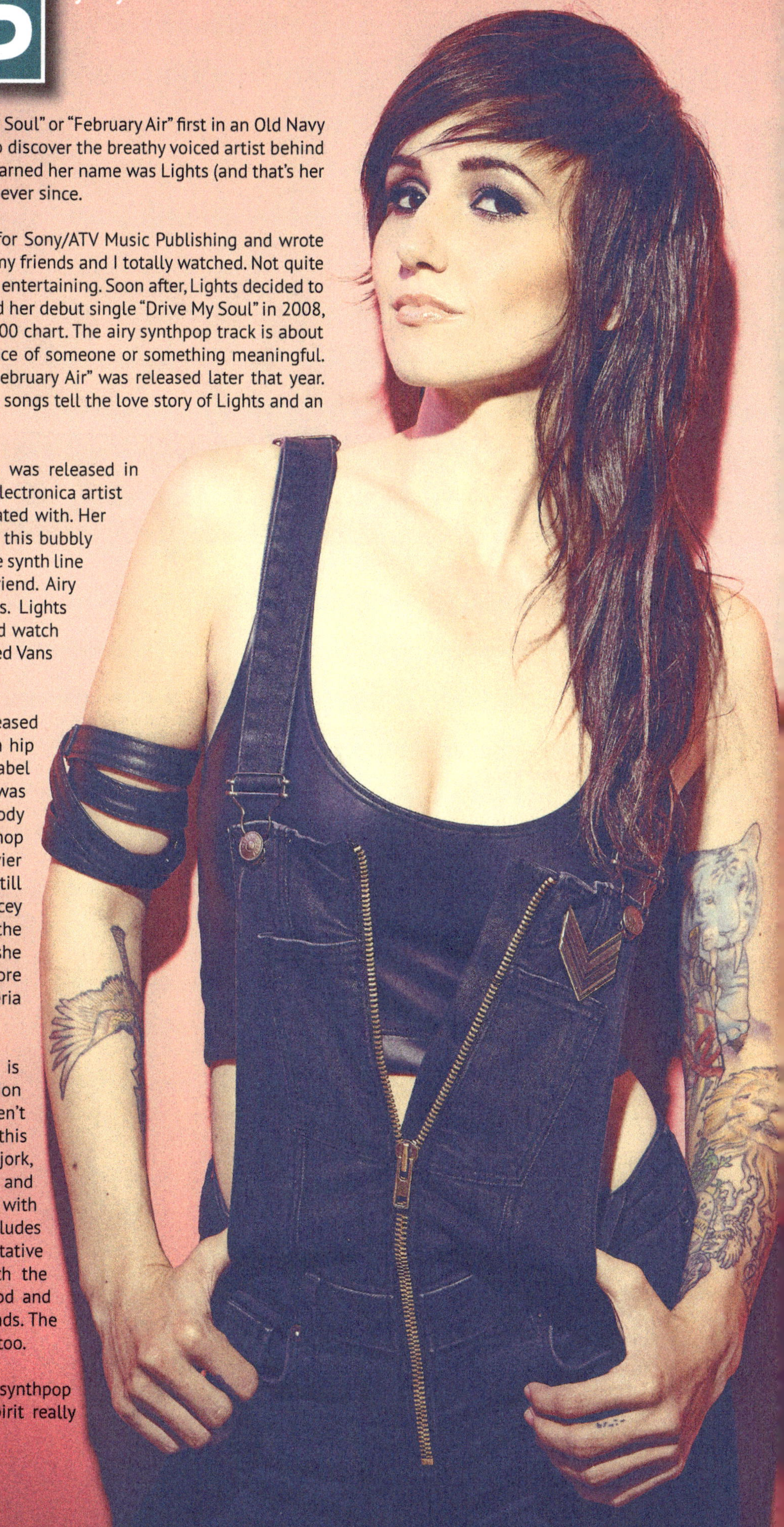

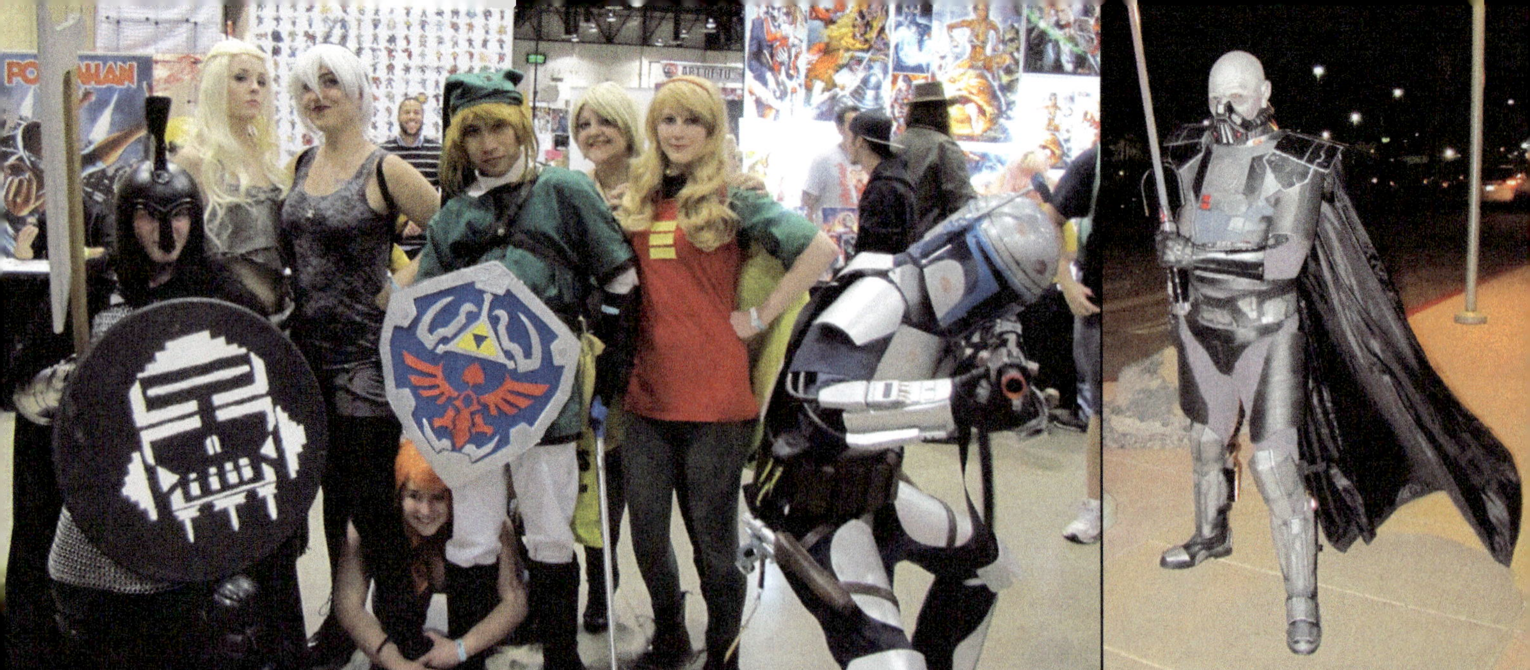

RENO COMIC CON 2014

By Kathleen Sharkey Reno's convention center has never been truly grandiose at least not by *Con standards (ie. Gencon, Dragon*con, Comic*con). As a geek/nerd/gamer I had never expected my little town to host any of the big boy *Cons. Then, a few years back, we won the right to have the Science Fiction convention come to Reno. Reno-vations was an exciting time for me and my friends. Science fiction writers, artists, cosplayers, actors and a whole slew of amazing innovations came to our little slice of the world. Perhaps the success of that one little chance helped put us into the minds of *Con folks because in 2014 we were blessed once again, but this time with the honor of having one of the, admittedly, numerous satellite Comic *Con conventions. I was more than elated.

The non-room side of the convention center was split into five parts. The first being a gigantic room for ticketing, the second was the "floor". For those of our readers who have never been to a gaming/comic or other type of convention the "Floor" is generally the place where various sellers are located. This can include artists, game manufacturers, toy sellers and trinket pushers. The over 75,000 square foot floor held comic book sales, artists of every type, costume designers, sword and shirt sales, jewelry, toys, anime, the list just kept on going. Then in the back of the hall at red draped tables were the guests of honor. Jewel Stait, Kaylee from Serenity, Lou Ferigno, Bruce Campbell, Norman Reedus, and even William Shatner, we felt honored that our town got to host such celebrities.

In the individual rooms were another whole variety of things. The stars either got together to give talks or they had individual meet and greets in these rooms. In the larger room there was a zombie laser tag going 24 hours. In still others writers, artists and a variety of other people got to give talks about comic books, art, breaking into art, writing, cosplay and a variety of topics. There were talks that included children and talks that were a little racier. But on top of it all were the costume contests, one for adults and one for kids. The costumes, as you can see from my pictures, varied from whimsical to stunning. It was obvious that the attendants of Reno Comic Con had a ton of fun creating costumes for the show.

The radiating Comic Cons around the United States in 2014 brought the vast convention to people who might not have ever gotten a chance to experience this type of convention. But would the attendance at the Reno Comic Con place it on the return map for Comic Con 2015? Attendance records showed over 10,000 people attended the Reno Comic Con more than bursting the expected numbers. So if you happen to be in the Reno area the weekend before Thanksgiving 2015 come on down to the Convention center and get your Geek on.

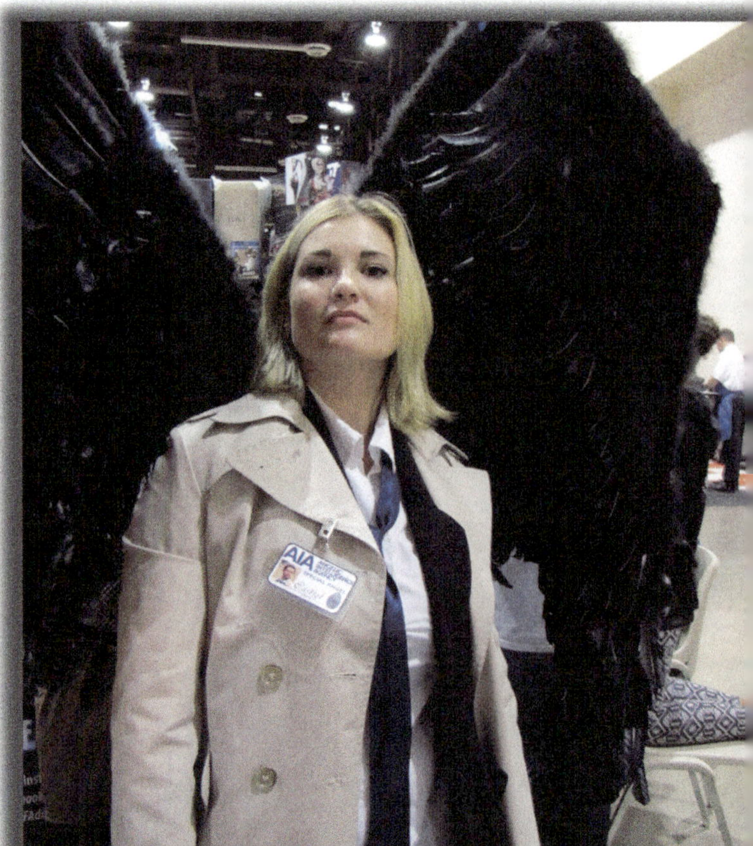

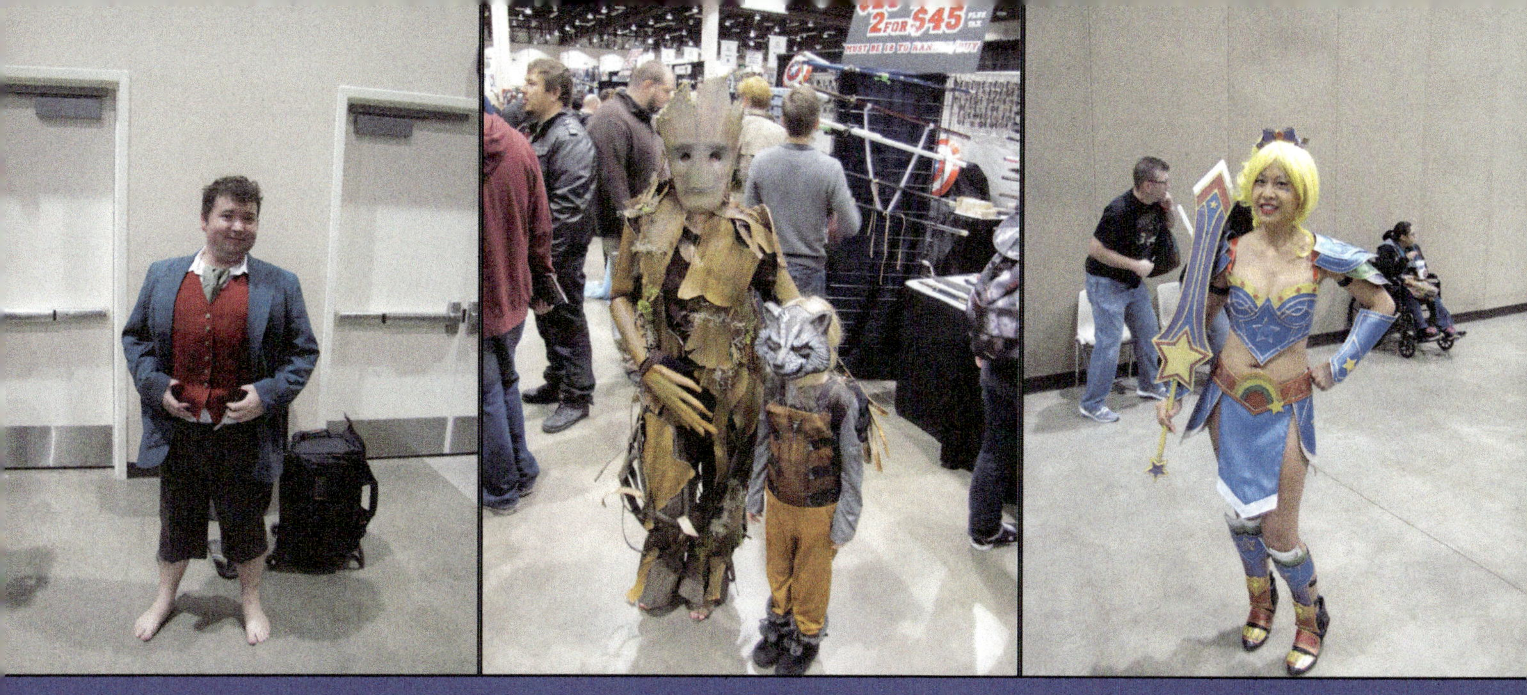

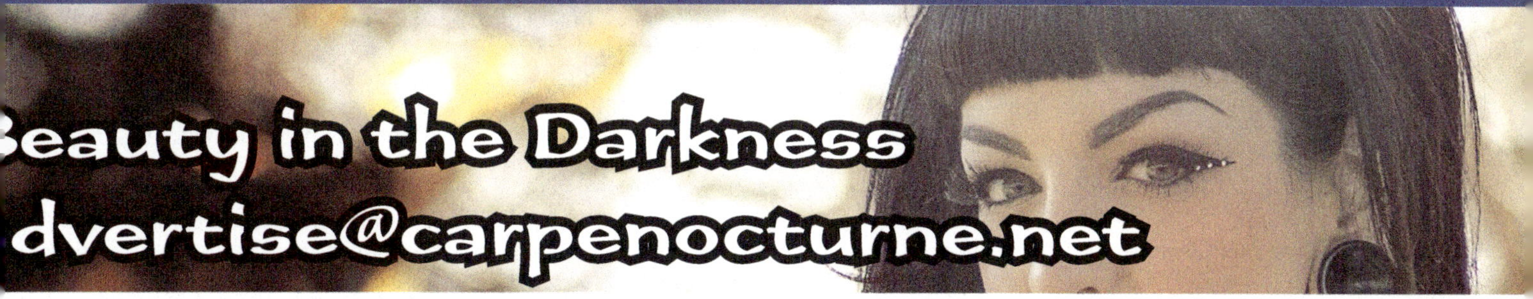

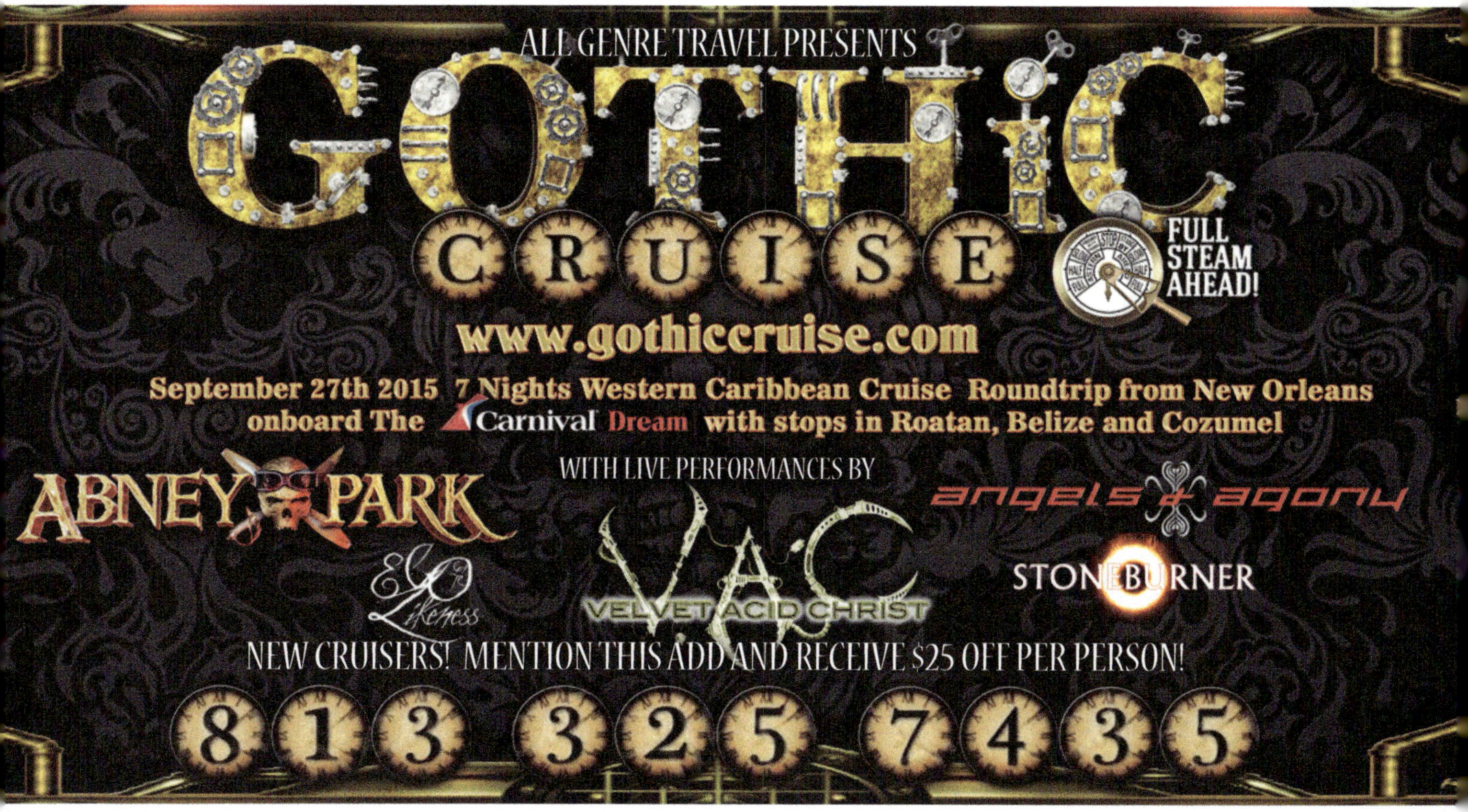

RAKS GEEK

By Yasaman Vrd'dhi

In a Galaxy not so far away, we have aliens, asteroids and Raks Geek. Get ready for one of the most interesting belly dance fusion styles of today. Meet Dawn Xiana Moon, the Producer of the Raks Geek group, and learn how her belly dance group came about and how sci-fi is a part of this belly dance style.

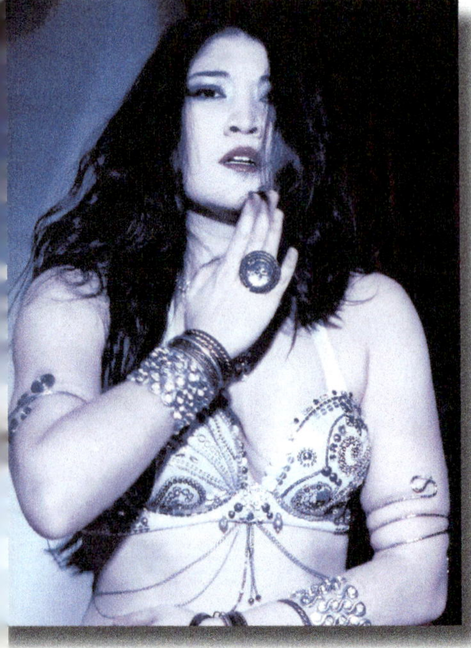

[Carpe Nocturne] *What does the name "Raks Geek" mean, and how did you come up with it?*

[Dawn Xiana Moon] "Raks" is an Arabic word often used as a proper noun by belly dancers - it translates literally to "dance." In the context of belly dancing, you'll often see a dancer call herself something like "Raks Yasmin." So we're "Raks Geek," or "dance of the geeks."

[CN] *What made you come up with this style of Belly Dance? Would you call it a Style or just a theme for belly dance performances?*

[DM] Raks Geek started out as a theatrical production. We're professional dancers and fire spinners, creating a show by and for our fellow geeks. It has expanded into a proper dance company that performs at cons, festivals, and various venues. As dancers, the members of the company come from different backgrounds: Kamrah was a competitive martial artist for over a decade, and her belly dance style varies from tribal fusion to Lebanese. When he's not doing his own style of tribal fusion, Lee Na-Moo performs with Joel Hall Dancers, a regional contemporary dance company (i.e. ballet, modern, jazz). And then there are the fire spinners, some of whom don't have a dance background at all, but they certainly know how to handle flaming swords and fans in ways that will make your jaw drop.

[CN] *Who makes up your group? And do you perform solo as well?*

[DM] The group started as a collaboration between Read My Hips tribal belly dance and the Chicago Fire Tribe. At this point, the cast rotates a bit, depending on our performance needs. But what stays constant is that we're geeks and professional performers. Our current core is incredible. Kamrah, whom I mentioned earlier, will be teaching at this year's Tribal Fest (for belly dancers, this is the equivalent of playing at Lollapalooza), and she's also a research scientist. Lee Na-Moo is a modern dancer and also won the Chicago Oriental Dance Competition. He's taught his version of tribal fusion belly dance in Argentina and Spain. Michi Trota is a fire spinner and one of the organizers of the Chicago Full Moon Fire Jams. Every month when it's warm enough, they perform for a couple hundred people on the shores of Lake Michigan. For the last few years, she and I have been giving talks about women and minorities in geek culture at universities (the University of Chicago) and cons (C2E2, Wizard World, Chicago Comic Con). She's also the Managing Editor of Uncanny Magazine, a new science fiction publication that's featured work by people like Neil Gaiman. When I'm not dancing, I'm a singer-songwriter. I've released two albums and played in 10 states, and the music hovers between folk and pop with influences from jazz and traditional Chinese music. I'm also a UX designer and front-end web developer.

As you can see, it's a pretty amazing group. I'm lucky to work with these guys, because they are absolutely fantastic at what they do.

[CN] *Where do you get your costume ideas?*

[DM] We actually like to work in concepts. It's difficult to say whether the music comes first or the conceptual framework does. Both of those things lead to costuming, which comes later in the process. Some of our ideas are funny - a video from one of our productions

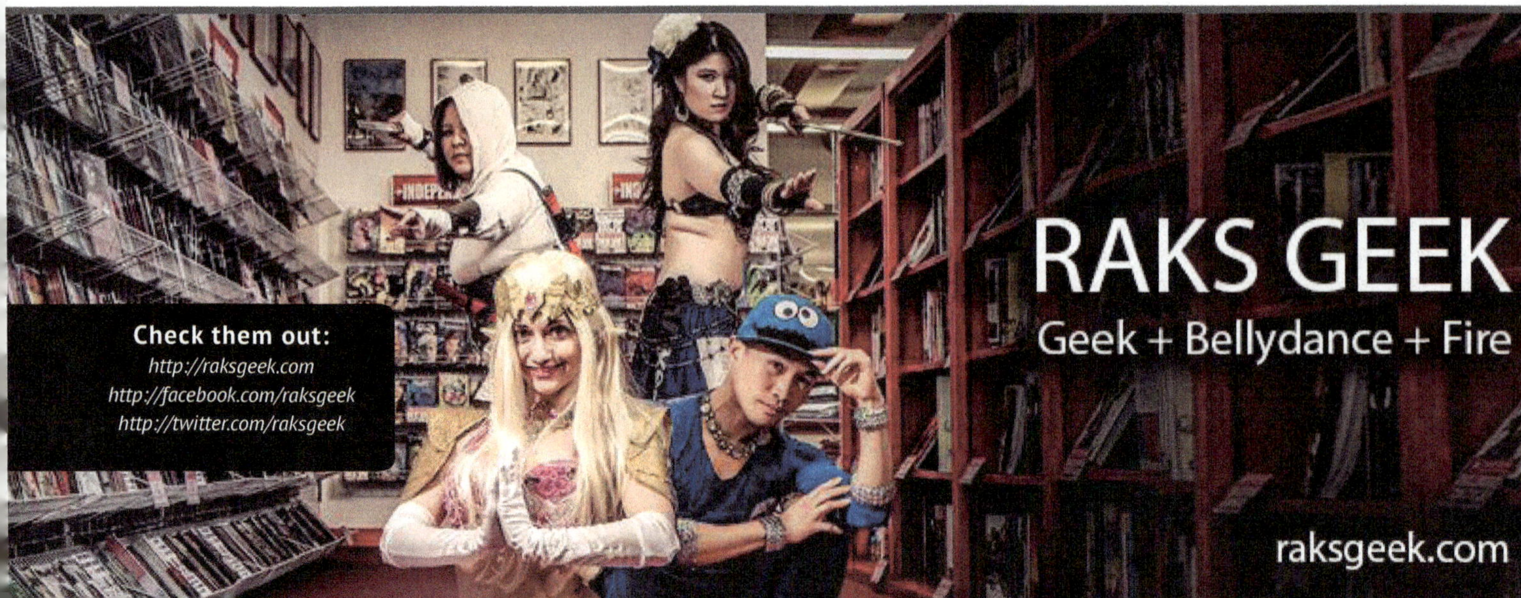

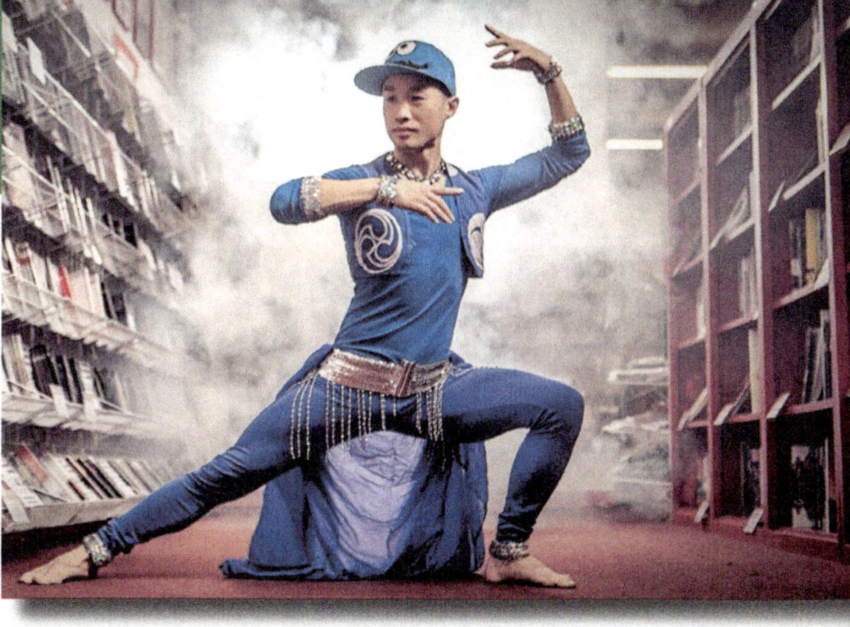

went viral, and it features a Wookiee belly dancing to a four-piece Klingon band playing an original song in Shyriiwook (the Wookiee language). Some are dark - we do a trio choreography mixing Lost Boys, Saw, and Nine Inch Nails. And some are pure fun - I often perform as the TARDIS to remixes of music from Doctor Who.

[CN] *It looks like Raks Geek is inspired by sci-fi? If so, how? And what other things inspire it?*

[DM] We love science fiction. I grew up watching Star Trek. My father is an engineer and a nerd himself, so I've watched Star Trek as long as I can remember. Back in the early days of the internet, I was on the Compuserve forums playing text-based Star Trek sims (i.e. Dungeons and Dragons without the rulebooks or dice). Other members of the group have similar stories. Depending on who you talk to, you'll also find an obsession with comics, Battlestar Galactica, horror, Babylon 5, Firefly, video games, Doctor Who, Star Wars, and hard SF literature.

[CN] *What is your Belly Dance background?*

[DM] I actually started as a swing and blues dancer. I taught classes in lindy hop, East Coast Swing, and blues dancing for years. Since blues is a dance form that makes strong use of body isolations, as a blues dancer you'll often hear about belly dancers and how they're able to isolate even more. So one night I went to the Source of All Movement Knowledge (i.e. Youtube) and looked up "belly dance". I got a sense of the different styles, from Egyptian to cabaret to American Tribal Style (ATS). One of the groups particularly piqued my interest - they were amazing. After watching a few of their videos, I realized they were from Chicago. And they taught classes. It took me a year to finally show up, but once I started I was hooked. The group was Read My Hips, and I was promoted to their professional company four years ago. We perform over 100 shows a year everywhere from Alhambra Palace (the largest restaurant in North America) to Chicago's Field Museum. Most of what I do as a belly dancer grew out of ATS and tribal fusion. My style is a modern, American form of belly dance that incorporates elements from flamenco, Bharatanatyam (classical Indian dance), traditional Middle Eastern folk dances, and hip hop.

[CN] *Your Performance name "Dawn Xiana Moon" is unique. What does it mean?*

[DM] I'm Chinese. "Xia" is a Chinese word that translates to "the glow of the rising sun" and "na" translates to "beautiful."

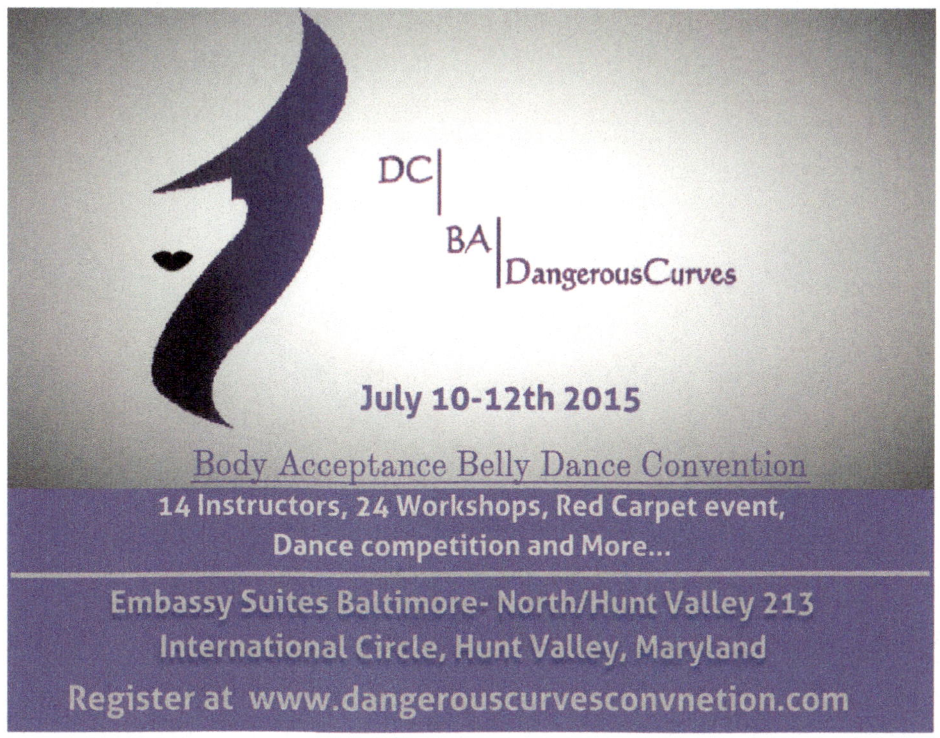

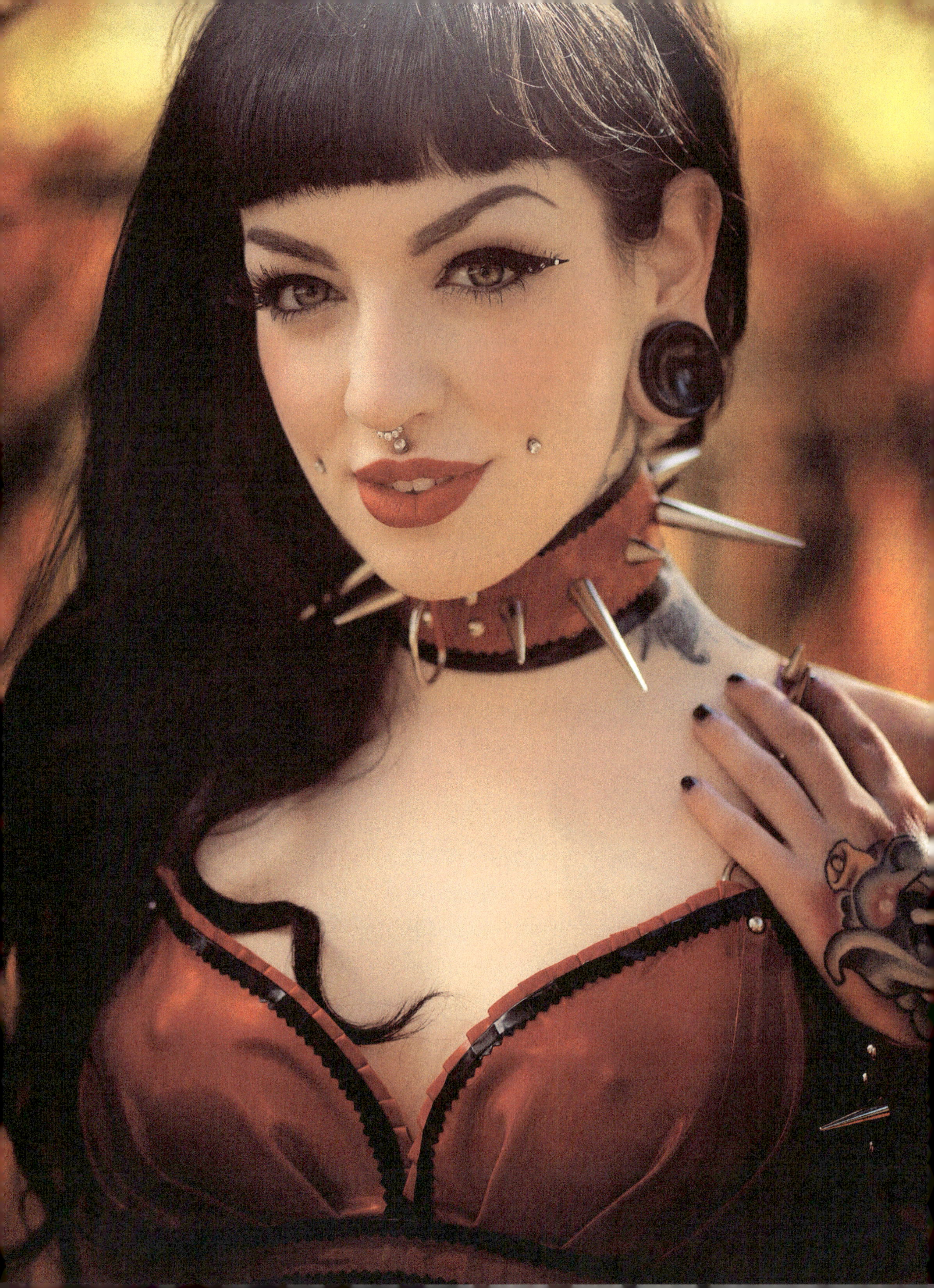

"CHERRY BOMB"
Twisted Visions Design

By Chantele Smith

This design is inspired to be red hot sexy!!! You will stand out with mouth-dropping hotness. Want to feel sexy for your night out to a fetish event? This design is perfect for that. The design is red with black inverted crosses and spikes with a badass chick look. The photo shoot was a lot of fun and the day couldn't have been more perfect. The location was at Hawrelak Park in Edmonton Ab.

The accessories shown in the set are the Cherry bomb collar, cuffs and spikes
 The big spikes are 3 inches long, with adjustable straps in the back of the collar by buckles. High quality nickel is used for the metalwork. And black zigzag trim is used to boarder the collar. The spike cuffs also have adjustable straps with nickel metal attachments and spikes. The cost for the set is $80.00

The cherry bomb top has a small ruffled trim boarder and snap buttons on the back. There are adjustable straps with spikes layered on the front. It is red latex with black zigzag trimming as well. The cost for the top is $140.00

Cherry bomb inverted cross high waist bottoms is red with black zigzag trimming. There are inverted crosses on the front and back. There are triple layered ruffles around the legs plus snap buttons on the crotch so you can easily undo them when needed. The cost for the waist bottoms $200.00

This design is made to order, so as to fit your size and Available in custom colors. All spikes are high quality nickel. The latex is 0.40mm - 0.60mm and high quality which makes it good for sensitive skin. Orders are available on etsy.com under Twistedvisions666

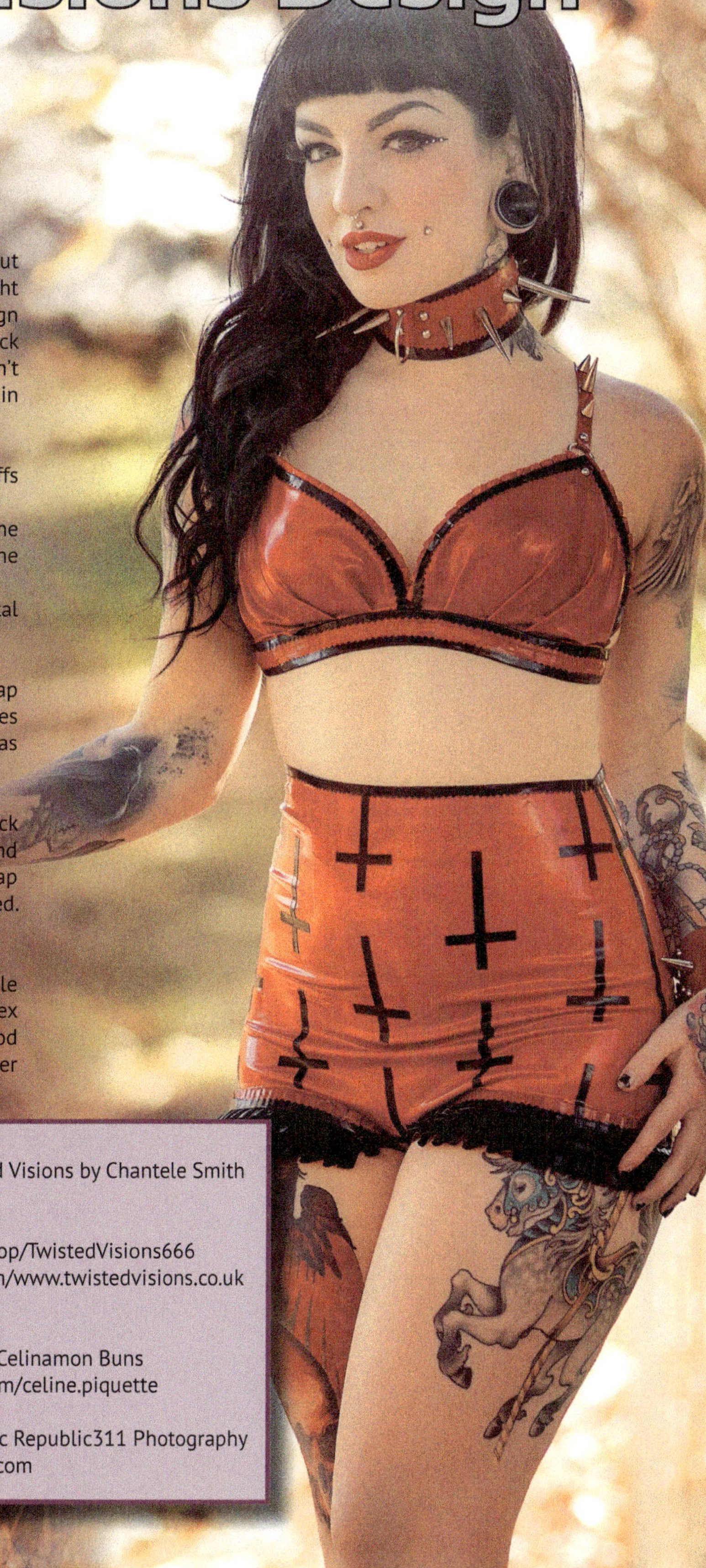

Credits
- Latex Designed; Twisted Visions by Chantele Smith

Shop online
https://www.etsy.com/shop/TwistedVisions666
http://www.facebook.com/www.twistedvisions.co.uk
Web site coming soon!

-Model / Hair / Makeup; Celinamon Buns
https://www.facebook.com/celine.piquette

-Photographer; Ferd Isaac Republic311 Photography
http://www.republic311.com

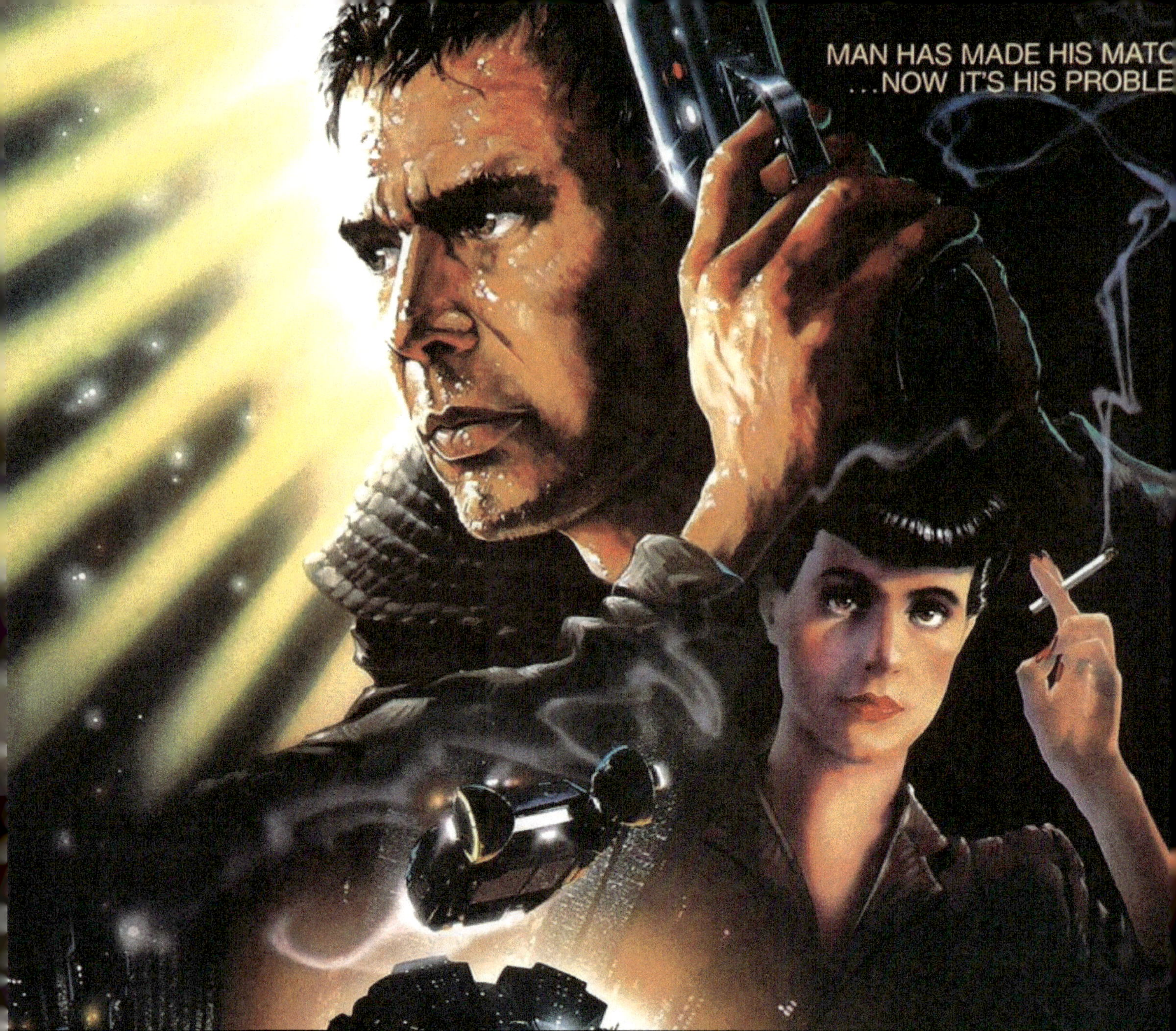

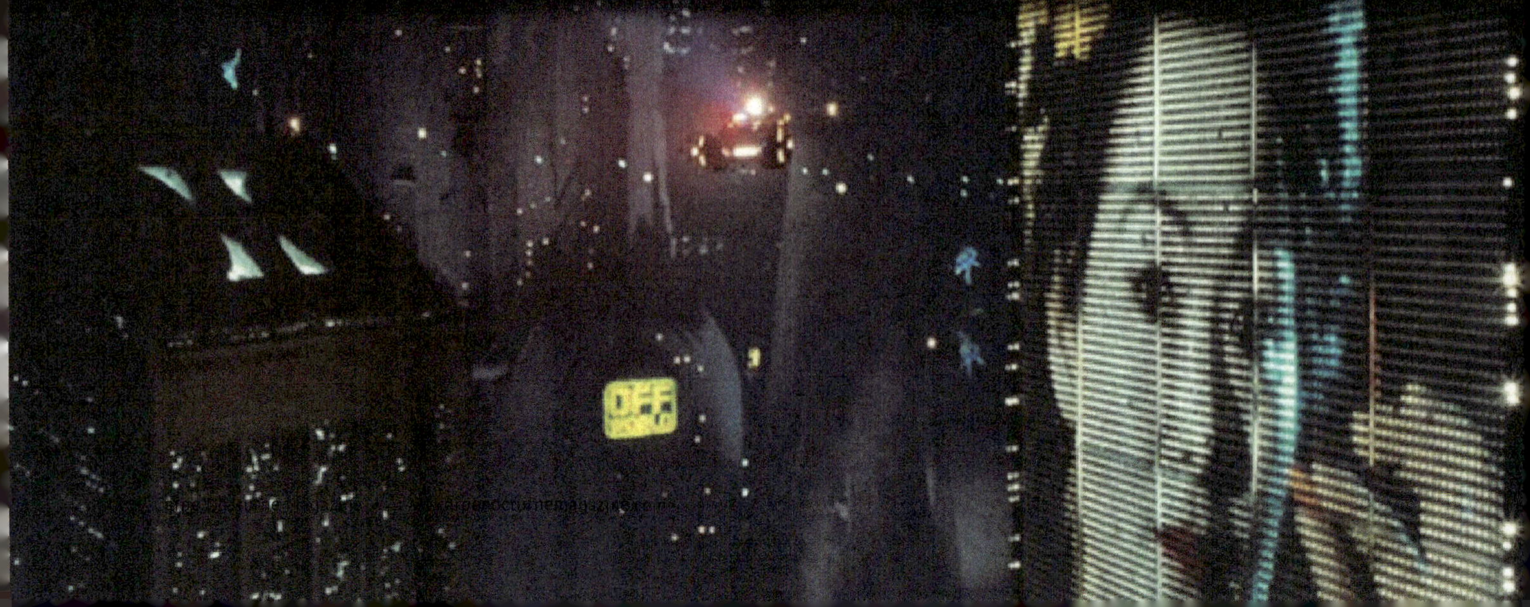

MAN HAS MADE HIS MATC
...NOW IT'S HIS PROBLE
TEARS IN THE RAIN:
OFF WORLD

A LOOK BACK AT RIDLEY SCOTT'S *BLADE RUNNER*

By Katie McKensie

@moonrisesister

We are only four years away from 2019, also known as the year of the world of Blade Runner, and we are nowhere near the nightmarish dystopia that director Ridley Scott envisioned on the big screen. Scott's Los Angeles is a grim and wet metropolis, teeming with larger-than life advertisements, clusters of high-rise buildings, and gritty street vendors hawking their wares to the poverty-stricken dregs of lower-level society... ok, apart from the flying cars whirring across the screen, Scott's look into the future may not have been that off-base. Adapted from the novel Do Androids Dream of Electric Sheep? by Philip K. Dick, who died the year Blade Runner was released, Scott's 1982 cinematic masterpiece is not only a certified cult classic but it is also a visual and thematic influence on nearly every science fiction film released in the last three decades.

Set in a time when androids have been created to serve humankind, Blade Runner examines the relationship between man and his dangerously rebellious creation along the lines of Mary Shelley's Frankenstein, but with a futuristic edge. Known in the film as "replicants," the androids look and act like human beings; the only way to detect one, in fact, is to administer a question-and-answer test that measures emotional responses in the test subject. Programmed to have a finite lifespan of only a few years and sent to colonies outside of Earth to work, replicants pose a threat when they become self-aware and insist on being reprogrammed to live out a longer and more fulfilling existence. Four such replicants, led by an inspired Rutger Hauer, have returned to Earth in order to seek out their creator – the head of a corporate conglomerate who harbors no intention of fulfilling their demands – and must be terminated before their mission claims a mass of human lives.

Enter the protagonist of our story, a harried cop known as a "Blade Runner," whose task is to track and kill the renegade replicants. Played by Harrison Ford in his action-hero heyday, Rick Deckard is modeled after detectives from hardboiled crime novels of the 1930s and 40s: gruff, nonconformist, and cagily seduced by a femme fatale (Sean Young), who in this case happens to be a replicant. As Deckard becomes more embroiled in the plight of replicants, he begins to question the morality of his assignment – and eventually, his own humanity.

The definitive neo-noir, Blade Runner is a visual marvel in terms of how it transplants mid-century pulp fiction into an alienating, dystopic future environment. Ford's Deckard and Sean Young's Rachel look and sound as though they've stepped off the pages of a Raymond Chandler novel; on the opposite end of the visual spectrum, Daryl Hannah is a space-age cyberpunk goddess as replicant Pris. The film as a whole is not perfect – at times it is sluggishly paced and wanders into an excessively philosophical dimension – but if remembered for nothing else, Scott's unique approach to art direction and set design secured Blade Runner's influence on countless science fiction films for decades to follow.

Thirty-three years after the film's initial theatrical release, Blade Runner exists in our modern world in many different varieties: whether you've seen the initial U.S. release, the "international" cut, the first "Director's Cut" (devoid of the painfully deadpan voiceover narration from Ford and the tacked-on 'happy' ending) – or the most

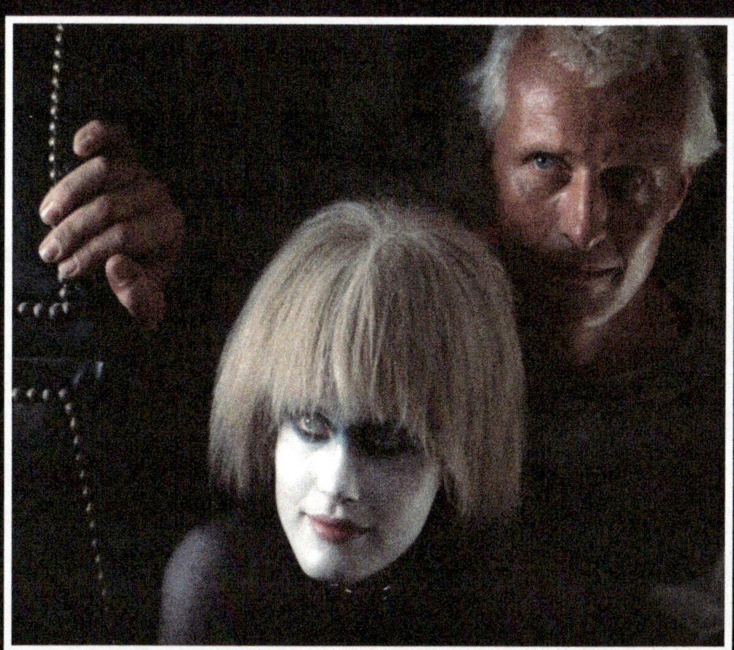

recent incarnation, the "Final Cut" – the film is ever-changing, and open for examination in ways not previously possible. The most famous subject for debate surrounding the film – whether or not a certain main character is, in fact, a replicant – is still being deliberated by fans old and new, who find intrigue not in definitively answering that question, but in pondering what the answer would imply about the future of the human race. The genre of science fiction, perhaps more than any other subject-specific forms of storytelling, often poses the loftiest questions – and it is our search for answers that brings us back to stories like Blade Runner, time and again.

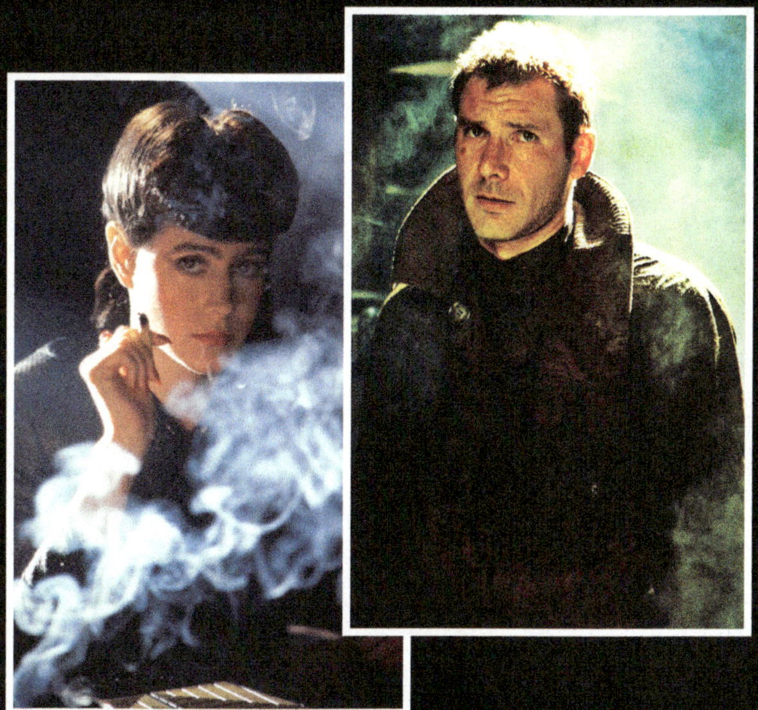

OONA, VINA, LEIA

By Isolde de Mortimer

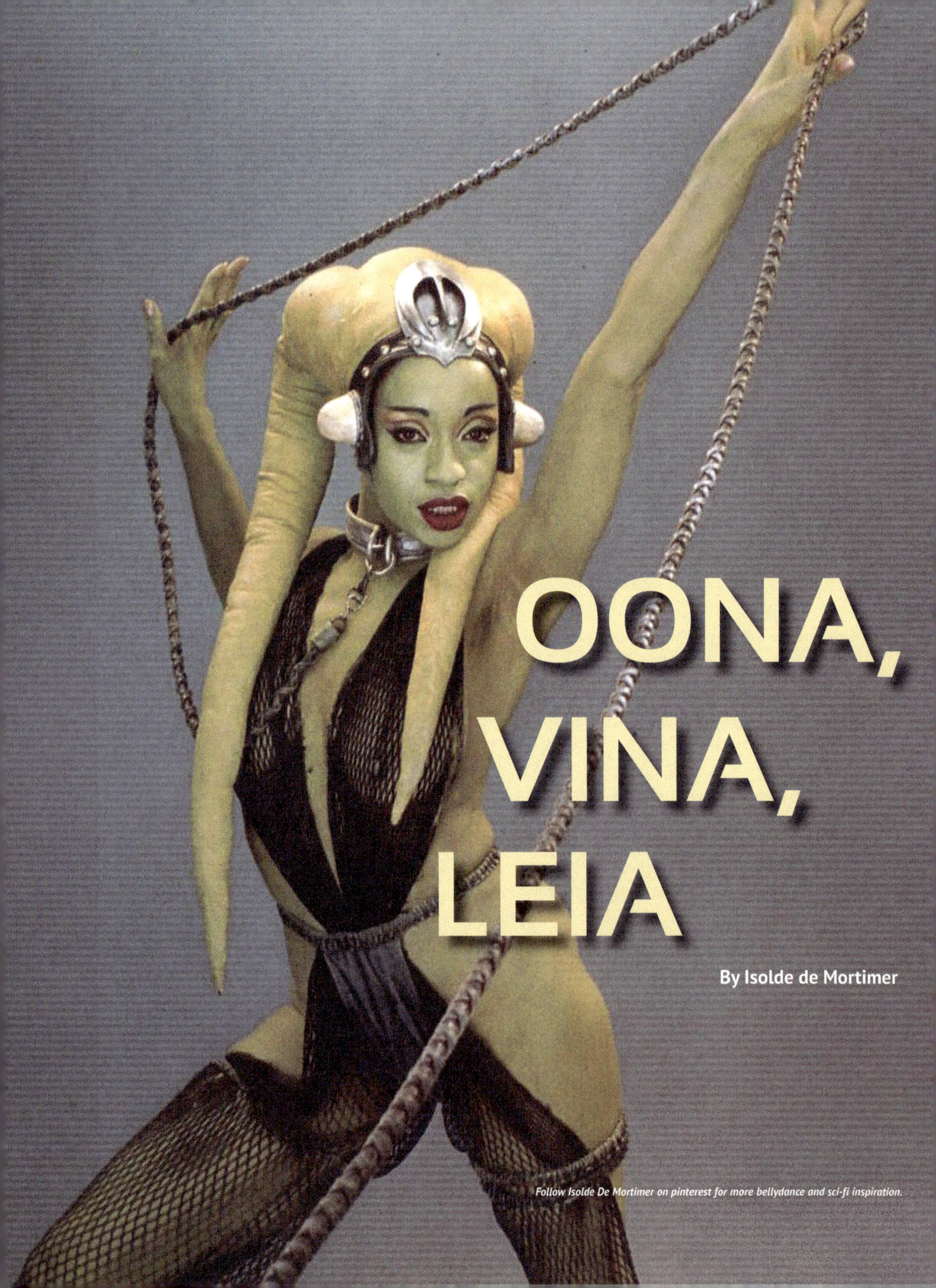

"We come spinning out of nothingness scattering stars... the stars form a circle and in the centre we dance." - Rumi, 13th Century

Ready to dance in a galaxy far, far away? Before you shake your cosmic thing, you'll want costuming and makeup worthy of an intergalactic empress.

First take your audience into account. Will you be dancing an edgy sci-fi inspired number for an audience of serious belly dance fans? Then hints of sci-fi in your costuming are all you need. Look to Jessica 6 from Logan's Run and Firefly's Inara Serra for costuming inspiration. Shimmery, floaty fabrics and metallics with sharp lines and angles will give you that galaxy girl feel without alienating your audience. That might sound like a costume you already own and by simply adding some chunky jewelry and sci-fi-looking accessories, you'll be set.

If you'll be dancing for a group of sci-fi fans you can be more specific in your characterization. Princess Leia's golden bikini from Star Wars fame or Leeloo's "bandages" from The Fifth Element are iconic. Any costume that would suggest either of these characters will be instantly recognizable for any sci-fi fan. You don't have to copy their unforgiving costumes exactly. Make tweaks to create a more dance friendly version or one that's more flattering to your figure. Flesh-toned mesh could be a real lifesaver here!

For some campy, classic cheesecake, look no further than cult classic Barbarella, a wide-eyed yet tough girl who has a variety of weapons in her arsenal. She wears distinctive black and white paired with silver accents and strategically placed sheer panels. Even more vintage and arguably more alien would be Theda Bara's giant beetle-looking headdress from her turn as Cleopatra. While not actually a sci-fi film, the part Egyptian, part art deco, part insect shows that a few simple touches can take you from belly dancer to futuristic femme fatale.

If you'd like to take your costume to the next level, glow-in-the dark fabric or battery powered led lights can be showy! These can be added to a costume you already have which is a nice time-saver and can be removed later to conserve resources. Glow-in-the-dark paints are available at craft stores and allow more versatility than

sewing with luminescent fabric, but are a more permanent option. And there's always the possibility of costume malfunction when you use gimmicks so test, practice in your costume, and retest.

Of course, not all alien women are sparkly and sweet. Maybe you're thinking more of a fighter like Trinity from The Matrix or Defiance's Irisa. A ripped tank top or tattered sports bra paired with cargo pants, embellished with pieces of plastic "armor" and studs will give you a soldier feel. A few spikes on your costume or your jewelry will create a grittier bounty hunter look. Add a knife or laser-style gun strapped to your leg (or for a prop) and you're a warrior princess.

Some of the most popular sci-fi women have rather neutral makeup. For example Princess Leia and Lieutenant Uhura from Star Trek aren't very sci-fi as far as their makeup. But if you want to carry your theme into your makeup consider your venue. If you'll be dancing on an elevated stage with lightning, then little crystals or blue eyebrows may be too subtle to read from afar. Simple and graphic will work well. Think over-the-top exaggeration; extra long, extra color, extra thick, as in lashes, liner, shadow. Something as simple as extending your colorful shadow and liner from lids to hairline, angled upwards like Princess Aura from Flash Gordon, makes your makeup unusual without a lot of fuss.

A quick way to be more otherworldly is by adding unexpected texture or color to your face like turquoise contour or glitter on your lips. If glitter isn't your thing, a simple texture technique is laying fishnet or lace over your skin and applying loose pigment on top then lift off the fabric. Go with a shimmery color for a more glam alien or earthy colors for a more animal-human hybrid. You can also draw your own scroll or lacy pattern with liner or paint it on with pigment and extender.

If you just want to be sparkly and ethereal, look to Blade Runner's Zhora. Her overall shimmer and loads of crystals is easily replicated with body shimmer, flat backed acrylic gems, and eyelash glue. Want to be more edgy? For a more human-machine fusion like Star Trek's 7 or 9, take a trip to the hardware store for small, lightweight,

flat-backed washers and gears and adhere with body glue. Small spikes or studs from the craft store will also work.

Pris from Blade Runner sports a bold black stripe across her face that is simple yet effective. With some imagination you can change the black to another color and play with the placement and width. Just under the eyes or tapered ends angling up or down. Layer on glitter or gems or outline in another color depending on the look you're going for.

For supernova impact you can paint yourself silvery green like Oona from Return of the Jedi or Avatar blue. The application will need to be flawless so get help for those hard to reach places. Body paints and glitter that glow are also available. Wide stripes painted on arms and legs would show better than a bit sprinkled on your eyelids.

Specialty lenses may not be apparent in a large venue, but in a more intimate setting where you can look audience members in the eyes they'll have the desired effect. If you're comfortable dancing while wearing them, they'd be a great addition to your costuming.

Don't forget to dress-up your hair with an unusual style, color or sparkle. Cinnamon rolls not required! Wigs, clip-in extensions, hair tinsel are some of the ways for a quick and temporary hair change. Always practice in full costume to make sure you have everything securely in place. A flying hairpiece would distract you and your audience!

If you chose to mix details of your costuming and music proceed with caution. While the green seductress Vina from Star Trek dancing to music from Star Wars could be entertaining, a Princess Leia bikini paired with Leeloo's orange unkempt hair could be confusing. Combining complete themes within each element is safer.

Keep your elements clear and plan appropriately for whom you'll be dancing and where. Complement the venue, theme of the performance, and the setting. Live long and belly dance!

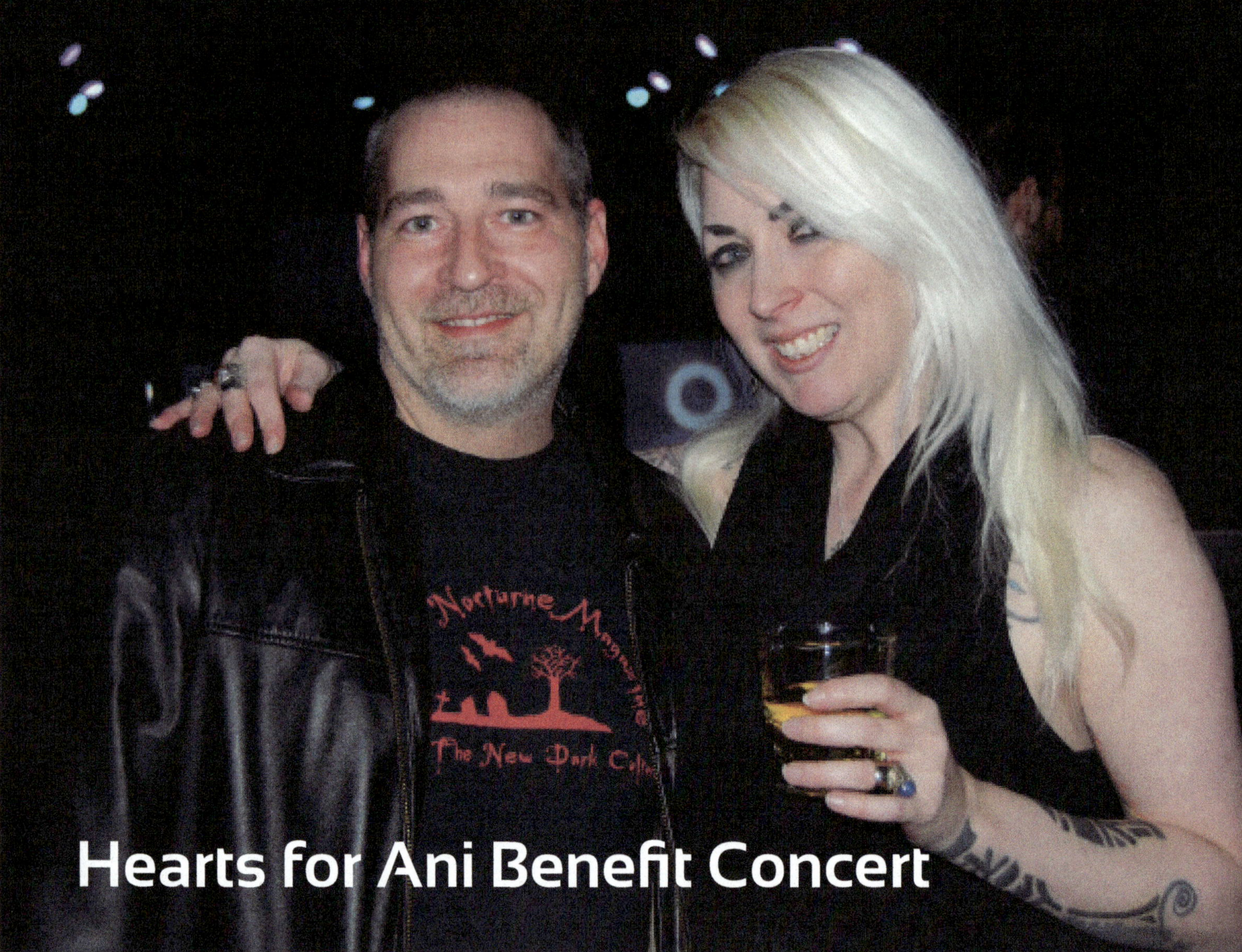

Hearts for Ani Benefit Concert

By Michael Jack   On December 5th, I was fortunate enough to attend a benefit concert held for a young woman named Annika Horn. Annika was a victim of a violent attack in her home. Stabbed over twenty times, she wasn't expected to live. The night of December 5th was not only friends coming together to help a remarkable woman in her time of need, but a celebration of the person she is and continues to be. I got a chance to meet this amazing woman that night, and experienced a concert unlike any I have ever attended.

The location of the event was Tellus360 in downtown Lancaster, PA, and the venue was donated by the establishment. The mood was upbeat and casual, with band members intermingling with the crowd. Everyone were friends that night. With my best friend and photographer, Eleuterio Santana in tow, I made a beeline for Donna Lynch. I am a huge Ego Likeness fan, and have spoken to her via Facebook several times. Donna is a sweetheart, extremely intelligent, and amazingly talented. She is also a lot taller than I expected. I guess it's hard to gauge when she is standing on stage. I am not going to run down the conversation, but it definitely was a highlight for me.

Before long, Donna's husband and EL partner, Steven Archer, took the stage. Stoneburner was about to perform. If you have never heard Steven's solo project, I suggest you do. The music is mesmerizing and so completely different. I've said it before, and I'll say it again, Steven Archer is a genius. He also makes me dizzy watching him. The guy never stops moving. I was excited to see belly dancers accompanying Stoneburner on stage. As I learned, Steven contacts the local troupe of each city, and has them perform along side of him. That night it was Troupe SYN based out of Hershey, PA. You were amazing, ladies!!!

In between bands I got a chance to meet and speak to J. Ward, now retired founder of COMA magazine. He made the trip up from Baltimore to attend the event. It was fun to talk shop for a while, and the conversation proved insightful. He was also a heck of a nice guy. I'm glad I got to meet him.

I don't remember the exact time Ego Likeness took the stage, but apart from attending the event to support Annika, they were the other reason I was there. In fact, the entire reason I knew about the event is because I follow Ego Likeness. The performance itself, what can I say? It was the second time I have seen Ego Likeness perform live, and the concert was every bit as amazing as the first time I had seen them. Donna Lynch is such a gifted singer. The highlights of the performance for me were "Aviary" and "Thirty Year War." They are just two incredible songs.

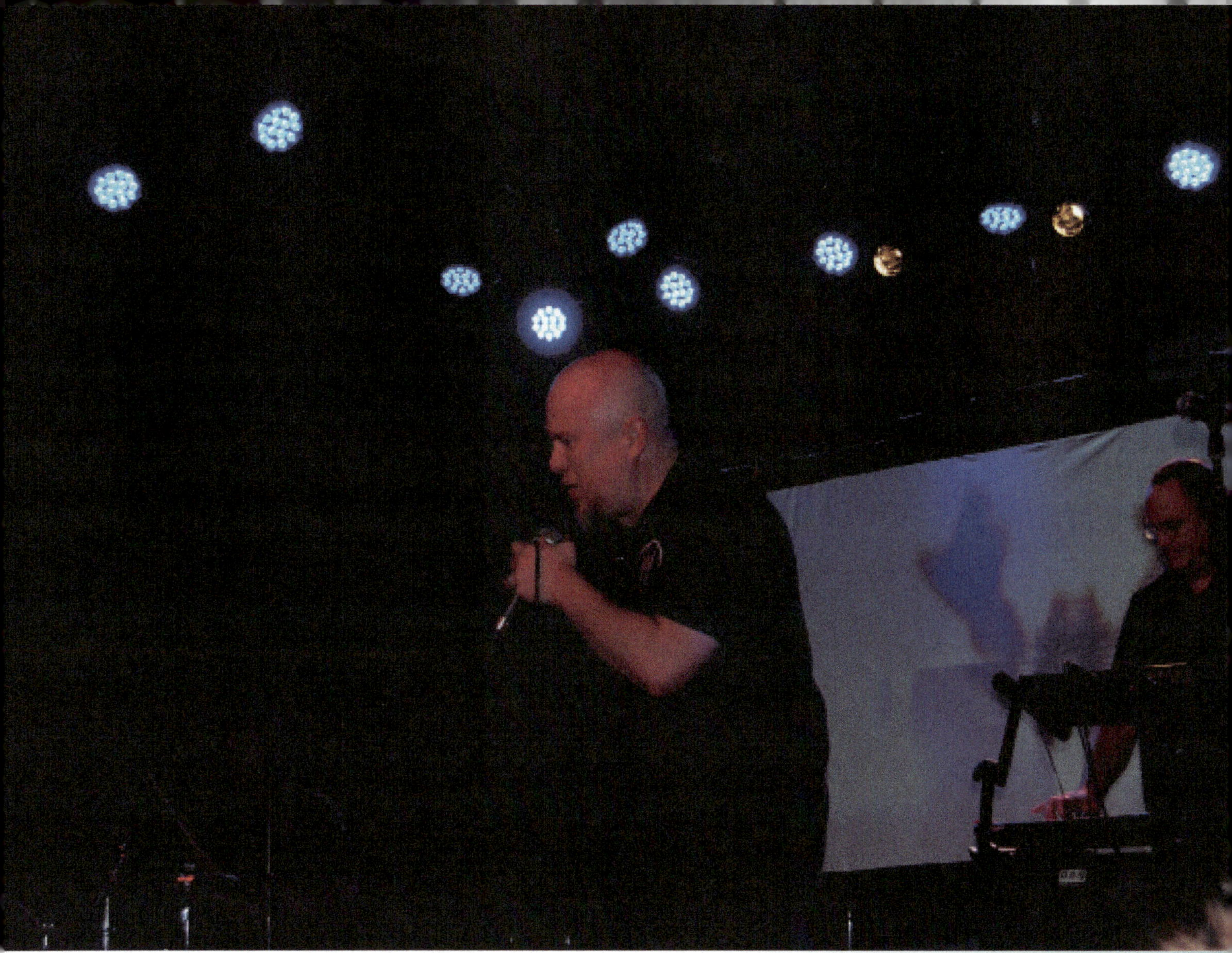

As everyone waited for Assemblage 23 to take the stage, I made my last few rounds of the evening. I got a chance to speak with event organizer Daniel Joseph McCullough, who did such an amazing job, before he took the stage and thanked everyone for attending. I also got a chance to speak to Annika herself, and she truly is an inspiration. If I could describe her simply, it would be charming, sincere, and genuine. I walked away from the conversation feeling fortunate I was able to be there and help out in a small way. It was truly uplifting to see her smiling and dancing, just like we all were.

It was past midnight when Assemblage 23 took the stage. Everyone was beyond psyched, and for me, it was the first time I would be experiencing them live. Assemblage 23 were fantastic, and I will definitely go back to see them when they come back around. The evening ended with a few surprises for the fans. The biggest was Donna Lynch joining Assemblage 23 on stage, and performing Bruderschaft's "Forever." What an amazing combination of talent. It was a once in a lifetime experience, and I was there to witness it. The evening ended around 2am, and by that time, I was tired, yet elated. Again, I'm glad I was able to attend, see an incredible show, and support such a courageous woman. This is one concert I will never forget.

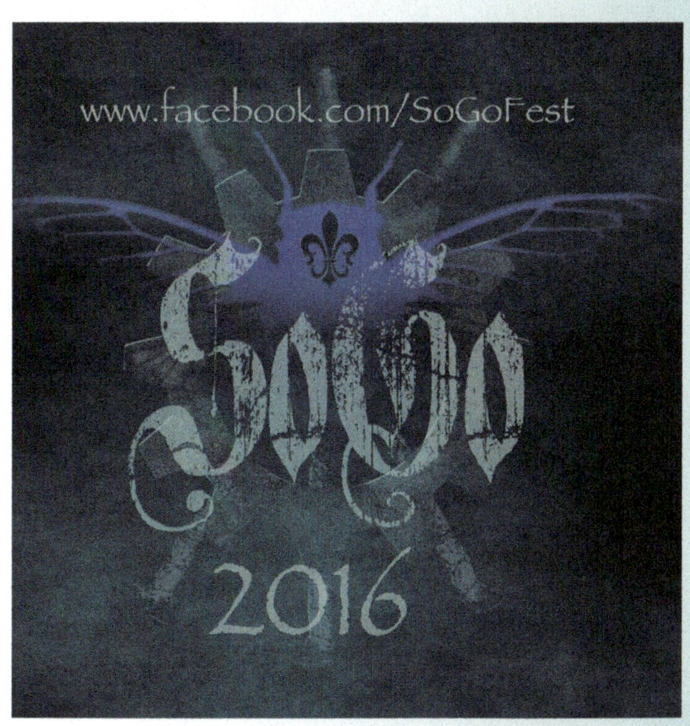

MUSIC

By Dawn Wood

My Life with the Thrill Kill Kult's long-awaited new release was unleashed in May 2014, followed by a steady 6 week tour of the United States. I was fortunate to catch their show in Philadelphia and my band opened for them in Seattle. The last Thrill Kill show I caught was in Seattle in 2012 and this new tour was a bit scaled down, lighter and *warmly funky*. Their support tour opener, DJ Toxic Rainbow, sets the mood for a dancier version of TKK. (DJ Toxic Rainbow won the *Beatport.com* THRILL KILL KULT "Kooler Than Jesus" remix contest, and has since done various remix work for the band and Groovie's side-project DARLING KANDIE.) Amongst old TKK favorites: a remixed version of "*Swine and Roses*", a fun call and response to "*My Life with the Thrill Kill Kult*" and my personal favorite "After the Flesh" from "The Crow" Soundtrack.

The new CD is the band's 13th studio album entitled: "*Spooky Tricks*" It is fun, interesting and certainly versatile enough to be played at any club. The influence of 70's electro music and some spaghetti western-esque guitars grace the collection of music. My personal favorites being: "*Neon Diva*", "Hell Kat Klub" and "*The Way We Live Now*".

The current lineup of My Life with the Thrill Kill Kult is: Groovie Mann, Buzz McCoy, Mimi Star, Justin Thyme and Westin Halvorson (whom Carpe Nocturne has featured in previous issues with TKK, Desillusion and Endless Sunder) . The band has progressed with an assortment of members over the past 25 years. Taken directly from the biography on the Official Thrill Kill Kult Website: It was in the fall of 1987, in a neighborhood Chicago bar. Artist and performer Franke Nardiello met with newly transplanted Bostonian musician Marston Daley over drinks. They crafted a shocking and lurid film concept, MY LIFE WITH THE THRILL KILL KULT. Inspired by a shared love of tabloid tales of sex, kitschy horror and exploitation films in the style of Russ Myers, the concept came naturally. The name was ripped straight from a British headline Nardiello had noted while living in London. With limited experience and resources the film was scrapped, but work on its accompanying soundtrack continued. Legendary Chicago record label Wax Trax! Records were drawn by the hard beats, distorted vocals, rich instruments and bizarre film samples. They released a three song EP in 1988. The full-length album, *I SEE GOOD SPIRITS AND I SEE BAD SPIRITS,* followed the same year. People seemed to love it almost instantly, and so, their dreams of celluloid became a reality on vinyl.

In the spring of 1989, Nardiello and Daley took on the names Groovie Mann and Buzz McCoy (respectfully). They recruited band members from bar stools and created a back-up group of singers/dancers dubbed the BOMB GANG GIRLZ. They jammed the crew of nine into a van with musical and stage gear alike, and hit the road. The tour had a "Cabaret From Hell" vibe and it aroused the curiosity of the kids and media, establishing THRILL KILL KULT as one of America's premier industrial/electro acts.

They continued to fuel the underground club dance floors with tracks like "*The Days Of Swine And Roses*", "*Kooler Than Jesus*" and "*A Daisy Chain 4 Satan*". The Parents Music Resource Center (PMRC) was appalled. It wasn't long before Groovie and Buzz started experimenting, combining disco bass with wah-wah guitars and dabbling in big bad burlesque brass. The result was SEXPLOSION! (1991). It was lusty and dangerous, giving them their first taste of commercial success with "*Sex On Wheelz*" and attracting a whole new set of fans.

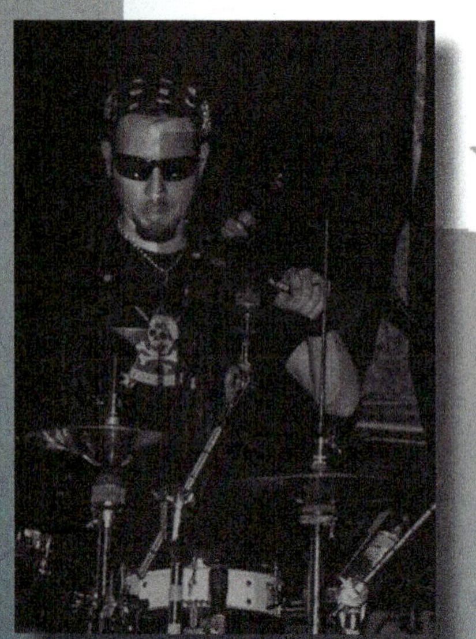

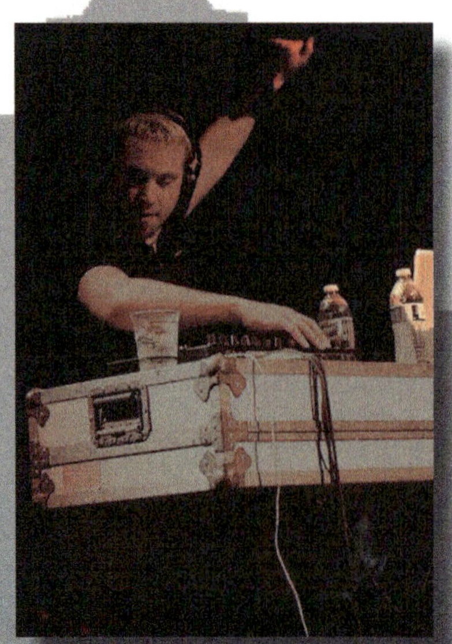

The explosion of popularity found TKK on Interscope and in 1993 they released 13 ABOVE THE NIGHT. Like all of their releases, it had an overpowering cinematic quality so it wasn't surprising when Hollywood took notice. The duo found themselves writing for an assortment of soundtracks like Paul Verhoeven's "*Showgirls*" and Ralph Bakshi's "*Cool World*." They even stepped in front of the camera for a cameo in the cult classic "The Crow" to perform the song "*After The Flesh*".

In 1998 MLWTTKK signed to Rykodisc, who reissued their Wax Trax! catalog. And later, GAY, BLACK & MARRIED (2005), an homage to the 70's disco era, and the depraved strip-lounge-rock fest, FILTHIEST SHOW IN TOWN (2007).

They have released 2 albums on their own label, SLEAZEBOX MUSIC, as well as a BOMB GANG GIRLZ cd titled *A TASTE 4 TROUBLE*, written and produced by Buzz McCoy. It features the formidable long time vocalist and dancer Jacky Blacque, with a guest appearance by Groovie Mann.

Still a favorite among directors who are looking for sexy sleaze, their music is frequently in both major and independent films and television, most recently in Sexy Evil Genius (Lionsgate) But it doesn't end in with the studio, film and tv, Groovie and Buzz still take the KULT out on tour extensively along with a rotating cast of depraved characters. In 2010 they re-created their role in the "Sextacy Ball" tour along with Belgium's outrageous *Lords of Acid*. In 2011 they performed at the "Wax Trax! Retrospectacle" show in Chicago, with old label mates Front 242 and Revolting Cocks. And the fall of 2012, the KULT celecrates their milestone 25th anniversary with a 7 week tour of the States.

MY LIFE WITH THE THRILL KILL KULT continue to morph and stretch the fabric of music as we know it, always remaining true to the KULT and true innovators.

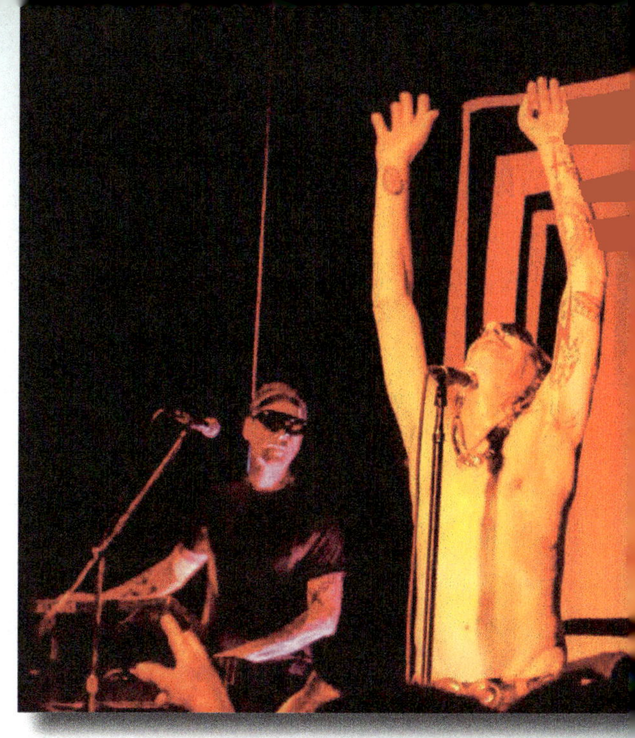

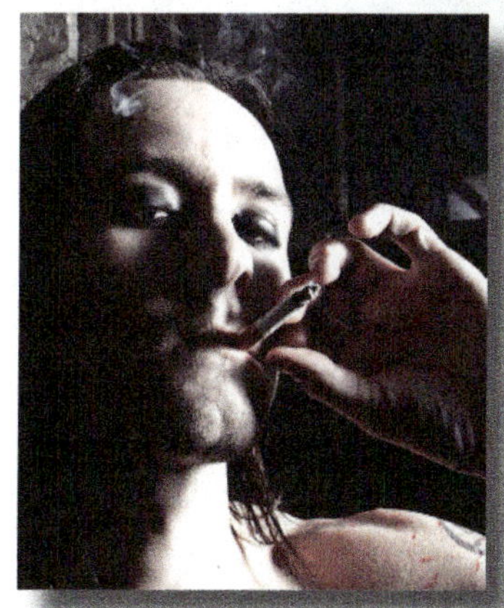

The new CD is a must have for your Thrill Kill collection:
http://mylifewiththethrillkillkult.com/store or Available on Amazon.com
www.facebook.com/thrillkillkult
http://mylifewiththethrillkillkult.com

Photos by:
Against the Grain: www.facebook.com/againstthegrainphoto
Fierce Bad Rabbit Photography: www.facebook.com/fiercebadrabbitphotography81

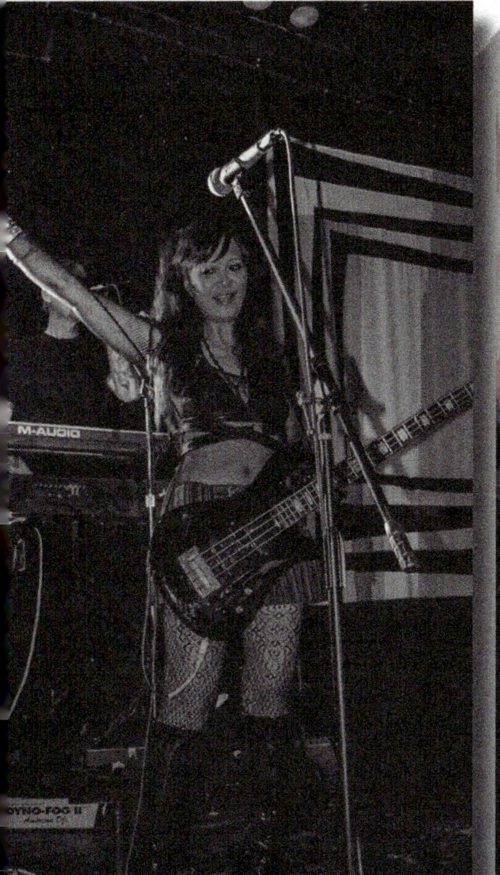

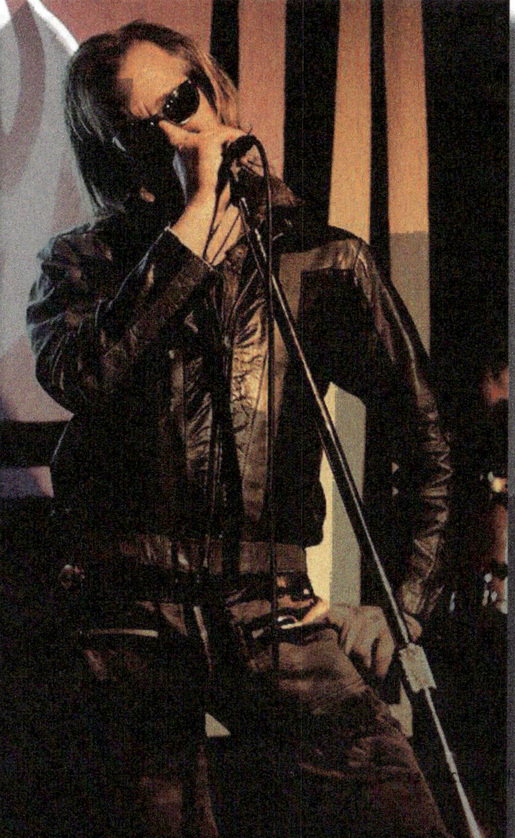

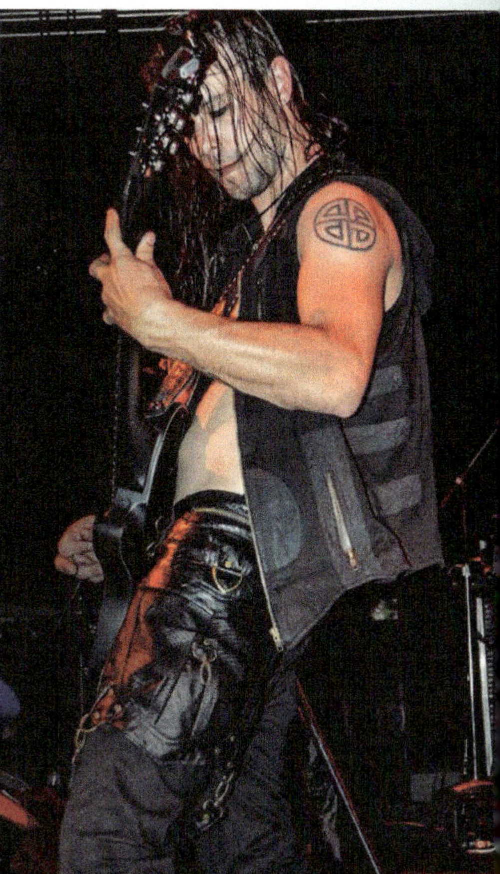

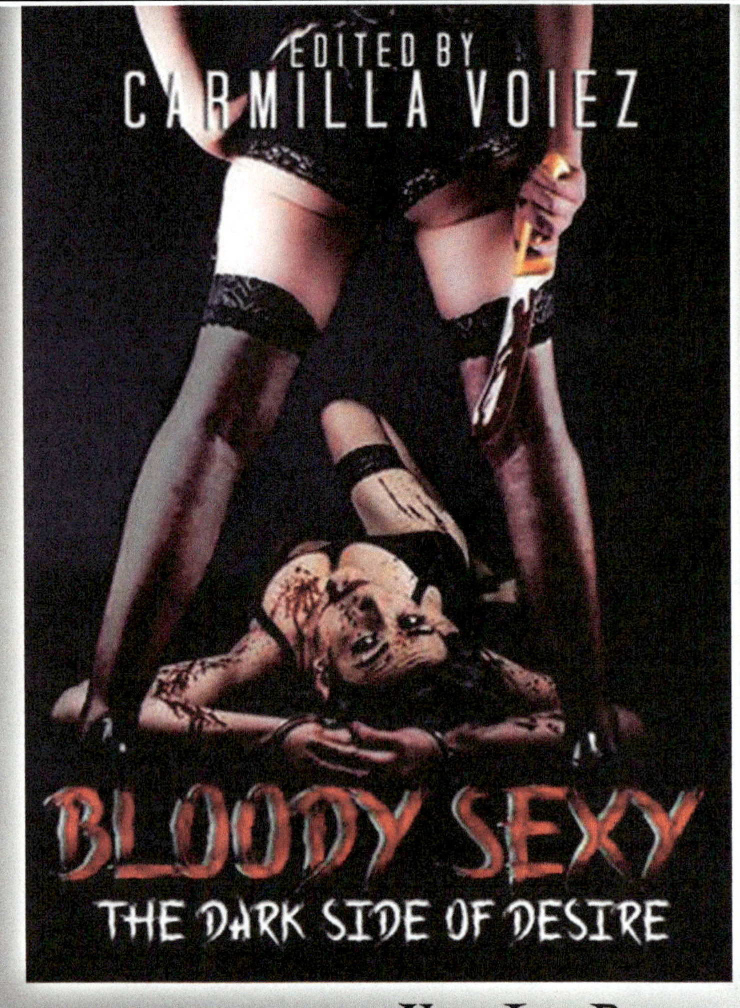

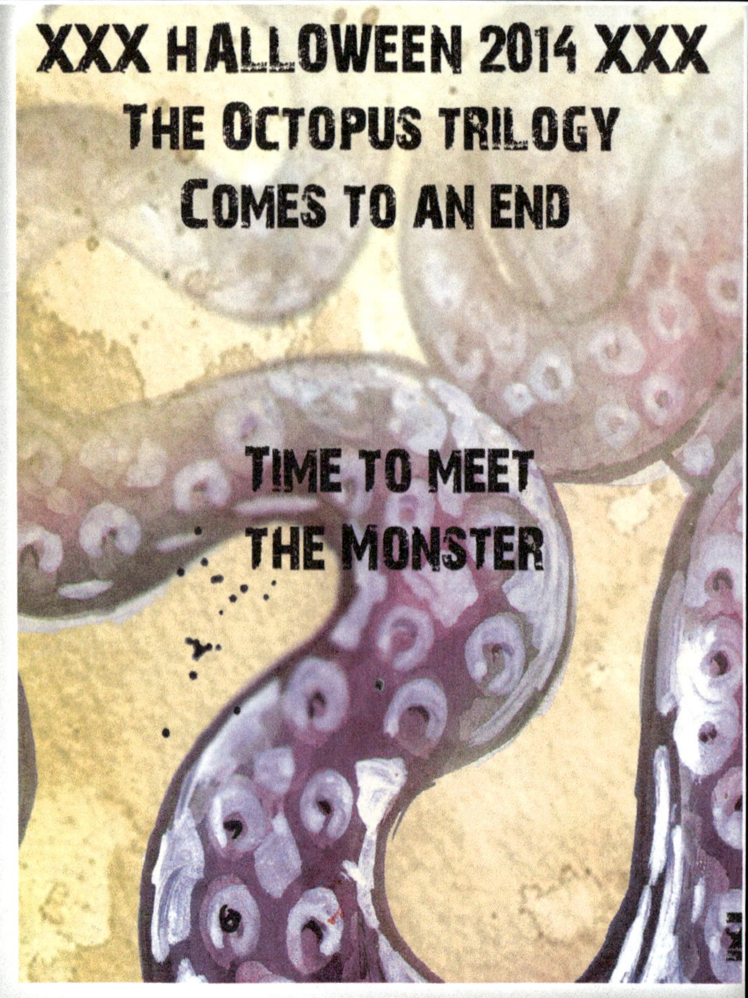

Available through Hot Ink Press

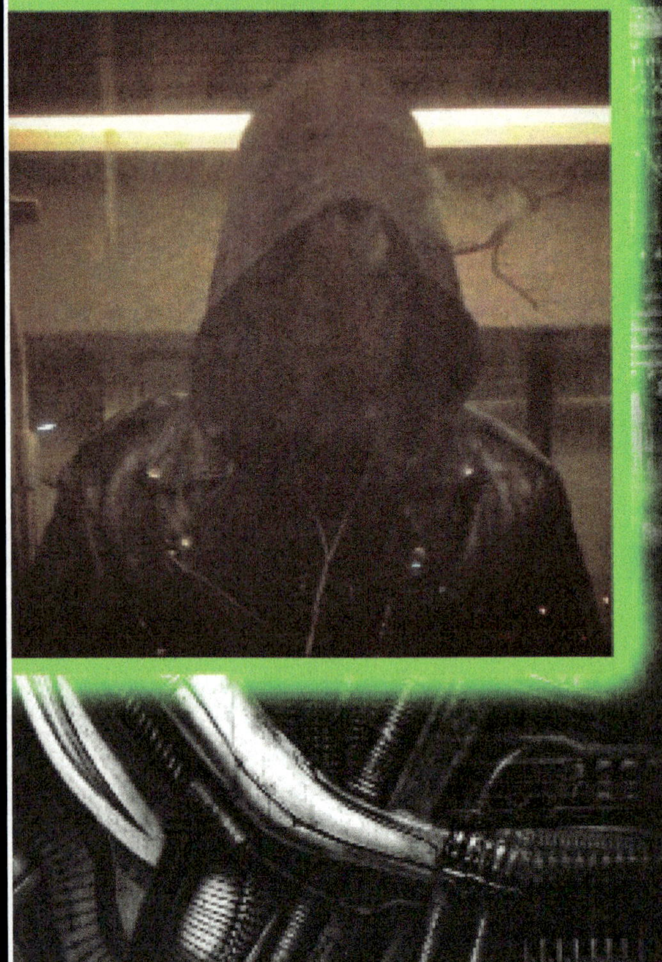

XXX ZOMBIEBOY'S TOP 13 XXX
SCI-FI Horror Films

1: Alien
2: Aliens
3: Event Horizon
4: Creature
5: Split Second
6: The Black Hole
7: Pitch Black
8: Predator
9: The Blob
10: Them
11: The Thing
12: Creepozoids
13: Every Frankenstein Film Ever

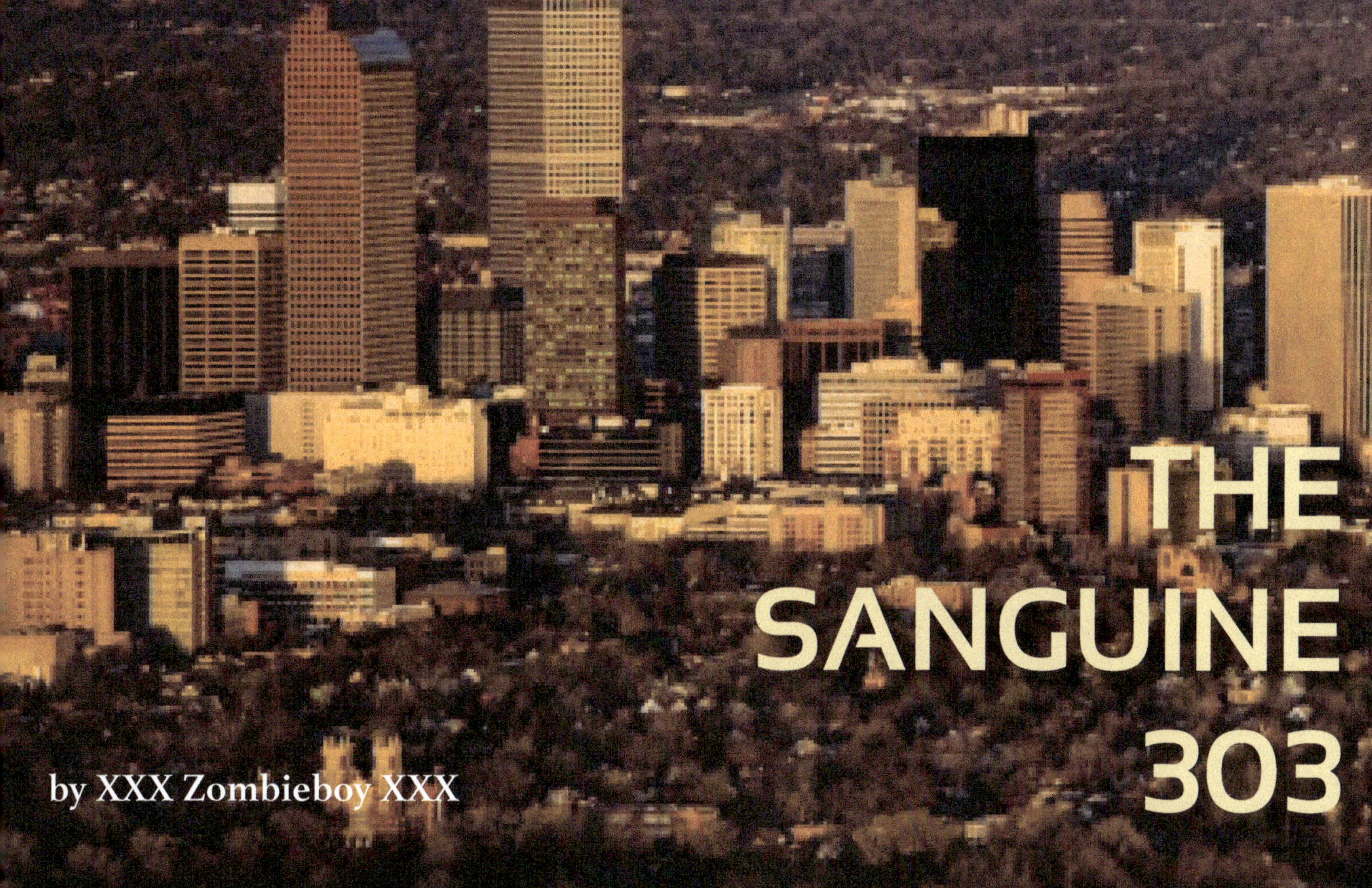

Braving the long and treacherous snowy highways across America, I sought a new home in a far away place, different from the one I knew. And upon entering the State of Colorado, though I had visited before, I had no true idea what to expect of my new home. I envisioned a great number of Western images, mountains, wide-open vistas, and more snow. And I thought to come across a few ghost stories and maybe some graveyards marked "Boot Hill". Truth be told I did find some of these things. What I did not expect to find was a place not only comfortable in the summer months but incredibly beautiful; a thrumming metropolis full of art and culture. I knew even less about the scene I was walking into...

by XXX Zombieboy XXX

I was pleasantly surprised to find one that not only thrived, but is widely tolerated, celebrated and welcoming. Here the people make eye contact and smile on the sidewalks. There is a band playing, a show to see, a club night to attend and something interesting to do every night. There is a bar on every corner, each with its own unique feel. And there is an air of weirdness lurking just beneath a layer of normalcy. There was also a darker side that did not hide on the streets. With tales of ghosts and haunted sites, dozens of haunted houses in the Halloween months, numerous creepy abandoned warehouses, a thriving Goth scene, and even the site of the Shining itself. Now as I face yet another move and another adventure, I wanted to share with you what I have come to think of as the Sanguine 303. And a number of the kind local celebrities, artists and musicians were awesome enough to take the time to share with me their thoughts on this place nestled against the Rockies.

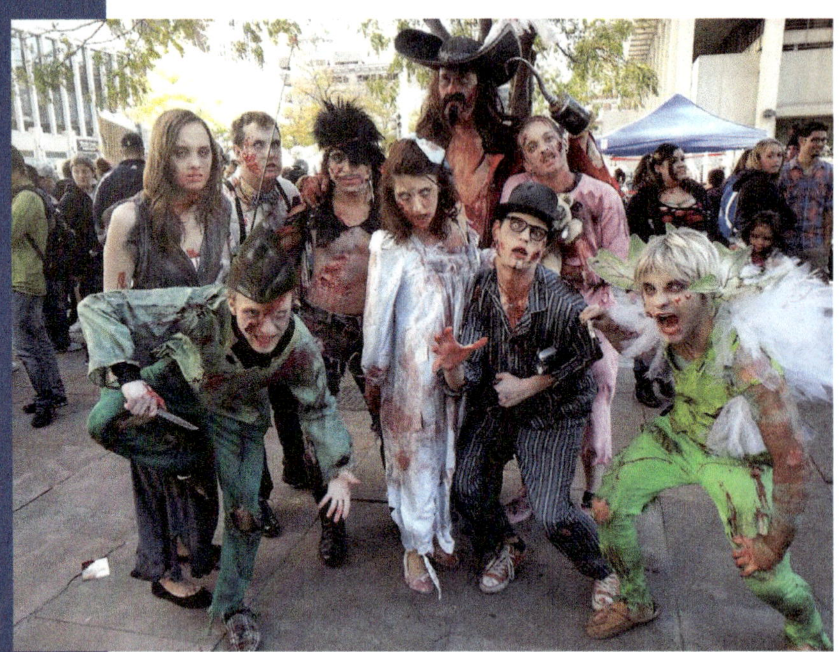

[XXX ZOMBIEBOY XXX] *One of the fascinating aspects of Denver I have discovered is that it seems almost everyone I have met here is from somewhere else. Are you all natives or do you hail from another local?*

[Isibella Mircalla Karnstein] Yeah you are right; I actually am from London, England.

[Amunet Isfet] I was born in Sidney, Nebraska.

[Cynthia Kalam] I've lived in Denver for over 21 years, so I consider myself a native but as previously mentioned, I was born in Cali. I am, however, of East Indian descent. Both of my parents are from Bangladesh, a tiny country on the Indian subcontinent. While I was born and raised in the states, my heritage greatly influences my life and many of my interest.

[Kimiko VonWyrd] I am from Denver. Born here and raised here, and I will probably die here unless Norway opens up its immigration possibilities a bit.

[Erik Kosnar] I would consider myself a local here, as I grew up predominantly in the Denver area. I find that most people who move here from out of state, especially recently are seeing what a strong scene Denver has always had, and in a lot of ways, while the current scene is different, it's also very much the same.

[Desiree Albee] I am a native!

[Rufio] Rufio is a proud openly gay native of Denver Colorado. He is proud to live in such a progressive state that is now a key destination for many artists such as his self. He has managed high designer fashion boutiques in leading city's such as Boston. He as well has a soft spot for Louisiana in doing up to 3 years of relief in New Orleans after Hurricane Katrina. The southern hospitality, Culture and Mystery of New Orleans inspired Rufio in living as a humanitarian and give appreciation for his community. His mission in Denver now as a leading multi genre artist is to develop Denver and bring the performing arts community of all creeds together. In Hope of Denver one day leading the nation in developing and leading the nation with its own style full of eccentric music, dance, art and entertainment for every one.

[Desiree Albee] Since I spent my whole adult life in LA I feel more like a non-native. When I moved back I only knew 2 people and had to start over with building friendships.

[Isibella] A certain gentleman with a very sexy American accent...

[Amunet Isfet] My parents moved back when I was about 4 so my mom could be closer to her parents.

[ZB] *Did you find Denver to be welcoming to your respective lifestyles and interests?*

[Isibella] Absolutely, Denver is incredibly welcoming for people who indulge in alternative lifestyles and fetish, I've always thought that.

[Cynthia Kalam] Denver has a great Goth/alternative scene. Most of the people involved are very sincere, friendly, and open. Denver's a great place to live if you're a little brown Goth girl who does paintings in blood. Alas, my strange ways have found me friends in Denver rather than repelling them!

[Erik Kosnar] I do have a comment on this. As a local guy, I'm always impressed by how many people find Denver to be a very accepting place, with a wide variety of lifestyles and interests for people to take part in. To be completely honest, it makes me proud to live here, and scared to live most anywhere else.

[ZB] *And did you find the scene to be inviting or did it take time to find your place?*

[Kimiko VonWyrd] I got into the Goth scene officially back in the late 90's, and yes, there were more options back then, but there is definitely plenty of ways to express your inner spooky kid. We are one of the few cities left that have multiple Goth nightclub nights. We have weekly nights, lots of monthly nights and plenty of places where the dark hearted can patronize and feel at home.

[Rufio] Denver Goth scene was very welcoming for Rufio as a young lost boy first introduced to the nightlife scene in 2005. Instead of first openly coming out as a gay male in the LGBTQ community; Rufio found his place regularly every Sunday at the "Church Night Club" one of Denver's leading Goth industrial nights.

[ZB] *What are your first/favorite memories of bands you've seen in Denver?*

[Erik Kosnar] I will always have an interesting perspective on this, since I was in a band from the late 90s until currently. When we started playing around 2000 there was a huge spurt of bands in the Denver area all going at once. People like Fiction8, Caustic Soul, and several others not only became great experiences watching and playing in shows with, but the scene was always supportive of everyone. That still makes the Denver scene a great place for local and out of state music. Most of my friends make a point to come to Denver on tours because the crowd is always into it.

[Cynthia Kalam] Hahaha, I have so many stories, two of my favorite shows from the last couple of years were Locura Fest in 2013 and Nick Cave and the Bad Seeds last summer at the Buell. I loved Locura because I got to hang out backstage and watch all the bands play from the side of the stage. I also got to spend time hanging out in the grass and having beers with my favorite band, HIM which was awesome! I loved seeing Nick Cave because even in his late fifties he never fails to put on a great show. He kept serenading me at the Buell during the show, which made me all twitterpated and brought out the little teenage schoolgirl in me; then after the show, came up to me and kissed me!!! (I don't usually kiss and tell, but that was too awesome!)

[ZB] *And since being here would you say that the music scene for Goth/industrial/metal and like genres is thriving still?*

[Kimiko VonWyrd] I think the genre is transitioning and we must transition with it. As far as Denver specifically I would say that we have one of the top gothic/industrial scenes in the US. As far as number of places that are not only 'Goth friendly' but cater to the sub-culture, Denver is high on that list. This didn't come by accident, there is a small army of people who work at it every day to keep us on the map.

[Cynthia Kalam] I'd say that it depends on the night you go out, but for the most part, I say yes. Denver's got not only a big scene, but also a very closely-knit community. Everyone seems to know each other, whether you like it or not sometimes!

[ZB] *What are some of the hidden treasures regarding music that you feel more folk should know about? Such as bands and artists?*

[Isibella] She's not really all that hidden, but Emilie Autumn is an absolute treasure in the world of alternative music, so unique,

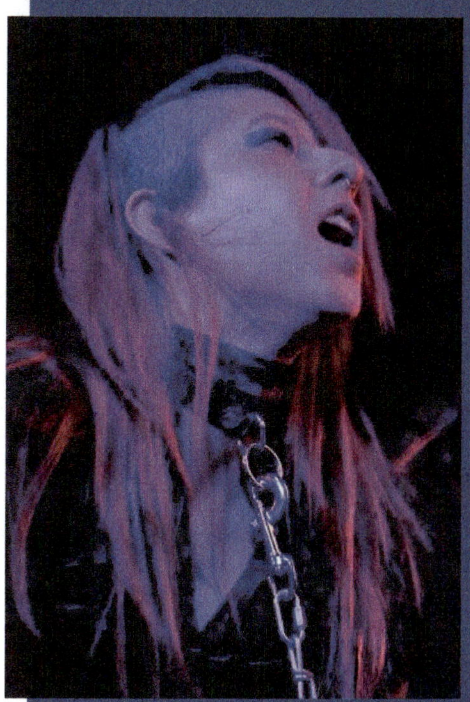

AMUNET ISFET

PROFESSION
By day: Receptionist at a veterinary clinic in Denver.
By night: Dancer, performer, artist.

BAND/NIGHT/CLUB/ETC
Bands are far too many to list.
The Church, Milk Bar, Syntax, Trax.
Any shows the strike my fancy.

BIO
I grew up in Commerce City. I was always drawn to the darker, romantic side of life. I didn't venture out into the club scene until I was about 20. From there my world was opened. I became exposed to a broad range of different aspects of the culture as a whole as well as introduced to some great music and talents. I have and still am enjoying many opportunities to preform with some truly great talent!

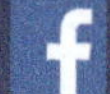 **Amunet Isfet**
St.Kittrn

I wish she'd get far far more recognition for her work.

[Cynthia Kalam] I love cheesy Gothy stuff from Finland. HIM is of course pretty popular, but some lesser-known bands from there are The 69 Eyes and The Rasmus. They have some really great stuff I would love to hear played in clubs. There's also a super obscure band I'm loving lately called Katie Cruel. I found them because their song,

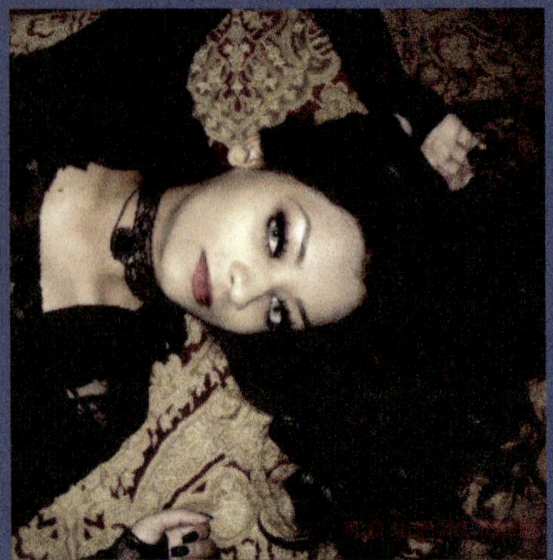

CYNTHIA KALAM

PROFESSION
Teacher, Artist, Poet, Dancer, Model, Paranormal Investigator

BIO
I was born on New Years Day in Los Angeles and moved with my family to Denver when I was three years old. I'm a graduate of University of Colorado Denver and currently work as a guest teacher for Denver Public Schools. In my spare time, I hunt ghosts and get into crazy shenanigans with my bestie, Isibella. In Denver's alternative scene, I am known for the work I've done modeling for dozens of photographers, and go go dancing at numerous events. I am also a bellydancer and enjoy shaking my hips to the sounds of the exotic East, which is where my family comes from. Currently, I am also working on a project that I'm really excited about. This summer, I will be releasing my first full length book of poetry and short fiction, entitled Nightshades of Eden which contains a set of illustrations which I have painted using my own blood.

"This is Not A Love Song" was played in the trailer for some seedy French film about a teenage prostitute. Unfortunately, I was only able to find two songs ever released by this artist, but those two songs are well worth listening to because of Wendy Rae Fowler's and haunting voice and the dark, sexy bass lines.

[ZB] *I've been to both the Church and to Milk. Both have been wonderful experiences along with certain monthly nights like Ominous. Yet I understand that the scene used to have many more clubs. Some open every night. What are some of your favorite old/current club nights and why?*

[Kimiko VonWyrd] Ominous and Sanctuary Radio put on some good nights month after month and try to keep things fresh and interesting. Milk Bar is a great weekly night and the Church is an institution at this point. The two old clubs I miss dearly are Onyx and Rock Island. Onyx was like the gothic version of Studio 54. It was debauchery incarnate and hit at the right time for the Denver scene. Rock Island was a great space, hosted great bands and had some really awesome DJs that introduced me to many of my favorites. It was a sad day when we lost those places.

[ZB] *What do you think caused the loss of some of the older nights?*

[Cynthia Kalam] Probably because of power struggles and rivalries, which is unfortunately, still prevalent even in the few remaining Goth nights/events in Denver.

[Rufio] Rufio is proud to say that the leading Goth/industrial event coordinators, performers and promoters are all in sync as a community to promote each other's events as a whole rather than competition. We are all very excited for what the future of what comes of Denver in the next years doubling the population from corners of the U.S.

[Kimiko VonWyrd] After you do it for so many years, people move on. Money gets tight, the neighborhood gentrifies and rents go up, who knows. Good things don't last forever, and neither did these places.

[ZB] *There are many other clubs, bars and café's that have dark or just unique settings. What are some that you enjoy? What are your favorite bars and such that aren't clubs?*

[Cynthia Kalam] I love Double Daughter's Salotto, which is probably where I'll be hosting my book launch party. I had always wanted to go there since before I could drink, and for a while I was living very close by, so I would pop in a couple of times a week to unwind and have one of their unique cocktails, with names like Severed Goat's Head, Fuego del Abajo, and Teddy Bear Orgy (which comes garnished with a stick of four gummy bears). The most impressive part of it is the decor. It's got a massive set of gold doors at the entrance, and the inside of the bar is utterly gorgeous. It's got two enormous black dead trees from which hang dozens of ghostly white doves. There's a row of booths leading up to the loft, all of which are shaped like huge blood drops, and the barstools look like they are dripping blood to match. The fence surrounding the loft area is made of axe handles, and behind the bar, there is a large water filled sculpture that looks like something that belongs in a steampunk boiler room. I just wished they'd play better music in there, though it also depends mainly on who is behind the bar choosing the tunes.

[Erik Kosnar] Denver definitely has plenty of bars, and there is a different flavor for everyone. If you want Metal and great beer, there is always TRVE. It's definitely one of my favorites. Atomic Cowboy has a good environment, with great pizza. For a strange atmosphere, Mario's Double Daughters is awesome.

[ZB] *There are also a few surviving gothic/metal clothing stores and some that have moved on. Tell us about these if you would?*

[Rufio] Rufio actually has his own personal team of leather and seamstress that design all of his dancers costumes and outfits. He loves to buy all of his bondage gear from the crypt and Needs off Broadway.

[Erik Kosnar] Fashion Nation has been an institution in Denver for many years. When it comes to clothing for the dark side, they are my one stop shop.

[ZB] *Then there are events all around the year. Some are publicly well known given all the winter sports and micro-brews in the area. Not to mention the legalization of ganja. But there are others not so well known catering to the darker aspects of art and music. Tell us a little about some of these events and when they are.*

[Isibella] I think I am guilty of hosting just these kinds of events, more so than my public events. Think *Eyes Wide Shut* in mansions with copious amounts of naked girls.

[Amunet Isfet] The Exile 4 fetish ball on August 29th would defiantly be one to check out. Greatly looking forward to the Colorado Goth festival on May 1st.

[Erik Kosnar] Denver's Kink/BDSM scene seldom intersects with the Goth scene in Denver (I hear this is odd?) but Exile has been going for the past few years in August and is one time you can expect to see everyone from both scenes mingling.

[ZB] *Have any of you staggered down 16th street during the annual Zombie Walk?*

[Rufio] Rufio every year is apart of the zombie crawl joining the several thousand other zombies along. Last year me and my crew of friends dressed up as Zombiefied Peter Pan Characters.

[ZB] *Not to beat an already beleaguered dead horse but any thoughts on the effects that the legalization of marijuana has had on the 303?*

[Amunet Isfet] I think that it has enabled a group of individuals to come together to get rid of a stereotype and by being able to show that there are real benefits to this plant.

[Kimiko VonWyrd] I think it's awesome for our city. I'm not a big smoker of it myself, but I am of the firm belief that the legalization is what is making our economy the best in the country. People moved here for the jobs and the freedom and stayed once they realized it's a really cool city. Come for the weed, stay for the amazing microbrews, restaurants, museums, culture, clubs, outdoor activities, beauty, and nice people. Somehow I don't think the Denver tourism bureau is going to pick that up as a slogan.

[ZB] *I know much of the spooky and haunted places surrounding many southern cities such as New Orleans. Yet I did not expect to experience this as much out here in the west. Yet, like New Orleans it almost feels like you cannot wave your arms around without smacking a ghost in the face! If you have any good Denver ghost stories I would love to share them with our readers.*

[Amunet Isfet] Oh, I have quite a few. The old apartment I used to live in on 13th and Pennsylvania has some stories. One of the times something spooky happened I was sitting in my living room watching a movie when all of the sudden I hear this whooshing sound. I couldn't make out what it could be so I walked through my bedroom towards the bathroom. Now, it had a claw foot tube with faucet handles that you had to crank to turn on. Both handles had been completely turned on. No one was home but the cat and me defiantly couldn't have done it.

[Isibella] I'm doing a ghost hunting TV show currently, and I think we have found a lot of places are quite haunted, had taps turning on by themselves in the underground bar in Colorado Springs. Had a glass of wine thrown in mid air and smash on me at V bar in the Springs. Lumber Baron inn in Denver is also quite haunted, as well as the infamous Stanley Hotel at Estes Park. Though that's a little more ghost tourism, but I did genuinely sneak into the basement of the concert hall and got myself accidentally locked in for half the night with their poltergeist known as Lucy! Not so fun, terrifying in fact!

[Rufio] My grandparents built there own Mansion on 50 acres of land. I remember as a child seeing fast shadows speeding by, coyotes starring at me through the windows, owls always landing on the ledges of the patio and snakes getting into the house. Toys without batteries would go off and standing furniture would move out of place. My mother sold the house after my grand parents passing. It was said that because of the plateau and high lands of the mountains that the surrounding area used to be an Indian burial ground.

[ZB] *What is the spookiest place in Denver?*

[Isibella] The spookiest place? I honestly don't even know if it is haunted, but if you go to Charlie Browns, there is the hotel attached next door. If you want to go to the rest room you have to leave the restaurant, go into the hotel lobby, then through a door into a stairwell and turn right. I think that stairwell gives me the creepiest vibe of any area in Denver, and I've been to a lot. All the hairs on the back of your neck stand up and It's like you feel that something is just going to leap out at you very fast. I've always felt that way in that place.

[Cynthia Kalam] Within Denver, sometimes I think it's my house! It was built in 1886 and actually has a creepy little dungeon-esque cellar! I don't know much of the actual history about the former residents, but I think there's an interesting energy in it. Though I love living there, the feeling of being watched by a spirit and unexplained noises in the middle of the night will make you kind of paranoid. Makes for excellent writing inspiration though! I also live going for cemetery walks. Mt. Olivet in Wheat Ridge and Fairmount on the outskirts of Denver are really big and have some gorgeous spooky scenery.

[ZB] *Anyone heard of Hatchet Lady?*

[Cynthia Kalam] Yes! I have always wanted to investigate Hatchet Lady Bridge but thus far have not the opportunity. It is a very distinctive "Colorado" ghost story.

[ZB] *I understand that one of the parks in the city was actually the inspiration for the movie Poltergeist?*

[Erik Kosnar] That would be Cheesman

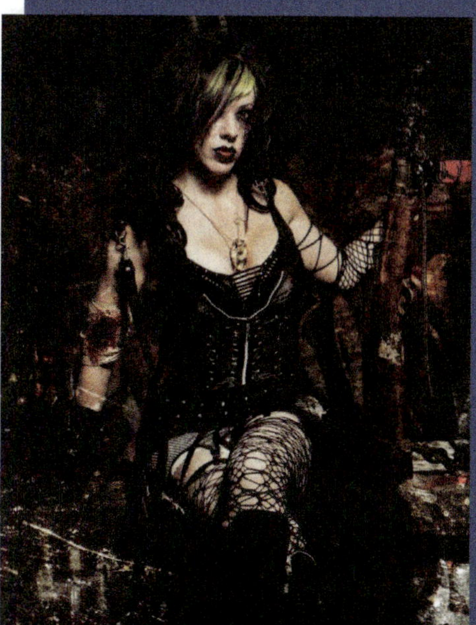

DESIREE ALBEE

PROFESSION
Creator, and Curator/Director of Repent at SIN Sundays, Club Promoter, Club set designer, Goth Bartender for MILK and CHURCH, Bartender and Bottle Service for SOCO Nightlife District, and Hollywood, CA go-go dancer

BAND/NIGHT/CLUB/ETC
Repent at SIN Sundays, SOCO Nightlife District

BIO
I grew up in on the outskirts of Parker in a small place called Elbert County. Parker, at the time, looked much different. There were dirt roads all the way to 1-25 and a gas station that doubled as a grocery store. To some that sounds horrifying, but I loved growing up there. In high school I was a cheerleader with a passion for art. When I graduated at 17 I moved to LA, CA where I went to school for Fashion Marketing and Design. I lived there for 12 years and was a big part of the scene there as well. I was a go-go dancer for 4 different Goth clubs, bartender, ran an adult toy store, was a buyer for a lingerie store, and had a clothing line. I moved back to Denver at 30. I became involved in the scene very quickly and wanted to bring a bit of LA to Denver. There are so many exciting things that are coming down the pipe for future projects.

 **Repent at SIN Sundays**

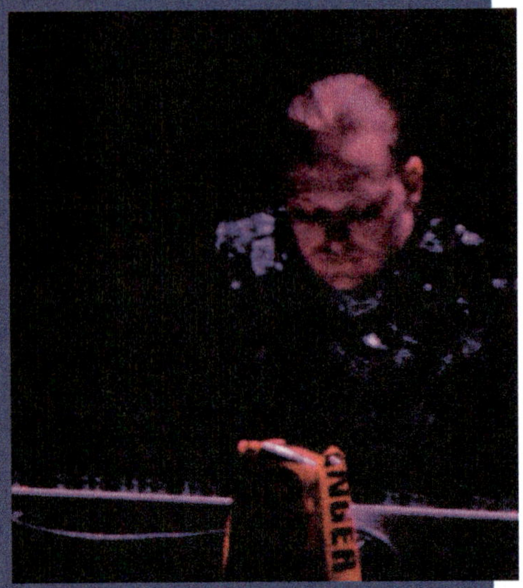

ERIK KOSNAR

PROFESSION
Musician and Graphic Designer

BAND/NIGHT/CLUB/ETC
Clouds Reign, Darker Days Tomorrow

BIO
Starting out in the Denver Goth scene in the mid 90s, the music immediately took hold of me. I was in the Band Emergence from 1999 until 2006, and Darker days tomorrow until the current time. My new project, Clouds Reign is set to take off soon, and it's very exciting.

Park. They moved the headstones, but not the bodies.

[Kimiko VonWyrd] This is true. Loose inspiration but yes. It used to be a cemetery and rather than dig up all the bodies and move them they just built the park over the top. It's supposed to be very weird at night with lots of orb sightings and such.

[Amunet Isfet] I know that the changing had been based on the experience of Russell Hunter while living on 13th in 1968.

[ZB] *Halloween is certainly very celebrated in this city. And the Haunted Houses are magnificent! What are some of your favorite haunted houses or Halloween/Samhain/Dia De Los Muertos events?*

[Kimiko VonWyrd] I used to run a haunted house so it was kind of my business to know the good ones. I will always have a special place in my heart for Frightmare. It's built in an old farm up in the northern suburbs. It's where I learned my chops as a haunted house actor and realized I have a pants wetting fear of stilt walking clowns with

chainsaws. Go figure. I hear that 13th Floor has a night after Halloween that you sign a waiver and it is full contact monster attacks. That may just be a rumor, but it makes my inner haunt running businessperson wince. Dear gods, the insurance nightmare...

[Desiree Albee] I bartend at the Goth clubs, and Halloween is my favorite! I love it more that Christmas! I look forward to seeing the creative costuming!

[ZB] *There is also a very thriving fine art and folk art community here. Are there any artists of the more gothic persuasion that you would like to give a shout out to?*

[Kimiko VonWyrd] I love the art of Kevin Eslinger and off the top of my head he is the only "fine" artist that I can think of. I've purchased some great art from galleries around Denver from local artists, but never got their names. There's a guy who does these great 'plague doctor in urban settings' types of things and I love his stuff. No idea who he is though.

[ZB] *Another aspect of the area is that it feels very liberal and welcoming to all lifestyles. At least on the surface. What are your thoughts on this?*

[Desiree Albee] Yes. Denver is very welcoming to its LGBT community. Repent is a wonderful example of that. From the team of people that help me put this show together to the go-go, performers, emcees, DJs, and vendors we pride ourselves in having a very diverse show that embraces ALL lifestyles.

[Kimiko VonWyrd] I would totally agree with this. You will always have some kind of bigoted asshole in any city, but I think that Denver is a very good place where all people are accepted. There are hangouts and places to go in many subcultures and lifestyles and on a random weekend night you will see all kinds of people just being themselves and not worrying (at least outwardly) about being attacked or hated on. It's kind of refreshing.

[Erik Kosnar] Denver used to be thought of as a rather right wing place. Since the mid 90s though, it's become incredibly liberal. As I have traveled around the country, both for work and as a touring musician, I can truly say that in my experiences, Denver is one of the least repressive places I've ever been.

[Cynthia Kalam] I certainly agree with that statement; Denver is very welcoming and you can see all varieties of people here in all shapes and sizes with all sorts of beliefs.

We all coexist here.

[ZB] *To the outsider who has never been out west or to Denver but may be considering moving to the area, what advice would you impart to them and what else would you have to say about the Sanguine 303?*

[Erik Kosnar] I like to tell people that Denver is one of the most fun and rewarding places to live. There is a thriving scene for just about everything and it's beautiful here. It's part of the reason rent prices are on the rise. Everyone is figuring that out.

[Kimiko VonWyrd] There are two things that I've heard that weird people out when they come to Denver. #1, people will actually acknowledge you when you pass them on the street. It's not a huge over the top thing, but they will nod, or smile or make eye contact. If you need recommendations or are lost people will usually go out of their way to help you. We are friendly without getting in your personal space. #2 the weather is wonky. It snows in June, and is 80 degrees in February. As I'm typing this it is 72 degrees outside in the beginning of February. It has also been known to do 2 or 3 seasons in the span of one day. I would like to think that most people who come here to scope it out will be pleasantly surprised. Denver may not

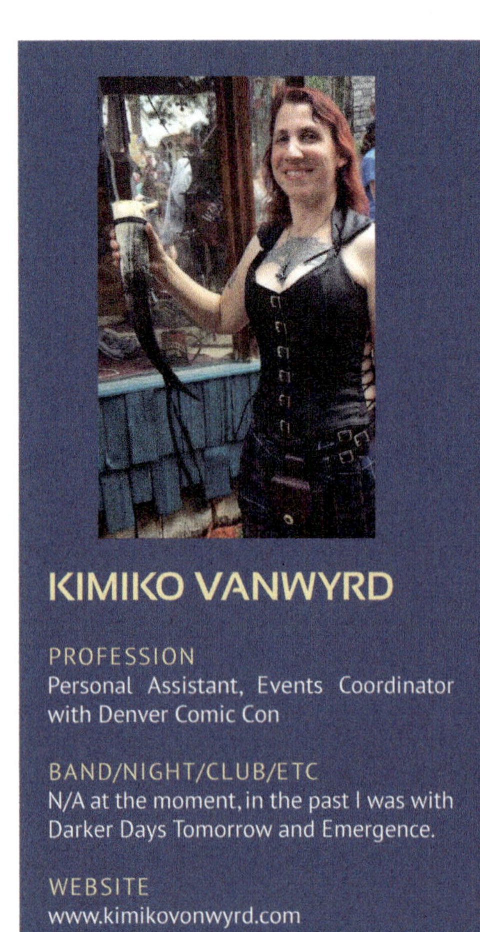

KIMIKO VANWYRD

PROFESSION
Personal Assistant, Events Coordinator with Denver Comic Con

BAND/NIGHT/CLUB/ETC
N/A at the moment, in the past I was with Darker Days Tomorrow and Emergence.

WEBSITE
www.kimikovonwyrd.com

have the slick reputation as a hip, exciting paradise, but that's almost what makes it better. There's not that level of pretention that comes with living in a "cool" town. We just do what we do.

[Desiree Albee] The same advice I'd give anyone moving anywhere. Be friendly, positive, and leave the high school "Mean Girl" mentality at home. You should always be yourself while being respectful of others. We are all different, and that is what is so beautiful. Of course clicks exist. But, you don't need to adhere to one to win friends.

[Rufio] Don't be shocked if someone opens doors, picks up trash, smiles, greets, says thank you, shares all in one day.

[Amunet Isfet] You will fall in love with the majestic, powerful mountains and the calming stillness of the prairie. The roaring bustle of the city and the dark, velvet blanket of the moon. A community of people who truly embrace not only people, but individuals. Our state is in the embrace of many great teachers and healers for many different aspects of life. That in itself is a reason to come to the 303. The Sanguine 303 is alive and well. So come take a bite.

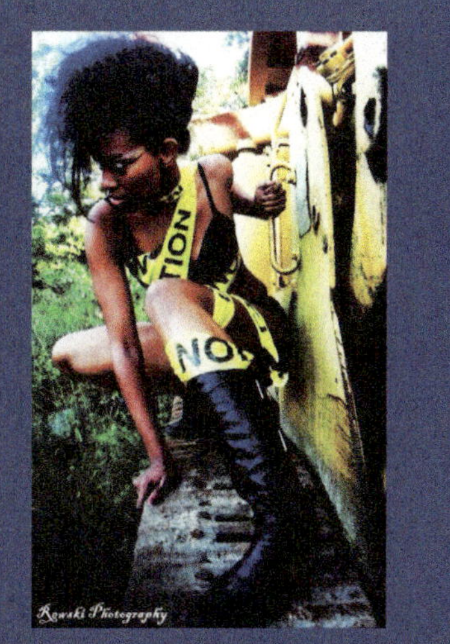

LUNA MINUIT

PROFESSION
Model, musician, artist, dancer, aerialist

BAND/NIGHT/CLUB/ETC
I am an art-addict. Better yet, I am a performance junkie. My passions lie in the arts, all of which can and are performed at least on some level.

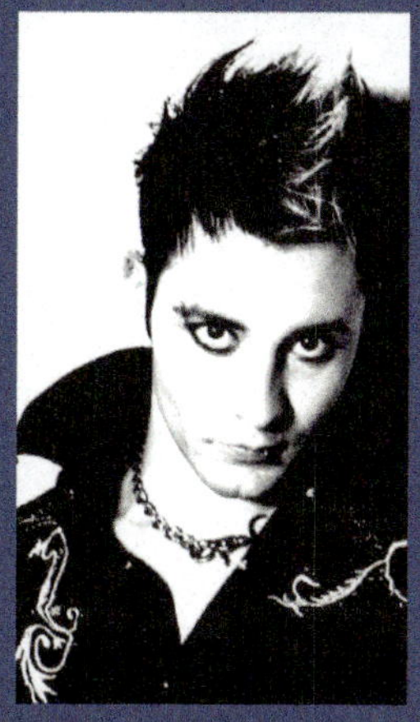

RUFIO

PROFESSION
Salonnière

BAND/NIGHT/CLUB/ETC
Performing Artist/ Angle Grinder/ Burlesque/Fire/Whips/ Stilits/ Gogo/ Event Coordinator

BIO
Rufio has been a leading male performing artist, social/equal rights activist and event coordinator in Denver for the last 5 years. As a classically trained percussionist he performs beat by beat with an appreciation for all musical styles such as Dark Alternative, Electronic, House and Hip-Hop. Rufio leads his bold brand of dance with eccentric costuming, striking stage performance and energetic technique.

WEBSITE
www.corkycaresfoundation.org

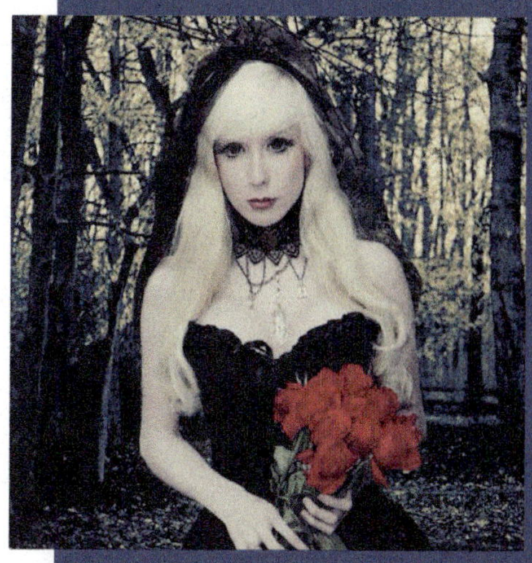

ISIBELLA MIRCALLA KARNSTEIN

PROFESSION
Salonnière

BAND/NIGHT/CLUB/ETC
Isibella's Parlor Presents events, and The Chateau.

BIO
I moved to Denver from the UK a couple of years ago, had always had an interest in alternative things and lifestyles. Started throwing nightlife and fetish/vampire events at Church nightclub, then had the pleasure of working with Father Sebastiaan last year for Endless Nights in New Orleans, then began hunting ghosts for a tv show and now running a website devoted to sexy cat girls! We also run a circus themed camp on the front row of the Burning Man festival known as Brûlée (Shout-out to Daniel, Gio, Angel, Jeff and Peter!) Been loving every minute of it.

WEBSITE
http://www.cirquedukinque.com
http://www.ghosthousegirls.com/
http://www.thechateau.org

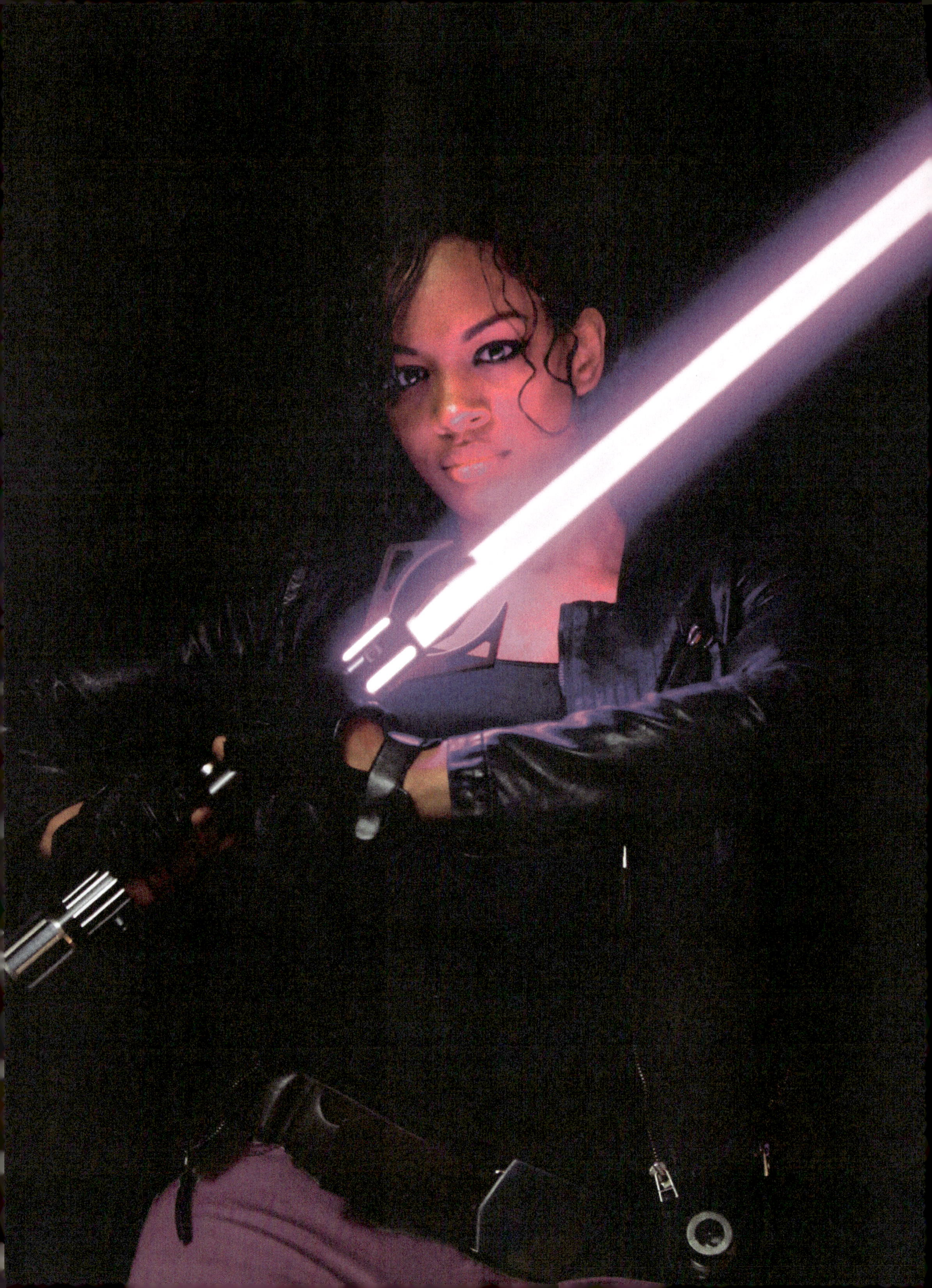

LUNA MINUIT

By XXX Zombieboy XXX

Our cover model for this issue hails from a far away land called Tallahassee, FL and has been slowly taking over the world ever since. A multi-disciplined and skilled artist, dancer, performer, singer and model, Luna Minuit stands poised to not only take over every artistic form she lays her hands on and mind to, but also to make us re-define our terms for each one! Luna was kind enough to take time out from her incredibly full schedule to talk with us about the Lunaverse!

[ZOMBIEBOY] *So, model, cosplayer, aerialist, dancer, choreographer, full time job and even learning the violin! I don't know how you found the time to talk to us but we are very grateful that you did! Thank you!*

[Luna Minuit] Thank you, Z! I'm thrilled to chat with you and humbled that you would like to indulge the ramblings of a silly!

[ZB] *The honor is ours! So let's start with your modeling. Is that something that always interested you?*

[LM] Well, not to get too lost in an artsy discussion so quickly, but when I was growing up, I dedicated myself to the art of dance. I hardly gave a thought to the idea of producing any visual art. As a child, I had an antiquated idea that models were untouchable, ethereal beings, born into beauty and wealth unlike the rest of us mere mortals. Of course, as I grew older and was exposed to the world (as wonderful and terrifying as it is), these ideals began to melt away. Models and photographers became more human. Due to a brief period of illness preventing the performance of my usual art form, I had a resounding moment of realization. One of those moments when you feel the epiphany ka-klunks into place in your brain...and then all of a sudden all of the electricity was flowing. I realized that models were human. Any human would do. It was both the minimum and maximum requirement. In addition, I realized that modeling is an art much like dancing... just slower. Every movement between the shutter clicks, miniscule or grand, is fraught with intention, creating another shape and image to tell a story through the viewfinder... in just a pinpoint in time. Bringing to life the visions of the photographer, the model, the designer, the make-up artist...all to convey a message. Whether it is beauty, isolation, or emotions.... But then there was another ka-thunk in my head. "Wait, a minute...I'm human!" I can do this! The idea remained a whisper in the back of my head as I continued to fantasize that I could be the person on the other side of the lens of my photographer friends. Then one day, I was asked (very casually) to model for a friend of mine who needed to test a new camera, and it seemed to work out. I am sure you hear it as often as I do, but I truly model for the fun and thrill of the challenge.

[ZB] *And going over your body of work you are very eclectic in both theme and visual style. Is there a particular aesthetic you prefer?*

[LM] Oh wow! I love it all! Honestly, I get most passionate about creating challenging images and aesthetics. Creating simplicity in a world of chaos, or bringing an array of subtle elements to a seemingly simple and stark photo. Being that my psyche tends to lean toward the darker aspects of existence, I am pulled toward those aesthetics as well. I find beauty in darker shoots, and run-down settings. Abandoned buildings, or tombstones reclaimed by nature intrigue me. I like the idea of contributing to the image and motif in the most natural way possible. That is not to say that I don't love to get decked out in my platforms, fishnet, corsets, and gloves for some quick shots!!

[ZB] *You worked with a body painter for this issue. It appears to be a growing trend. What are your thoughts on it and what was the experience like?*

[LM] It was cold!! And also incredibly rewarding! We had a ton of fun. It was my first experience working with a body painter on such a large project, and we had a blast. Tim Weiss with Tim's Airbrush (http://www. timsairbrush.com) was amazing to work with thanks to his easy-going nature and effortless professionalism. We spent the time chatting and listening to music as he artfully transformed me from a girl hanging out in her pjs on a Saturday, to a creature that may or may not have been related to a Xenomorph. I certainly understand why it is a growing trend. It can create the Russian Doll effect in photography. Art within art. I would do it again!

[ZB] *And with the recent passing of Giger I think it is not only a beautiful photo shoot but also a lovely salute to a great artist. Are there any photographers you have worked with you would like to give a shout out to? Are there any you hope to work with?*

[LM] Z, I have been incredibly fortunate to work with so many wonderful photographers! I must give a special shout out to Rewski Photography. Kayla was the first person ever to ask me to model for her, and I got lost in who I became through her lens. My first glimpse at how much I enjoy modeling. It all began with her. Her work has only grown exponentially since then, so please check out her page! I have also had the pleasure of working with Rob Timko Photography (http://www. timkophotography.com), Cindy Walker, Micco Photography (Facebook), No Signal Photography (Facebook), and of course Erik Kosnar, who also deserves special mention for capturing the somewhat biomechanoid girl you see in this issue.

[ZB] *Moving on to your aerial performance. As this is still a relatively underground form of expression, can you give those readers unfamiliar some background on the art form?*

[LM] I have certainly been met with every reaction in the book upon mentioning my involvement in the aerial arts!! For those who are not familiar, aerial arts are performed on aerial apparatuses, such as trapeze, lyra, aerial fabric/silks, sling, hammock, straps...believe me, the list goes on and on. Almost everyone can recognize these from a circus, and most notably, Cirque du Soleil. So...Yes, that.

[ZB] *What made you wish to become an aerialist?*

[LM] It all began with Cirque du Soleil marathons played on Bravo every few weeks or so. As a little girl, I would be sure to watch every single show that was aired. I was completely enamored by every little detail in the choreography, costuming, production, but most of all, the skill of the performers. More often than not, my parents would stumble upon me attempting (and not particularly succeeding) to contort myself between the sofa and the wall as I watched the performers from an impossible angle. It eventually became commonplace in my house. I often watched sections of the productions upside down as I attempted to train my own back bends and handstands. Eventually, I was able to attend a live show in Las Vegas, which only fueled my fire. We all realized it was only a matter of time and in 2009, I finally had the opportunity to join a local circus. Using my dance skills to gain a foothold, I took off from there. I climbed, swung, and dropped from anything within my reach. Eventually, I moved to Denver, where I was able to structure my training in a much more efficient way, focusing on aerial fabric and rope. I have since expanded my training trapeze, lyra, and rope/harness, with ambitions to conquer every apparatus made available to me at a professional company member at Iluminar Aerial in Broomfield, CO (www.iluminaraerial.com). For me, there is nothing quite like bringing the emotive expression of ground dance into a vertical plane where together, the possibilities truly seem to be endless.

[ZB] *You mentioned in passing how much you dreamed of performing Aerial with a band. Any particular bands?*

[LM] Oh boy, I hope I don't embarrass myself here! Yes, you are absolutely right...I have always had a bit of a secret desire of adding an aerial component to the live performance of any one of my favorite bands. Admittedly, I have always dreamed of doing a fun piece on stage with perhaps my favorite band of all time, Ego Likeness, however I do get quite shy (and socially awkward) at times and have never mentioned any such desire...until now. Gee thanks, Z! I have also (silently) entertained the idea of performing with Bella Morte just as much as with the others. That said,

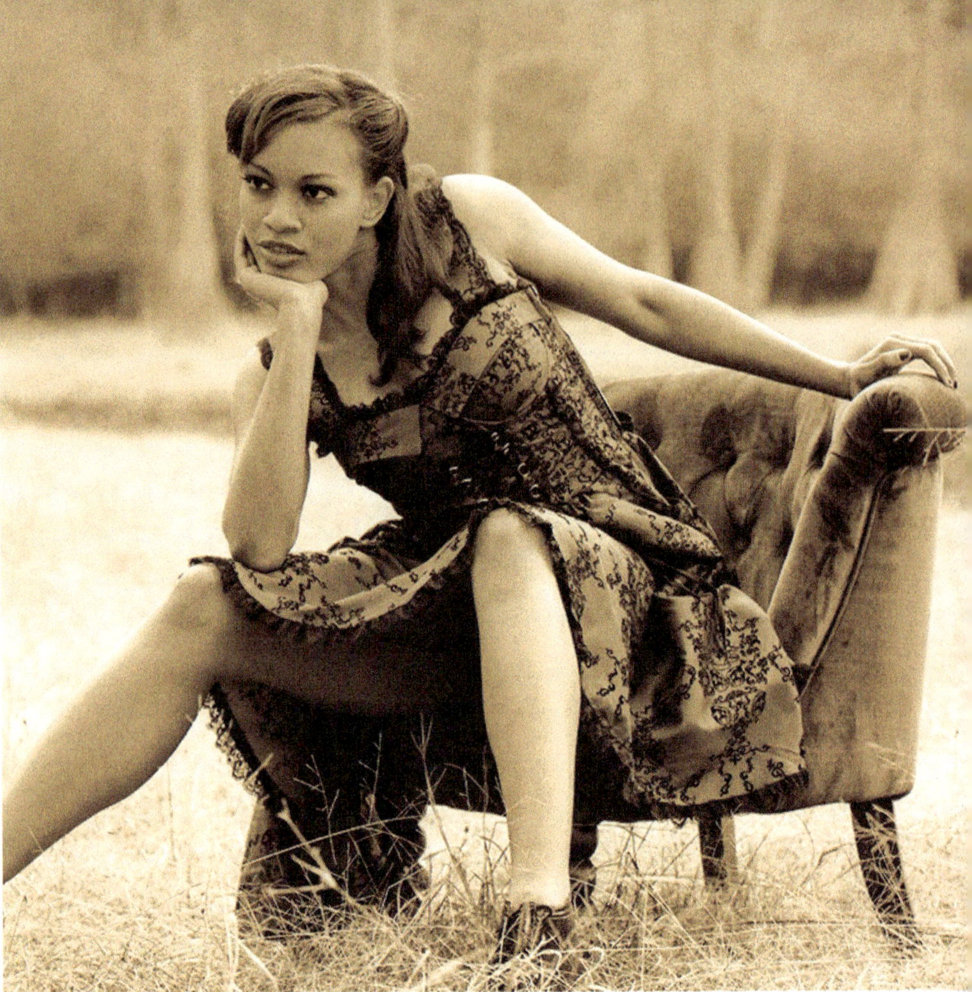

a brand new musical project will be hitting the scene soon, so please stay tuned!

[ZB] *And on that, what are some bands that really make you want to dance?*

[LM] Such a huge question!! Do you have time for me to list them all?? My musical tastes vary madly. Bands that make me want to dance? Hmm...it comes down to one thing. Does their music make me want to move? If it becomes a struggle to stay still while listening to them, I consider that a highly positive sign! A brief list would be Ego Likeness, IAMX, the Crüxshadows, Gary Numan, Sisters of Mercy, the Cure, Wolfsheim, Covenant, Ministry, Skinny Puppy, Deadmau5, De/Vision, Ladytron, Icon of Coil, Frontline Assembly, VNV Nation...this list could probably go on until my fingers fell off. I admit...a not-so-guilty pleasure of mine are the cheesy dance remixes....Don't judge me. I do hold a few songs sacred, however. Basically, if you are in Denver hanging out at one of the Goth/alternative or 80s nights, you will likely see me on my feet dancing until the lights come up!

[ZB] *You mentioned a new musical project. You're a singer in a band now yes?*

[LM] I am! It is an incredibly exciting new endeavor! I have always been inspired to sing in a band by female vocalists, such as Donna Lynch (Ego Likeness), Chibi (Birthday Massacre), and Emily Haines (Metric), but have been waiting for the right band to come along with the right sound. Not many people know that I come from a very musical family with plenty of experience in contemporary music, however my background training is predominantly classical. I have been performing classical or musical theatre intermittently since I began singing at 6 years old. That said, the bulk of my classical music training involves instruments. I am beyond excited to bring my experience and ideas to the contemporary scene in a big way! When my musical partner approached me regarding our new project, Clouds Reign, I didn't skip a beat on taking him up on the offer! It is so empowering to contribute my own sound and style to the music we are creating.

[ZB] *Tell us about the band and the sound you are developing?*

[LM] First of all, Clouds Reign is a very new project, but I think we are going for a powerful mix of aggro and synthpop. Stylistically, we plan to pull elements from a lot of different places musically, and given some of the new design tools in the studio, it should be a wonderful mix of melodic and dissonant sounds. This...is going to be fun! My partner, Erik, has many years of experience in the musical industry. He founded the band Emergence in 1999, and started a solo project called Darker Days Tomorrow in 2006. I am incredibly confident that Clouds Reign is in great hands!

[ZB] *Ever thought of singing while doing aerial?*

[LM] It has absolutely crossed my mind!

[ZB] *You're also a huge nerd and I mean that as a compliment. Isn't your dog named for a Dr. Who character? What other shows do you enjoy?*

[LM] Yes!! But don't worry, I own it! Let your nerd flag fly, I say! Yes, my mini Australian Shepherd, named Bannakaffalatta (AKA Bana), has interesting coloration in her eyes which make her look a little like a cyborg. The logical conclusion was to name her accordingly!

I am shamelessly a fan of pretty much all sci-fi, horror, fantasy, historical fiction, etc. You caught me! I am a fanatic about literature (script and film) and I do love some video games and many tabletop games. It is a wonderful method to lose myself in the worlds others create in order to unwind from the chaos of reality.

My favorite shows include most British sci-fi, many of the recent popular American shows, Battlestar Galactica (old and new), Star Trek (duh), Hemlock Grove, Sherlock, and many, many more. My list of favorite films would likely require an appendix. These conversations generally go on for hours (and have), so if anyone wants to chat anything nerdy, find me online and hit me up!

[ZB] *Which leads to cosplaying. You were quite a hit at DraconCon last year I hear. What was your costume(s) and what characters do you dream of tackling next?*

[LM] Last year's Dragon*Con was an absolute blast! That is to say, it was even MORE of an amazing experience than usual! I can hardly explain in words how incredible and rewarding it was to walk about in such fun costumes! Akasha (Queen of the Damned) was by far the most fun I have had as a cosplayer at the convention. Gail (Sin City) was another great hit! The exciting news is that I have even bigger plans for Dragon*Con 2015, with a few surprises up my sleeve. Come find me if you can!

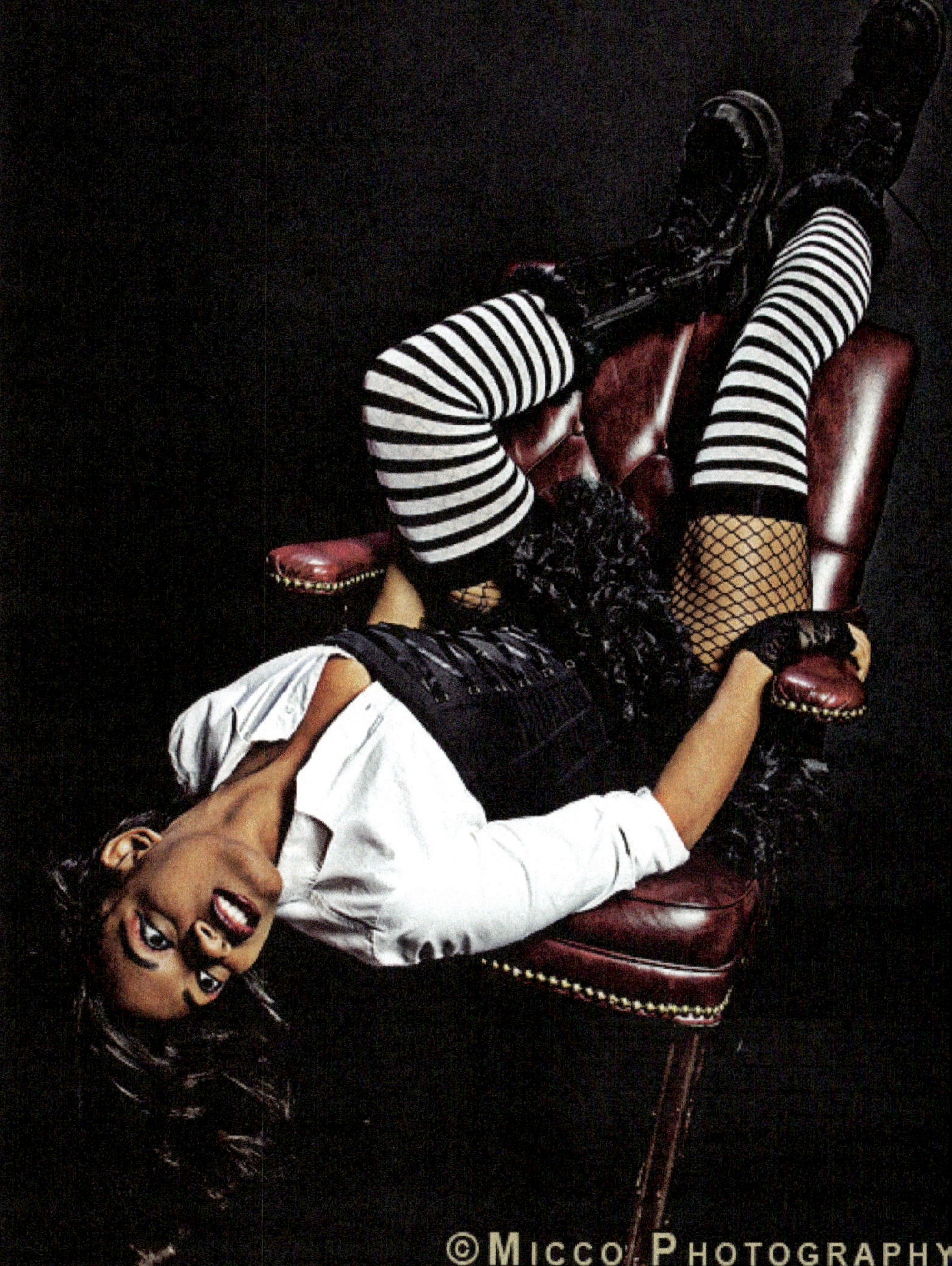

[ZB] *You are also a multi-faceted dancer. You wear many hats Luna! Give us some of your dancing background?*

[LM] Well, dance has been a major role in my life from a very young age. If I step back and look at my life thus far, I would have to say that dance and music are the two most important aspects to my creative and artistic fulfillment. I began training in classical ballet, and very quickly introduced lyrical ballet, jazz, tap, and hip hop to both my performance and competition repertoires. Utilizing motion as an art form comes as naturally as sitting in front of a piano and creating a composition out of silence. I often find little ties between the two. Music is as much of a performing art as dance, in completely different and yet similar ways. In both areas, it often feels as if I lose control.

If I give myself over to the impulses of my brain, the movement and music will flow from me in the most satisfying way. I would not trade that feeling for anything in the world!

[ZB] *And now you are a Go-Go dancer at several Denver nights correct?*

[LM] I am! Yes, you can catch me on the go-go boxes from time to time at both the Church Nightclub for SIN Sundays (Facebook), and at the monthly alternative event, Ominous (Facebook), which is held at Tracks Denver. Both nights are themed, which brings the alternative Denver community together in a fabulous way! Costumes everywhere, with corresponding décor to transform the nightclubs into another world. The DJs are pros at giving you exactly what you need to keep your feet on the dance floor! I always have a wonderful time dancing with both teams.

[ZB] *All this on top of having a full time job. To quote [Darth] Vader, "Impressive. Most impressive!" So where else do your ambitions lie?*

[LM] Oh, I have plans... Although, it is worth noting that the best opportunities have always surfaced outside of each and every plan I have ever made. I will be starting my graduate degree this year, which is very exciting! I have some languages I am still learning, and much traveling to accomplish, but for now...I am very excited with where this swift current is taking me! It will be an exciting ride for all of us, so don't forget to follow me on Facebook!

[ZB] *What's next in the Lunaverse aside from world domination?*

[LM] Well, you hit the nail on the head, Z! Given that a lot of my focus is going toward Clouds Reign and my aerial arts, I would say that I am pretty content with my current workload. However, be sure to keep your ears to the ground! I may just have a couple of surprises in store for you spooky Carpe Nocturne followers!

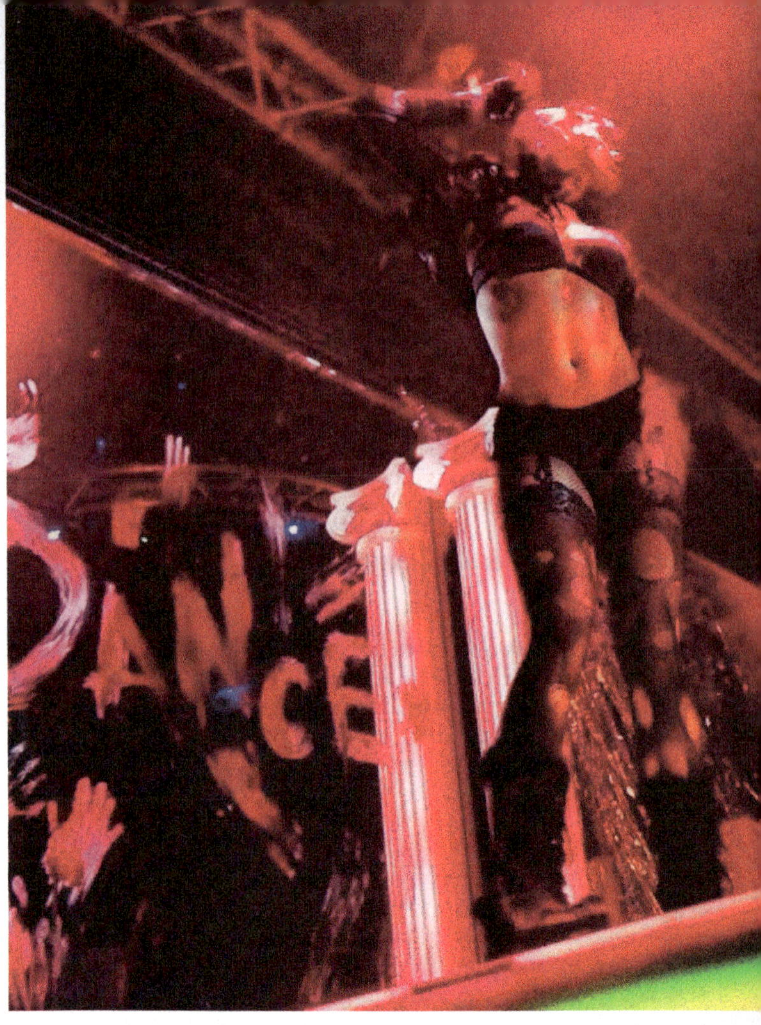

Photography Credits

Tim's Airbrush: *www.timsairbrush.com*
Rewski Photography *Facebook: Rewski-Photography*
Rob Timko Photography: *www.timkophotography.com*
Cindy Walker *(Facebook)*
Micco Photography *(Facebook)*
No Signal Photography *(Facebook)*

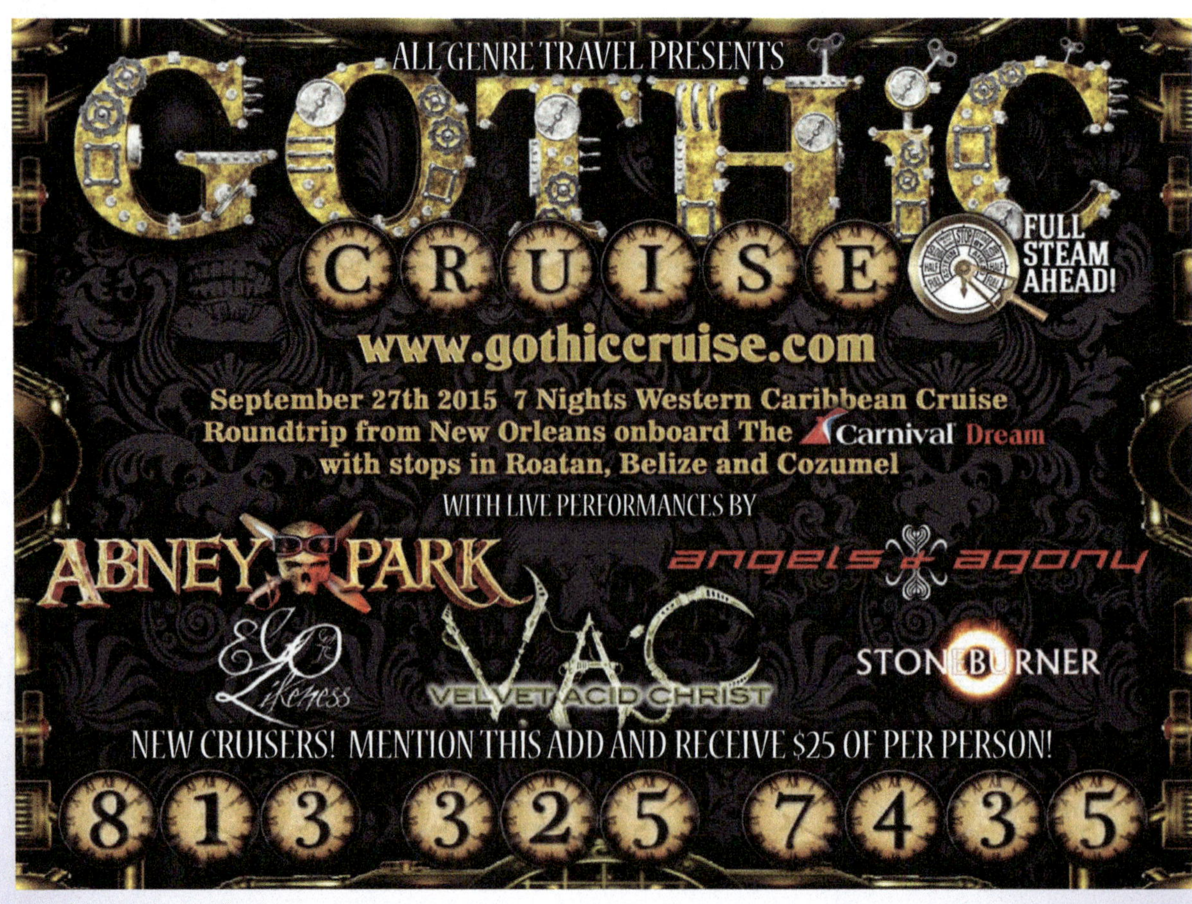

The Surreal, Sensual Works of HR Giger

By Zahara's Tangled Web

Last year, we lost the brilliance of HR Giger, when he passed away in May. "Hans Ruedi" was the creator of the terrifying monsters in the Alien films, and is credited with giving the film franchise its Biomechanical aesthetic. But HR Giger was much more than a "monster man". He was a prolific artist, sculptor, and interior designer; truly a master creator for nearly five decades. He had his own Giger Bars (the two remaining ones located in Switzerland), and the Museum HR Giger opened in Switzerland in 1998.

It was his book Necronomicon that inspired the Alien world and was his first large movie project. He won an Oscar (Best Achievement in Visual Effects) in 1980 for that film and proceeded to provide design work for Species, Poltergeist II and A. Jadorowsky's unrealized version of Dune. Giger has several film projects to his credit, which are listed on his website.

His images were the perfect match for musicians and bands looking for unique and surreal cover art. Two of his paintings for Emerson, Lake & Palmer were stolen in 2005, and according to Giger's website, a $10,000 reward is still being offered for the return of the paintings. Yet Giger did more than just provide album cover art for the music world. He also worked with Debbie Harry (lead singer of Blondie) to create music videos for her solo album. The video for "Now I Know You Know" features his biomechanical imagery on the body stocking worn by Harry, as well as large paintings as background pieces and one of his chairs. The entire video can be found on YouTube and you can also find some interviews with Giger and Harry.

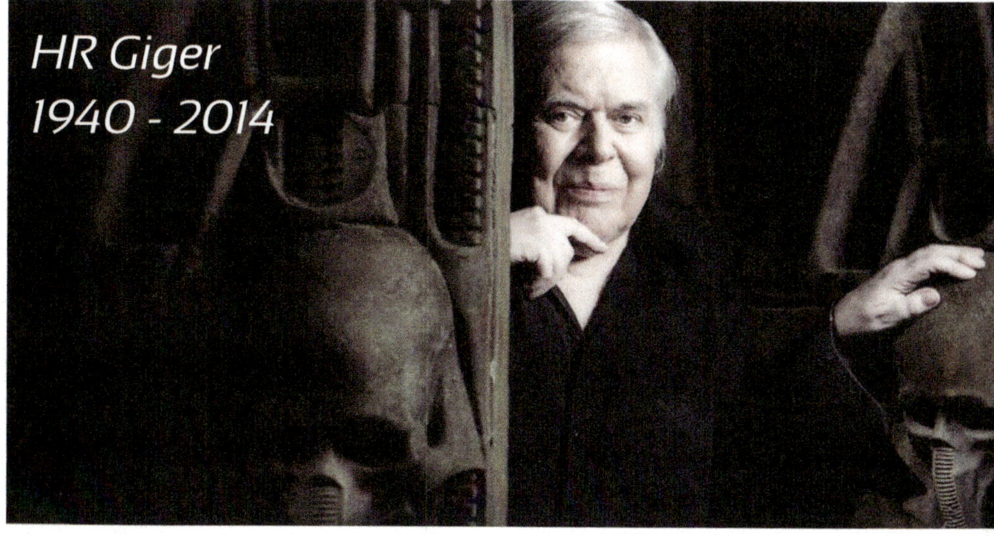

We gain another glimpse into his creative genius when Giger is commissioned to create a microphone stand for Jonathan Davis of Korn. According to his website, Giger said, "Since the music has always been the most important thing for me and I must, absolutely, like it before I can work with a band, or even agree to let them use one of my old paintings, first I listened to all the Korn CDs they sent to me." Giger was a collaborator, wanting the stand to be completely functional for the singer by watching videos of Davis performing and noting the singer's movements on stage and his use of other microphone stands.

Giger's paintings are showcased in his books, such as Biomechanics and Necronomicon I & II. But it wasn't enough for him to paint or sculpt his visions; Giger also wrote stories. Readers will learn much about his horrific imagination by delving into The Mystery of San Gottardo. More than a collection of art, Giger weaves a disturbing tale of horror that is upsetting and difficult to put down. His paintings were also used in the HR Giger Tarot by Giger and Akron. All of these works are available through Giger's website.

The art world lost more than just another artist when Giger left this world last spring. We lost a visionary who was unafraid to be master of his work and servant to his dark muses. He was a collaborator who encouraged his colleagues to push boundaries and expand beyond their preconceived notions of what's possible. His incredibly detailed art is sleek and beautiful, yet unnerving and (in some cases) viscerally unsettling at the same time. The collection of his work at Museum HR Giger is certainly just a small representation of his overall creativity. He will definitely be missed.

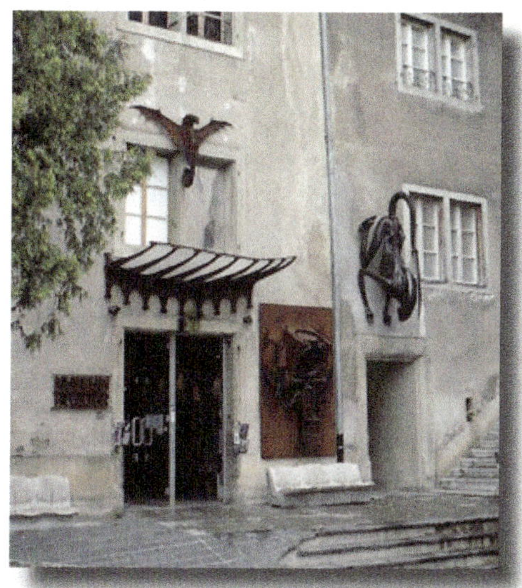

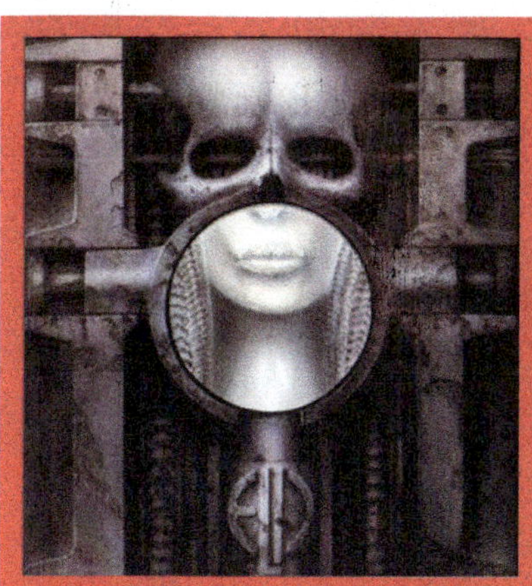

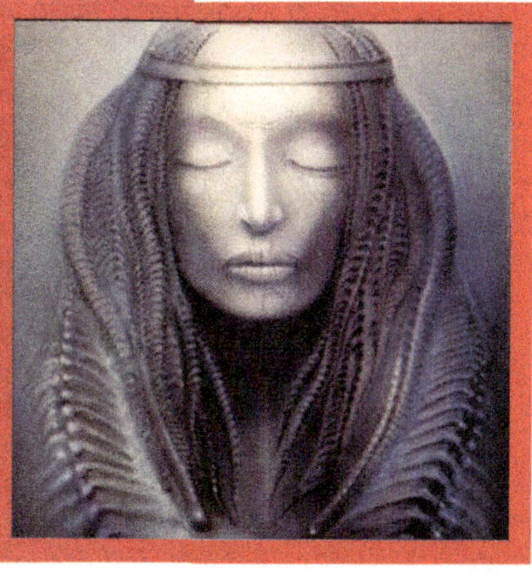

ORION SLAVE WOMEN:

The First Sci-Fi Bellydancers

By Jezibell Anat

In many ways, belly dance and sci-fi are at opposite ends of the fantasy spectrum, but they share some developmental parallels. Both became part of the cultural landscape of Europe and America in the late 19th century, amidst a time of rapid industrialism, exciting new technologies, and global expansion. The negative side of this progress was the European colonization of other parts of the world, leading to the boast that the sun never set on the British Empire. The justification for this imperialism was that the Europeans were bringing the benefits of civilization to backwards peoples, highlighting the age-old dichotomy of the progressive, rational West versus the languid, mysterious East. Along the way, the belly dance (a folk dance of ancient origins) was polished into a stage art for Western audiences.

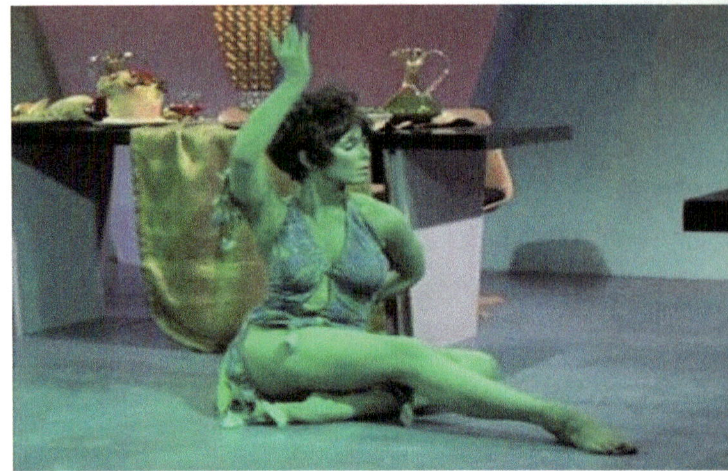

European explorations of both current and past societies of the Middle East and Asia formed the rudiments of what would become the sciences of archaeology and anthropology. These intellectual advances of the Victorian era inspired a unique genre of fantasy fiction based on science, imagining time travel, outer space, and alien races. In these futuristic worlds, the marvels and wonders that were once the result of magic could be accomplished through technology.

Despite the extraterrestrial settings and emphasis on rationality, sci-fi was very much influenced by the mores and attitudes of its home culture. In the beginning, sci-fi was a male-dominated field, so it's not surprising that there are still vestiges of Victorian attitudes about women and dance. The iconic sci-fi belly dancers are the Orion slave women, described as "sinuous green dancing girls" who feature in several episodes of Star Trek. When I first saw them, I loved their green skin and flowing hair but was very put off by their status as slaves. But as the story unfolds, we discover that these women are not actually slaves but enslavers - as they dance, they emit pheromones that compel men to do their bidding.

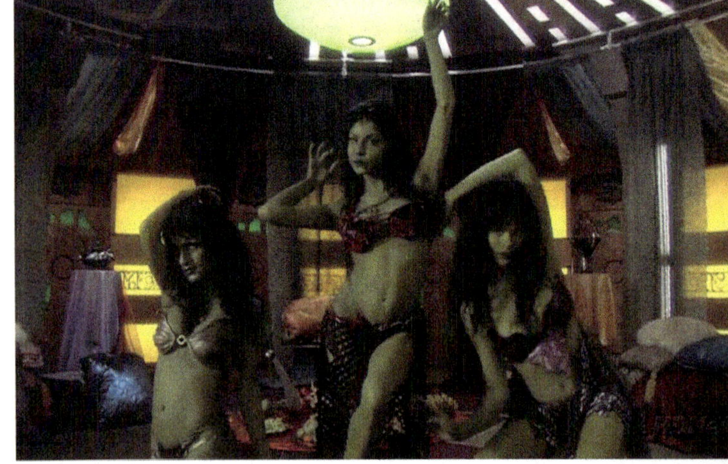

In the first Orion appearance, Susan Oliver plays Vina and performs alone on a sumptuous stage. Both the setting and her style of dance are reminiscent of the old Hollywood sword and sandal epics. In a later episode, Yvonne Craig plays Marta. Craig was trained as a ballerina and is the most technically accomplished of the dancers, with a few belly dance moves layered over her arabesques. In another part of the episode, her character unsuccessfully attempts to poison the Captain.

On Star Trek Enterprise, the Orion women appear as trio Navaar (Cyia Batten), D'Nesh (Crystal Allen), and Maras (Merina Fortunato), where Commodore Mendez says "they're like animals, vicious, seductive. They say no human male can resist them." Attired in shiny bikinis with a bit of skirt, the trio dances beautifully, performing an elaborate choreography by MTV Music Video Award winner Travis Payne.

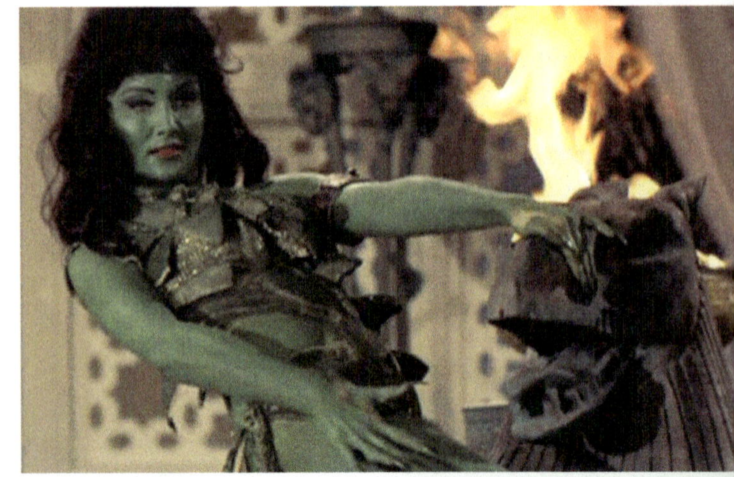

As Fortunato says, they "move very slowly, very seductively. I would like to compare us to snakes – we like to slither and creep around, versus a human. So we're a little sneaky. The three of us are trying to get something accomplished, and each one of us has our target, so to speak, to try to manipulate them to get what we want in the end."

These Orion women hearken back to the depictions of harem girls and odalisques by the Orientalist painters of the 19th century. Orientalism is the romanticized portrayal of Middle Eastern, North African, and Asian cultures by Westerners, with stereotypical sexist and racist overtones. In this view, women and non-whites are considered unintelligent and inferior to white men because they are more instinctive and closer to animals in their nature. The Oriental female is perceived as sensual, exotic, and dangerous, an image that has been projected into dancers from Salome to Mata Hari, and (in sci-fi) upon the Orion slave girls.

Both the Orion dancers and the harem depictions of the Orientalists also glamorize slavery. It is true that in some societies slaves had rights and could live well. For example, in the Ottoman Empire, the Sultan's mother, the Valide Sultan ruled the harem, and she was often a slave. But overall slavery is a brutal system of subjugation. Even though the women in the Ottoman harem lounged in luxury, they were captives, trapped in an environment of jealousy and rivalry, and all were subject to the whims of the Sultan and his mother.

In the Star Trek universe, Orion is a planet of raiders and traders outside the Federation. In this context the Federation represents the organized, sophisticated West, and Orion is the chaotic, backwards East. The Orion women are bred to be alluring, so that they can make deals to benefit their people. So, even though they may be ruling the men through sexual allure, they are trafficked, and are used to captivate other men. And once the effects of the pheromones wear off, their appeal is gone.

However, the femme fatale offers an aspect of glamour and power that still appeals to many modern women. Whether we admit it or not, many of us would like to be so beautiful and alluring that we could be perilous to men even if we didn't want to be. But we also want to be more than our physical attraction. We want to be smart and creative and powerful without the gender limitations that have been imposed on us for centuries.

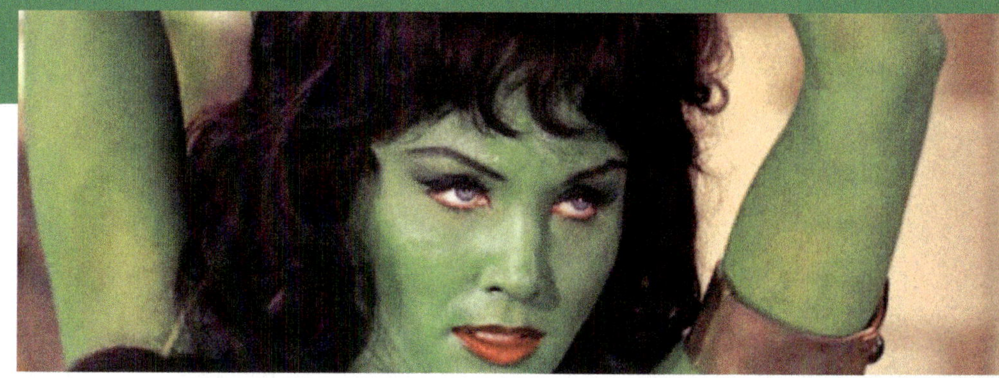

The cultural irony of belly dance is that it originated in parts of the world where women are oppressed, yet it has become an empowering and creative art for Western women. Contemporary belly dance encompasses many forms and fusions, some of which are incomprehensible to those who perform the authentic Middle Eastern style. Through this dance, we can honor and express our sensuality, but also incorporate our wit, our intelligence, and our emotional depth.

Today, sci-fi belly dance can be a new realm to explore, where dancers can break through the stereotypes to become scientists and warriors, or even portray members of exotic alien races who are not defined by their sexuality. Let's lose the old cliches and engage the art.

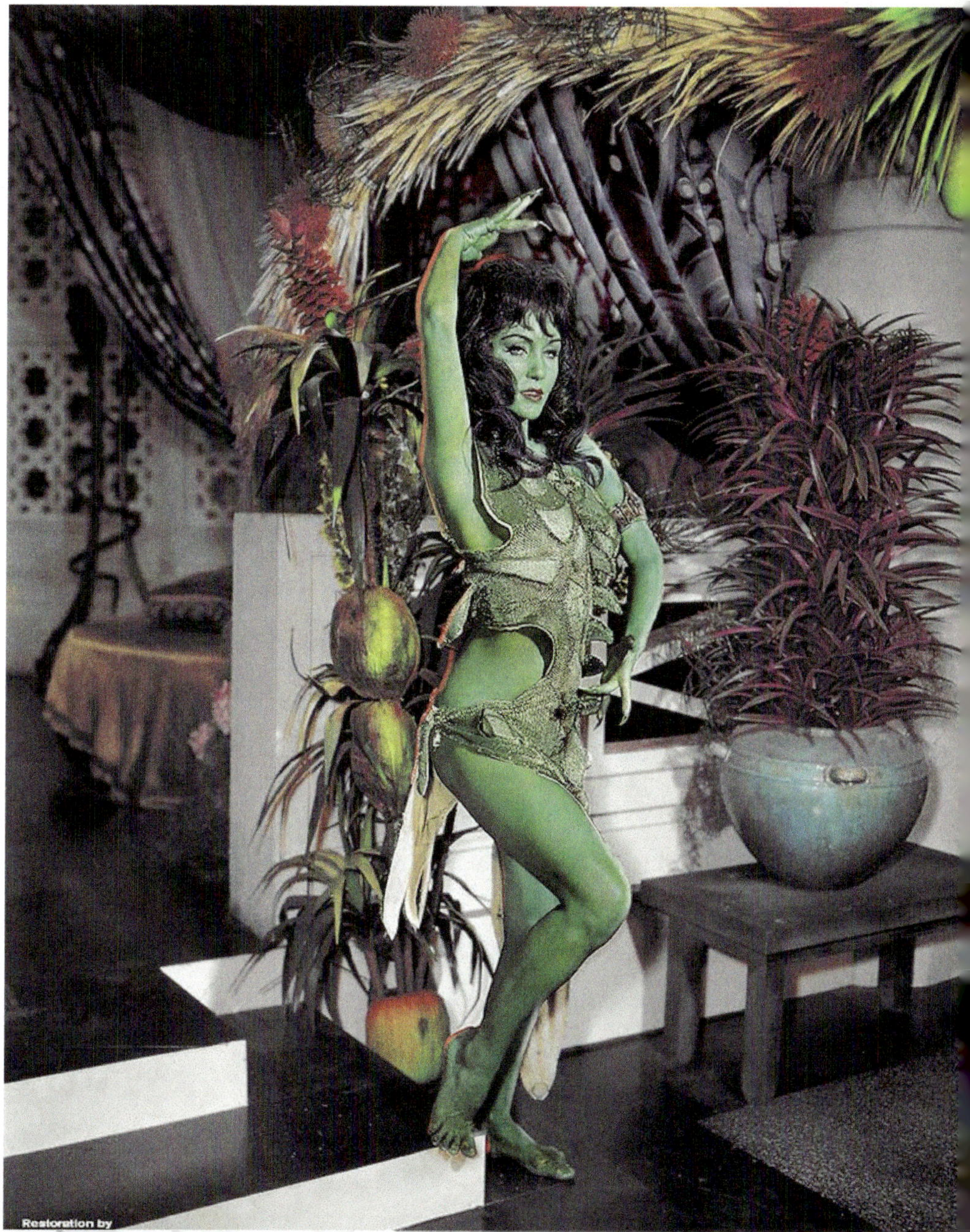

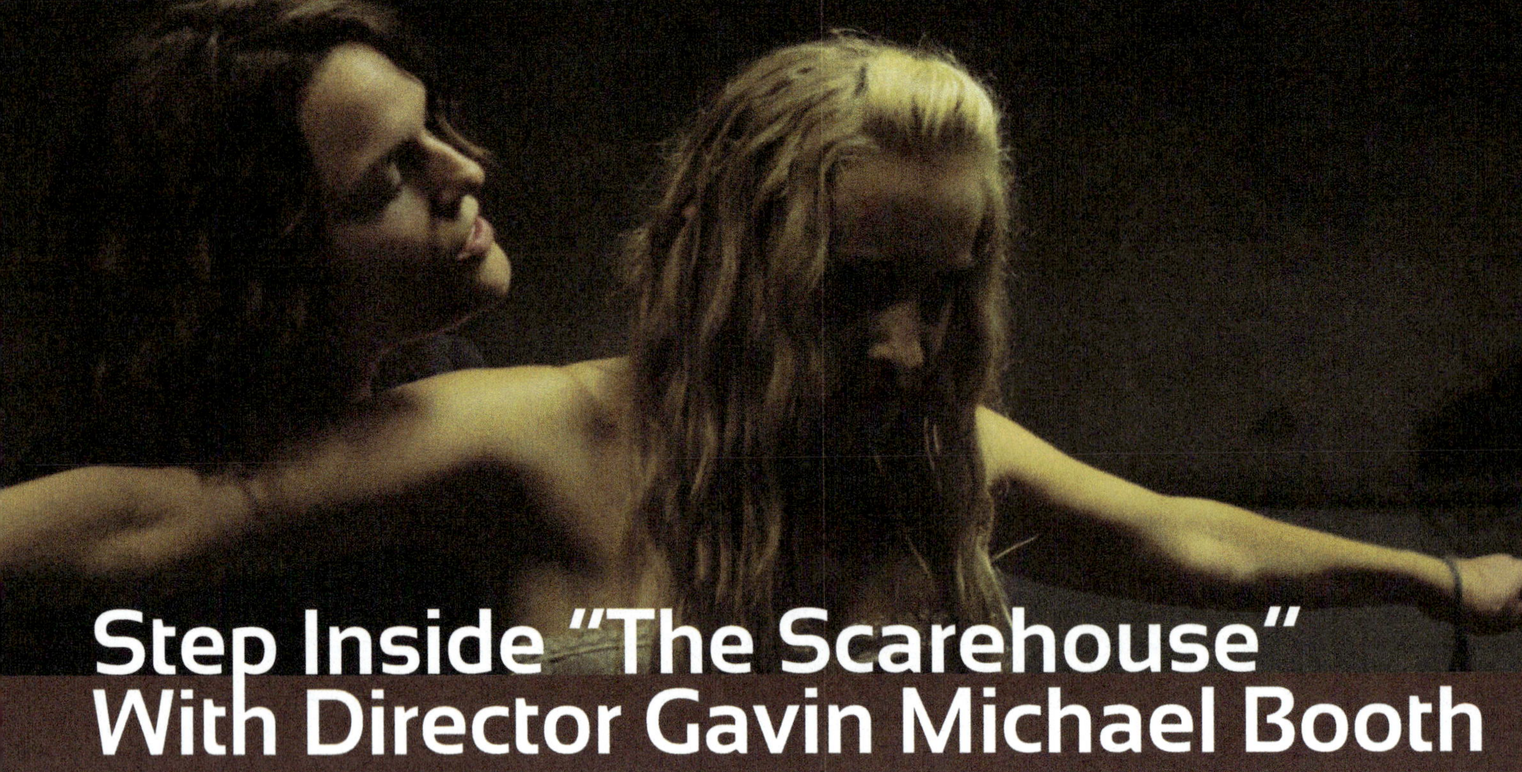

Step Inside "The Scarehouse" With Director Gavin Michael Booth

By LinnieSarah

From music videos to horror films, writer/director Gavin Michael Booth is making his mark in the industry one project at a time. His most recent film, *The Scarehouse,* is an independent feature that was picked up by a major Hollywood studio and has been gaining considerable critical and fan traction. Booth sat down with *Carpe Nocturne* to discuss *The Scarehouse,* indie film, and where he is headed next.

[LinnieSarah] *You've worked on everything from music videos to short films, and now, you've moved into the horror world with The Scarehouse. What has changed about your technique and style from genre to genre?*

[Gavin] Generally I just try to bring the sensibilities of each genre to the table. It is more of a feel than a specific technique. Sure, you're going to have moodier lighting some times, other times call for handheld, kinetic camera movement to create the urgency. It really does vary. With *The Scarehouse* I wanted the haunted house itself to have a lot of atmosphere and then let the characters play inside that. Other than a few chase scenes, the movie is shot entirely on a locked tripod or on a slow moving dolly. We wanted to approach the film that regardless of how much suspension of disbelief is required to buy into the basic concept and over the top revenge plot, the characters are grounded, they could be people you know, they have morally conflicting thoughts. With that you want to make each frame about the characters and not so much about how cool everything around them may or may not look.

The Scarehouse is the first film where the soundscape that is present in 90% of the film was super important to me. The sounds of the haunted house, the sounds of the other patrons going through the haunted house. I wanted it to very much always be in the audience's mind. Corey and Elaina are always one step from being discovered and very boldly committing these crimes within earshot of people that could discover them at any time.

Part of prepping for *The Scarehouse* and shooting in this location was the fact that I had already shot a half dozen music videos inside this building. I knew some of the lighting schemes I would want the DOP to employ. One of the videos I shot in there was a Grindhouse style zombie video for Emma-Lee (Shadow Of A Ghost) so in essence I had already made a horror film there and had a head start style-wise that I could carry over into this film.

[L] *The Scarehouse* was produced on a relatively modest budget and received a lot of positive attention from studios. How did it feel to get that kind of love as an indie director?

[G] $200K is not a lot of money to make a movie. Especially since our approach was to make sure we paid our crew better than a slave's wage and we went with union actors, which sucks up a lot of an indie budget. We felt it was better to have people well fed and well paid and that would bring out the best in their hard work to give us their all in each department to get what we wanted on the screen.

The fact that Universal agreed to take the film on for the U.S. at script stage and that D Films here in Canada along with Telefilm Canada were involved right from my elevator pitch is absolutely thrilling. There is no better way to describe it. It's the ideal for a lot of us struggling to "make it" as filmmakers, to have the major players that have released all of our favorite films get behind the projects we are creating. For me it is always about looking forward. We cracked this door open, we've released The Scarehouse in a big way for a little film and that is super exciting but what comes next? How can this opportunity propel this cast, this crew and closer to home, my next scripts, projects into a larger arena?

[L] *What inspired the idea behind* **The Scarehouse?**

[G] A very close friend of mine, Shawn Lippert, owns and operates a haunted house attraction in Windsor, Ontario - my hometown (directly across the river from Detroit, Michigan). I was taking a tour of his attraction during the daytime with all of the lights on. All of the scare magic was gone. I was fascinated learning how these "haunts" work. You only need a small group of people to keep changing costumes and leapfrogging through the building's narrow halls and trap doors, changing costumes sometimes as they move, in order to

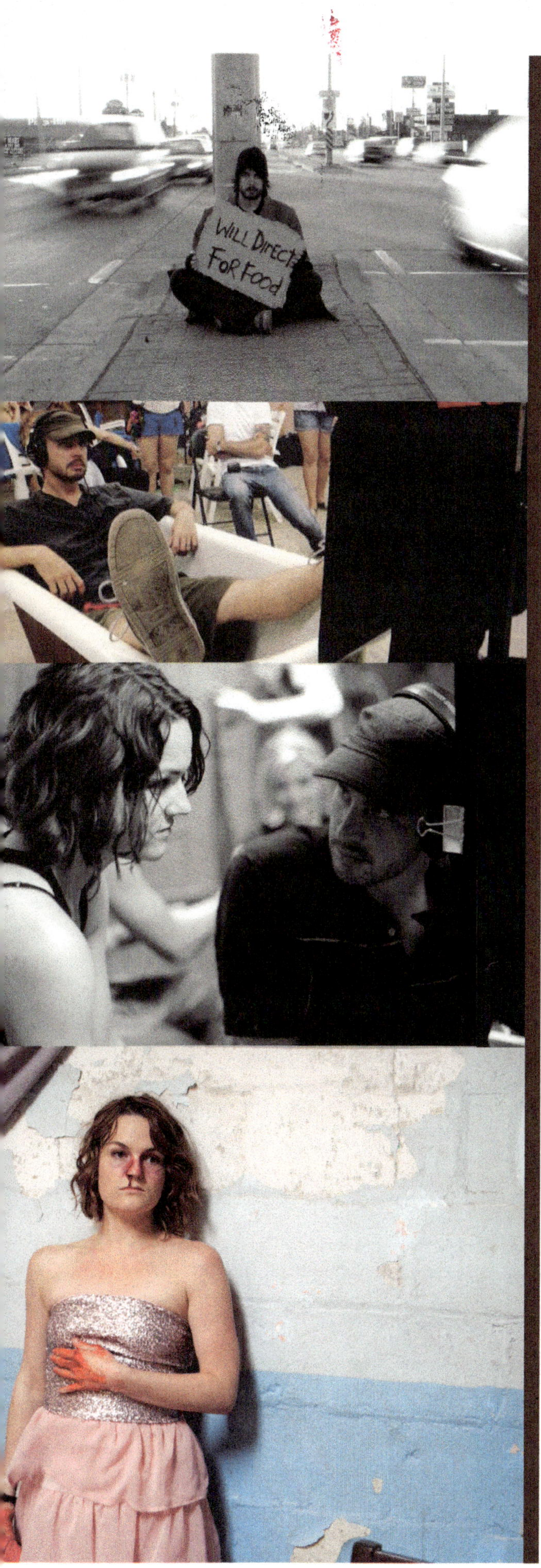

make it feel like dozens and dozens of different people are terrorizing paying customers. Truly all smoke and mirrors.

I had been close to film a script I wrote called *Four Shots* which was a super edgy movie about student's perspectives of being trapped inside of a mass shooting scenario in a high school at the time. I said to Shawn that day that if I was a disgruntled kid that had that evil streak in me, I wouldn't storm a school with a gun, I would open a haunted house, invite everyone I felt I needed revenge on down for a special preview night and then take care of business inside the dark hallways. You would have a total home court advantage inside a maze you built. I half joked you could even hang the bodies on display in plain sight and other people coming through the funhouse would just think it was awesome make-up effects.

That was it. I literally wrote it down on a Burger King napkin and filed it away. When there was interest from D Films I called Shawn right away. We worked out a deal to shoot the film inside his haunted house, which is called Scarehouse Windsor by the way! I was too lazy to think of a better title. It is a working titled that stuck. "Gavin what are you working on?" "Well it is this revenge story that we are going to shoot inside of The Scarehouse." Eventually it just made sense. Shawn became our production designer and resident haunt expert. We used some of his exact set-up, built other custom rooms and we were off to the races. It was concurrent with scripting the movie. I would dream up a room or scenario and call Shawn and ask if we could make that happen for our budget. It was a really exciting project to work on from that perspective.

[L] *Canada has always churned out some amazing horror films (Black Christmas, Visiting Hours, Tucker & Dale vs. Evil) but never seems to get the respect it deserves. Why do you think that is?*

[G] That that old adage of if a tree falls... if a Canadian film is made and no one sees it, did it ever exist? There is a really sad fact that we have a hard time getting Canadians to watch Canadian films, so what chance do we stand with the rest of the world tuning in? There's obvious factors like the American studio system and the big star system for movies dominating the public's knowledge of what films there are to watch.

When I saw *Black Christmas* as a kid I didn't know it was Canadian or American or anything. It was just a movie I rented at my video store. In December, I had an invite from Anchor Bay to see a 40th Anniversary screening of *Black Christmas* here in Toronto. Truth be told - until that invite I didn't know the film was Canadian (nor that it was directed by the SAME Bob Clark that directed *A Christmas Story*)!

[L] *What are your favorite horror movies?*

[G] *A Nightmare On Elm Street.* (actually I quite love the 3rd one too), *The Blair Witch Project* (mildly obsessed with well done found footage films having a few original ideas of my own), *Child's Play* (it was my anti-Toy Story growing up - locked all my toys in the closet each night before bed) and *Poltergeist.*

[L] *Who do you consider your inspiration as a filmmaker, horror or otherwise?*

[G] Kevin Smith (mostly *Clerks* and *Red State*) - he was the guy that when I saw *Clerks* when it was first released on home video - I read about how he made the film for so cheap it clicked in my brain - "I can do that, I can save/raise 20k and go make a movie". I think it was the first independent film I had ever seen. Why does it look so cheap? Why is it black and white? Why do I love this film so outside of the box even though some of the acting is pretty bad? It really was a defining moment for me.

Everything for me since then has been about not worrying about budget and finding away to get it done. My most successful music video with international praise and millions upon millions of views was made on a budget of $700.00. Tell the story with the gear and the crew and the access to whatever you have at the time. Make the story great,

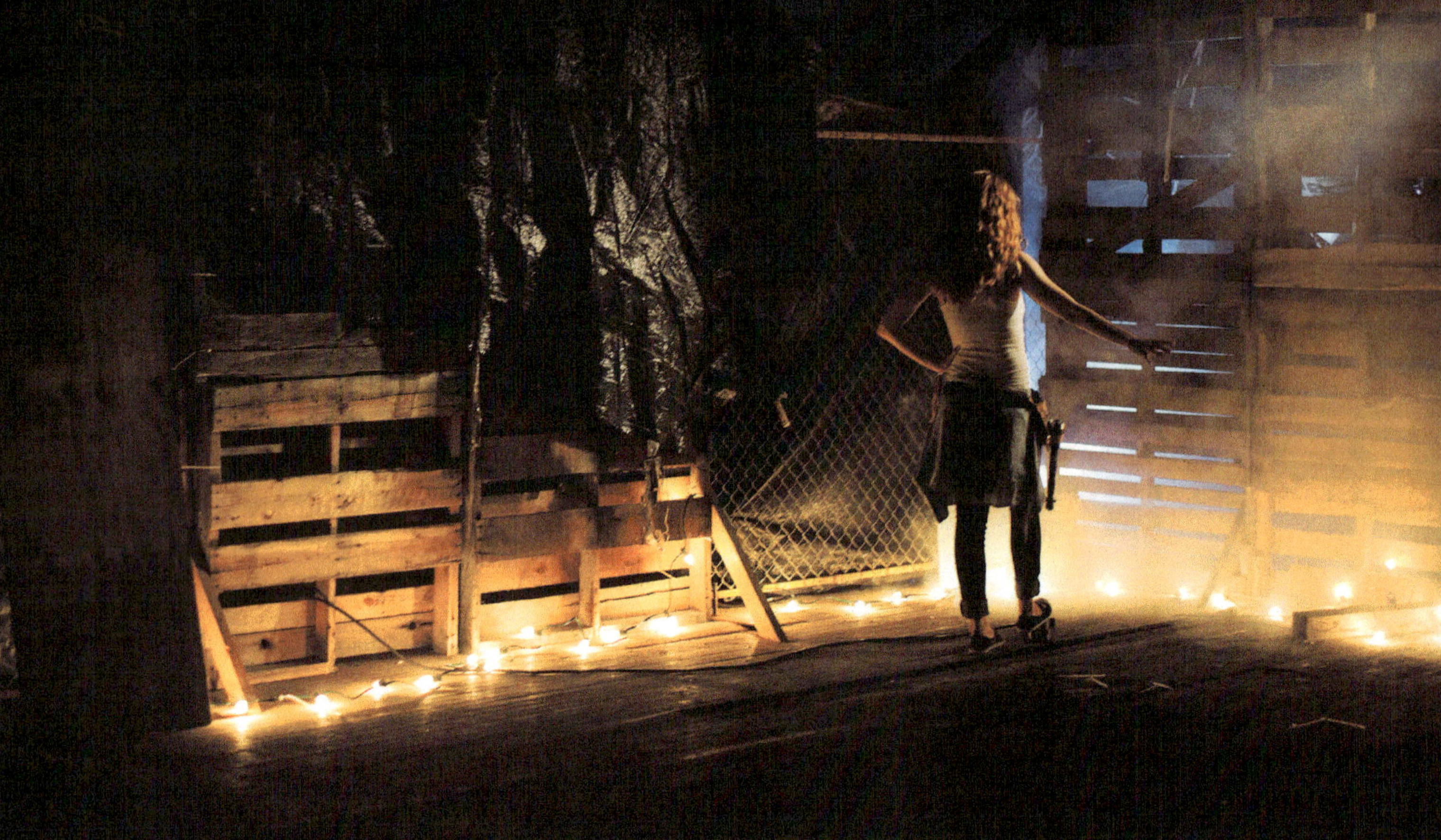

work on your script to tell a story people will want to watch and everything else is mostly forgivable by the viewer. I still love *Clerks* to this day as a film but more so it was my bible in the sense it gave me the religion I needed to believe I took could walk the filmmaking path of the almighty Kevin Smith. I do not mean that in terms of success or personal - just simply that I didn't have to wait for permission from a studio or TV network or anyone to start making movies. There was this indie way to do it and the digital video revolution was about to happen so it was definitely the right time, right place for me.

[L] *What's next for you: more horror or another genre flip?*

[G] Well, that all depends on what gets funded by a studio or independently next! I have a slasher film by a Toronto writer that I really want to make. It is really outside the box while staying inside a very familiar and loved horror playground. There's some traction with that project. I have a soldier story that is close to moving forward and then on the opposite end of the genre universe I have a bank robbery comedy with a musical element to it.

Then there are more music videos. We just wrapped one for Gavin Slate that will come out soon and will be shooting the next Gavin Slate music video across America soon. I'm excited to get back into music videos again - I shot so few of them during the production and post periods for *The Scarehouse*.

Links:

Gavin's Music Videos: https://www.youtube.com/playlist?list=PL6CD2093B4B3E687B

Emma-Lee - Shadow Of A Ghost: http://youtu.be/7utJPmXOocs

http://www.scarehousemovie.com

The Scarehouse Trailer: https://www.youtube.com/watch?v=IFe7FOSuX60

The Scarehouse Prank Video: https://www.youtube.com/watch?v=Bf9HNpxvedo

Gavin's Facebook: https://www.facebook.com/gavinmichaelbooth?fref=ts

Gavin's Twitter: @gavinbooth

Scarehouse Facebook: https://www.facebook.com/TheScareHouse

Scarehouse Twitter: @scarehousemovie

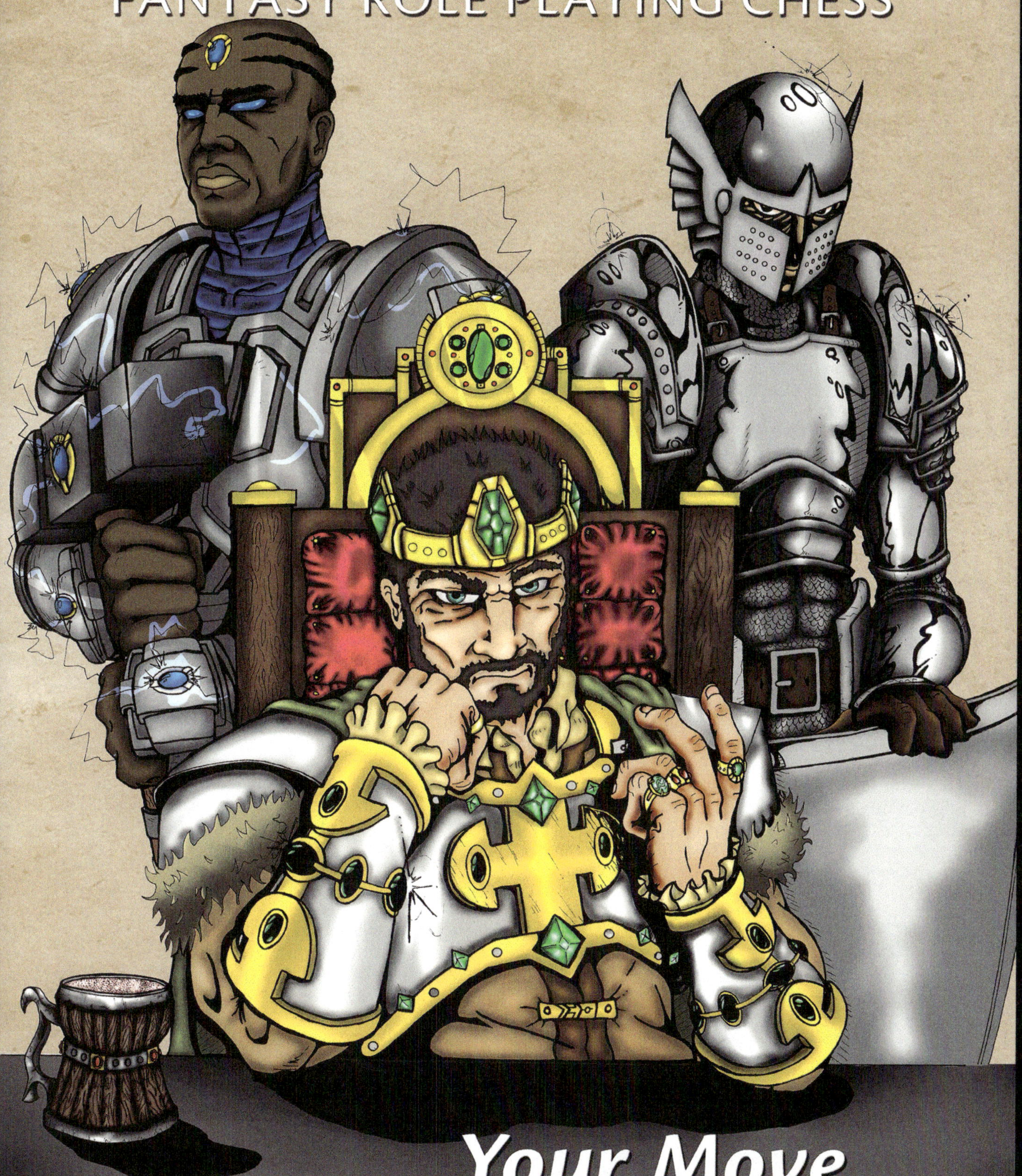

Cathedr'l
FANTASY ROLE PLAYING CHESS
Your Move . . .
FACEBOOK.COM/CATHEDRL
CATHEDRL.COM

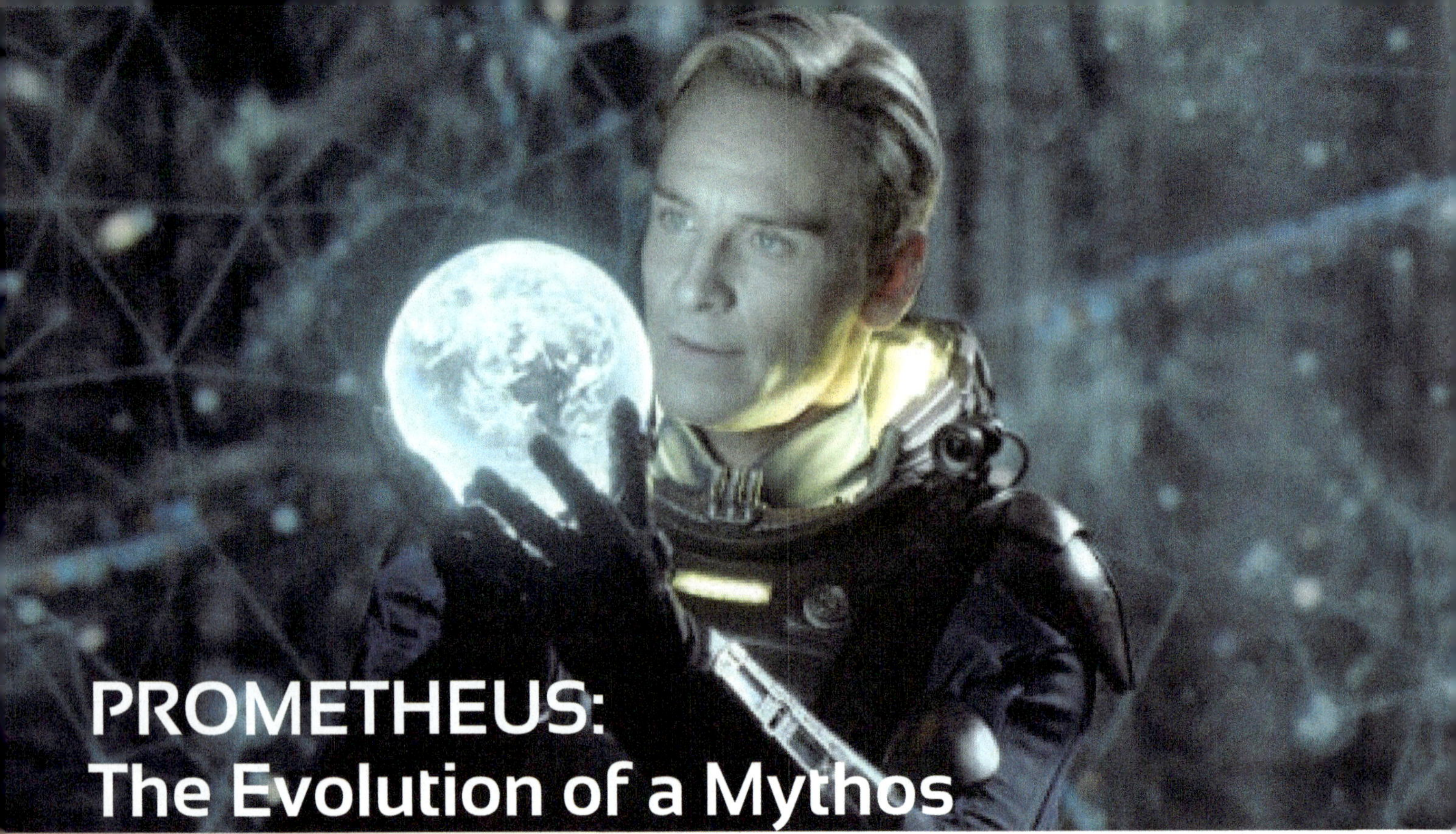

PROMETHEUS:
The Evolution of a Mythos

By K.A. Morris

Modern prequels to films that have created a universe of their own have had a rough go of it, specifically one that has as unique a universe as Ridley Scott's Alien series. I'm not even sure that I could name a horror prequel (or reboot for that matter) that's been met with open arms, especially one around which an established mythology has been formed.

It is to Ridley Scott's credit that no effort has been made to remake Alien in any form - preferring instead to pile on sequels with ever more expendable side stories, edible military personnel, and more creative ways for the Xenomorphs to acquire and dispatch those aforementioned snackables.

As a prequel, Prometheus has the devastatingly difficult job of introducing the origin of its species, and by design, the origin of its mythos. Prometheus is an evolution story - In Greek mythology, Prometheus ('forethought') was a Titan who is credited with the creation of mankind, and for defying the rule of the Gods and giving Man the gift of fire - the act that allowed for the birth of civilization. Sacrifice for progress, and quite literally sacrifice for the survival of a new species, is how we begin.

I've heard several theories about what influences Scott brought to his imagining of the origin story of Alien, from 2001: A Space Odyssey (which some also argue gave birth to science-fiction itself) to the Cthulhu Mythos. As I've been in a bit of a Lovecraftian mode lately, it's the Cthulhu Mythos that I'm going to address first.

Usually, whenever people see tentacles, one of two things occur: those among the faithful are the first to screech jubilantly "Ia! Ia! Cthulhu Fthagn!" while most everyone else looks on in horror because they've seen too much hentai and know where this might be going. Prometheus definitely has its share of tentacles, and it's not surprising that this is how we are first introduced to the creatures thriving in the alien spacecraft.

Lovecraft's work in general feeds off of a feeling of unease, of looming dread - it's not so much about the actual terror, but the growing of it, the weight of it. Prometheus is full of the feeling of crushing doom, and it's not until the end (just like in The Call of Cthulhu) that we are actually introduced to the physical manifestation of this horror.

Lovecraft's work also centered around the concept that the thirst for knowledge is the search for the ultimate horror - or more bluntly - "curiosity killed the cat." The same is true for the Prometheus and her crew: they are in search of the ultimate knowledge of mankind's creation, to answer the unanswerable with all the hubris and vanity of a failed creation grown too big for its space boots. I would argue that while it is obvious that Ridley Scott is inspired by Lovecraft (as is H.R Giger), I see about as much of Cthulhu in Prometheus as I see fake moon landings in The Shining.

However, leaving Lovecraft behind for a moment, what intrigued me the most about Prometheus was the focus on the generative

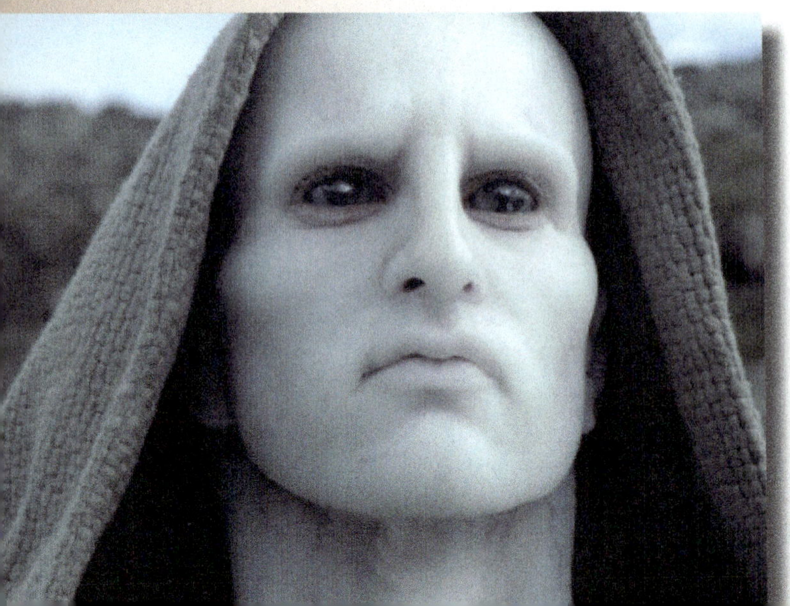

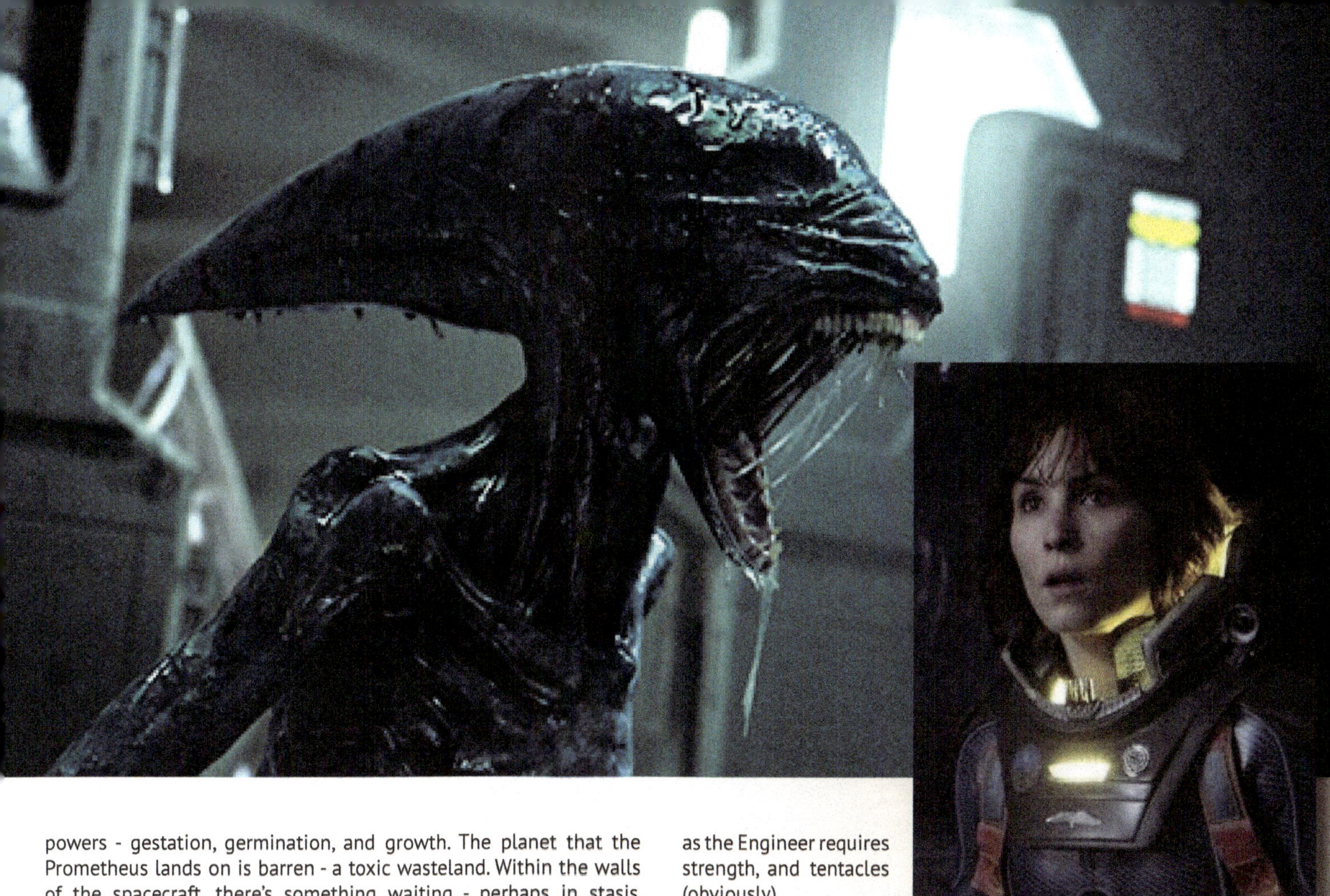

powers - gestation, germination, and growth. The planet that the Prometheus lands on is barren - a toxic wasteland. Within the walls of the spacecraft, there's something waiting - perhaps in stasis, waiting to be nudged into action. Shaw and her team are the perfect catalyst for that action - to be completely creepy about it, they are the perfect petrie dishes. Contaminating the setting with their deliberate clumsiness: perhaps it's the addition of their breath, body heat, skin oils, pressure from their feet - any number of stressors on the dormant environment that bring it suddenly and terrifyingly to life.

The canisters in Prometheus aren't the catalyst for life anymore - they are a catalyst for death created by the Engineers to destroy their human science experiments - and like anything past its expiration date, I wouldn't recommend making anything you plan on serving to guests with these ingredients. It is this drooling black muck that has me fascinated - primordial ooze filled with the building blocks for a myriad of life forms, depending on what they happen to come into contact with. Infiltrating the soil, the water, there's no limit to what can be produced and sometimes it all depends on the host.

Humans are extremely unique organisms with a steady core body temperature, moist orifices for entry, mucous membranes, and cavities that can incubate any manner of alien life with amazing alacrity. The proto-alien lifecycle is a rudimentary one. Ingestion of the black ooze, even a drop, is enough to start the dominos falling. Ingestion leads to procreation, procreation to gestation, gestation to extraction, rapid growth after extraction gives us our proto-facehugger. Alarmingly large, I read a lot of criticism of the creatures introduced in Prometheus. And yes… I giggled a bit. However, when you stop to once again think about the fact that these creatures have been gestating inside HUGE beings, a tiny little face-hugger from Alien wouldn't even have made it to the Engineer's giant face, let alone been able to insert anything in its chest. So, once again, we have to consider the source. Used to incubating inside larger specimens, our squiddy proto-facehugger friend would have ripped Shaw to pieces had she not extracted it. Being able to overpower a being as massive as the Engineer requires strength, and tentacles (obviously).

At this point, we're all viscerally reminded of Kane's brutal face rape at the claws of the face-hugger in Alien - what did it take to get from the massive creature to the slim, spidery terror that we all know and love. Evolution is the answer. In Prometheus, it's "survival of the biggest," but by the time our mythos has aged to the point of Alien, it's now "survival of the adaptable." Now for my favorite part. In the theater, when the proto-chest burster appears, the theater erupted with two reactions - audible groans/facepalms from one section of the crowd and a chorus of "YESSSSS'" from the rest - I was in the YESSSSSS section. Maybe it's all the years I've spent doing anthropological study, but evolution fascinates the f*ck out of me. This little proto-alien, fully formed and trying out it's baby xenomorph gazelle legs and double mouth is the beginning of a very beautiful thing. No seriously, that's actually how I feel about it. Once again, the look of the creature is tied to its host - the massive form of the Engineer can incubate an almost fully grown creature, where the human form cannot.

Necessity is the mother of invention, and the same is true for evolution.

The canisters full of the black mucus of death become the field of Alien eggs, the need to gestate spore inside a host becomes a fully formed creature with its own propulsion system, and fully formed infant aliens become chest-bursters that grow quickly once freed from their fleshy prison. Infants grow into Xenomorph Queens and the cycle continues.

Breed. Feed. Expand. Evolve… Delicious.

K.A. Morris is an author and editor living in Vancouver.

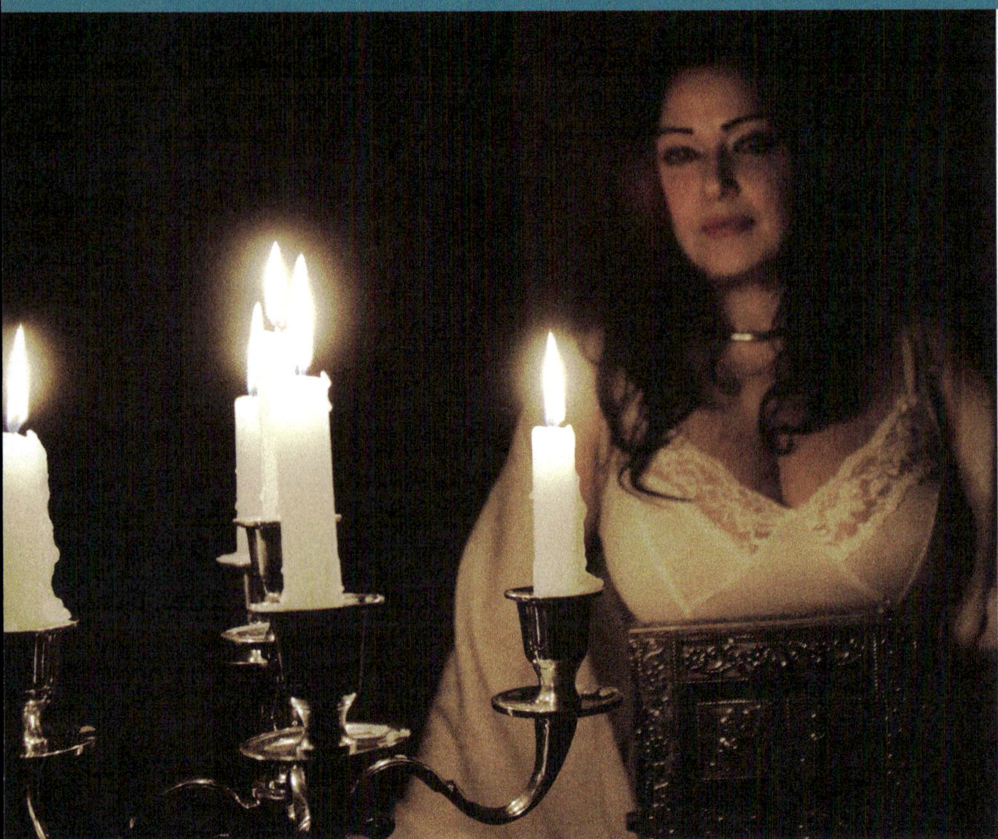

MUSIC

By Asylum Attendant

1.) I'm sure a lot of people remember The Danse Society from the 80s. Musically, what features has the band retained from its origins?

Paul Nash (P) - I personally think the band has retained the unique sound it had in the 80s, fusing vocals, drums, bass, guitar and keys in many interesting ways with, as always, a dark edge. We enjoy a mix of powerful and atmospheric textures and that still shines through in our music today. There is a definite parallel if you remember our first ever AA single "Clock" (an up-tempo powerful spikey dance track) and the brooding dark atmospheric "Continent" and compare that with our recent AA single release "If I were Jesus" and "Sound of Silence". You can see the musical similarities, although of course the sound has evolved over the 30 years or so and has a much more modern edge to it now.

2.) The band has gone through many changes over the years. Paul, as the only remaining founding member, how do you feel about the current line-up?

P - I am absolutely loving our current line-up of Jack (on Bass), Sam (on Keys) and Iain (on Drums). They are excellent musicians that bring something new to the melting pot when it come to writing songs. They have incredible ideas and I am really looking forward to everyone hearing the tracks from the forth coming album! Maethelyiah has an amazing voice and tops off the sound perfectly and I think the recent refresh of the line-up has brought in a new energy (maybe because they are all younger) that really adds excitement to the sound both on record and live.

3.) Why did you decide to cover Paul Simon's "Sound of Silence" and what do the lyrics mean to you?

P -Good question! I was watching The Watchmen film (again) and the funeral scene (which features the original track) got stuck in my head. I had an idea to re-imagine the guitar line and feel of the song by making it slower and we tried it out at rehearsal and developed it from there. I was really happy with the way it turned out - it is a fantastic song and of course the lyrics are incredible. Personally the lyrics' meaning to me are about the way we sometimes feel when things seem dark (but not necessarily in a bad way).

4.) Your music videos are very artistic and entertaining. Are the visuals just as important as the music?

Maethelyiah (M) - I wouldn't say they are as important as the music but they certainly are the immediate way to get our music out there. People seem to react more quickly when they have the chance to see what they hear. Having the whole band playing live in our newest videos gave the chance to display what really the band is about: love, dedication and chemistry. The company that deals with the video making (I.A.P. UK) has always been keen on researching and producing videos to a high standard. Also, we had the chance to collaborate with award winning artist Callum Nash who's ace when it comes to translating ideas into images. He's the same artist that designed the White Rabbit on our T-Shirts, and also features on our video White Rabbit. Nothing is ever improvised or left incomplete. Our supporters deserve the best.

5.) I really got a kick out of your humorous new song "If I were Jesus". How did you come up with this anti-Christmas song of sorts?

M - I wrote it in 2004 but for some reason "If I were Jesus" only emerged when I brought it at rehearsals a few months ago. I'm pagan but I respect other religions (as long as they are mutually respectful). I don't have problems in celebrating Christmas but I'm sure that if Jesus Christ was due back on earth he wouldn't be too impressed by the way his life is used for speculation and persistent business orientated activity. I find the way the Catholic Church uses his image rather disturbing, starting from having his death displayed as a logo...seriously I prefer the Christ Buddy in Dogma (the movie). I find it much more respectful and in theme with the message of love, compassion and support that he really meant to express.

6.) Maethelyiah, I see that you write surreal novels as well as songs. What inspires your magical writings?

M - A good chunk of what I write is inspired by true facts and stories. Until 2001 I have travelled as much as I could and met the most controversial and different kinds of people. "The 5 Monsters" was written after a good 5 years spent interviewing and researching after cases in the Death Row. There's many references to the paranormal world because that's home for me. I'm writing a new novel now that explores the world of BDSM and domestic abuse and no, it's nothing to do with 50 Shades of Grey. I can assure that, because it's based on a true story.

7.) What's your favorite thing about live shows?

M - On a mere technical point of view, I like the eternal challenge. I think that you don't really know a musician until you go live. The mutual support, the skill, the work under pressure and the way we deal with the daily technical issues is rather revealing. I was supposed to hate the tech issues we had on stage in our last gig (Bristol last year) and instead, I had a really good laugh with Paul and Dave on stage. It was incredible. The show always must go on. On a more emotional point of view, nothing beats the feedback and the response people can give us directly. The interaction is best. I realise sometimes I'm too concentrated into what I am singing that I sort of "forget" where I am but that's part of being volcanic and passionate as I am. But, once I'm back on Earth I love chatting to people afterwards.

P - Playing live is a way to convey your songs in an intense, exciting and real way. Being on stage adds an extra edge to the music and the feedback we get from the crowd is inspiring and motivating to keep on doing what we do. Also it helps bond the band together as we are all 'in it together' to have a great time and enjoy the music - I love it!

8.) The concept and artwork for your album Scarey Tales are both very imaginative. Why did you choose a fantastical theme for this album?

M - The cover art was made by Italian esoteric painter (and very dear friend) Danilo Capua, who's been a friend of mine for the last three lives. His way of capturing the Lovecraftian spirit in his pictures is out of this world. The song "The Tale" was inspired directly by H.P. Lovecraft stories. The painting seems to have Cthulhu peeping out of the clock. It also seems to have The Scarecrow showing himself to the observer. The novel that Paul (Nash) and I wrote was inspired by Lovecraft in part, as well as we wanted to feature all the elements that each song was representing (The Wolf, White Rabbit).

P - When the initial songs were written for Scarey Tales a theme began to develop, and we were inspired to look musically and lyrically at dark fantasy tales, and it just developed from there. The addition of the cover painting by Danilo and long poem that myself and Maeth wrote fit in perfectly with the theme, as sometimes these things do. It just all came together at the right time.

9.) Which bands/artists would you like to tour with in the future?

M - Peter Gabriel, Steve Wilson, Ultravox, Trent Reznor, Gary Newman, Adam Ant. If I could resurrect Ian Curtis, definitely Joy Division. There's many more amazing artists and musicians but the list would be too long to mention.

P - There's too many to mention, but any band that is creating fresh original and exciting music would be fine with me. There are some great new bands out there as well as some reformed bands that are making some fantastic music. Top of my list would be Killing Joke (again), QOTSA, Muse, Royal Blood, Band of Skulls, Gary Numan, NIN, Death Cab, The Cure, Depeche Mode, Elbow, Portishead, Radiohead...

10.) I heard your new album will be out around Easter time. What can you tell us about it? Any surprises?

M - As it seems to be our tradition, the songs are very different from each other, so you can expect tense songs as well as more spacey atmospheres. At the moment we have half the album baked and there's some really freaky moments. I feel like calling this band a sort of Tardis because there's all sorts of sounds, older and newer, that keep our style reinvented, where everything can happen since we are not concerned to stick to a "genre".

P - It's going to be EPIC lol - so far, we have as always a very eclectic mix of songs but all retain the signature darkness, power and atmosphere of The Danse Society sound. I think at this point the album will be released around May/June fingers crossed. I am really looking forward to everyone being able to hear it!

11.) Where can fans come and see you in the coming months?

M - As we speak, we are restarting our tour in March this year to promote our new AA single "If I were Jesus/Sound of Silence" (on purple vinyl) in Sheffield. We will then headline the Sci-Fi Festival in Scarborough, Dark Waters Festival in Nottingham and the Calvert Stock Festival in Devon. There's many more dates to be confirmed and will definitely include London as well. Just keep an eye on our website (the only reliable resource of info for The Danse Society since 2011) at www.thedansesociety.com.

Thank you, and thanks to all the supporters and fans that managed to keep up with the many stages of The Danse Society. We are certainly working hard and honestly to deliver our best tunes. The Danse Society has reinvented itself since 1980 and that is still going.

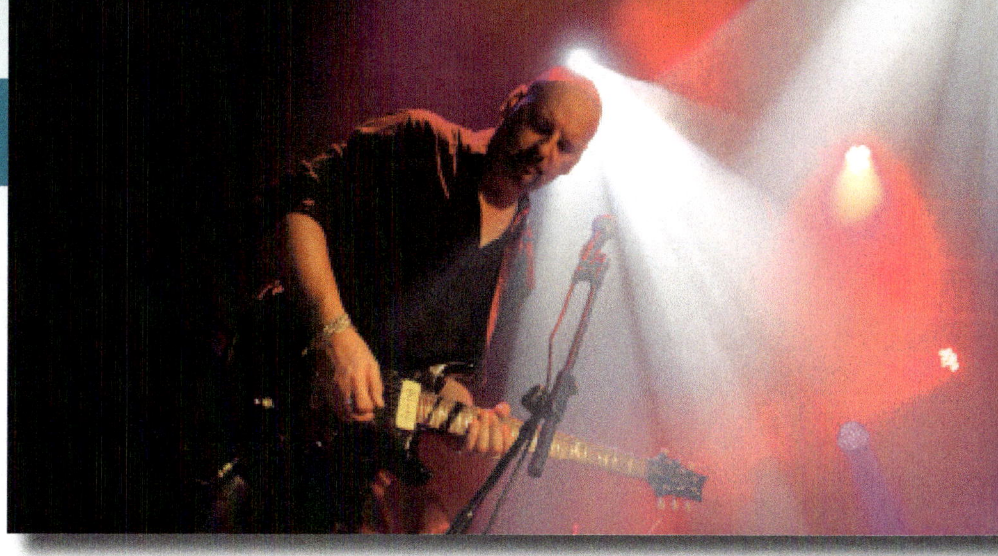

BELLYDANCING

By Yasaman Vrd'dhi

In a Galaxy far, far away there lived a dancer who fused a ancient art called Belly Dance with her own people's dance, and so was born Raqs Sci-Fi. Now that would really be sci-fi if this fusion of belly dance came to be in that way. In the world of belly dance, there are many fusions that are created every year and Raqs Sci-Fi is one of them. What is Raqs Sci-Fi you ask? It's belly dance fused with science fiction concepts and music. The costumes are based from different sci-fi movies, books and even characters created by the Dancer.

Are you interested Raqs Sci-Fi? Then I have some tips on how you can get into this new creative version of belly dance. First, if you are not already into sci-fi (and I think if you're interested in this style then you just may be), look to sci-fi movies, books, etc. to get some ideas as to what characters you would like to base your next performances on. With movies you can get visuals and music ideas, and in books you can also get a feel for the character's personality. Also if you are creative (and it sounds like you just might be), then take ideas from your own creative mind and write your very own character. That's how I do it at times.

Now the music: as dancers we know how important the music element of our performance is. We connect with it, we dance it, we recreate it. For Raqs Sci-Fi, you would look info sci-fi based music. I look all over the Internet for different music in this field. Like I said before, you can reference sci-fi movies for this as well, as they will have albums for most movies, and www. youtube.com can be your best friend in this instance. Just put in something like "sci-fi music", and all kinds of sci-fi based music will show up, giving you hours of music to study and listen to.

The costumes: now to the costume design, you may need to get creative with your hands in this area, since there are not a lot of belly dance stores out there that will just have a wookiee belly dance belt and bra set sitting around. Yet do not fear if you are not

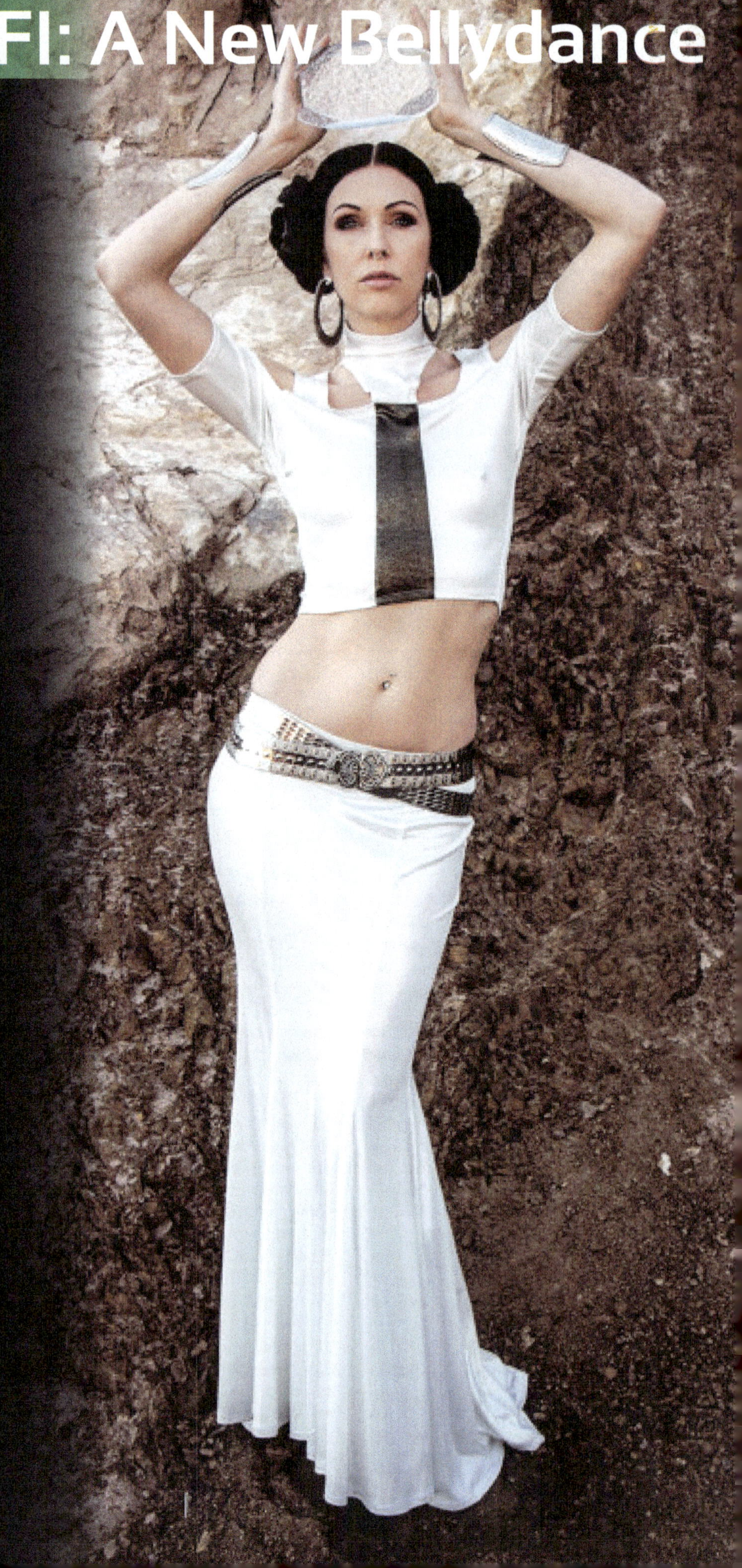

so good with a needle, there are some costume designers out there that can save your bleeding finger tips (look for links at the end of this article). When thinking about your costume, think about how you can fuse (let's say) a Jedi look with a belly dance look. Fusion is the key here. You will want to get across your fusion of sci-fi and belly dance.

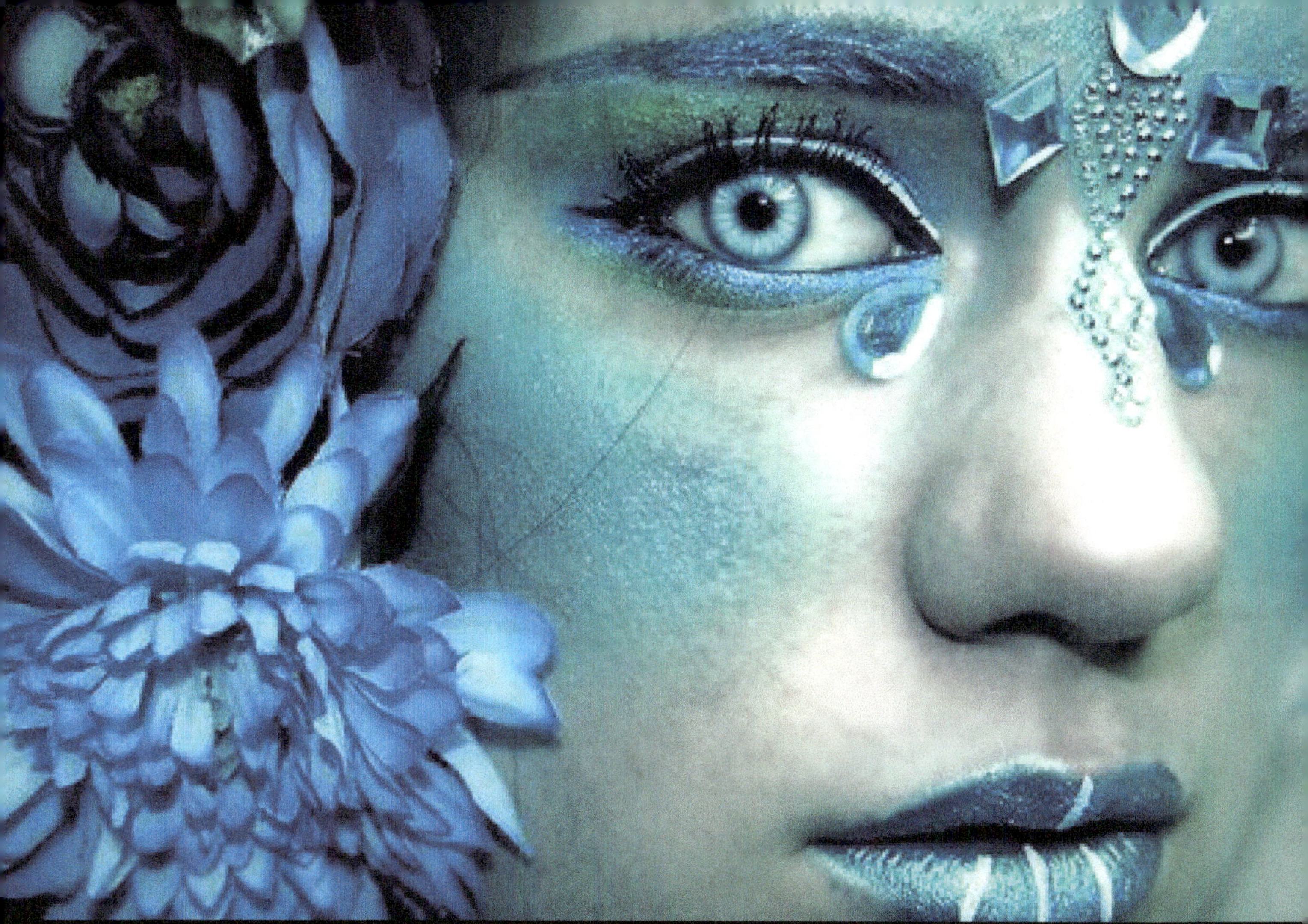

The make-up: let's face it, not everyone's a make-up artist, so get some nice ideas from pinterest.com. There are videos on youtube that can even teach you how to do sci-fi make-up. I like to use EYECONS Metallic-Powder and Bindis (by Jessica Dances). Her make-up kits work great for amazing looks, and for sci-fi, you will need amazing. Your make-up should be based to your character and the story you're telling.

So are you even more interested than ever? Well, if you are, how about giving it a go? Turn on your sci-fi geek, and your belly dance shimmy because you can put the two together, and get your Raqs Sci-fi on.

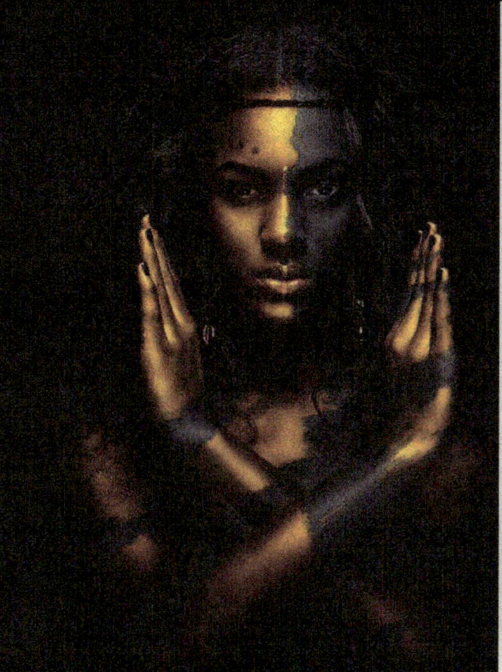

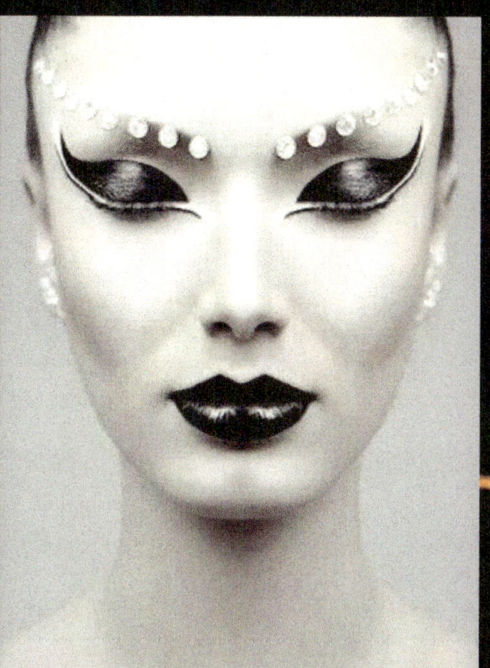

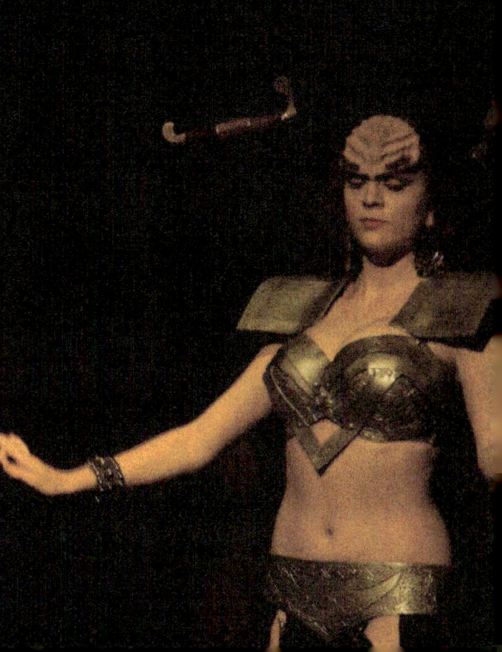

CANDYLUST

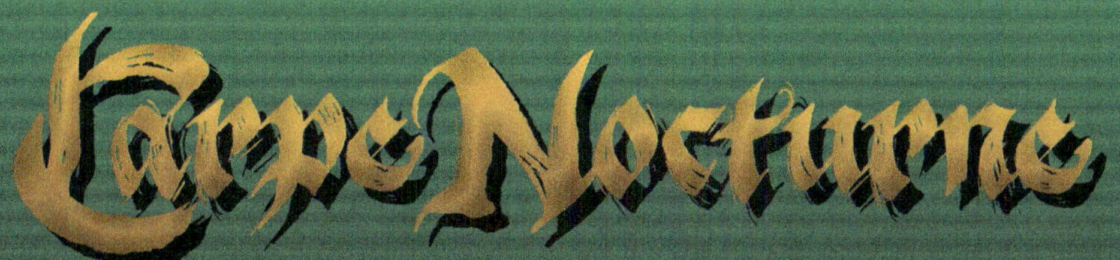

/vis(ə)rəl/ -

coming from strong emotions; not pertaining to logic or reason

---

Visceral Attractions is Carpe Nocturne's official Fashion insert, spotlighting the most unique and decadent counter-culture fashion out there. Every quarterly issue features full page spreads of fetish and cosplay photographs to the theme of Goth, Fantasy, Sci-Fi and Steampunk.

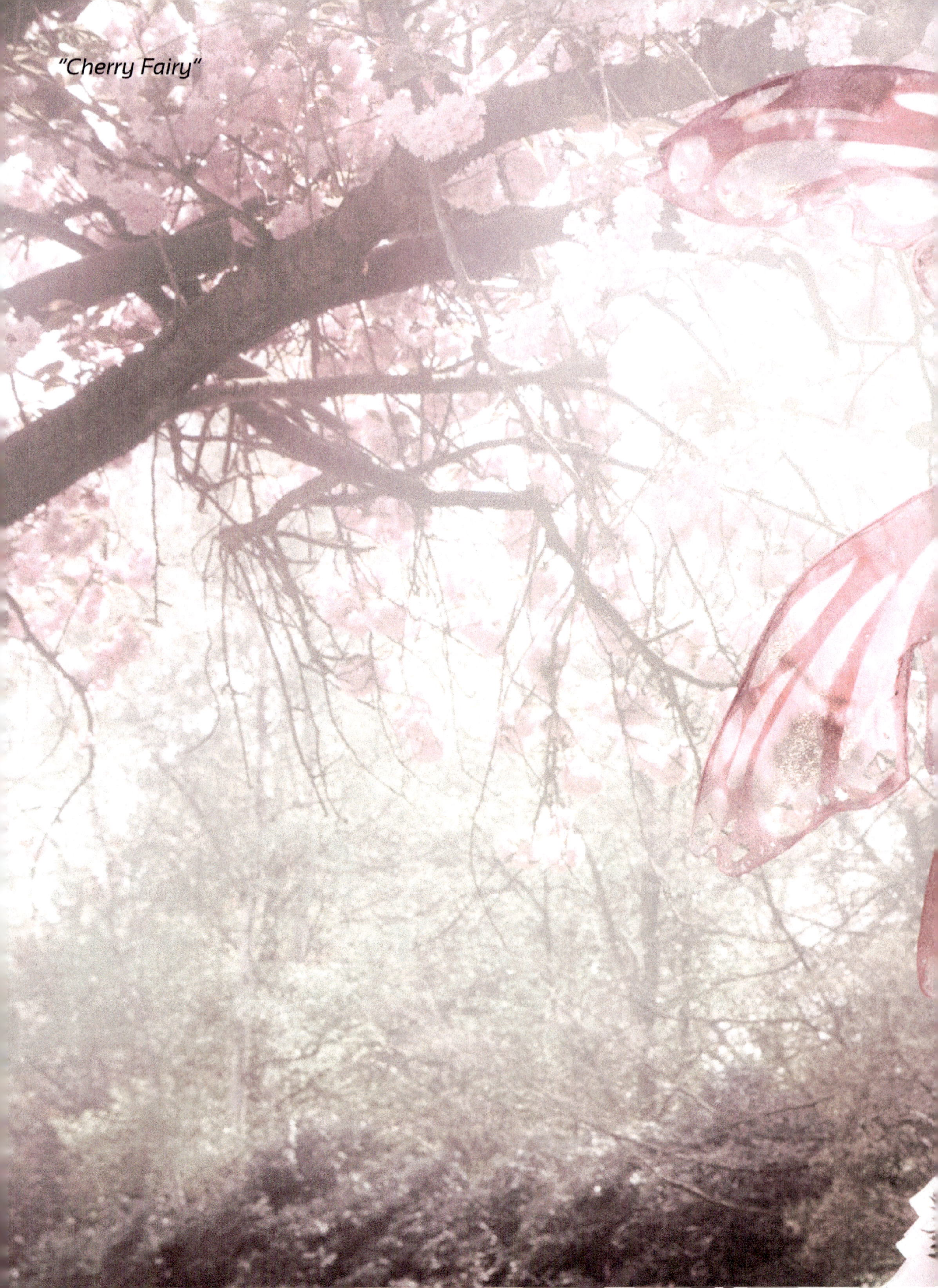

"Cherry Fairy"

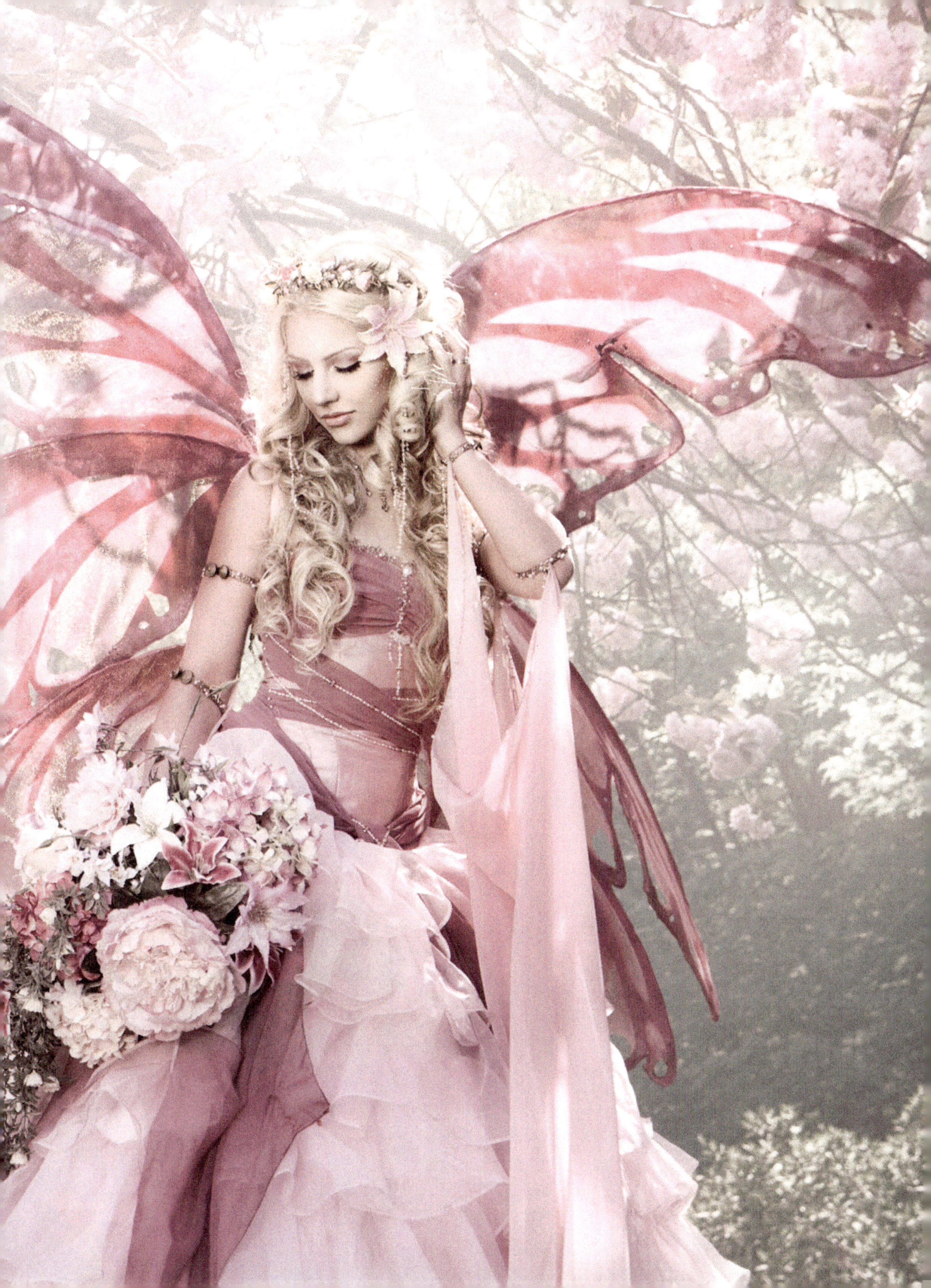

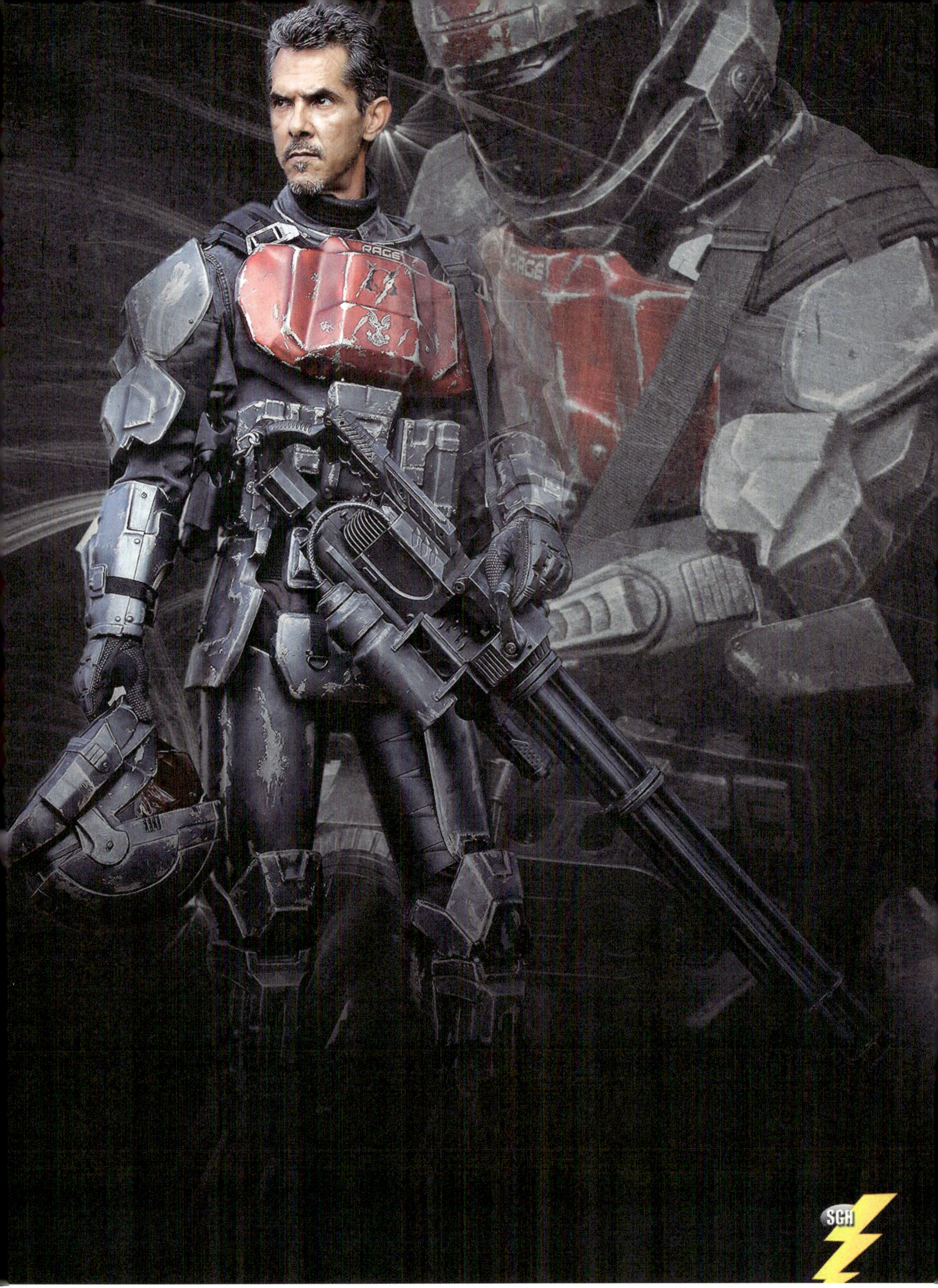

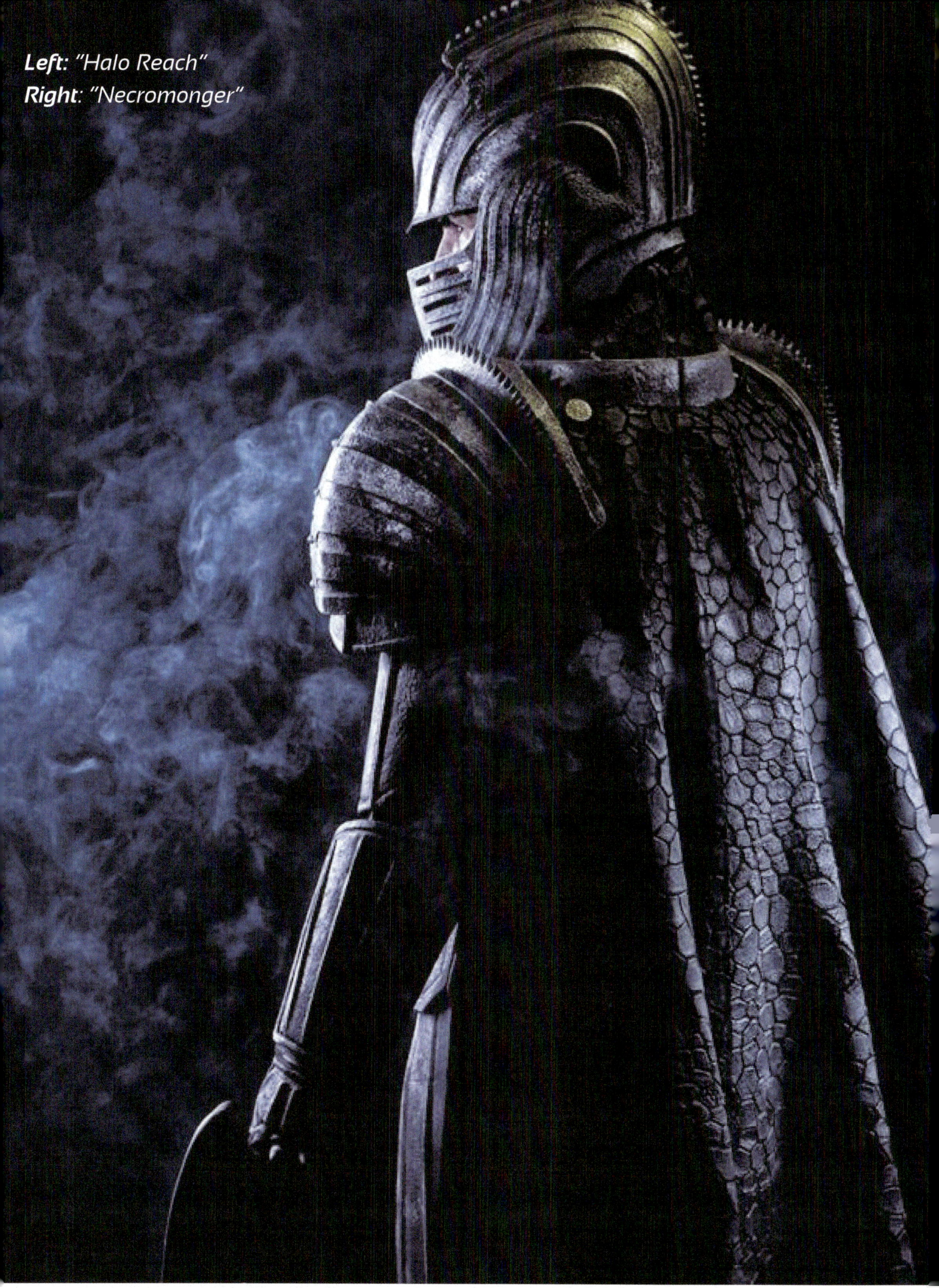

Left: "Halo Reach"
Right: "Necromonger"

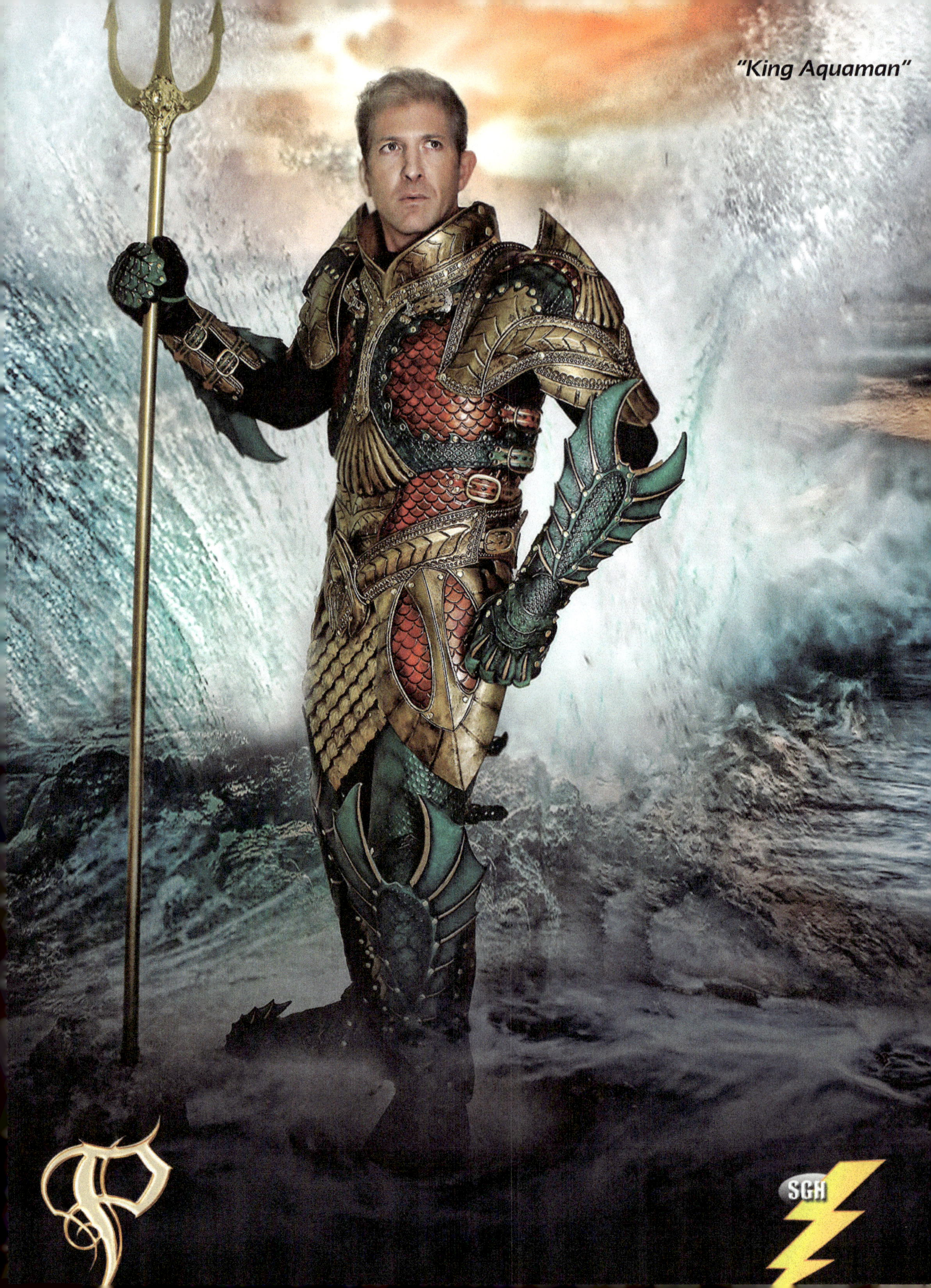

"King Aquaman"
SGH

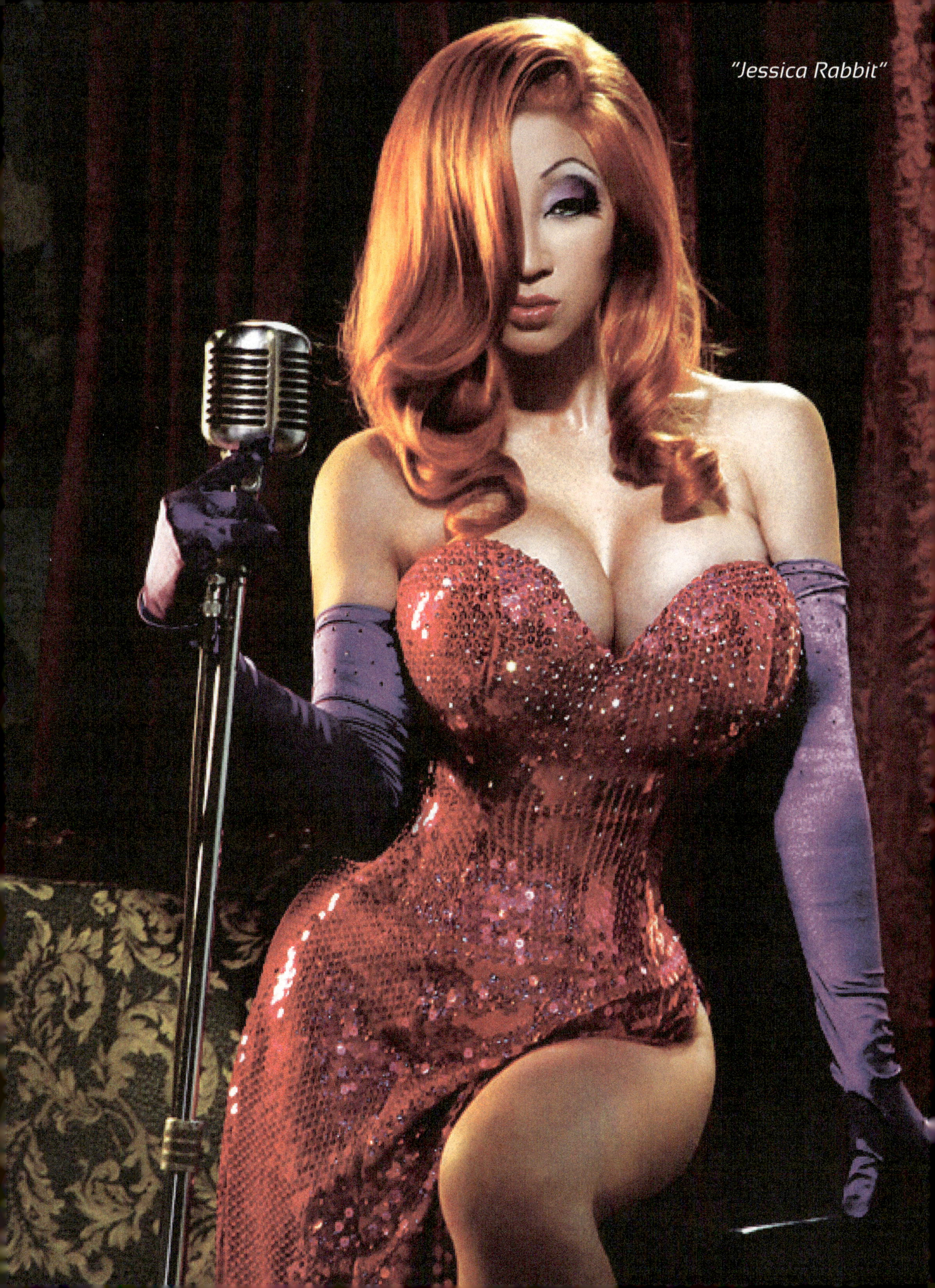

"Jessica Rabbit"

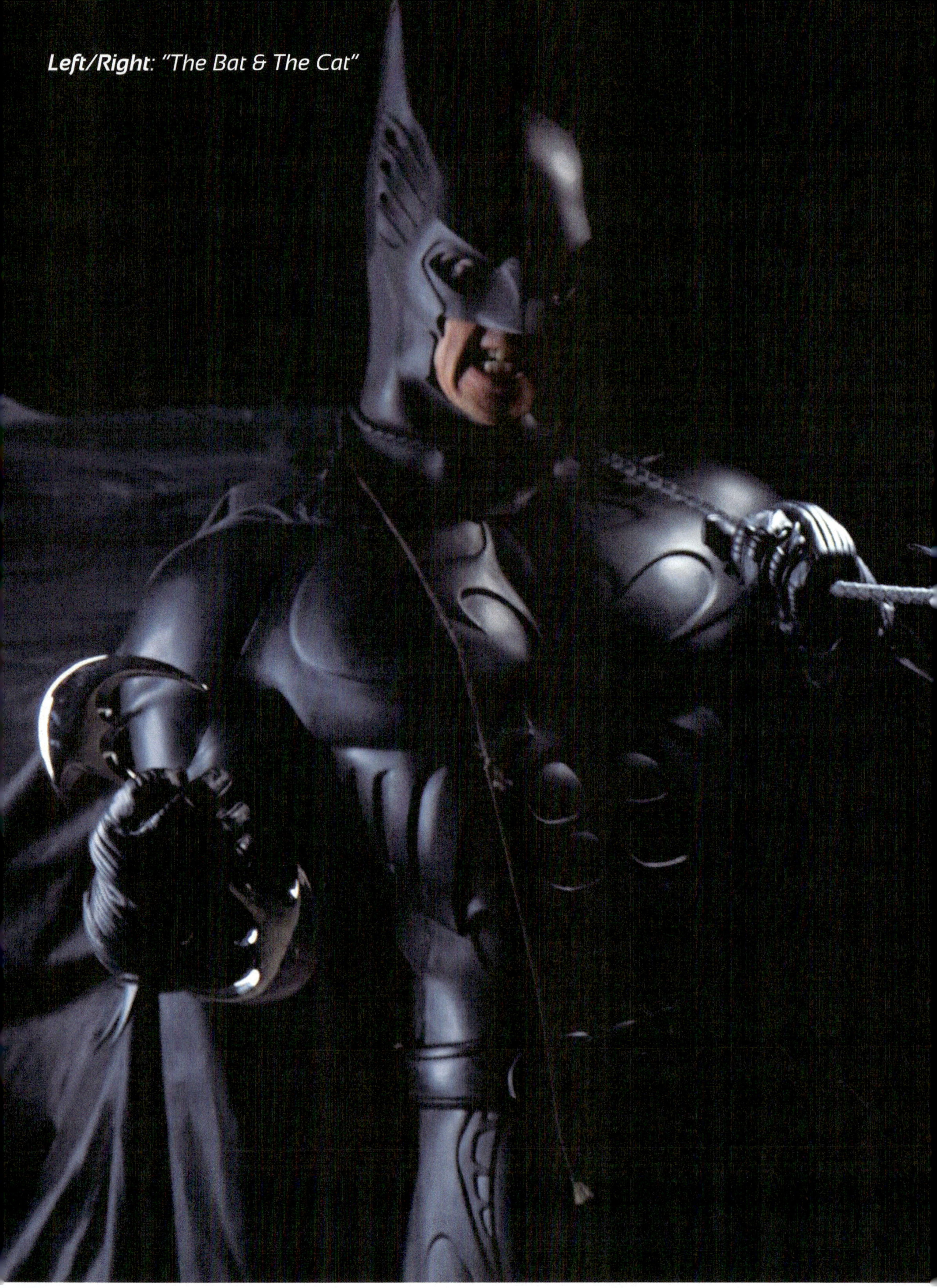

Left/Right: "The Bat & The Cat"

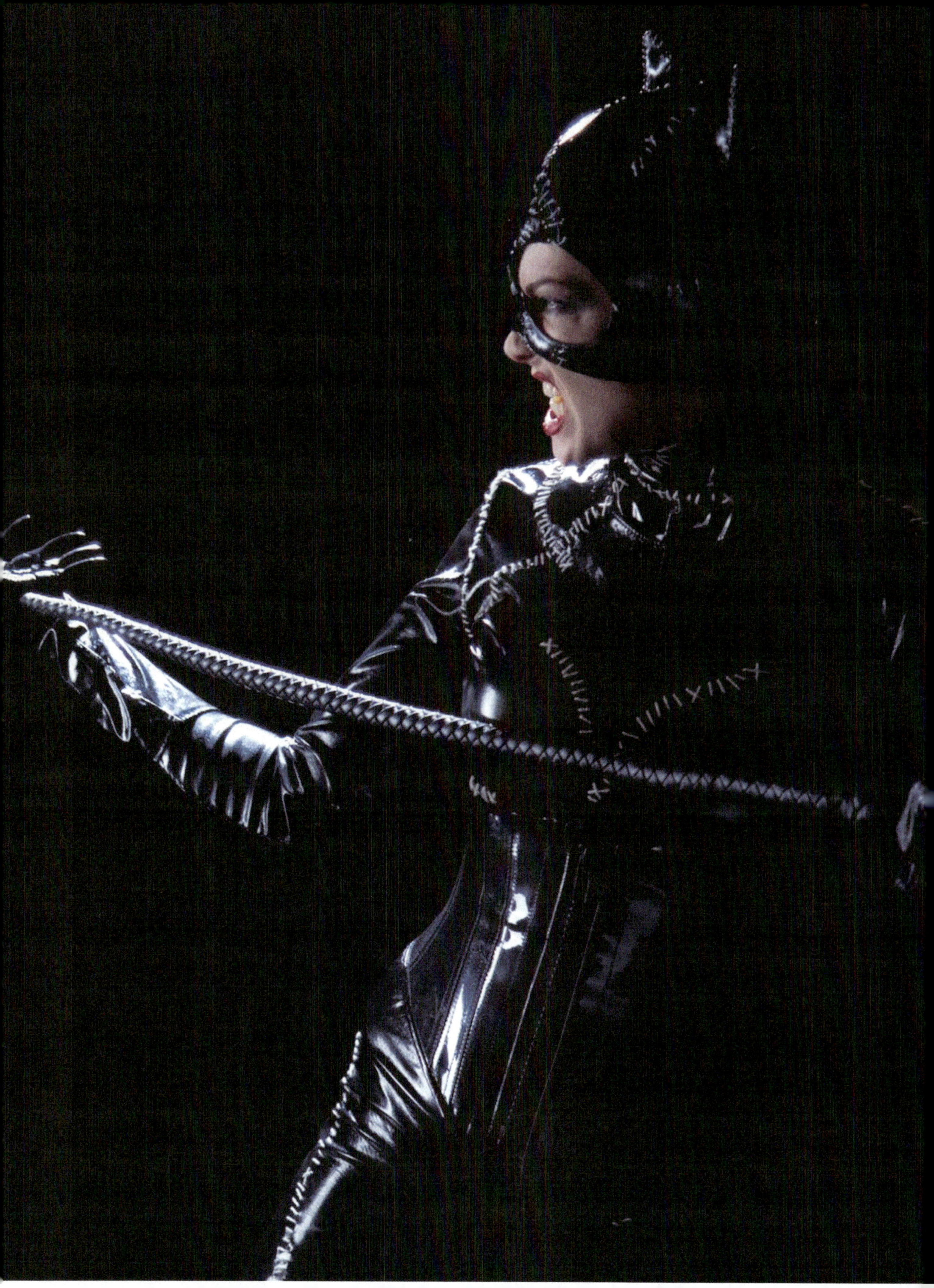

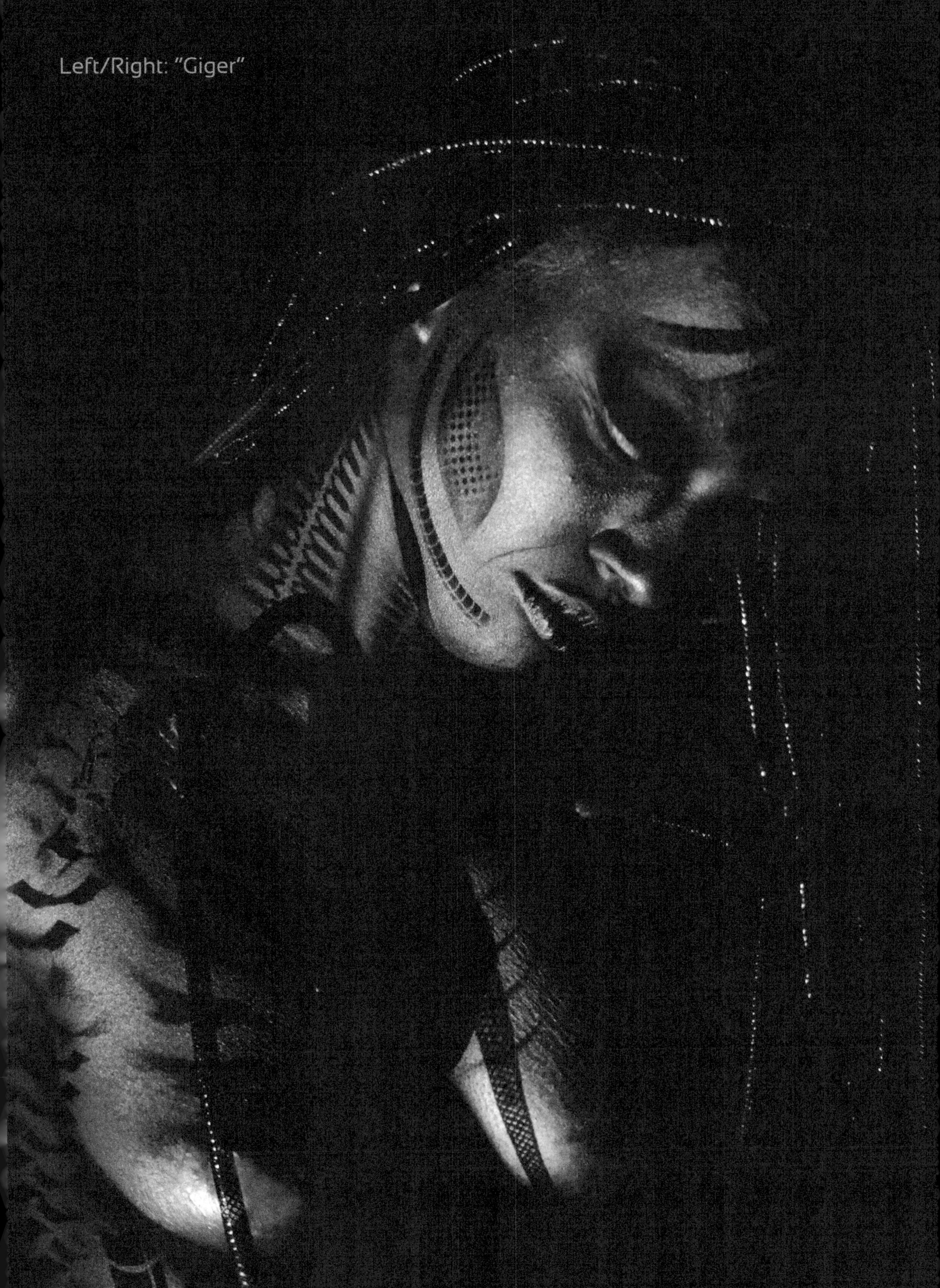

Left/Right: "Giger"

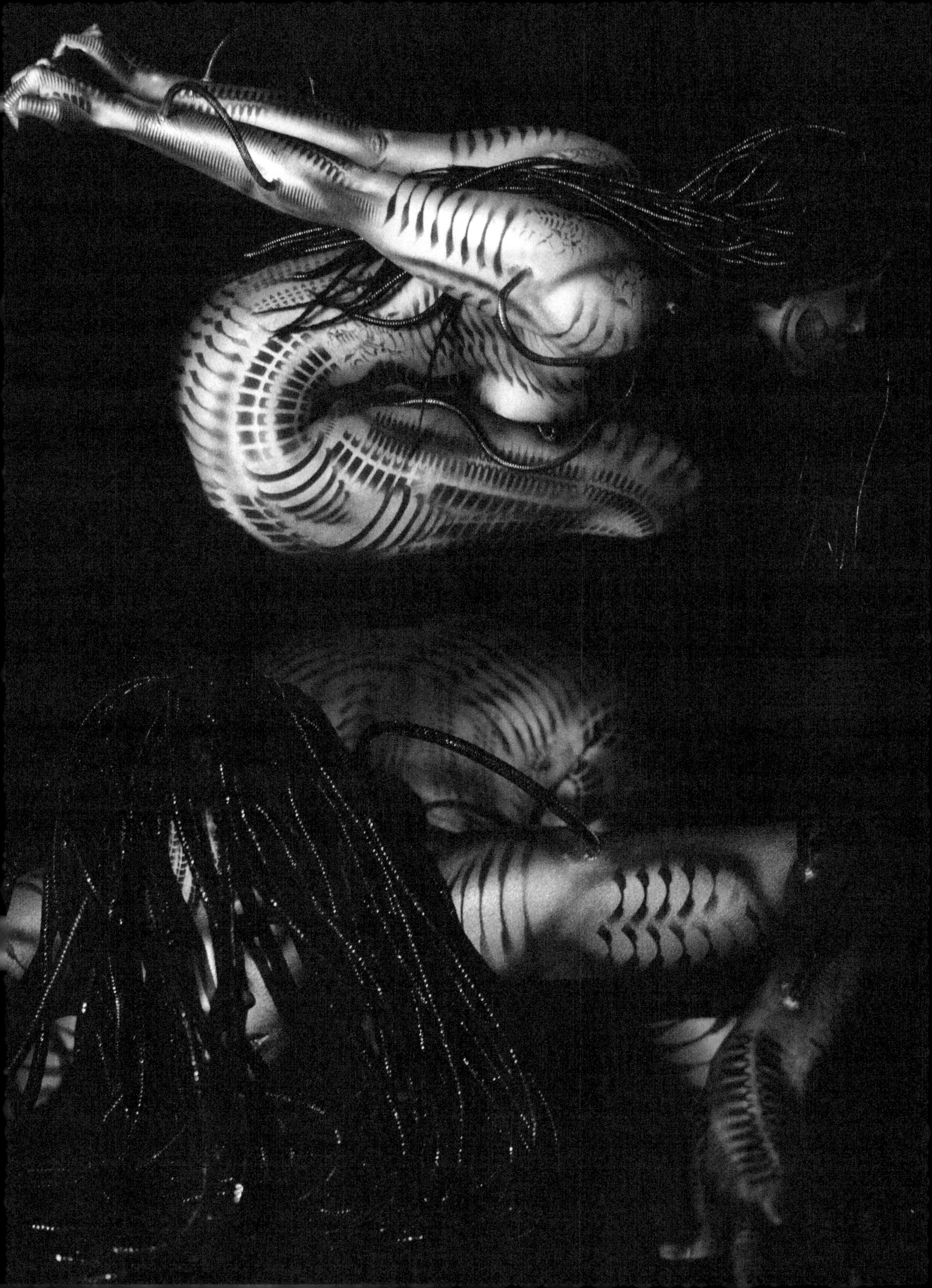

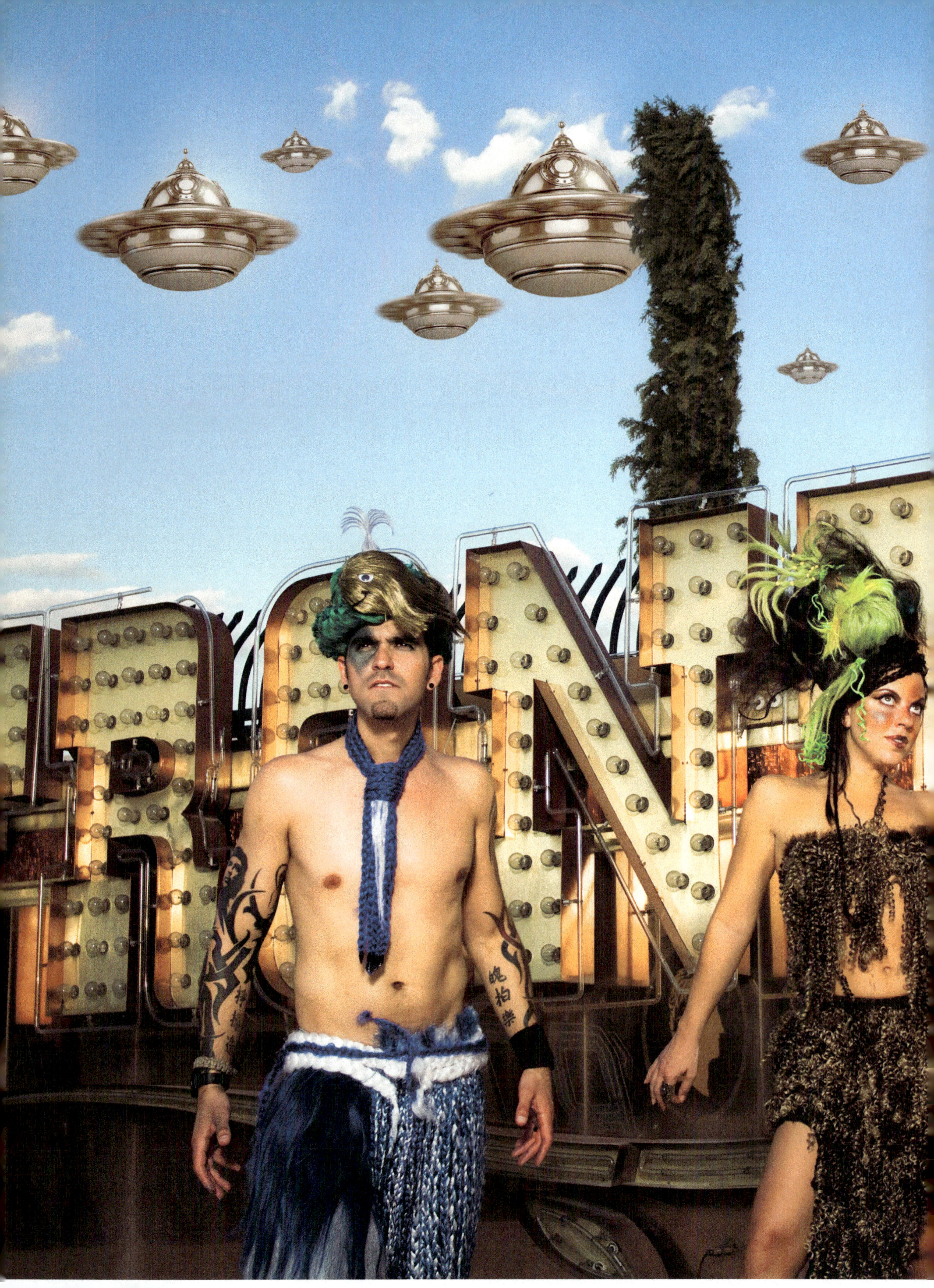

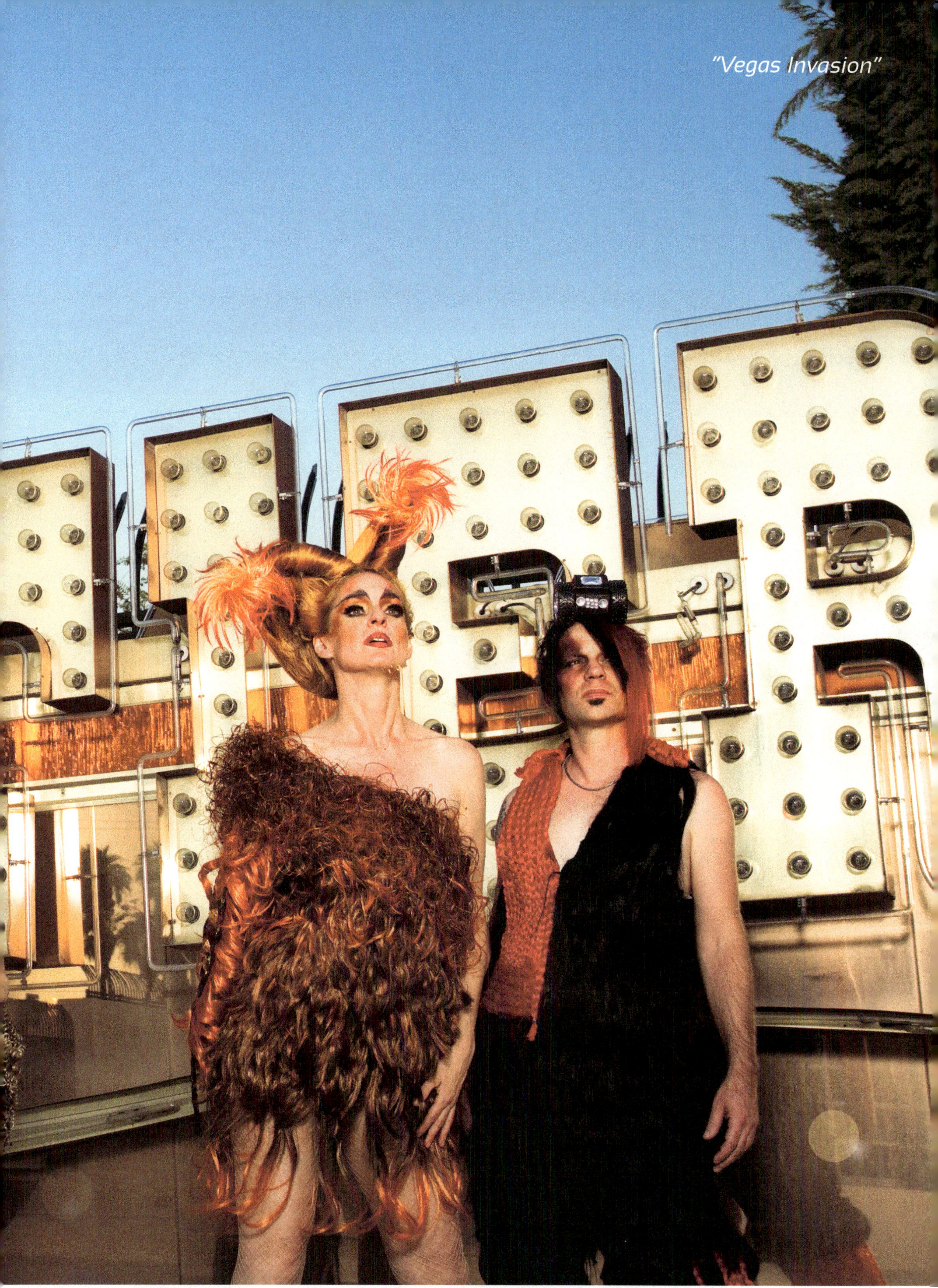
"Vegas Invasion"

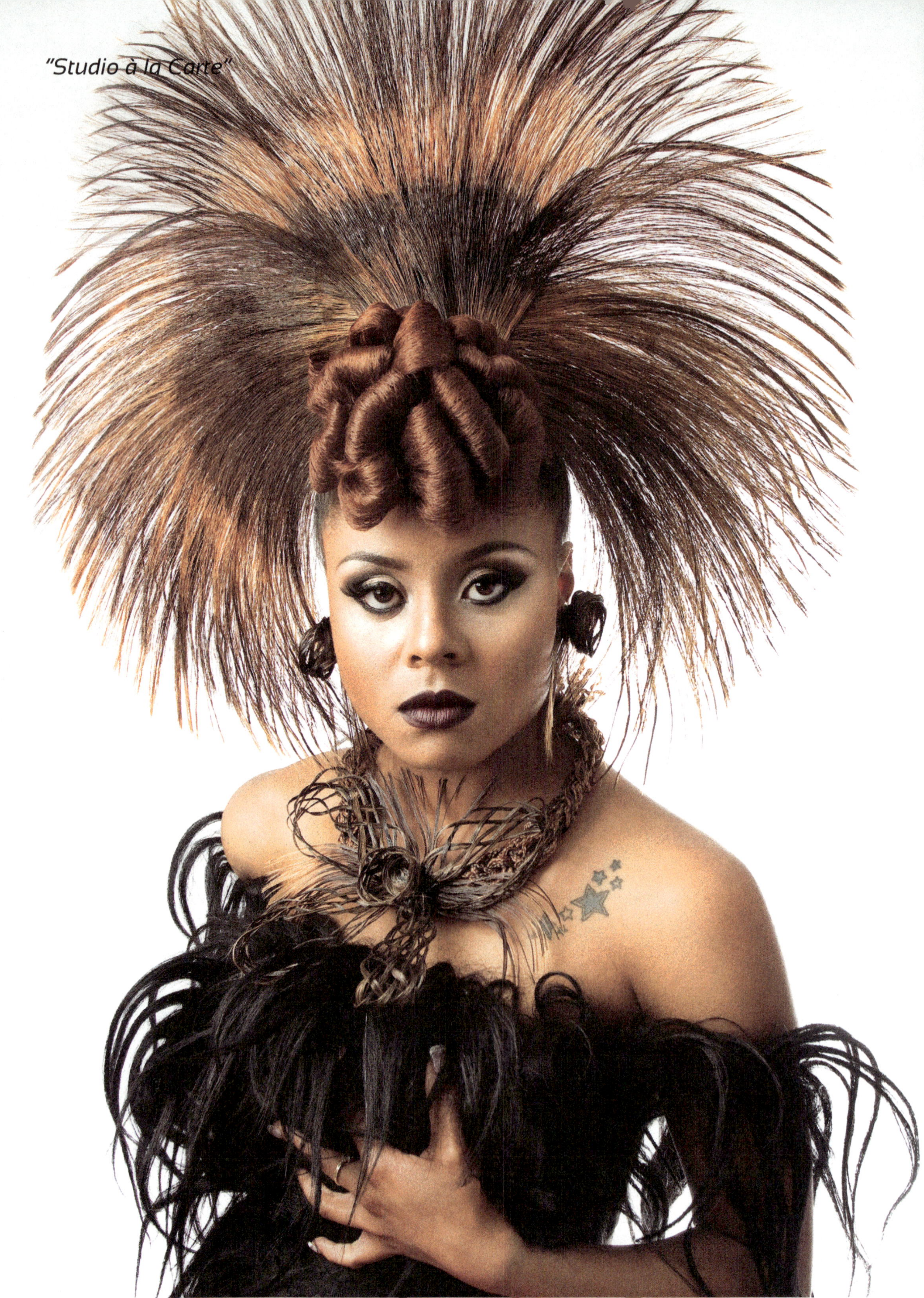

"Studio à la Carte"

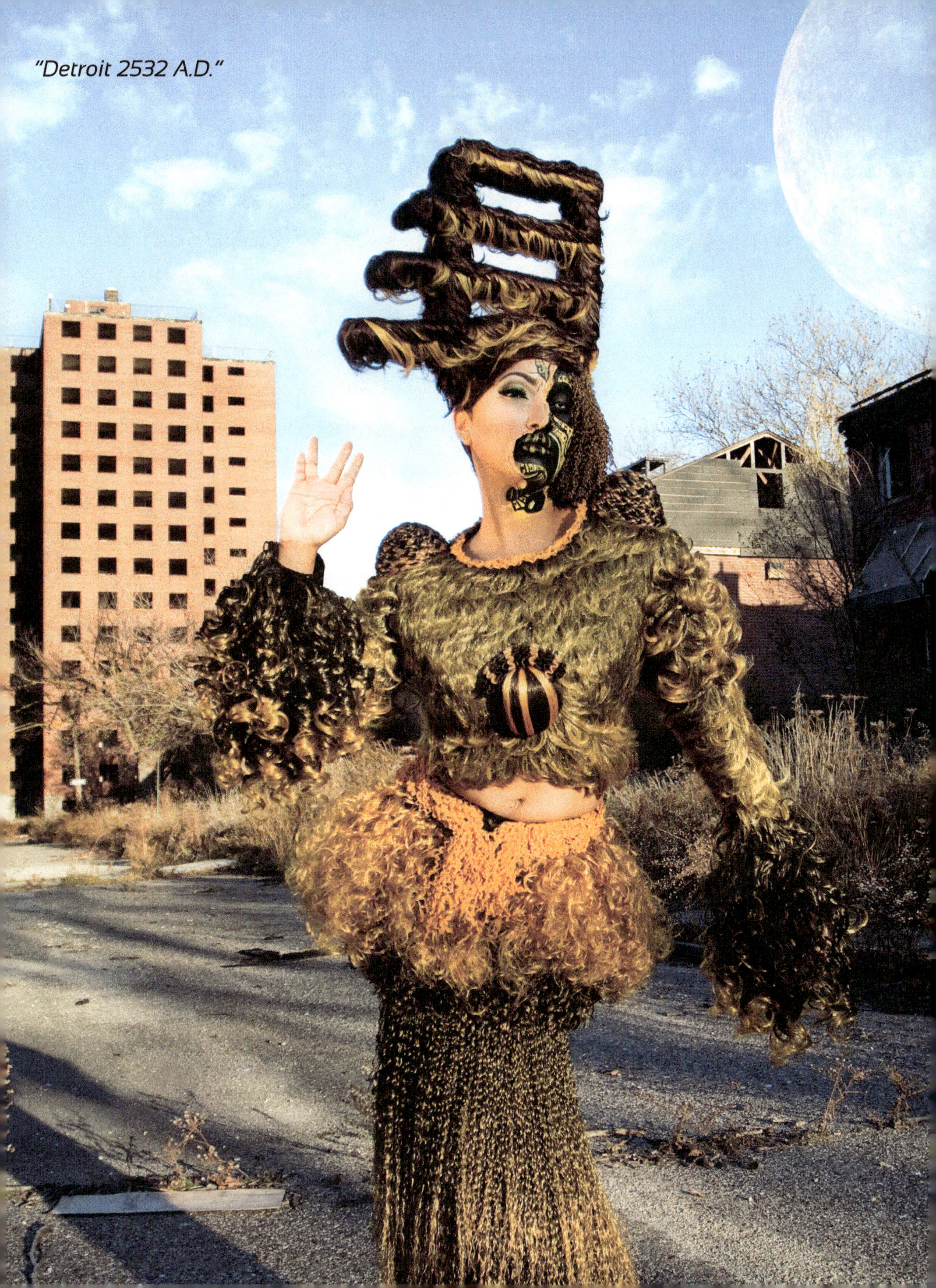
"Detroit 2532 A.D."

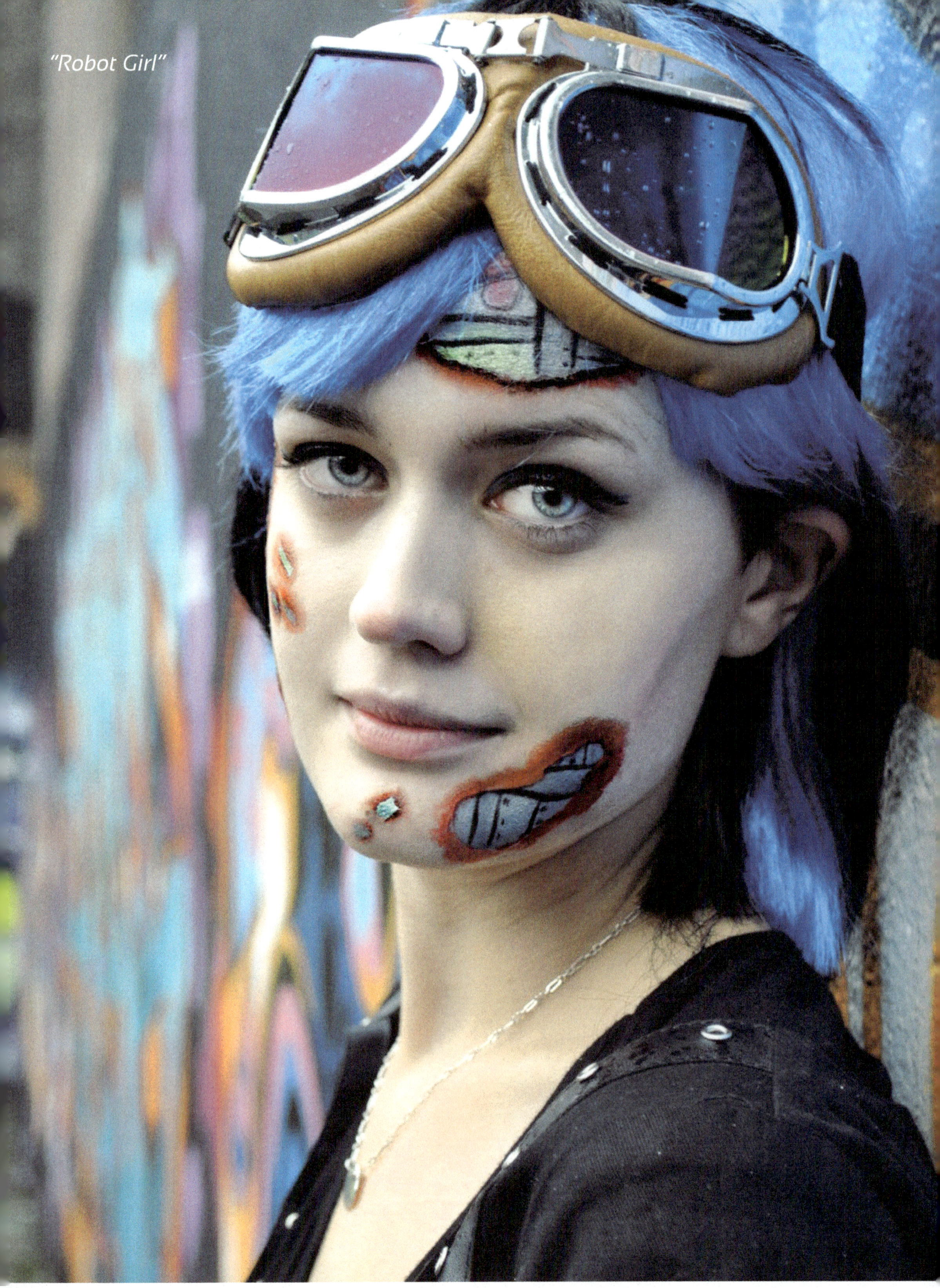

"Robot Girl"

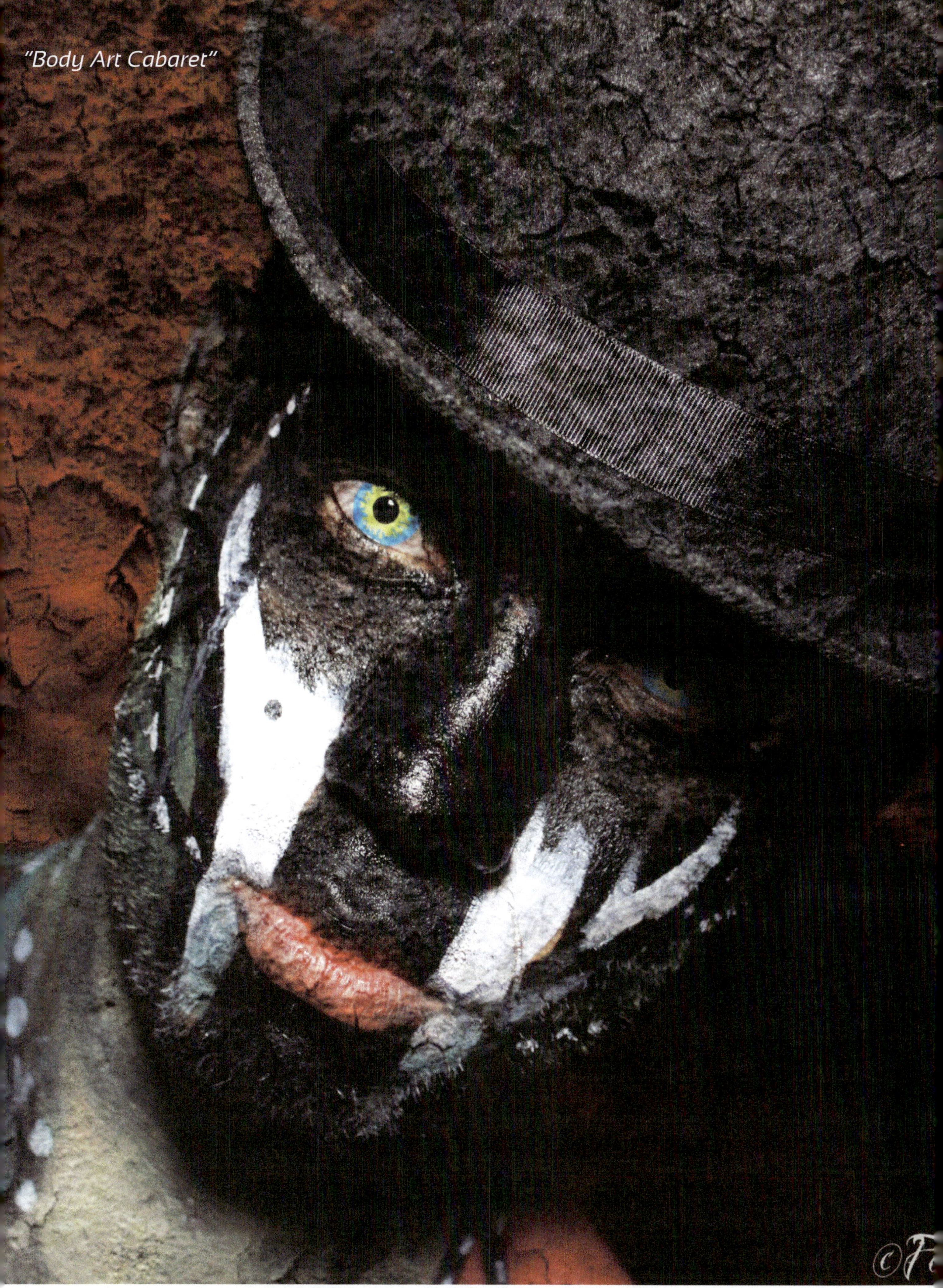

"Body Art Cabaret"

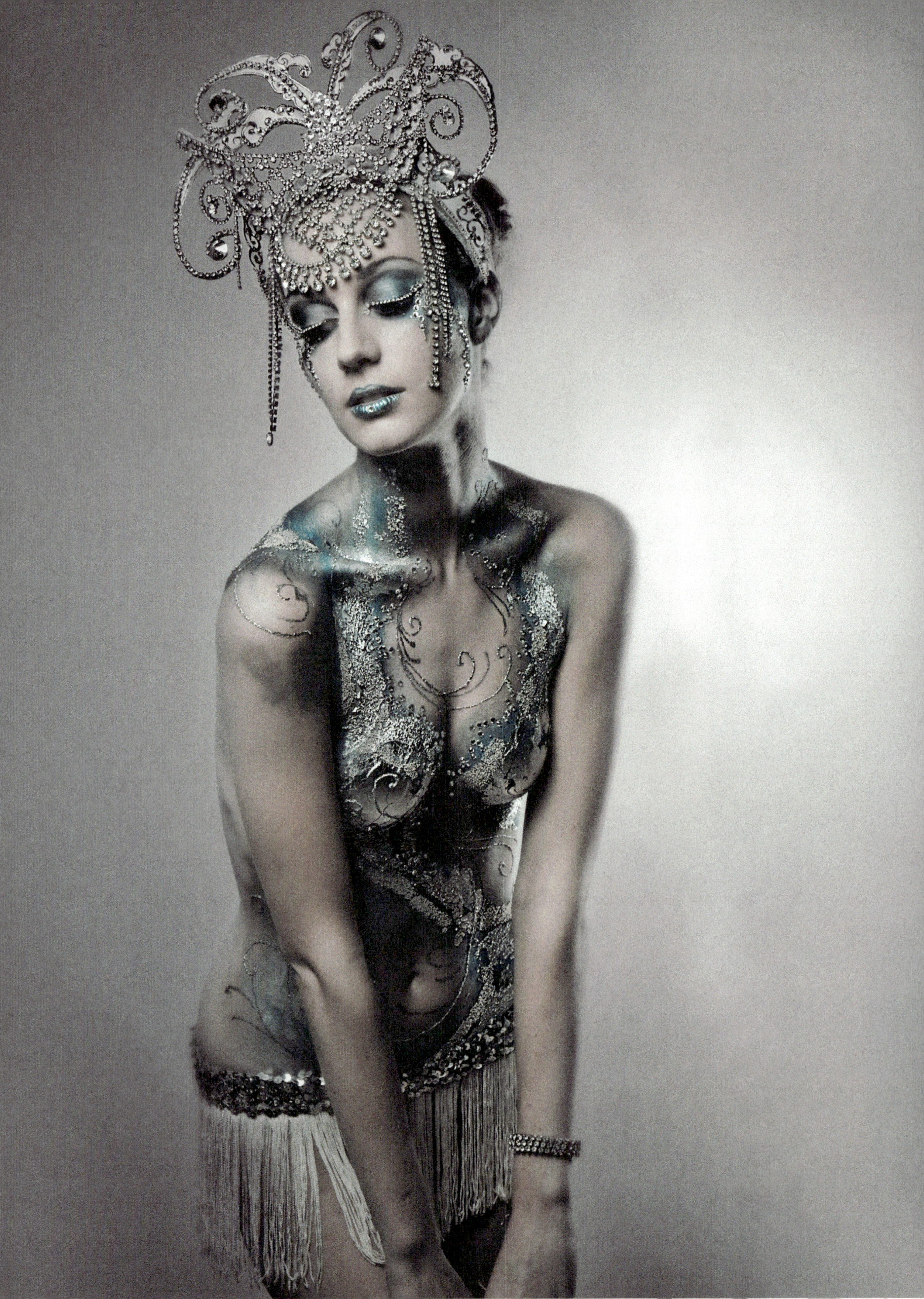

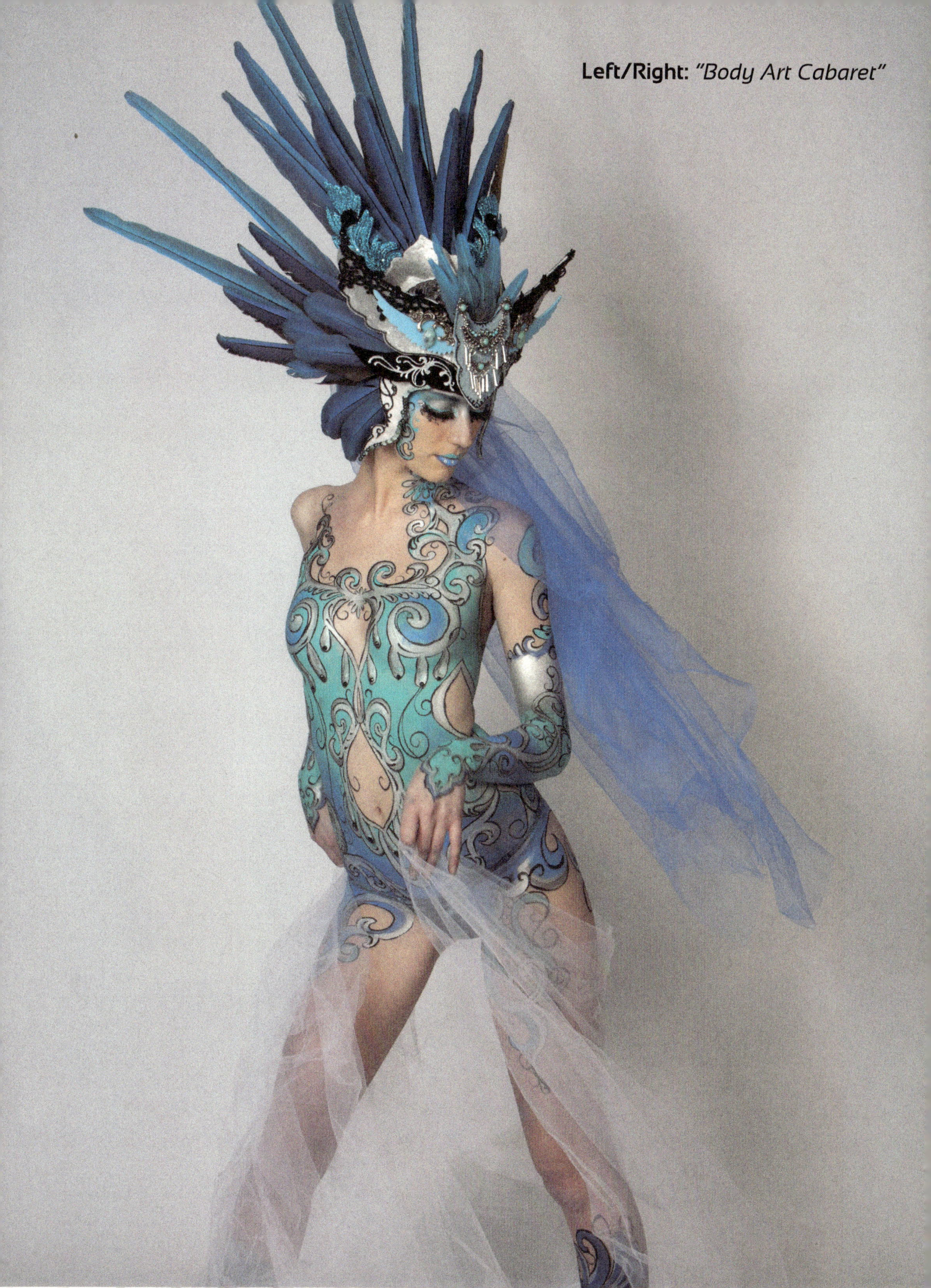

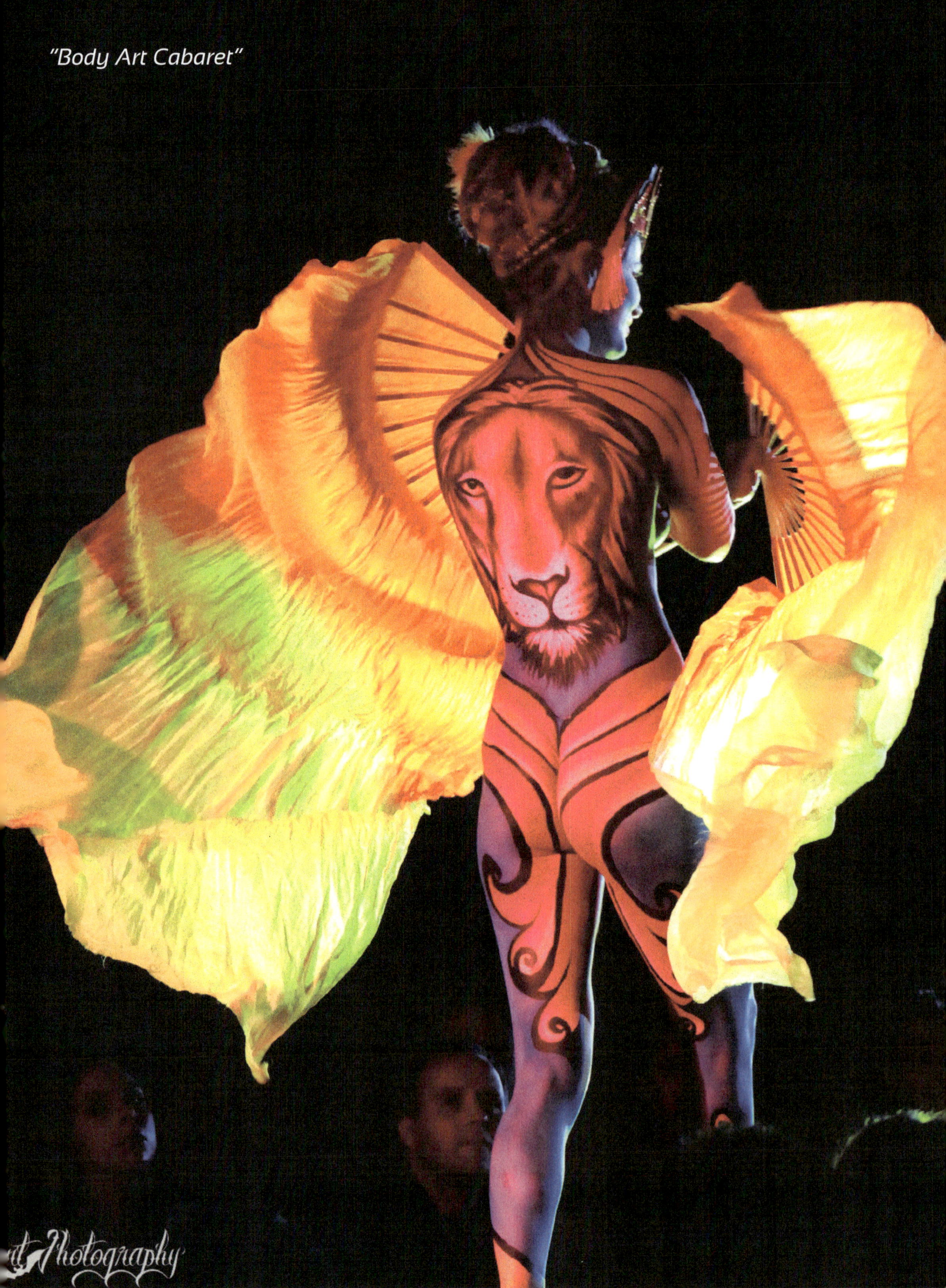
"Body Art Cabaret"
Art Photography

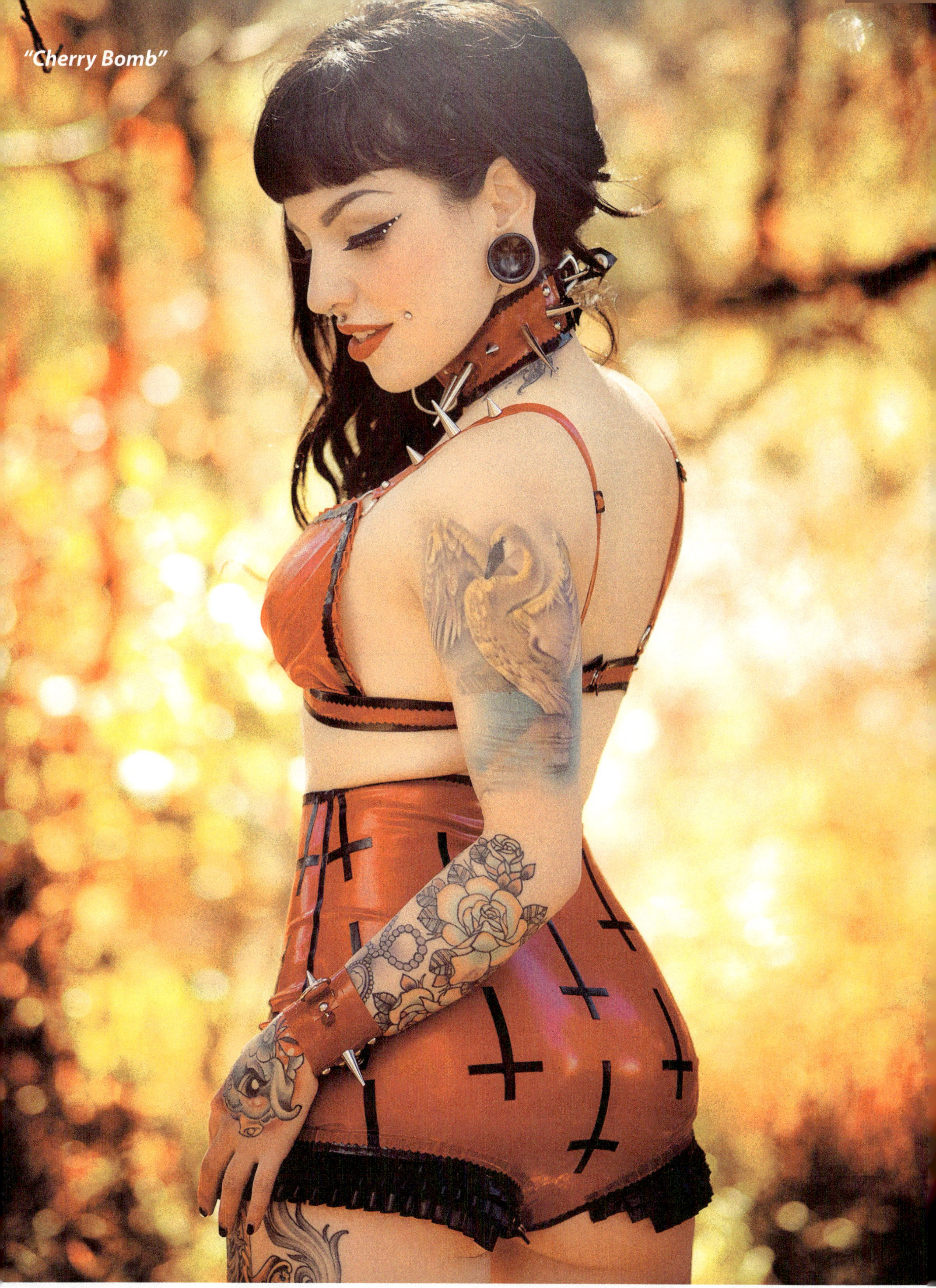
"Cherry Bomb"

CREDITS:

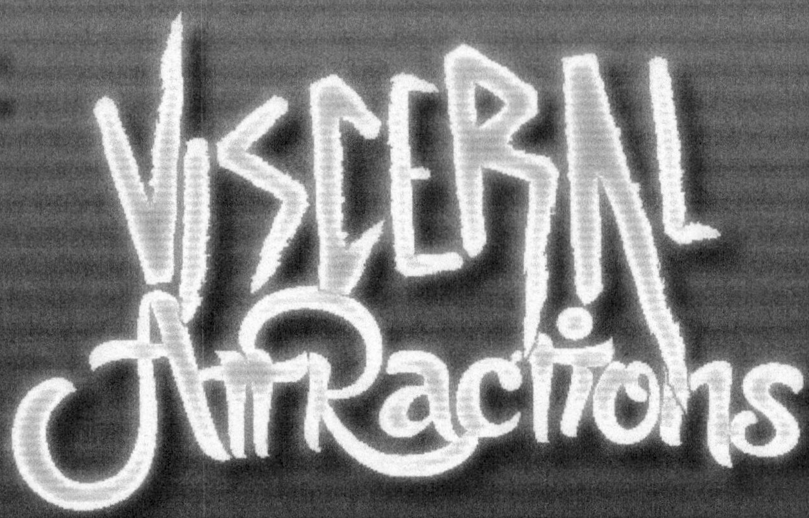

If you are a model or a designer and would like to have your photographs featured in Visceral Attractions, please contact the editor at fashion@carpenocturne.net.

'Cherry Fairy'	Designs by Fairytas www.Fairytas.com
'Halo Reach' 'Necromonger' 'The Bat & The Cat'	Carlos Blanchard Facebook: Catwoman in Miami www.facebook.com/medievalbatman
'King Aquaman'	Designs by Prince Armory www.PrinceArmory.com
'Jessica Rabbit'	Yaya Han Photo: by Brian Boling
'Giger'	Luna Minuit Facebook: Rewski-Photography
'Vegas Invasion' 'Studio à la Carte' 'Detroit 2532 A.D.'	Designs by Steven Noss Weaven's World – A Journey with Fantasy Hair www.WeavenSteven.com
'Robot Girl'	Photo: by Caroline Walsh Makeup: Zoe Ryan Lammers Model: Emma Roberts Facebook: Photos-By-Caroline-Walsh
'Body Art Cabaret'	Rosemary Kimble www.enrapturingentertainment.com
'Cherry Bomb'	Chantele Smith www.etsy.com/shop/TwistedVisions666

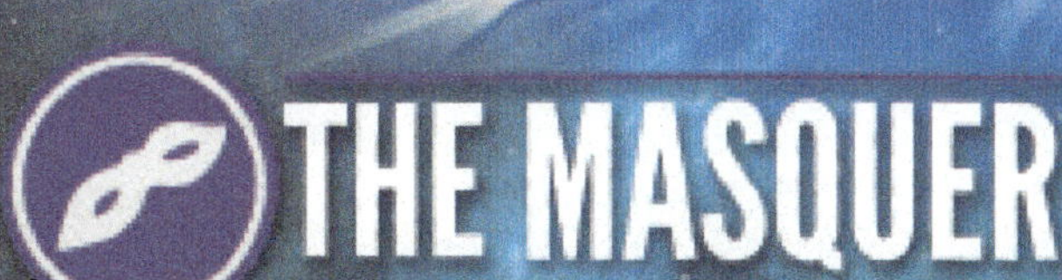

PRODUCED BY MARKSTERCON.COM
CO-HOSTED BY DRAGON FIRE EVENTS

TIME LORD PARTY II

ATLANTA • JUNE 12, 2015 • 9PM–3AM • 18+

THE MASQUERADE

- PHOTOGRAPHERS & VENDORS
- WHOVIAN COSTUME CONTEST
- DJ SERAPH & DJP GOTH, DARKWAVE, INDUSTRIAL, EBM
- THEMED DRINK SPECIALS
- TARDIS PHOTOS & MORE

POLICE PUBLIC CALL BOX
POLICE

SPONSORED BY
Carpe Nocturne

PHOTOS BY ATELEVENTHPHOTOS.COM
& WORKMAN REFLECTIONS PHOTOGRAPHY

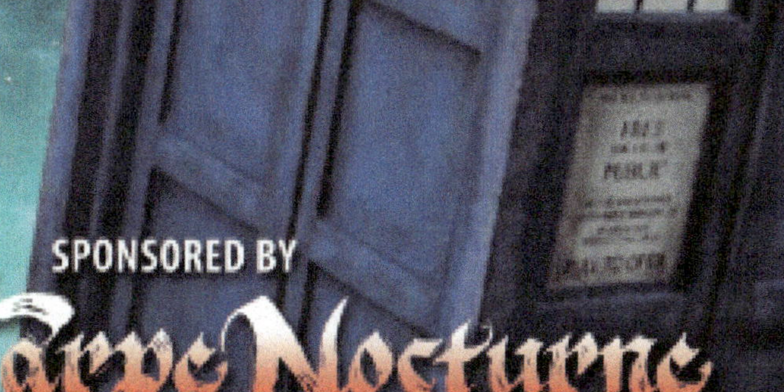

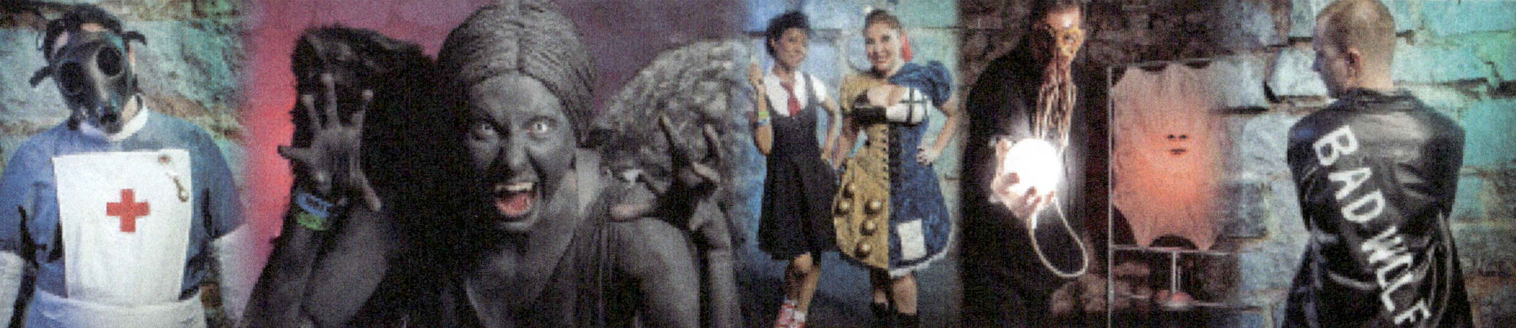

BAD WOLF

www.TIME LORD PARTY.com

VISIT MARKSTERCON.COM FOR FUTURE ATLANTA SCI-FI & GEEK THEMED EVENTS

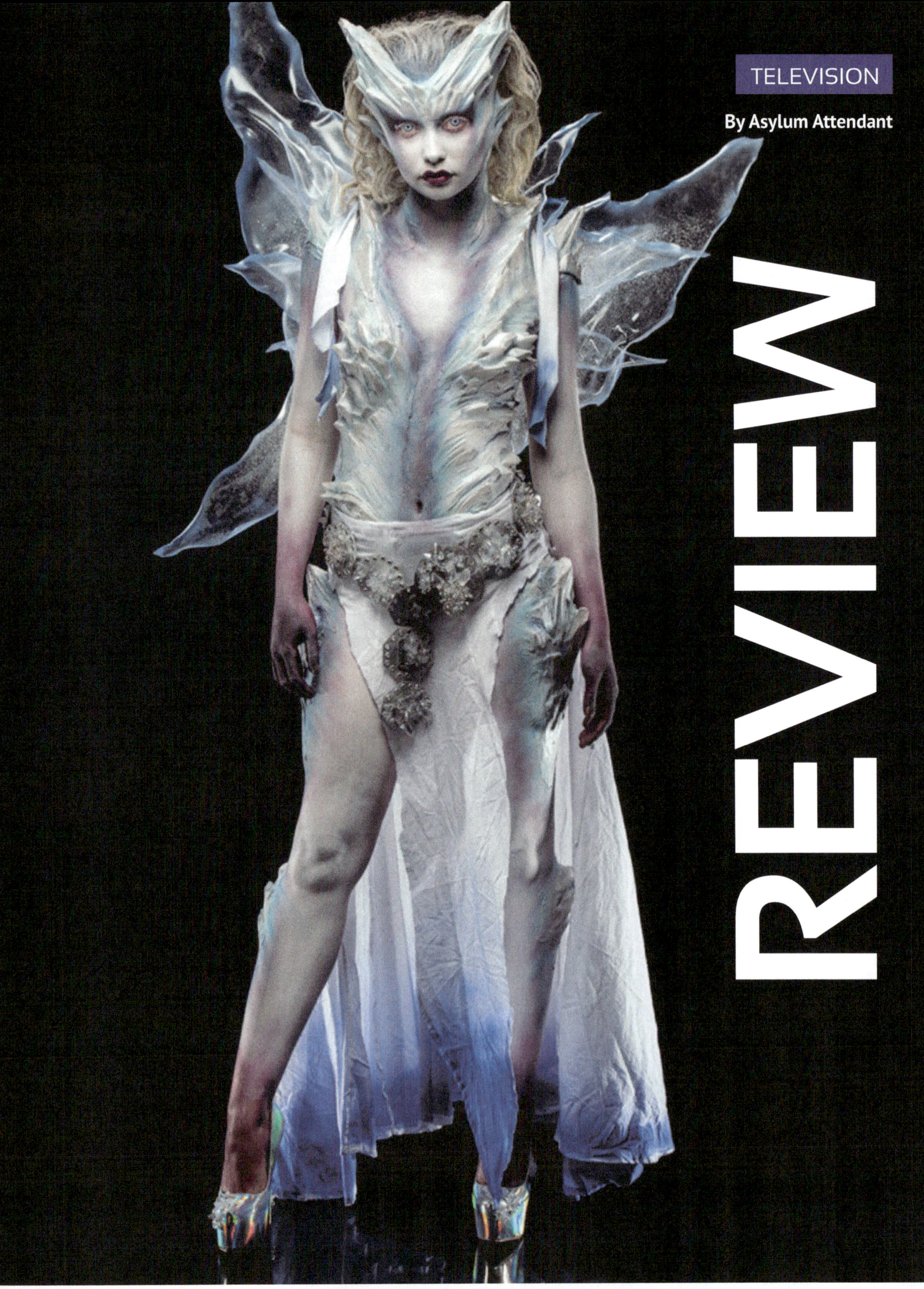
TELEVISION
By Asylum Attendant
REVIEW

FACE OFF

From fantastical sea creatures to whimsical royal playing cards come to life, the Syfy network's reality television show Face Off is truly from another planet. The planet of awesome, in fact.

The competition show first premiered in January 2011 and is currently airing its eighth season. Face Off revolves around a group of special effects makeup artists as they compete in weekly themed "Spotlight Challenges" to create their own full blown horror and science fiction film characters. The plot of Face Off is actually very similar to that of the fashion show Project Runway. The contestants travel to a certain location where they receive their challenge for that week. They then have a few days to construct their character. Drama ensues as contestants sculpt, mold and ultimately apply makeup and prosthetics on their models. A panel of expert judges decide the top and bottom looks from the challenge, sending one contestant home every week.

There's something for every viewer watching Face Off. If zany extraterrestrials and cyborgs aren't your thing, then tune in the following week for a Tim Burton tribute or Wizard of Oz character reinvention. Fairies caught in oil spills merge with Cyclops cheerleaders on a show in which any creature you can imagine has probably been crafted.

The witty commentary and brutal honesty of the judges is quite entertaining. Plus, judge Glenn Hetrick, who has designed makeup looks for shows such as Buffy the Vampire Slayer and Heroes as well as props and outfits for Lady Gaga, is just cool to look at.

Surprisingly, the contestants on Face Off all seem to get along and help one another. That's not typical in the land of catty reality television. It's refreshing to see a show focus on the art rather than using conflict to boost ratings. This artistic integrity is surely why the show continues to be renewed season after season.

If Top Chef is getting a bit dull for your taste, check out the sharp bite of Face Off. The demented clown episode is pure gold wrapped in your worst childhood nightmare. Do not watch it alone.

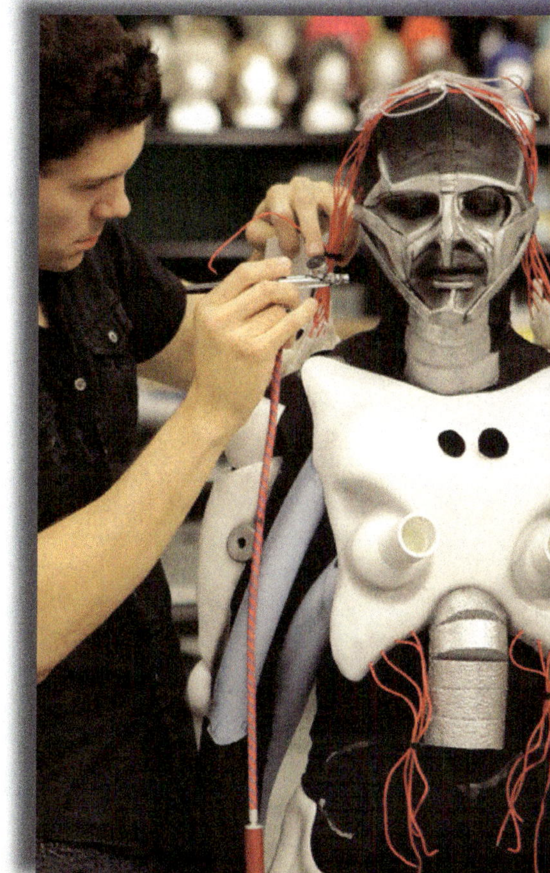

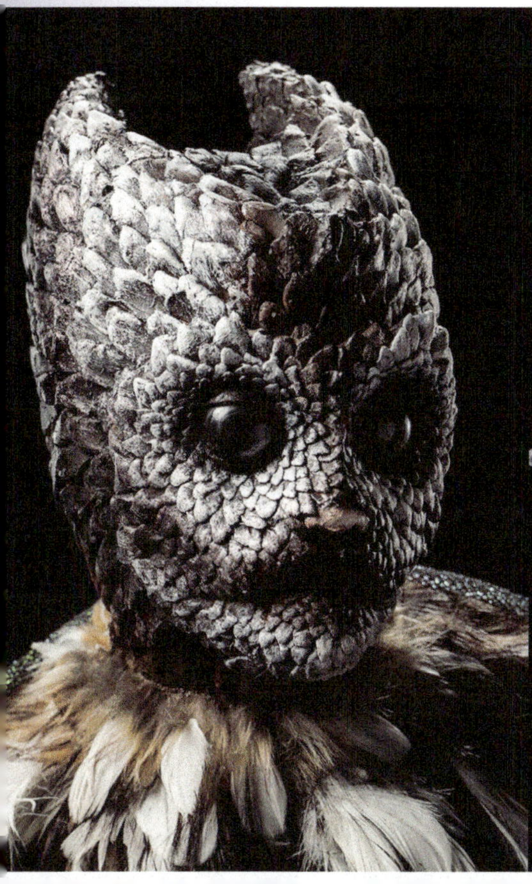

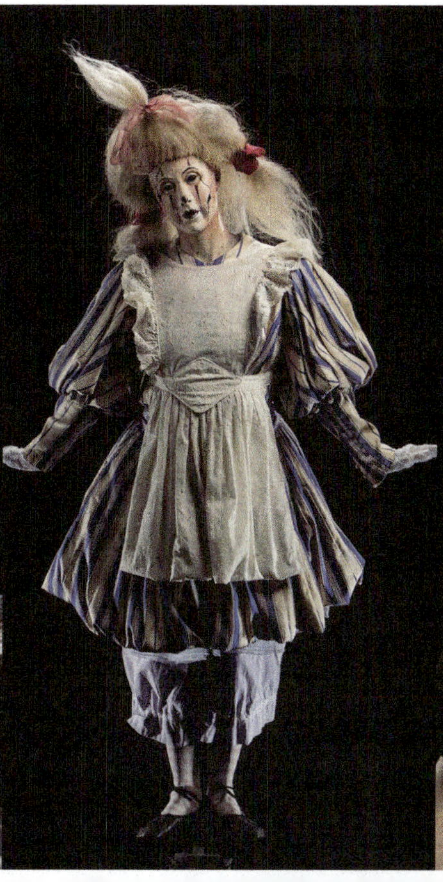

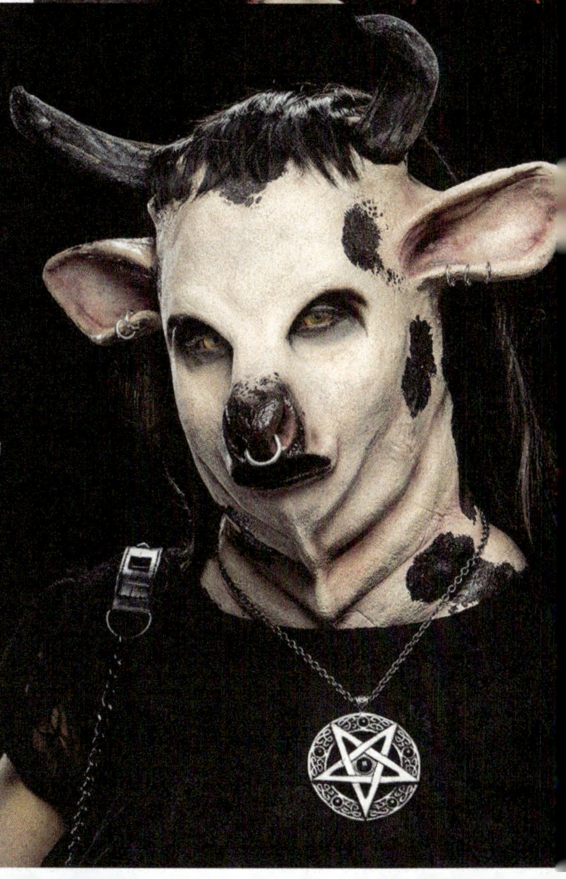

BRAINDANCE

By Michael Jack

There have been a lot of great concept albums throughout the history of music. The Who had many, Tommy being the most notable. Pink Floyd had several as well. The Wall is the one I remember best. Maybe the most famous concept album of all time is Sgt. Pepper's by the Beatles. Now Braindance is back after almost a decade since their last release. Their new CD, "Master of Disguise," is a concept album every bit as good as the ones I just mentioned. There is a clear progression of songs taking you along an epic journey of suffering and confusion. One song flows directly into the next, and builds a world of wonder around you. The vocals, the music, the controlled chaos of sound bites and movie clips all converge into a mind shattering experience you want to live over again and again. "Master of Disguise" is a CD I want to play for everyone, and share the brilliance. It is one of those albums where you discover something new with each play.

I began this journey, for that is what it is, with an email and a video. The video, "Lost," Braindance's first release off of MOD, mesmerized me with Egyptian themed artwork, faceless figures, and a story that only led to more questions. The song itself was incredible. I was already becoming hooked. I opened the CD and found more of a similar styled art along with a 16 page comic. I popped in the CD and began listening, and listening, and listening. There came a point when I sat there thinking, "How am I ever going to review Master of Disguise appropriately in three or four paragraphs?" It's basically impossible. I had only one option. I contacted vocalist Sebastion Elliot for an interview. He said yes, and I was spared many tormented hours of trying to do the impossible. A CD this great deserves all of the attention it can get.

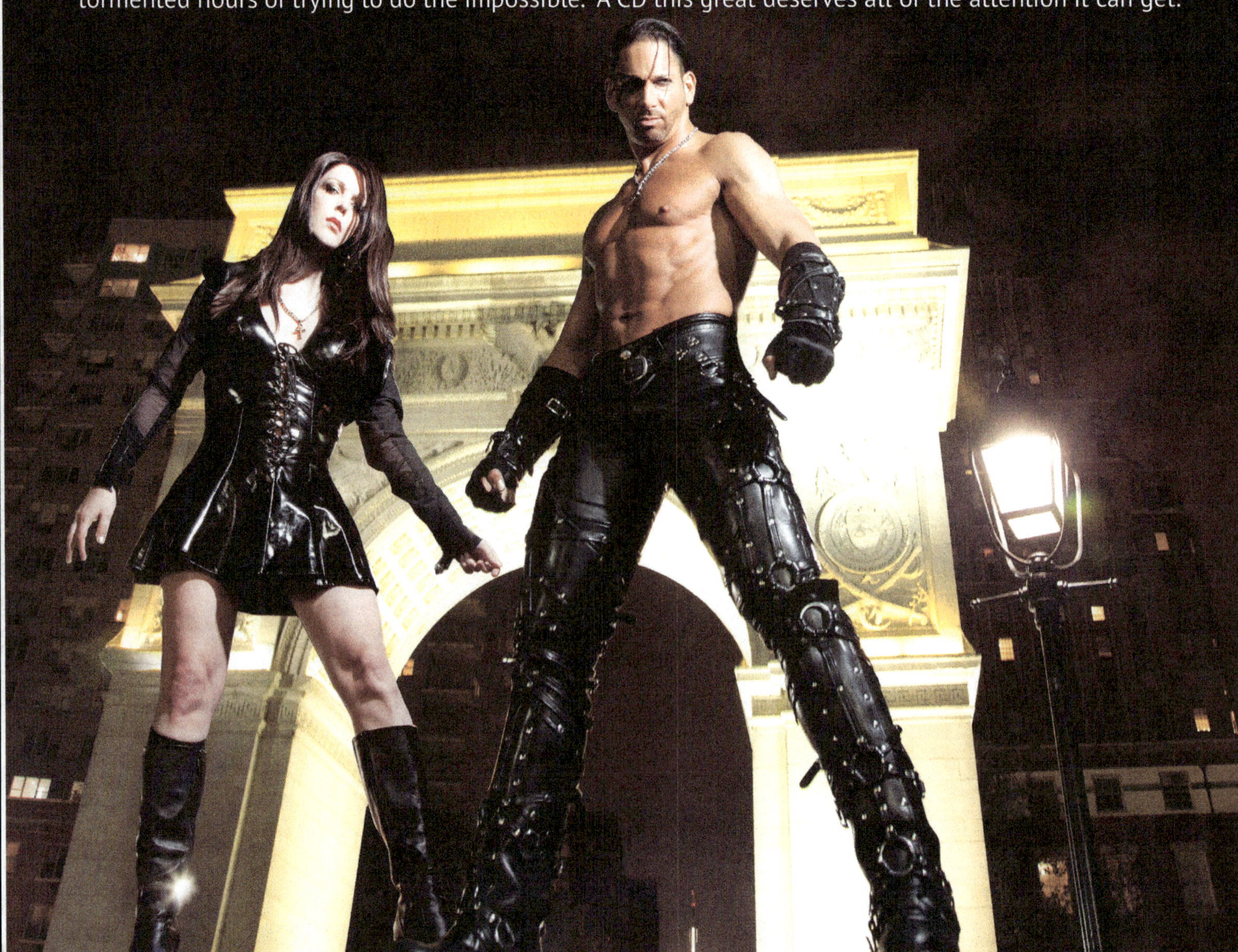

[MJ] *Where did the concept of Master of Disguise come from?*

[SE] It began long ago, with challenges I was facing in both my personal and professional life, and the unfortunate reality of having to frequently wear a figurative mask in order to 'maintain equilibrium,' as it were - as well as to regularly prepare for the possibility (or eventuality) of fallout for having done so over long periods of time.

This concept of sublimation and the subsequent disconnection and/or resentment associated with maintaining this duality blossomed into several associated concepts before morphing into a (hopefully entertaining) synchronistic science fiction/fantasyframework running parallel to the emotional underpinnings.

Although our lyrics always have clear underlying meanings for me, I do my best not to assign definitive conceptual thematic values in their presentation, because I believe listening should be somewhat
interactive. Insofar as everyone's experiences are different, so should their interpretations be. Running underneath this fictitious science fiction or fantasy framework, then, I still might see despair and desolation, whereas someone else might very well see a ham sandwich.

Having said that, however, Master of Disguise could still be defined
overall as a 'concept' album, in part because it contains a progression of recurring themes (clearly identifiable or not) and developing story arcs from start to finish. Without giving away too much - it tells the story of a alien monarch whose exposure to otherworldly influence results in the loss of identity and the difficult journey of self-discovery that follows - all against the backdrop of a parallel universe sharing similarities with both ancient Egyptian and Mayan culture and civilization.

[MJ] *Besides the music, there is some amazing artwork, and a 16 page comic that accompanies the CD. Explain how the visuals help to complete the concept of Master of Disguise.*

[SE] - Thanks for your kind words. For Master of Disguise, I did quite a bit of research on the history, religion, architecture, fashion, and overall culture of ancient Egyptian and Mayan civilization and society. I also spent a lot of time reading up on the history of written communication, from cuneiform and Egyptian and Mayan hieroglyphs and pictograms to Asian scripts, Cherokee alphabets and Anglo-Saxon and Nordic runes, and spent as much time reviewing archeological artifacts from around the world and their associated inscriptions. In particular, I focused on religious practices, burial techniques, and theories on the afterlife from ancient Egyptian civilization, drawing regularly from texts such as the Book of the Dead.

I spent of lot of time researching these different areas, because I wanted to convey the concept of identity loss and confusion under a
simultaneous barrage of apparently unlimited information, or dense communication. I wanted to convey those ideas visually wherever possible, and in as many creative ways as possible. By creating an alphabet from every alphabet every created, by re-creating significant
archeological artifacts within the packaging, and by creating a

story in the which there existed a parallel society whose nature of communication was as perplexing as identity loss is, I felt that I paid attention to the underlying emotional challenges as well as presented something unique that draws the viewer (or listener) in, and makes it interesting enough to stay for awhile.

There's certainly a lot going on - from the alphabet assembled and redesigned by myself and the mighty designer Kevin 'Pavement K'
Beard, to the 3D mural by the German artist Rainer Kalwitz, to the ten
page foldout illustrated by the incredible Joe 'Sweetrot' Simko, to the photos taken by Hristo Shindov, to the 16-page comic brought to life
by Simko and Kieran Oats, to the amazing printing by Ross Ellis.

For the 'golden glyphs', i researched 60 alphabets from the very beginning of recorded time and chose five characters per alphabet to replicate in order to create a 300 character custom designed alphabet. These characters, visually presented in random (or not so random) order could easily be taken at face value as solely a form of hieroglyphic communication (and perhaps a moderately attractive visual effect), but the message _behind_ choosing a visual comprised of a multitude of apparently non-compatible glyphs - and a main theme running through the entire album - again, is one of identity confusion amidst information.

Similarly, the ten page foldout features our protagonist shadowed by an imposing structure, flanked by pyramids, and standing knee deep in sand, presumably before a great expanse of imposing desert. At his feet are recognizable archeological artifacts, yet he apparently remains completely unaffected by their presence, or associated symbolism or meaning. In his right hand he holds a royal staff and a purple robe, remnants of a life that is about to be left behind. In his left hand he holds a amulet of undefined power that has clearly affected him. An amulet that has changed many hands across time, space - and four Braindance albums…!

The graphic novelette expands upon both the ten page foldout and the story put forth in the title track, 'Lost', and is meant to simultaneously set the stage and whet the appetite for the remainder of the album's concepts. Designed by myself, illustrated by Joe Simko and colored by Kieran Oats of Cadence Comics, the novelette begins the saga of our protagonist, who, upon discovering the aforementioned ancient relic, ends up questioning his entire existence and destroying everything around him.

[MJ] *Any thoughts of continuing the comic beyond the CD?*

[SE] Sure. Any thoughts on Carpe Nocturne sponsoring it..? ;)

[MJ] *You have added an amazing lineup for your live performances. First, how did you manage to collect so much talent, and when might we see a tour?*

[SE] Vora and I were finally able to get our hands on a genetic replicator and build our live lineup from the ground up, thereby eliminating all of the unpleasant attributes that are usually associated with working with human musicians. We were able to clone Kenny Grohowski, who has played with the Secret

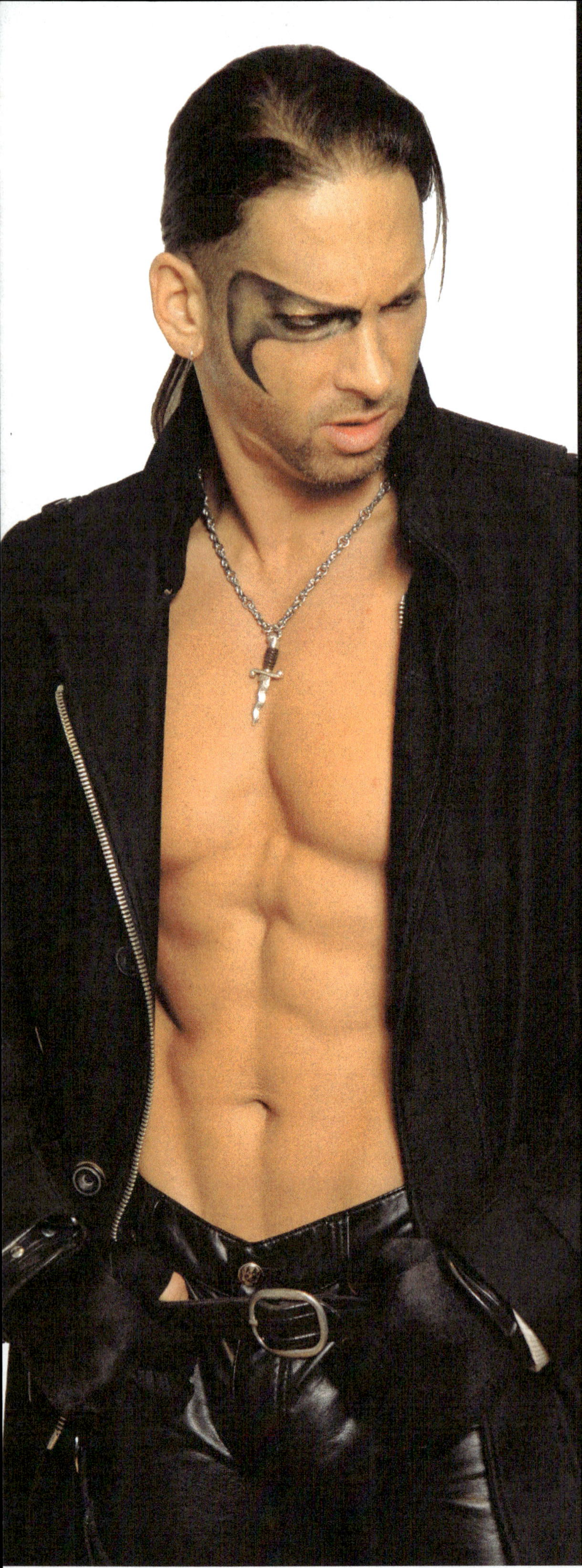

Chiefs and the Pastorius brothers, rhythm guitarist Tony Geballe, who plays with the League of Crafty Guitarists, bassist Eiki Matsumoto, who was with us from 1992 until 1996, keyboardist and backing vocalist Elektra, and two other backing vocalists to be announced. In addition to the cloning, we also provide a vast array of sumptuous finger foods and salty snacks during rehearsal that always keeps 'em coming back.

As you may already know, Braindance has always technically been an unsigned act, and we've been blessed with the learning of this wonderful business as we go. I feel very fortunate to have had so many people pick up on what we're doing, but doing it yourself takes a strong toll, especially financially, and as much as we love performing,
hitting the road without the proper support is not necessarily the way that I'd like to promote the material, aside from the obvious damage it would cause to other areas of our lives, including, quite possibly, the current promotional campaign for Master of Disguise. Having said that, we're currently lining up some local performances in support of the new material with the aforementioned team.

[MJ] *Speaking of talent, Vora Vor has some mad skills on guitar. What's it like working so closely with such a gifted musician, and how times a day do you sit back and say, "Damn, did she just do that?"*

[SE] Mad skillz - fo reals tho. It's been an honor and a privilege to work with - in my assessment - the only genius that I've ever met, and that assessment extends to the guitar path, through the village of composition, across the realm of music production and far beyond.

[MJ] *So how much are you bench pressing these days?*

[SE] Far, far less than you might imagine.

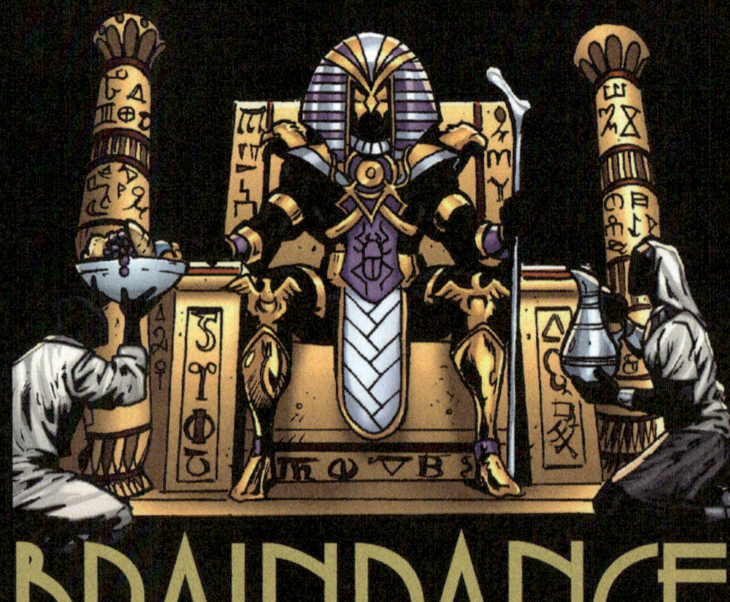

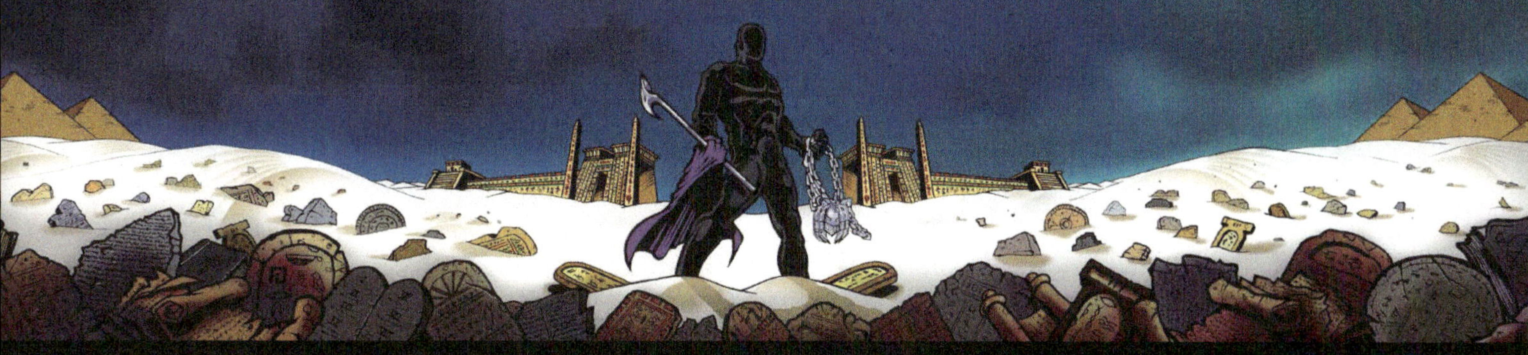

[MJ] *Going back to MOD, I was surprised by the amount of movie and TV clips you used within the songs. Where did the idea come from, and how long did you have to spend gathering them all?*

[SE] We've been sampling movie quotes in our recordings and performances since the inception of Braindance, and for this album, I knew exactly what kind of samples I was looking for, and what kind of movies I wanted them from. It took a few months to record and compile them, a few more to make final selections and designate placement, and still a few more to edit them together cohesively for the collages. In my mind, however - just like writing melodies or lyrics - I knew there would be a perfect fit for each intended space and up to me to find them.

[MJ] *With the video "Lost," you combined so many different visual elements to create, as you accurately state, "a feast for the senses." Where did the idea come from, what did director Tony Hanson bring to the table, and how difficult was it to pull off?*

[SE] 'A feast for the senses?' Wow. Obviously, I'll say anything to get people to check out the over-the-top, super cheesy video for 'Lost'. I knew that visually, I wanted as much as possible, and we were able to incorporate three separate story lines, costumed actors, green screen technology, set design and makeup, overhead outdoor shots, CGI effects, live performance, and VFX digital artwork created from the ground up.

I have to tell you - in our 23 years of doing this, there are perhaps a handful of people that haven't let us down, and an even smaller handful of people who've exceeded expectations. Tony Hanson of Fenix Studios is one of those people. I searched for five years for a video
director who could deliver a fraction of the ideas that i suggested, let alone take those concepts to the next level. All I found were guys who wanted to charge me a million dollars, or who wanted to slap their name and concept across every inch of it, or who couldn't return a fucking e-mail, or most commonly - guys who told me it couldn't be done. Tony and his exceptional team not only delivered, but also had the passion, the vision, the dedication, and the professionalism that allowed me to focus on what i needed to do, instead of worrying about everything and everybody, every step of the way.

In the video, the accompanying story for 'Lost' is quite different - incorporating a sinister character background of our monarch, a separate thread involving the priests and their magical influence, and overall, ending on a definitive moral high ground. Without a doubt, a different twist on the tale (other than the one told in the comic), that Tony suggested would be more effective in video form for viewers. And the visual elements that created 'a feast for the senses?' Konstantin Vilenchitz completed the animatronic rendering of the comic (both the official and full animated version), and all of the VFX, green screen, and CGI stuff took a full year of post-production from Tony's team before completion.

[MJ] *Your side project, Sentinel of Eternity, is so completely different than Braindance. How did it come about?*

[SE] I met Stephane and Salandre during the days of MySpace when they reached out with a Braindance friend request. At the time, I was on the lookout for an EBM project to lend my vocals to, and Stephane's compositions truly spoke to me. I responded with a proposition, and over the next year, worked closely with Stephane on arrangements, and then subsequently wrote and recorded the lyrics and melodies for the self-titled Sentinel of Eternity album.

[MJ] *Was it a challenge working in a completely different genre of music?*

[SE] Not unlike wearing another pair of pants, since not surprisingly, I'm a fan of all of the sub-genres that make up Braindance - goth, industrial, electronic, ebm, synthpop, progressive metal, classic metal, progressive trance, vocal house, and classical. I had been looking for a project with dense programming and multi-layered melodic composition like S.o.E. for quite some time, and jumped at the opportunity to put my lyrics and melodies over Stephane's dark soundscapes.

[MJ] *So what's next for Sebastian Elliott?*

[SE] Although Braindance is my priority, I would still love to do a house project ala Morillo, a trance project ala Van Buuren, or a electronic hybrid project ala Nero or Pendulum. Right now, I'm looking forward to performing the new Braindance material live, re-releasing 1994's Shadows and 1996's Fear Itself, and of course - reading the new issue of Carpe Nocturne. ;)

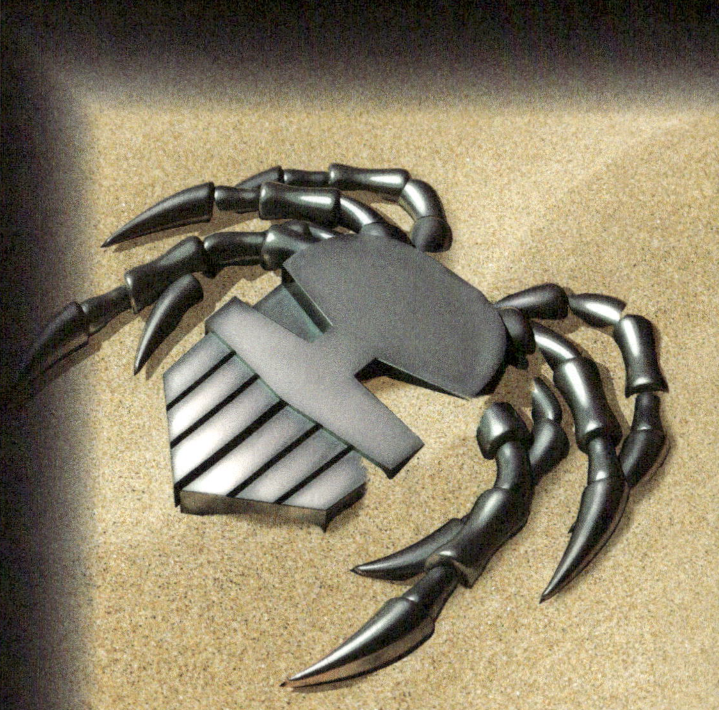

MUSIC

By Dawn Wood

I had the honor to meet Andrea Ferro and Cristina Scabbia and chat with Andrea of Lacuna Coil at El Corazon Seattle in late 2014. We chatted about the tour, album and where they are heading, as a band. It was a great pleasure to hear the Lacuna Coil story and Andrea's perspective. What a great conversation. Andrea is so incredibly humble and it is evident how Lacuna Coil fans around the world, are treasured by them.

[Dawn Wood] *Lacuna Coil emerged in 1994 in Milan. How would you say you have evolved since this time, as a band?*

[Andrea from LC] 1996/97. 1994 is when me and Marco, the bass player started to play together in his house, but just playing cover songs that we liked. So, it wasn't really a band, just me and him jamming in his house. 1996 we did the first demo tape. In 1997 we created the name. We have evolved by doing things we never expected to have happen as a band. Back then, we just wanted to send our demo out to a label and maybe get it released. We never expected to be professional musicians and have it as our career, especially coming out of Milan, Italy. It was not a story of other bands in rock and metal spreading around the world/touring the world. So, we were the only ones. There are some in other genres, but not really in ours. So everything that has happened over the years has been beyond our imagination at that time. As it happened, we couldn't believe, step by step and more than we could ever have dreamed.

[Dawn] *Earlier this year (2014) you announced some member changes to Lacuna Coil. As a musician, I understand this has the potential to change the energy of a show. Has this been a challenge and/or added something different to your sound/shows?*

[Andrea] Yup. Overall I think it has been a positive change because, it happened, not because we were not getting along. It's just that, after many years, if you are not motivated 100% to be on the road with this lifestyle, it gets really hard. For someone who doesn't want to be there, it is difficult for them and for us. We never came to the point where we would fight. We just sat down and discussed, in a very civilized way, the fact of losing the passion over it and dedication of the project, being away all the time, away from family. Our drummer was moving in a different direction, moving to the countryside and building a house, had a baby girl and a more stable life. Our guitar player moved here to North America, with his wife. Neither of them are doing music anymore. So, it was just a matter of life changing. It had nothing to do with not liking each other anymore. We decided to keep going with one guitarist. So for the next album we will work on writing with just one guitar and maybe more keyboards. And, our new drummer, Ryan, was already working with us for 7 years as a drum tech. He had stepped in to drum for our previous drummer when he had his baby girl, so Ryan was already touring with us. It was a natural choice to have him a part of the band. By the time we start working on our new album, after touring this year with the lineup, arranging and finding out what works, we will have a solution. This record has been a change in times for Lacuna Coil. We kind of closed a chapter, opened a new one and moved towards a new

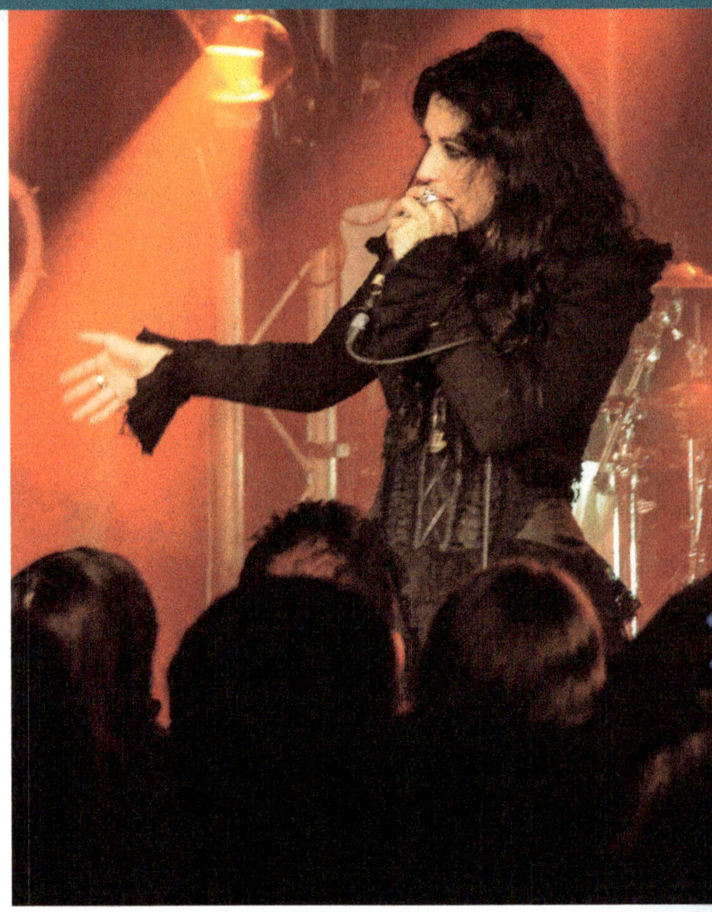

direction. It's very challenging, but also very motivating...refreshing.

[Dawn] *How long will Lacuna be touring in 2014/2015?*

[Andrea] We have four more weeks. Then, a Canadian tour. 6 shows on the West Coast. We touched most of the usual cities in the states. We are thankful that the fans are still coming out. After the Canadian tour, we will head down the East Coast before heading back to Europe. Then, we tour as co-headliner, in Europe with Motionless in White and a new project, Devilment. We will do a rock cruise in January 2015.

[Dawn] *Your new video for "Nothing Stands in Our Way" is a glimpse into behind the scenes and also some performances on tour. Tell us about the filming and where the footage was filmed.*

[Andrea] Actually, it was filmed in Jacksonville, Florida at the 2014 Welcome to Rockville show. The director asked if he could film footage of before, during and after the show and keep the camera on. He wanted to share the experience. Then it turned out so good, we wanted to use it for the video. It represents the band so well. The label loved it, so we said: 'why not?', so we used it and here we are.

[Dawn] *When you are on tour for such an extended period of time, how do you, as vocalists, stay healthy and keep your beautiful voices strong?*

[Andrea] The voice is the hardest part, because you get tired and easily can get sick. We try to not drink or just before a day off. We don't smoke. We do warm-ups before the show....and still we get

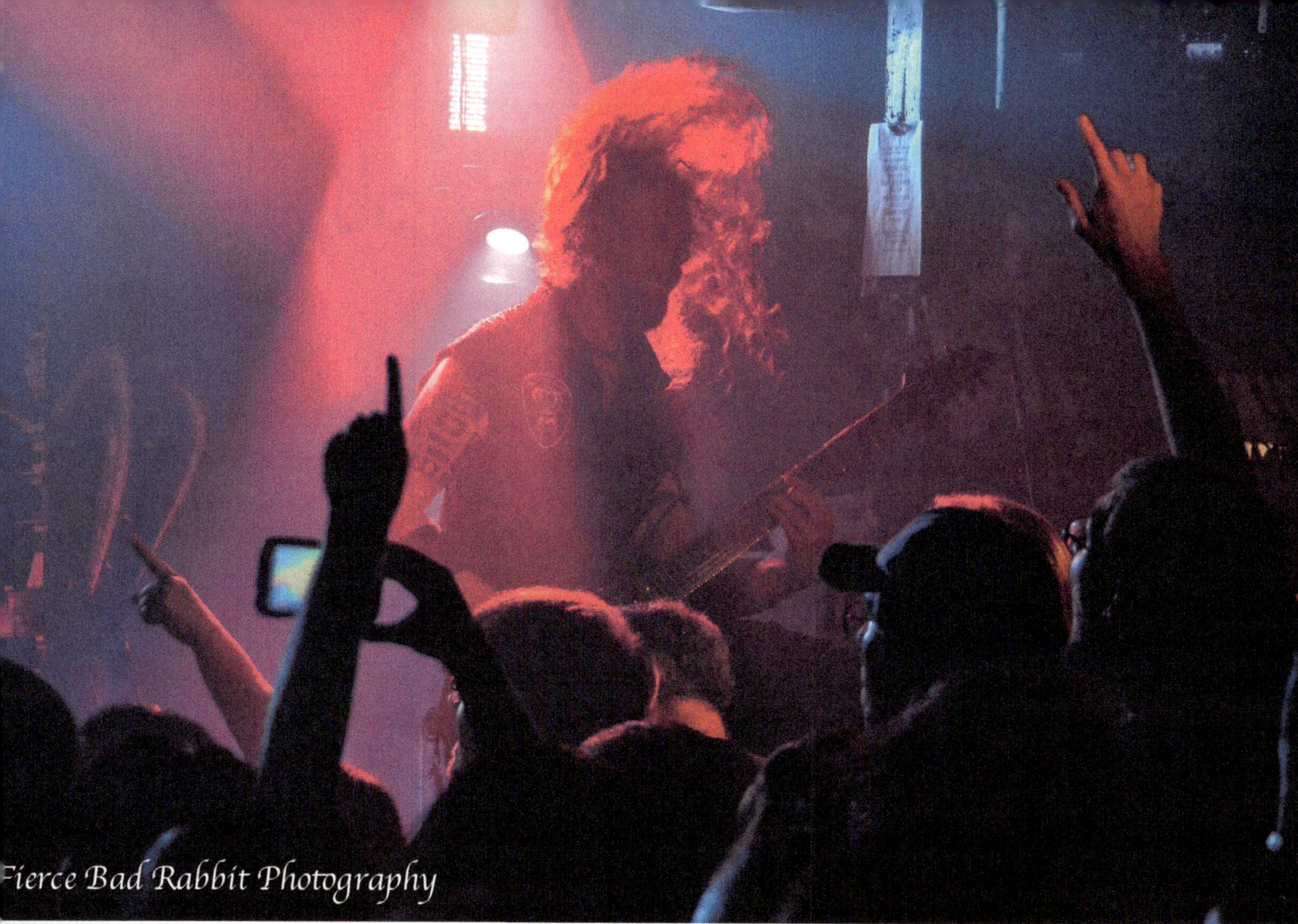

tired. It's part of touring, you know when you are on tour, certain gigs will not be excellent. It is what it is. It's part of being on tour? We try to stay well rested and not talk too much, when not necessary. We have never had to cancel a show because of the voice. We had to cancel a show for other reasons, but not for the voice.

[Dawn] *You have been quoted as having numerous influences and favorite bands from: Dying Bride, Linkin Park, Beethoven, Sound Garden, Meshugga, Black Sabbath, Gold Frapp, Cocteau Twins, Danzig, Nine Inch Nails, Type O Negative. I've noticed amongst your loyal fans: everything from Classic Rock to Metal, to Gothic/Industrial to Dark Wave to Pop to Electronic fans. This is such a broad spectrum and so complimentary to you as a band. Have you marketed to different genres or do you feel your "vast influences" have a part in winning your various audiences over?*

[Andrea] Linkin Park? Me? I wouldn't say them, but maybe someone else. Wait, I think our former drummer was into them. Nothing bad. I really like their albums, just not one of my influences. Black Sabbath, yeah! Danzig, Nine Inch nails, yes. That

is more MY kind of music. One band that every one in this band really likes is Faith No More. Faith No More has always been very open to all genres. Obviously we are coming from the Gothic/Metal Scene. When we started, we wanted to be in the same sound as Type O Negative or Paradise Lost. We evolved. We still fall into a Gothic-type band, but we aren't exclusively in that genre or at least what a Gothic band is now-a-days. Actually to be Gothic is a very broad spectrum. I think certain song chord progression can be considered dark. Even Black Sabbath can be considered dark. It isn't just The Cure or Sisters of Mercy or bands distinctive of that genre. Rammstein can be, in their way, dark. To me the vision of Gothic and dark is very open. Even Neil Young can be dark. Johnny Cash had songs very depressing and sad on certain lyrics. The Doors. To me, dark is not just a cliché. I love the Cure, Bauhaus, Joy Division, all those 80's bands. I love Alice in Chains. They are also very dark. I like the term dark better than Gothic, because sometimes Gothic is too much restrictive. Growing up in Milan, a lot of the city's monuments are Gothic and it is beautiful. It is just the view we have. So for me, dark is just a very wide spectrum

of music. For us, we have two singers and there is always a certain dark element to our lyrics and the keyboard arrangements. We don't want to fall into a cliché. But, whatever kind of album we do, still...there will be darkness.

[Dawn] *I interviewed Fred from DragonForce here at El Corazon last year and we discussed this topic. I am interested in your take. Do you notice a difference in popularity of Metal in the United States vs. Europe (the fans, radio play, shows, etc)?*

[Andrea] I'm a big fan (re: DragonForce). I think here you have more old kind of rock, not just in Metal but in general. While in Europe, it's more a certain part of people that really listen to Metal, but it is not as much in the Pop/Mainstream Culture. Here, Metal is up and down. There are moments when it is more popular. Even in the UK it is more of an up and down trend. In the rest of Europe there is more of a loyal fan base. There are trends of more modern and the classic, conservative metal. I think you need both sides for the future of the genre. Here, I noticed there will be a hot band and then in a few years, there will be another hot band. Also they have in Germany: Wacken. They sell out tickets the day they announce the bands. So many people want to go there because of all the bands, side shows and camping. You know you are going to have a good time seeing friends from all over the world. It's not even so much of seeing all the bands anymore. It is more of an event. It's a subculture. That's the difference, maybe. Here, there is starting to be more festivals too. Maybe 8-10 festivals, just here in the United States.

[Dawn] *Favorite cities/places to perform live in US and abroad?*

[Andrea] I think New York City, LA, Vegas. Playing in Texas is always good for us. It isn't necessarily one place. We have a good amount of fans here and we always have good shows. In Europe, playing in the UK is always really good for us. But, also France, Holland. Italy is always good, but in Italy there is always a good deal of pressure. This especially in Milan. It is always difficult to play in your home town. It's always a good show though. We did a show there last Summer for almost 10,000 people so it was great. So it is good there. It is just a lot of pressure because your good friends and family will be there.

[Dawn] *So what do you think of the way that the music industry is going? Is it something you are excited about or...any concerns?*

[Andrea] I think surely there are new ways and possibilities, but in general I think it is a much worse situation. And not because of all the downloading of music. That is OK, although that is a problem, of course, financially. It forces the bands to have to be on the road all the time and you have to release an album every two years, so there is no space. Sometimes I feel like we need some more time to finish an album. Nowadays, you are forced to end touring cycle then go straight into recording. If you don't feel it, it doesn't matter, because you have to. You have to get the album out and tour in order to be able to make a living. So I don't like it. We come from a previous generation in music where we had time to write an album. It could take two years. It was great because we really felt inspired. Now you have to because the market needs you to do it. You have so many bands today, but many of them are copycats. They may be good players, but many sound the same. Only the image makes a difference. I don't like that, because many bands don't have the time to develop their own personality. We got that because we grew up in a time where we have two, three records before we became a known band. We were able to grow from the cliché of sounding like our favorite bands to incorporating our own, more personal sound. You need time to do this. Today, if you don't make it in the beginning and get some attention, then you would be dropped. There are many more bands today but there are always those 5 bands which are gonna break out.

[Dawn] *Tell us a little known story/tour shenanigans about Lacuna Coil?*

[Andrea] Well, we have done a lot of interviews. I don't know that there is much that people don't know actually. There are stories we have from the road, but nothing so crazy. You mean something musically?

[Dawn] *Well yeah, if you want or something silly or something that seems completely mundane.*

[Andrea] Well, we really enjoy going to Walmart. Maybe because we don't have anything like that in Italy. We like to see the people there. There are things there more difficult to find, like in the typical supermarket in Italy. So we go there very often. So....yeah, that's one thing. (smile)

[Dawn] *That's actually pretty great. Just so you know, we enjoy it too. People watching there and just laughing, basically.*

[Andrea] It's really the whole situation. The people and the fact that it is open 24/7 and the fact that you have these old people, you know...working in front there, even very late at night.

[Dawn] *Yeah, the Walmart Greeters.*

[Andrea] Yeah! The Greeters is something that we don't have. Oh and the automatic carts where you can drive around.

[Dawn] *Haha. That is awesome! Anything else you would like to promote?*

[Andrea] Yes, you can check out our tour dates on our website. We are also very active on social media. Each of us have our own pages on Facebook, but are also on Instagram, Youtube and Twitter. In 2015 we will be on the Shiprock Cruise in Miami.

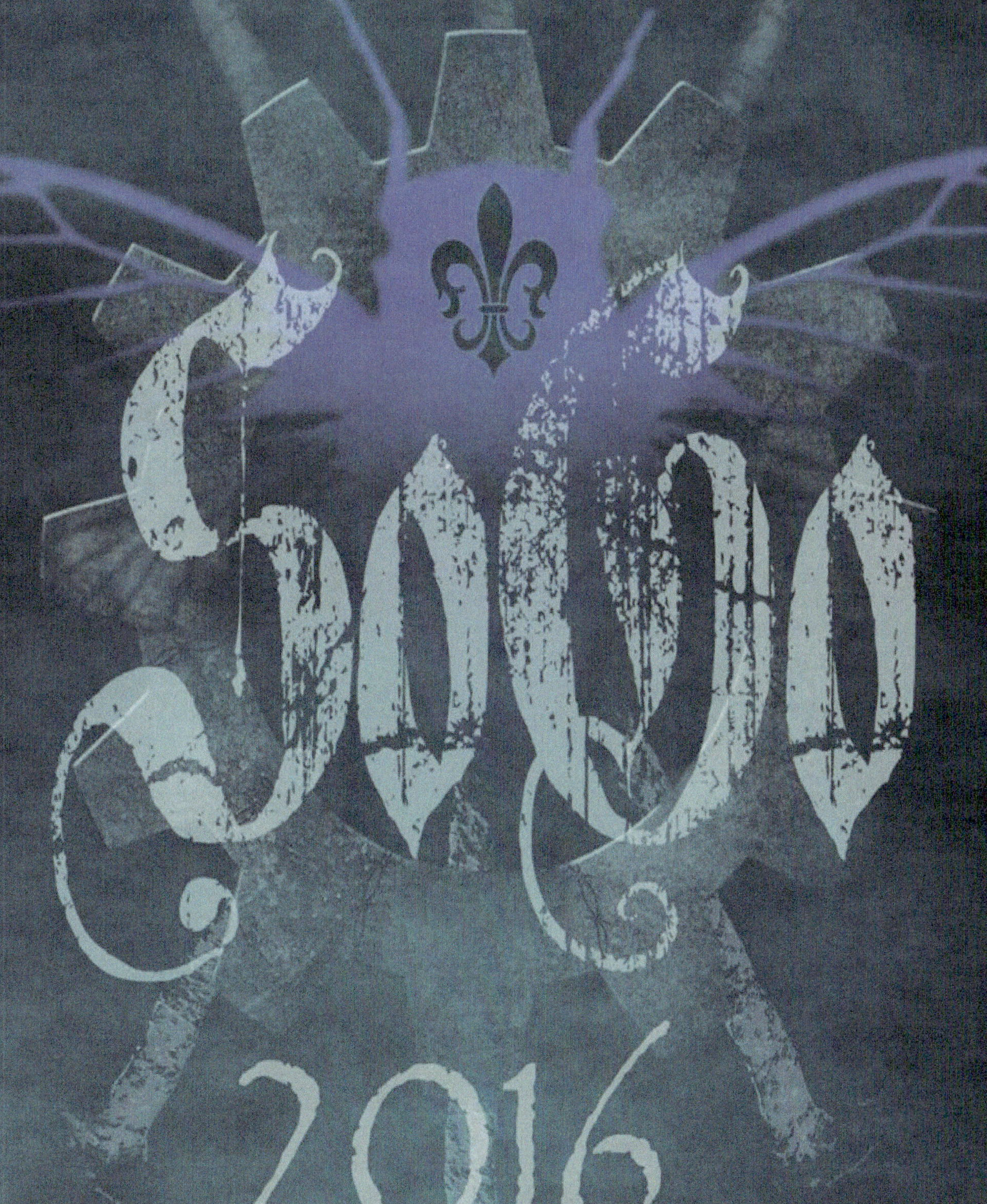

www.facebook.com/SoGoFest
SoGo
2016

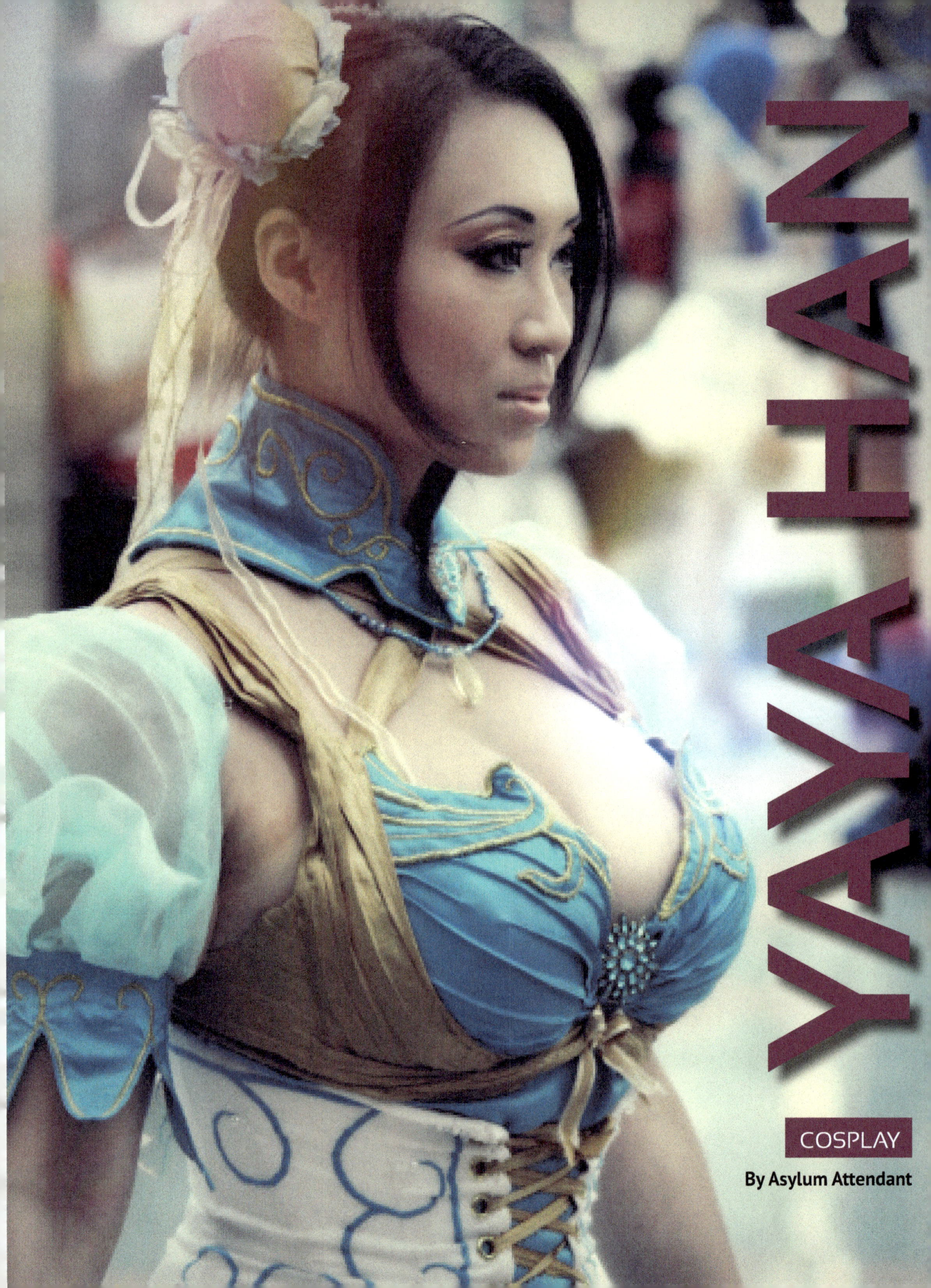

YAYA HAN
COSPLAY
By Asylum Attendant

From comic book superhero to sexy My Little Pony, costume designer, model and cosplayer Yaya Han takes Costume Play to the next level.

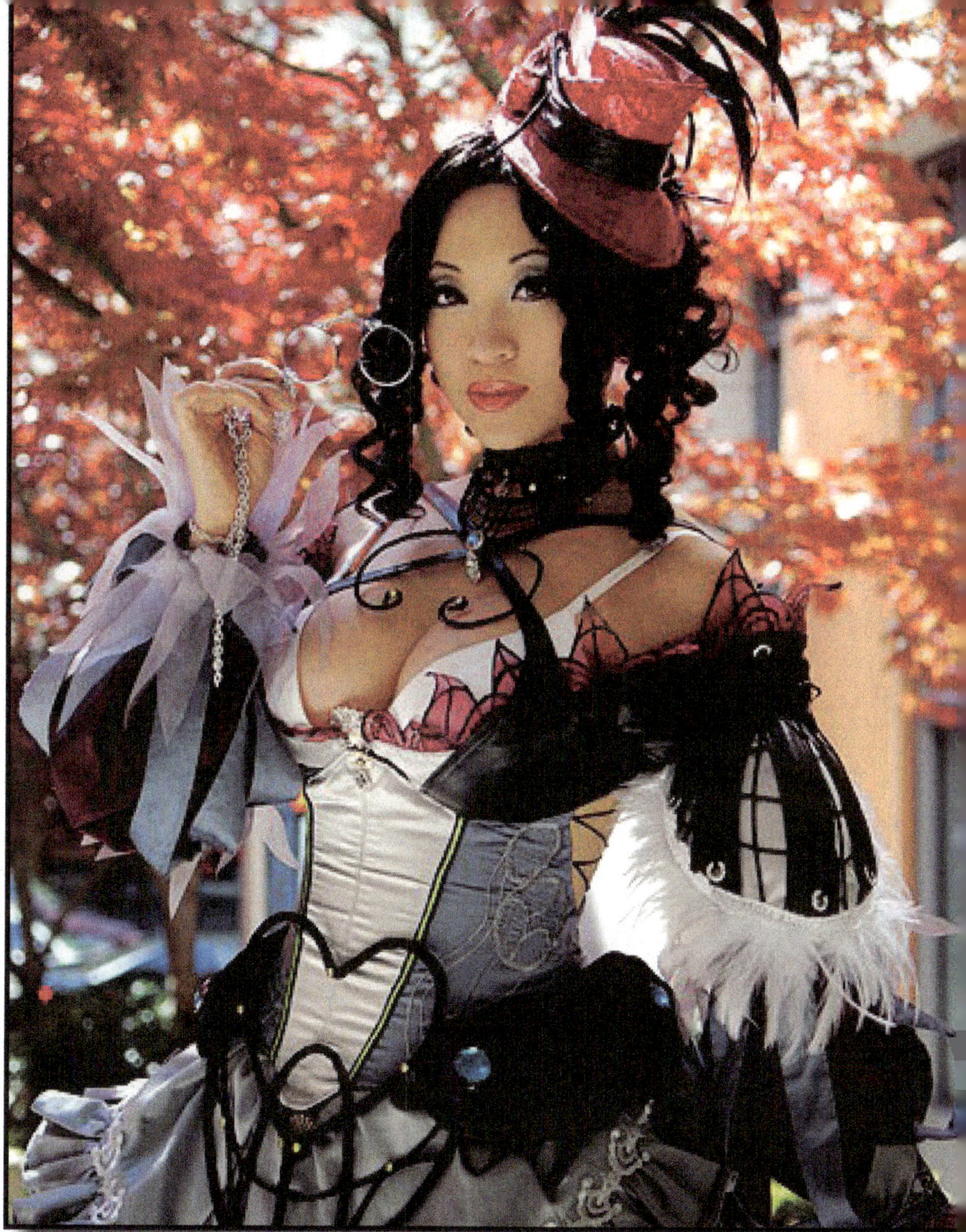

Yaya started out as a teenage anime lover and artist. After visiting her first anime convention in 1999 and discovering the wild world of cosplay, Yaya began to learn how to sew and create costumes of her own. At first, she made many mistakes. Over time, Yaya honed her design skills through trial and error and a lot of hard work. Amazingly, she has never had any formal training. 300 costumes later, Yaya has cosplayed as a bubblegum angel, a retro space girl and even a dark elf. Her costumes span the genres of sci-fi, comics, anime/manga, video games and her own original characters.

Yaya has an online shop in which she sells her cosplay accessories such as unicorn horns, cat ears and magical wings. At first Yaya took on full costume commissions, but she realized that she preferred to make affordable accessories for cosplayers that would encourage them to create their own costumes. Yaya had no option but to make her own costumes 15 years ago. There just wasn't a cosplay market yet. Nowadays, fans can buy high quality costumes from many designers. Nothing beats the satisfaction and fun of creating one's own costume from scratch, however.

Yaya has also appeared on various TV shows. She was a guest judge on the TBS competition show King of the Nerds and was featured on the Syfy show Heroes of Cosplay. Yaya has won many awards for her mind blowing costumes and characters and is a regular host, judge and panelist on the convention circuit around the world. Her photos modeling her cosplay creations are captivating works of art. She even has her own comic book featuring herself as the sassy superhero. How epic is that?! Yaya is such a dedicated designer and never leaves any details unfinished.

You can see photos of all of Yaya's cosplays and shop for the perfect costume accessories at her website, yayahan.com. Be sure to check her out when she comes to a Comic Con near you!

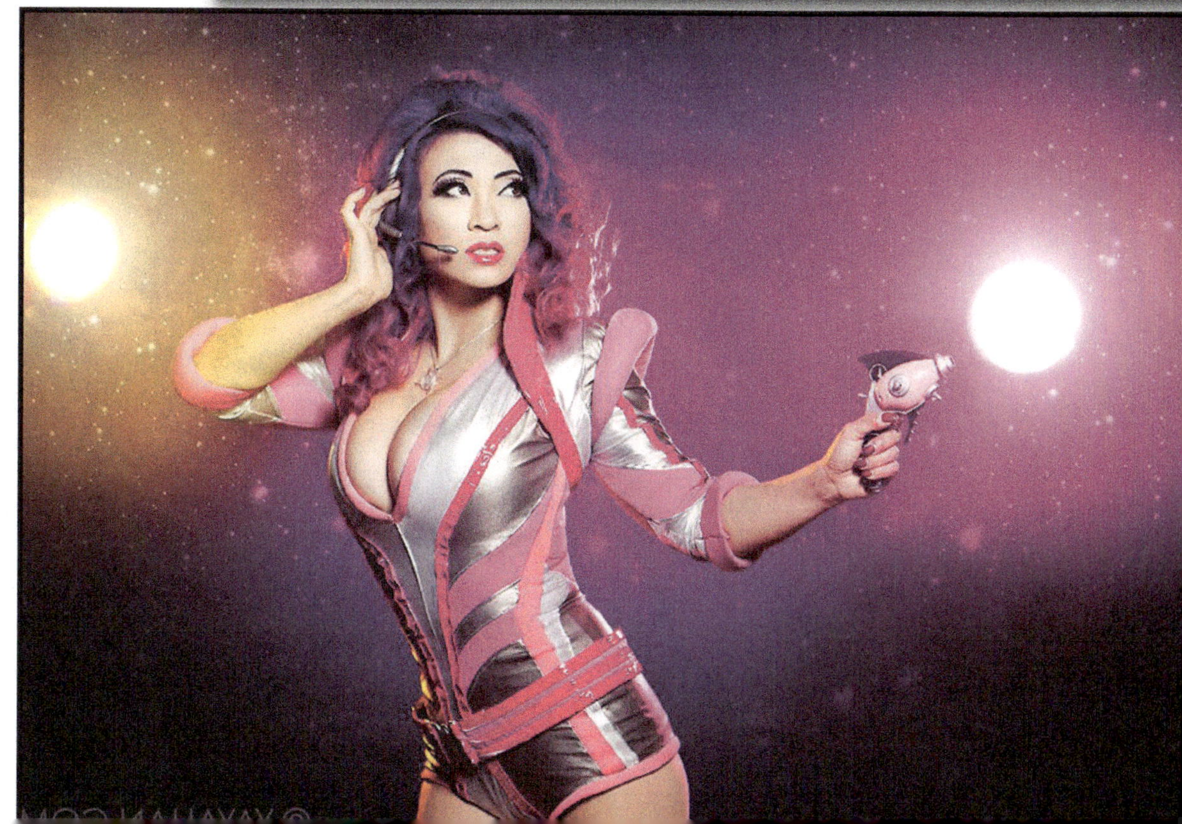

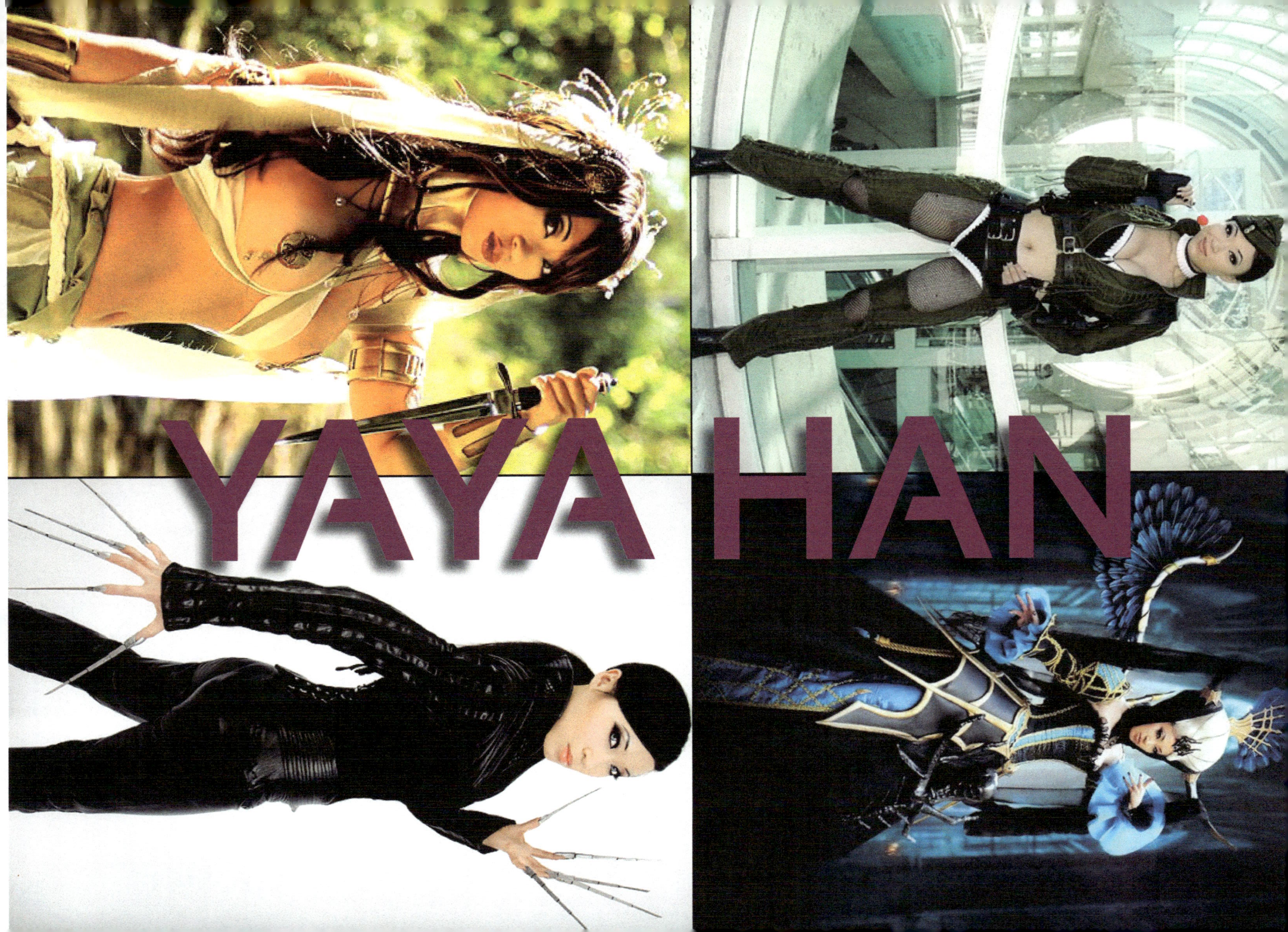
YAYA HAN

PRODUCED BY MARKSTERCON.COM
CO-HOSTED BY DRAGON FIRE EVENTS

TIME LORD PARTY II

ATLANTA • JUNE 12, 2015 • 9PM–3AM • 18+

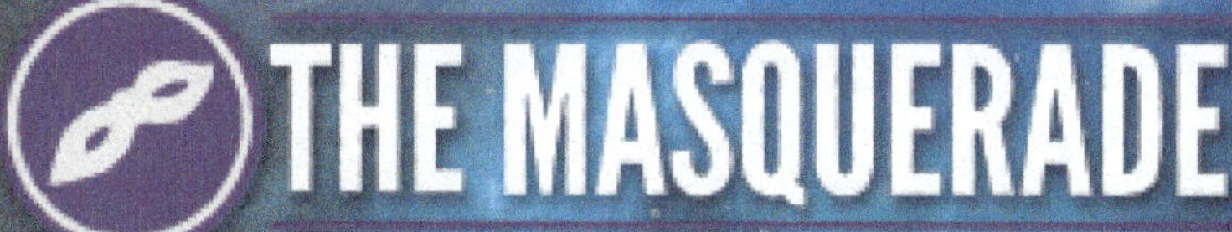
THE MASQUERADE

• PHOTOGRAPHERS & VENDORS
• WHOVIAN COSTUME CONTEST
• DJ SERAPH & DJP GOTH, DARKWAVE, INDUSTRIAL, EBM
• THEMED DRINK SPECIALS
• TARDIS PHOTOS & MORE

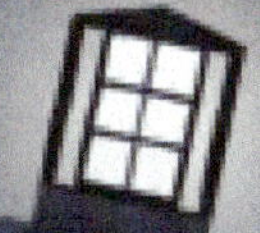

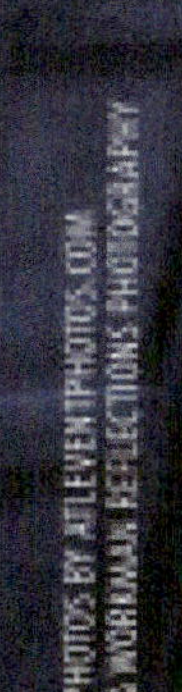
POLICE PUBLIC CALL BOX
POLICE
PHOTOS BY ATLEVENTPHOTOS.COM & WORKMAN REFLECTIONS PHOTOGRAPHY

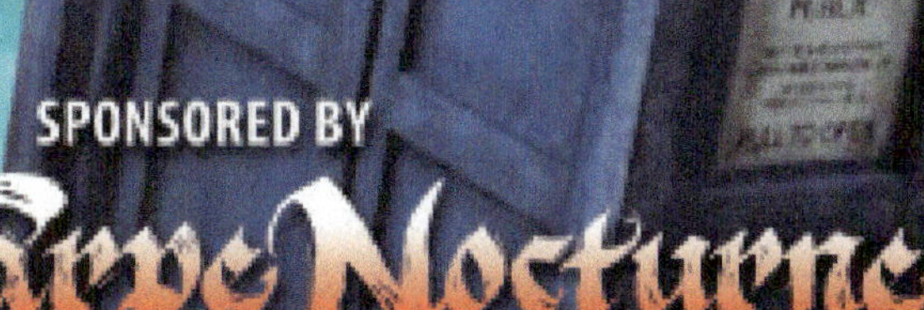
SPONSORED BY
Carpe Nocturne

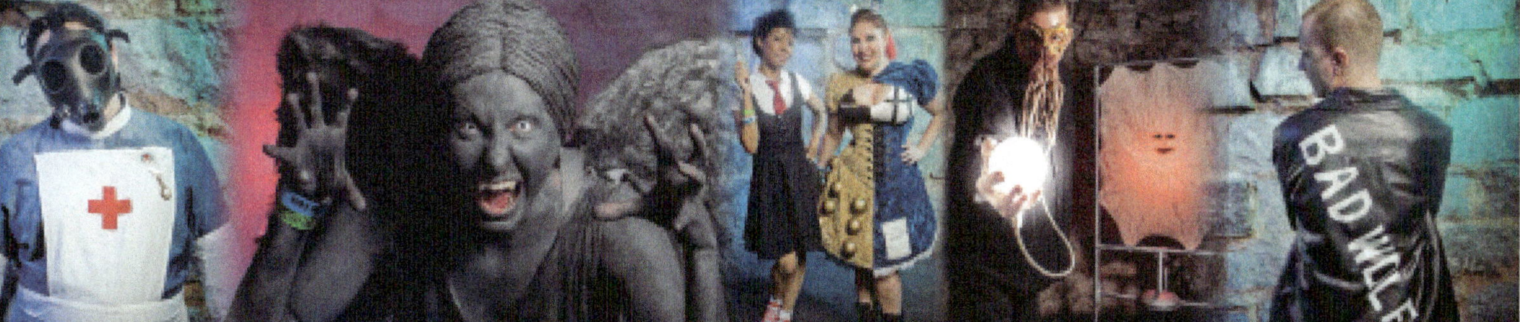
BAD WOLF

www.TIME LORD PARTY.com

VISIT MARKSTERCON.COM FOR FUTURE ATLANTA SCI-FI & GEEK THEMED EVENTS

By Michael Jack

[Michael Jack] *Congratulations on your new CD "Japanese Robot Invasion." Why did you choose this track to name your album after, and what is the meaning behind it?*

[Corpus Christi] Well a couple of years ago, we were looking to change the name of the band once called "Lovelorn" because of another italian female fronted band called ... Lovelorn. We had the option to make a drastic change or to add something behind Lovelorn. Finally, we choose option 2 and we kept "Japanese Robot Invasion" as a cool idea for a song instead.

[MJ] *For "Japanese Robot Invasion," there are lot of violent and horror themes to the lyrics. Where did you draw the inspiration from?*

[CC] The lyrics are actually inspired by the world around us. There are more horrors in the world than in our songs. Violence, sickness, addiction are everywhere and those are the main themes.

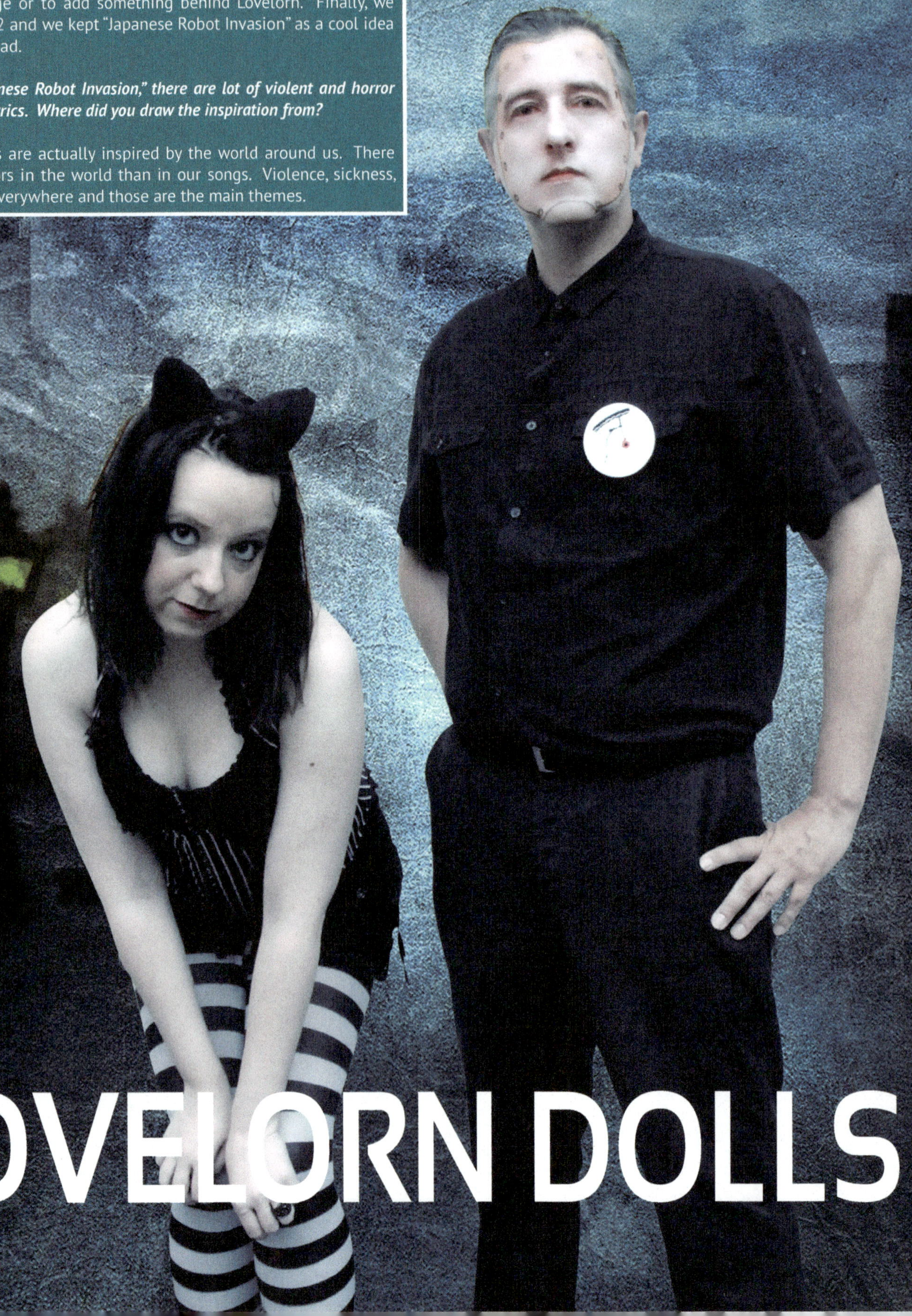

LOVELORN DOLLS

[Ladyhell] It's true it's not really happy themes, but there is always some light in the dark. I always try to bring some hope in the lyrics.

[MJ] *May we expect a new video or two from Lovelorn Dolls, and if so, to what song(s)?*

[CC] Well, it's not planned. Maybe if we do it ourself but at the moment it's too expensive.

[Ladyhell] If we had the means, we would make videos for Happy Valentine, The Thrill or Blood Moon.

[MJ] *"Japanese Robot Invasion" is definitely different from your previous album "The House of Wonders." For the new CD, you worked closely with Max of Helalyn Flowers. What did he bring to the Lovelorn Dolls sound, and how much of that change is attributed to his collaboration?*

[CC] For the first album, we were a bit stuck by our rock n roll roots. Electronic elements were only a layer on top of basic rock songs. For the second album, we wanted to include the electronic parts more deeply into the tracks. Max brought not only an extra eye but he added his own input and lots of synth stuff. I recently published on my Soundcloud the first demo of the song The Thrill, if you compare with the final version you can have an idea of his input in the songs.

[MJ] *Another thing I noticed with the new album, there is more diversity in Ladyhell's vocals. Was it deliberate, or just a byproduct of the songs on the album?*

[CC] It's deliberate. We brought an extra attention to the vocals. We were very relaxed with the recording of this album : everything was home made and we had constant contact with Max so we could make changes, re-record things without pressure of being in a studio.

[Ladyhell] I always try to vary my vocal lines, but I felt more free to explore some new areas of my voice. You also have to know my voice has changed after being pregnant twice. I can sing lower than before. So I was very excited to use that new skill (for example in Blood Moon).

[MJ] *One last question about "Japanese Robot Invasion" (but I could ask so many more)....I have made it no secret that I love your remake of "Just Like Heaven." Why did you choose this song to put on your album, and was it a challenge to make an iconic song so different from the original...but just as good, in my opinion?*

[CC] It was a command from our label to be honest :) They planned to release a compilation of The Cure cover.

[Ladyhell] I first wanted to cover "Lovesong" but another band was already working on it, so Alfa Matrix asked us to try on "Just Like Heaven," so that's what we did and it ended pretty good.

[MJ] *The irony of your names is not lost on me... Corpus Christi and Ladyhell, or good and evil in simplified terms. Is this coincidence, or if not, why the choices?*

[CC] It was a choice. We wanted to use nicknames related to religion. Our first bass played was Hindi Rose and the drummer was Gabriel Arkangel. Our live guitarist uses the nickname Sedjem which is the personnification of "hearing" (also known as God Ptah).

[Ladyhell] Of course this is full second degree, I'm not all bad and he's all good. Actually we are both very bad people ah ah ah !

[MJ] Besides the music, Lovelorn Dolls is known for some great artwork. Do you create any of it yourselves, and why do you choose the primary color of blue?

[CC] In my opinion it's important to associate a band to a design. The power of the image has never been so strong than now.

[Ladyhell] Corpus Christi is a very talented drawer, he already drew my portrait and I have to say that it looks pretty awesome.

The choice of blue is simple: the first artwork made by Gogo Melone for "An Intense Feeling of Affection" was blue, so we kept that color direction.

[MJ] *Going back to "The House of Wonders," I absolutely loved your unplugged version of "Save Me from Myself." Might we see any more acoustic songs in the future?*

[CC] Well we played acoustic for a show on radio but the new songs sounds better with the electronic parts. If you like those kind of unplugged maybe you can check the unplugged version of « Treasured Felony » which is a song written by Ladyhell for Skeptical Minds.

[Ladyhell] We have other unplugged versions, like "After Dark" in piano version and the cover of "The Kill" (30 Seconds To Mars) guitar voice only. We really enjoy doing this, so be sure you'll hear new unplugged versions very soon !

[MJ] *Unlike many bands, at least from what I have read, you have no burning desire to embark on a major tour. You do perform at big events like Eurofest later this year (congratulations by the way). What are your reasons for this decision?*

[CC] Well we won't tour at all. In fact, to tour, you have to pay the headliner so you can be in the tourbus... or follow the tourbus with your own vehicle... maybe I will break some mystical secrets but - when a band is picked to support a headliner- it's not because the headliner finds that the support is cool or promising. It's just about money. And yes, we do not make any money... we are loosing money in fact. So we have to limit the expenses to avoid problems with our wives and husband.

[Ladyhell] We've been asked several times to tour as a support act for very cool headliners, but the conditions are completely unaffordable for us. It goes around 8000 euros to embark on these tours. I'm trying to win the lottery but for the moment it hasn't been a success. The other reason is also that I'm the mother of very little kids and there's no way for me I will leave them on a long period to tour around the world. That's my way of thinking.

[MJ] *Last year you performed at Alt-Fest on the metal stage. I know your music can be placed into several different genres, so I was curious to see if you felt that was the correct stage for Lovelorn Dolls. If not, what stage would you have placed yourself on?*

[CC] We were "supposed" to play Alt fest but it was cancelled 3 weeks before the event... Once again the problem was about money : they did not made enough presales...

Well I'm not sure we should have played on the metal stage... the mainstage would be more appropriate. Not because it's bigger but in festival the mainstage is not dedicated to a certain "genre". However we've already played at metal festivals... female fronted metal of course.

[MJ] *Any last words for your fans?*

[Ladyhell] Repeating myself, but take the time to listen to us, and if you like it, share!

[CC] May the God of music be with you, always!

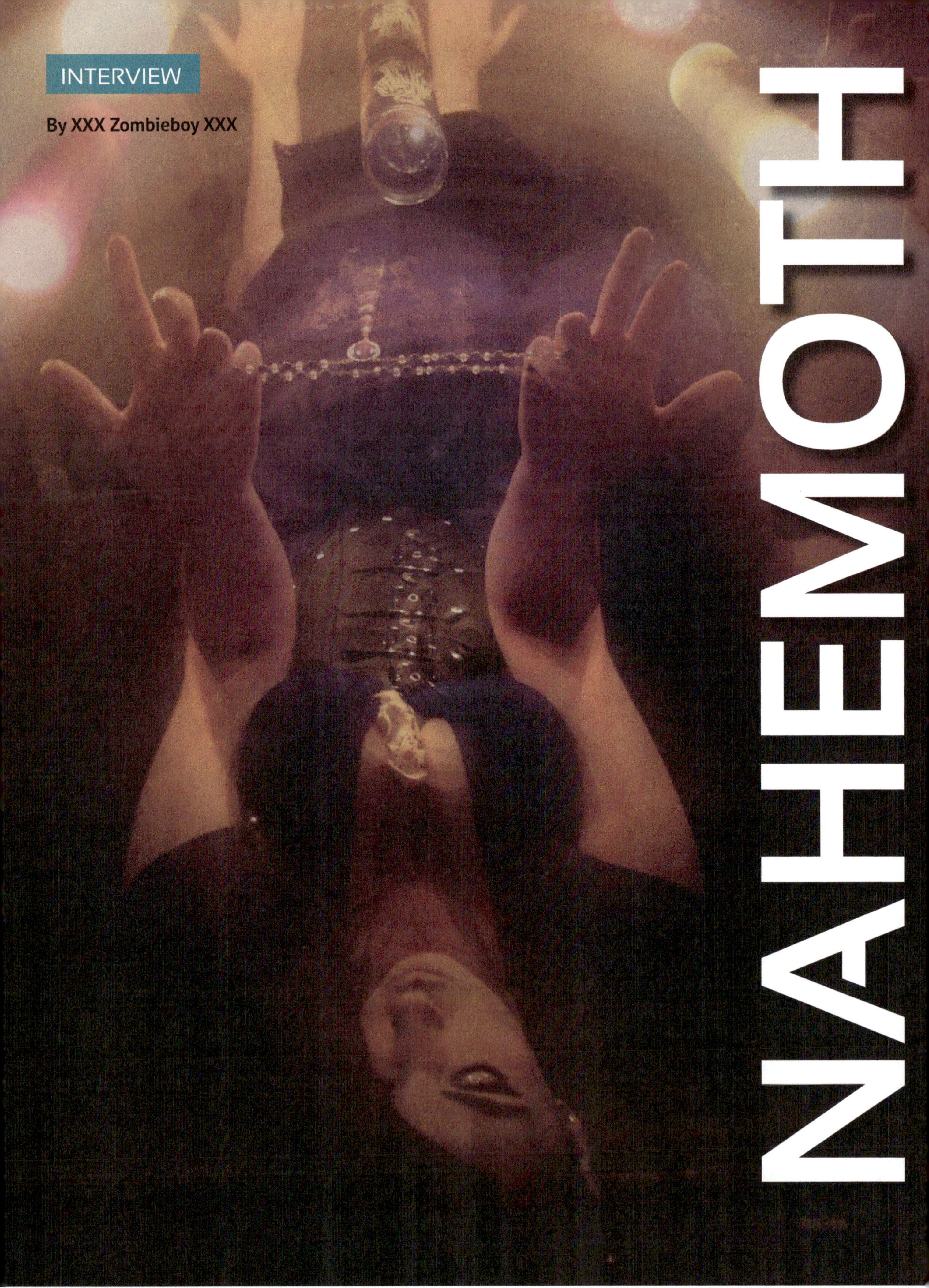
INTERVIEW
By XXX Zombieboy XXX
NAHEMOTH

It is like standing upon a vast and silent field of snow, Silent but for an endless steady wind that blows out of nowhere. The snowfield is featureless and seems to reach on forever. One walks out onto the field, aware of feeling eyes upon them, but turning around to face a danger only brings to a startling realization that the way behind is the same as the way ahead; an endless plain reaching far and beyond human vision. One begins to walk, and even the snow underfoot is silent. And the walker is unaware of the Leviathan writhing far below. Of the thousand seeking tentacles moving through the strata as if it were mere water. Reaching from the dark as a thought from the primitive man's mind.

The music of Nahemoth brings to me this vision. Amongst many others. It is atmospheric and beautiful and both calming and at times brutal. An eclectic journey that invokes visions and atmospheres of dystopic silence and vastness. Nahemoth are part of a growing subgenre of metal that some refer to as "Occult Metal".

I had the opportunity to host the singer Caine Del Sol and the keyboardist Scarlett Nova (also his model/artist girlfriend) recently in Denver. While showing them around the city and sharing in its many delights and vices he gave me a rare and somewhat privileged look into this underground movement that is growing in popularity with such bands as Ghost B.C., Purson, The Oath and Watain (the latter whom we would later meet that trip and enjoy the spectacle).

[ZOMBIEBOY] *For the uninitiated, what does Nahemoth mean?*

[Caine] The word? Nahemoth is the shadows that whisper in the dark, the ones that call the chosen, the children of Lilith, to the chosen path. Think of it as the dark conscience. Every aspect of the Holy Ghost inverted.

[Z] *Do you feel such have a direct impact on the music you create or is the title more in subject matter.*

[C] I believe, and my experience suggests that the Nahemoth and other entities of this path do exist in some form or another. And do speak to those who will listen. What we write is not of us. It's through us. It is much more literal.

[Z] *And can you tell me the goal and purpose of your music?*

[C] It's not easily explained, but the best explanation I can give is greater communication with the other side, increase in knowledge and wisdom of that which lies beyond our borders.

[Z] *Your music is image provoking and atmospheric. Is it written for the purpose of meditation?*

[C] Yes. It is written through and for meditation and it is specifically designed to invoke a sense of synethesia.

[Z] *And how do you prepare yourself to be open and hear or feel what you need to write?*

[C] That primarily comes from experience. Following the initial communication whether it is from a successful ritual or shall we say divine intervention such as a near death experience.

Scarlett enters the room with a sultry smirk.

[Z] *That or your girlfriend walks out of my kitchen playing on her iPhone.*

[C] Following such, the soul and the mind is left with an imprint. Once you have seen it you can't go back. And since that time, my life has been dedicated to reproducing that and perfecting it. So when I begin to write a song, I start with what I experience in one of those moments of divine communication. A tone, a word, a thought. And build from there, according to related concepts, frequencies, and sounds. It normally involves a lot of planning; mixed with an equal part of shall we say inspired improvisation?

[Z] *And do you write most of the instruments as well as the lyrics?*

[C] I write all of it. There have only been a few select songs that I have not written 100% of the music or lyrics. I normally defer to artists of a similar path for sections that are not mine to complete.

[Z] *And a little history of the band?*

[C] It was formed purely out of necessity. An expression of spirituality. And an experiment in how sound and light and imagery effect the brain. From there following a full length and several EP's I began to feel it was necessary primarily for the increased potency of the rituals and my work to begin playing live. That's when I found Mikhail, whose insight has been instrumental to bringing Nahemoth to the place it is now. Shortly afterward, I met Scarlett, whose passion for the Great Work has allowed us to shape the new era for Nahemoth, stylistically and spiritually. Other musicians have come and gone assisting me in various ways, but Mikhail and Scarlett have stayed, and we have been conducting an

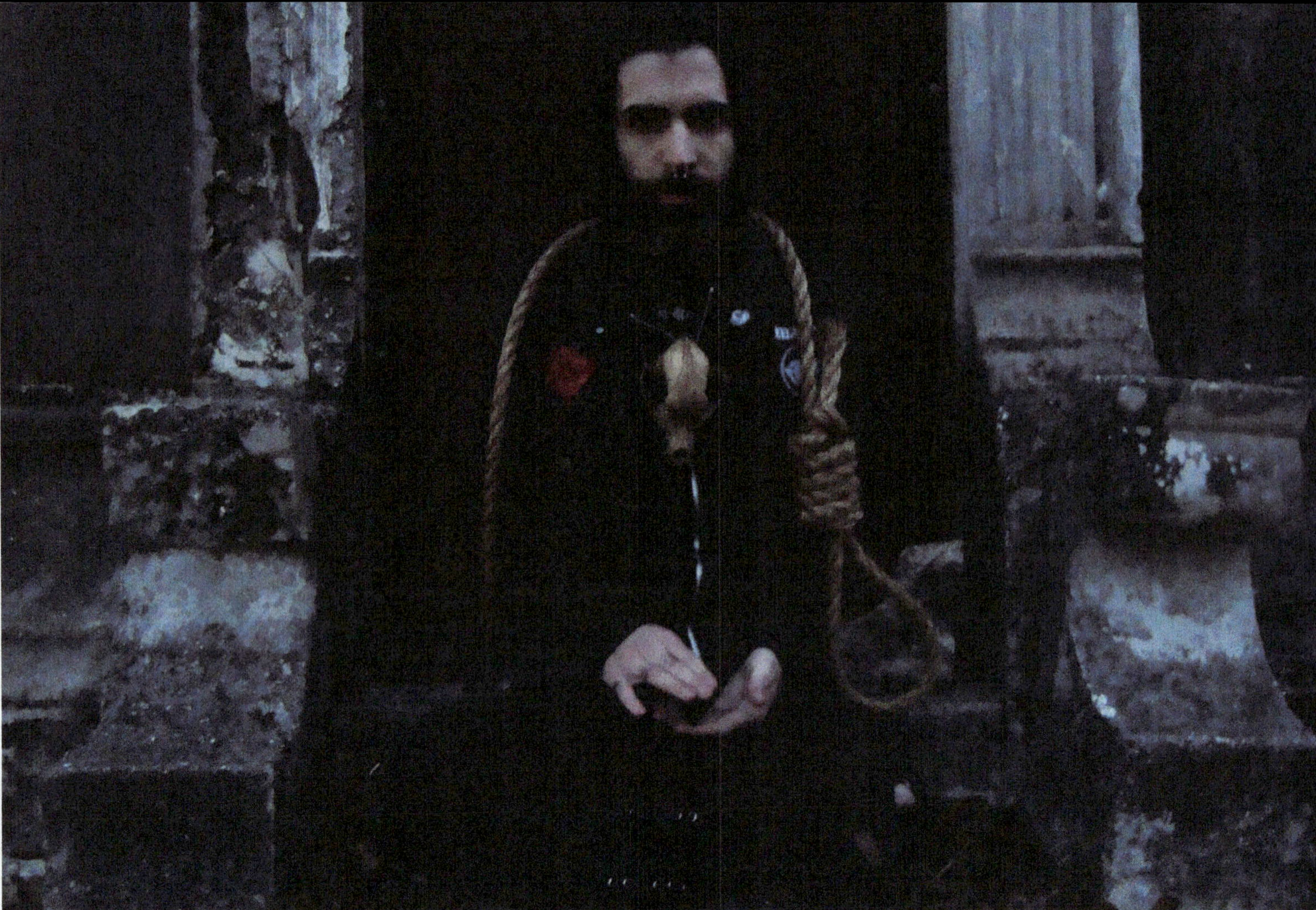

ongoing search for others who have heard the call to assist in the work. So what started as the impromptu ritual of an angry teenager ten years ago has been evolving into something much more than I could have imagined.

[Z] *How do you feel occult metal is progressing in the over all state of the genre and how does creating such music in a very bible belt region of America effect you and the genre?*

[C] The occult has always been a part of metal and the basis of rock, even going back to Robert Johnson and the blues or even the obvious references within the works of Roky Erikson. It is the Devil's music. However, recently such things have become more widely accepted. Those who practice are brasher in their statements. And others shall we say are "following the trend". On one hand this is a good thing. It brings a higher standard to music. The artists have such great passion and higher purpose for their work. On the other hand, there will always be sheep in wolves clothing. People like that make it harder for the legitimate practitioners. It gives the public the idea that it is all fake. Because one band or twenty bands in this popular label playing these big shows wearing corpse paint and talking about Satan or using symbols thought holy by various orders, stated that they don't believe or have shown themselves to not understand what it really means. People begin to believe that this means the one or two that do use real ritual practices and materials are also faking it. That it is fake blood. That they are saying, "Hail Satan" because it is just what you do. That the symbols you use are just pretty designs. This is also a problem in the opposite sense. Especially in America where in places like the Bible belt they use these examples to legitimize their fears and intolerance, making it very difficult for true art to escape and spread. The

greatest examples of this, we and others like us are demonized and discriminated against. Preventing us from pursuing greater forms of the work. Thus also, suppressing those who would become initiates and those that hear the call ignore it for fear of their life.

[Z] *So you refer to the greater quality of music by spiritual drive and yet the genre of Black Metal, not necessarily Occult Metal, is known for intentional low fi recording.*

[C] Yes. I see no discrepancy with this because low fi recording can become a very powerful tool. Much of the method used to influence the mind in a ritualistic or magical manner requires basically a wall of sound so that you may not hear everything that is going on but your body reacts. For this reason many bands as well as Nahemoth suggest to our listeners headphones and hi volume or live performances. This goes back to shamanic techniques, breaking the psyche, allowing the subconscious full authority by overwhelming the conscious mind.

[Z] *The occult is well known for being elitist and not wanting their knowledge or the music that they make to become popular. They want it to remain underground. How do you feel about this?*

[C] I highly disagree. In black metal, people tend to believe that the only authentic black metal is unsigned low quality very solitary music. In the occult, people tend to believe that the only authentic practitioners hide away in their temples and their secret lodges, and that there is no way that the common man could find them, and that the common man SHOULD not find them. While I respect the push for authenticity, and the maintaining of the secret nature of the highly sacred, I believe the knowledge itself should be open to all. Those who can understand will. Those who cannot will not be drawn. And in either case, it's very obvious that the attempts to keep either black metal or the occult hidden do not deter the swindlers and fakes.

[S] Honestly, the push for "underground only" by elistists is a close minded approach to the genre as a whole. When the pressure to only have "true" bands be the ones who are killing themselves financially to get their work out there, it causes a stigma that if you are financially succeeding by living off of your work and having your music reach further, that you are fake. A poor magician is a poor magician. As a culture we should embrace the bands that are pushing themselves harder and celebrate their success, especially within the genre of occult themed music. Though what is almost more depressing to see among the elite, is the idea that if any band is to experiment with a different style that is just as reverent and even more personal, that they are "selling out" or becoming "weak". A great example of this being "They Rode On" from Watain's most recent album "The Wild Hunt". As an occultist, that song spoke to me in a depth that can only compare to the anthem of devotion that is "Waters of Ain". It upset me to see the backfire they were put under for using a different perception and frequency to approach their same message. True fans, elistists or otherwise, could learn a thing or two from opening their minds to all messages that are given. Not just the ones that only come in familiar packaging.

[Z] *In this somewhat at least underground genre of metal, what would you say are your influences?*

[C] Not necessarily only from this genre of course. I draw influences from a very wide variety of music. The actual style does not matter as much as the passion that drives the musicians to create it. For this reason my primary influences I would have to say are The Devil's Blood, Opeth, Watain, and Johaan Sebastian Bach.

[Z] *On the subject of the worship of death, as you bring it up a great deal, can you provide us with a little insight on this?*

[C] Death... is a primal concept that has been worshipped through many cultures and in many different forms under many names. Modern practitioners have a great deal of variance in their opinions on Death. Some embrace it. And some even in the sinister path, shun it. I view Death, as the truest representation of the goddess. The crossroads of existence and the liminal point between life as we know it, and the unformed darkness beyond our perception. Thus while the true goal may be beyond death, the focus must be on Death. And that transition into the unknown. It is similar in concept to the very nature of the Hindu gods. It is a concept personified and given form, so that it might then be transcended. Death is the great Mother, Provider, and that which distinguishes. It is entropy and darkness in all forms. To worship Death while in life is to subvert the concept of duality. And to seek a foothold for Death is to enact the great and acosmic work.

A few songs to help introduce the reader to Occult Metal

Scarlett:
"Death Knows Where" by In Solitude
"On the Wings of Gloria" by The Devil's Blood
"Vermillion Clouds" by Year of the Goat
"The Wild Hunt" by Watain
"Force of a Floating Tomb" by Inquisition

Mikhail:
"Love Always Yiedeth" by Zero Kama
"Introducing the Brides of Christ II part B." by Mr. Vile Thumb
"Waters Of Ain" by Watain

Caine:
"Blood Current Illumination" by Acherontas
"Khanda Manda Yoga" by Cult of Fire
"When the Sky is Black with Devils" by Tribulation
"The Otherness of Being" by Nightbringer
"The Serpent's Chalice" by Watain

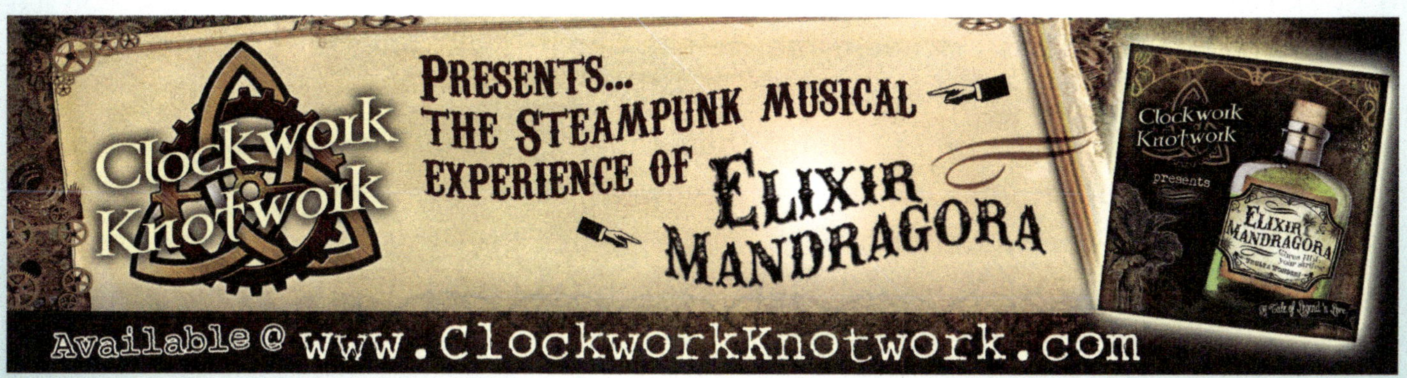

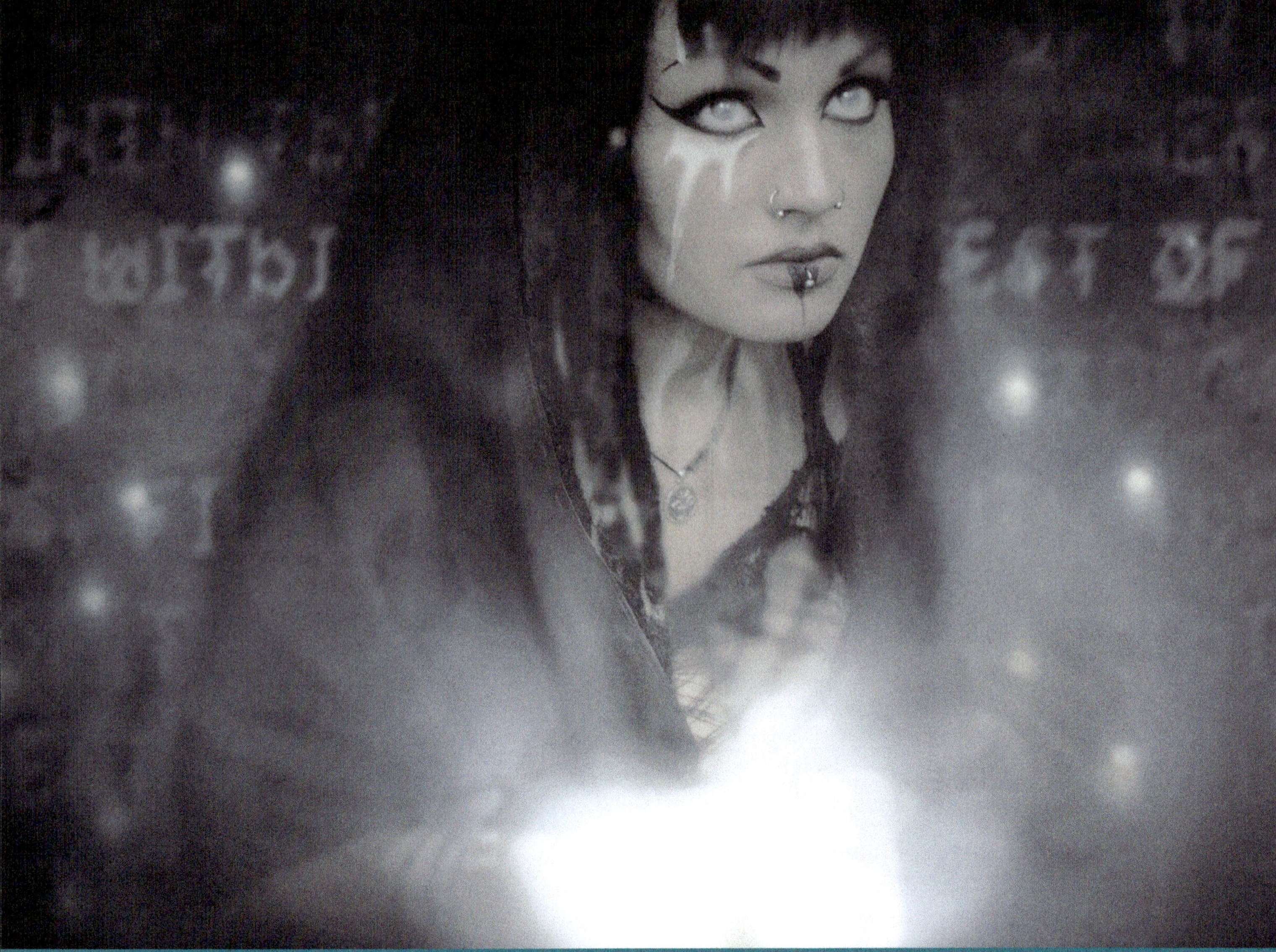

GILD THE MOURN

By XXX Zombieboy XXX

I have had the honor of knowing Gopal Metro for many years now. Running into him at several shows and conventions, particularly Dragon*Con. The man has never been anything but kind and open and friendly. And by my observation he is that way with everyone. As well as having the same effect on everyone. Positivity and energy. A very talented artist in many facets as well as a scholar intellectual, Gopal is not only fun to be around but fascinating to talk to, and enthusiastic in his conversations. His wife Angel with her grace, her charm and her kindness make seeing them together a light almost too bright to look upon and impossible to look away from. I know. Not exactly the description you would expect of two well-known Gothic artists. Trust me when I say this though. It does nothing to detract their macabre allure to the lush sound that as a family unit they have created in the project "Gild the Mourn."

[ZOMBIEBOY] *Greetings and Salutations my friends! Thanks for taking the time to talk with us!*

[Gopal Metro] Greetings, Zombie! Always a joy!

[Anjel Metro] Thank you for having us Zombie!

[ZB] *First, I would like to give you a heart-felt congratulations on the birth of a future rock star! How is fatherhood treating you and has the wee beastie been given the Gopal hair yet?*

[G] Thanks so much. Being parents is, hands down, the coolest thing we've ever done!

[A] Actually Kailasa (our son) was born with a natural mohawk. We joke that the years of hairspray-abuse our hair has endured altered our DNA.

[ZB] *Gild the Mourn has a lush and beautiful sound. How was the band developed?*

[A] Gopal and I decided to play around with writing a song, and the sound that came out hooked us. We both knew it was something really special. The product of that session became "Shade". The response was overwhelmingly positive, so we kept writing and producing and haven't looked back!

[G] We both have a deep passion for dark music and fairy tales, so we decided to continue creating more of the stories and music that we love. Ideally, timeless songs with dark and beautiful melodies; rich atmosphere that evokes thoughts of ancient lore, empty ruins, great battles and magical places; and lyrics that are rich in story, history and meaning. In other words, fairy tale themed gothic rock.

The Coffin, Best of 2014" podcast!

[ZB] *You release your music on Bandcamp currently. Will there be any CD releases in the future or do you plan to stay exclusively digital?*

[G] Our current plan is to continue releasing one to two songs per month, with a "Collected Works" digital album every October. As such, our primary releases will be digital, with annual Limited Edition CDs and Vinyl. For our patrons and hardcore fans, we also offer a killer annual subscription service offering a wide array of benefits. Readers, if you are interested, contact us for the details at gildthemourn@gmail.com!

[ZB] *Take us through the collaborative creative process of the band if you would?*

[A] We usually start by writing the instrumentals, then based off of the tone they set, we develop a theme for the lyrics. A lot of our stuff is inspired by either stories we hear or life events, so we use that as a foundation. We like to get creative too, and experiment with unusual sounds and synths. Our song "Shade" for example, has Tuvan throat singers in it, and our newest track "Greed" has our son's voice altered into a synth.

[ZB] *Is there any chance we will be seeing the Metro Family on tour anytime soon?*

[A] You will definitely see us on the road! Currently, we're in the process of creating a stage show that our fans will really appreciate. Of course, we have to wait until the little one is old enough to handle being on tour, so we aren't traveling quite yet. But, soon!

[ZB] *For the gear heads tell us a little about your toys and weapons!*

[G] Damn. I could talk gear for hours! But, I'll try and keep this brief.

[ZB] *I find it amazing to see a husband and wife team. Gives the rest of us hope for such an amazing connection!*
[A] Our relationship is really the proof that you never know what life is going to throw at you, but it could be totally amazing! We really stress open and honest communication with each other and that is the secret to our success.

[G] That kind of communication breeds trust, compassion and acceptance of each other's character strengths and flaws, as well as the ability to adapt, grow and change with one another over time. It truly is a joy to be able to create something lasting together. I wouldn't trade it for the world!

[ZB] *It is an inspiration to witness. And I hear Gild reached #1 on Gothic Paradise's charts as well as Best Newcomer of 2014?*

[A] It's true, and what an honor! To be named Best Newcomer by a group so integral to the scene is a massive compliment to our work and we couldn't be happier.

[G] Huge thanks to everyone at Gothic Paradise for the support! I'd also like send a "Thank you" shout-out to the wonderful John "Ichabod" Anderson, who honored us by including us on the "Out Ov

Our studio computer is currently a Macbook Pro. I keep burning up drives, so we will be moving to a dedicated iMac 27" Retina over the next few months. This means we will also be producing music videos soon, too!

I'm a HUGE fan of Ableton Live Suite and Max for Live. It is amazing what you can create with that software collection, straight out of the box!

Other key plugins include Omnisphere, the Korg digital collection, all of the TAL and Final Symphony stuff, Native Instruments Guitar Rig (useful when the little one is asleep!), iZotope Ozone 4 (I can't praise the iZotope team and products highly enough!), the SoundToys collection and few older Waves plugins. Our drums are primarily from a private sample collection that I've recorded and polished over the years.

Our audio interface is a PreSonus Firestudio Project, with plans to upgrade to an RME at some point. Our main preamp is a PreSonus MP20 with Jensen transformers. We also have a custom "giant killer" preamp that I built a few years ago and break out on occasion.

Our primary mics include a heavily modded Monoprice 600800 (using the MicrophoneParts.com RK-12 module and parts kit), an MXL990 (also using the MicrophoneParts.com mod kit and PCB, but with a RK-47 module), a modded Shure SM57 with bypassable transformer and custom impedance box that I built, along with an array of other more unusual mics that I've built over the years.

Still using my Ibanez SR885 bass, accompanied by a Luna Apollo electric guitar and a gorgeous handmade harmonium from the Biba Emporium in India. Plus, a whole array of strange instruments that I've collected or made over the years, including a number of DIY Arduino based synths and stompboxes that I recently built and have grown particularly fond of.

Alright, I think I'm done for the moment, but anyone reading this who wants to talk arcanum, feel free to hit me up at gopal.metro@gmail.com and we'll geek out!

[G] Thanks so much, brother. It was joy to see you, there, too! Andy (Deane) and Tony (Lechmanski) asked me to play the "Best of" release party in Charlottesville in 2013, which was a blast. At the time, there was talk that I might rejoin the band. I had just graduated from Full Sail University with a degree in music business administration and I helped Andy and Tony consolidate their online store, develop some new products and develop a social media marketing and business strategy, so rejoining made sense.

However, after Kai was conceived, communication between the guys and I broke down again and we went in different directions in mid-2014.

DragonCon was a show of chance. Bella Morte's touring bassist, Marshall (Camden) was getting married that weekend, so the guys hit me up for a one-off. At the same time, the Cruxshadows contacted Angel and I to see if we'd be interested in helping them at the Con. We love working with both bands and everything fell into place, so we came down. Definitely a great time. DragonCon is ALWAYS a great time. And, as an added bonus, I finally got to play a gig with the legendary Tom Coyne. I love that dude!

After that show, we went our separate ways again, then met by chance at a party Bella Morte played for a mutual friend and fan named Gavin. That was a strange night. This demon chick showed up and there were zombies everywhere and we ended up in this van! Did I ever tell you how much I like baseball bats?

[ZB] **Laughs* There is nothing like the feel of a classic Louisville Slugger when you are saving the world is there? And is anything happening with Brighter Fires?*

[G] Brigher Fires is very much a barometer of Andy and my friendship. Music is a core part of our friendship, and, like our friendship, I fully expect that Brighter Fires will be present in one form or another until we die. We have some unfinished songs in the works, but we do not currently have any plans to finish them up in the near future. Some day, though!

[ZB] *Are there any other musical endeavors, collaborations or ambitions we can look forward to in the near future?*

[G] Gild the Mourn is our primary project and takes full precedence. However, we are always up for collaboration! Angel recently sang on My Own Sorrow's ,"Part To Play" and we have been invited to contribute to a few other projects that are still under wraps. We are also always happy to produce, remix or contribute in other creative ways when time allows. Not to mention, we thoroughly enjoy appearing in awesome novels/graphic novels/comics that involve zombies, magic, demons and great storytelling! (Gopal sez: "Go buy "Zombie Come Reap" on Amazon.com, today!")

So, readers, feel free to contact us if you'd like to work together!

[ZB] *In front of the entire world I am not afraid to say I love you Gopal, and to thank you again for honoring me by appearing in my recent story to kick some zombie ass! You have other professional endeavors I believe. I am curious about Bluepulse Studios. What exactly does being a Product Strategist entail?*

[G] Bluepulse is a talent-rich up and coming video game studio founded by Rafa Fernandez and based in Charlottesville, VA. I serve on the advisory board for the company, where I focus on business strategy, high-level product development and product strategy.

To answer your question briefly, product strategy is a roadmap for a given product that defines the products targeting, pricepoint, development, deployment, mix (length, width and depth of the line) and planned life cycle.

Bluepulse is only one of the companies I work with and consult for. In one capacity or another, I have also recently advised or developed strategy for Bella Morte, The Cruxshadows, Ships In The Night, Centric, Krellware, CoshX Labs, Tinkersmiths and quite a few others.

When working with artists, my primary goal is to help them develop revenue streams and either cross the gap from independent to managed/signed or to help them become independently self-sustaining, depending on their goals.

When I work with startups and not-for-profits, my objective is to help them define and achieve their goals and attain sustainability.

I absolutely love business and marketing strategy and I'm always thrilled to work with people who are passionate about their art, mission and vision!

[ZB] *I think it is amazing too that you work with 501C3 Not-for-profit organizations, musicians and artists. It is nice to see someone with such passion as well as so much training and education, put forth that badly needed energy and support! Going back to your band... Goth, Synthpop, Deathrock, EBM, Post-Punk, Electronica, Fairy Tale music, man you have crossed many styles! What influenced you to explore so many forms and disciplines? And what do you feel you have yet to conquer?*

[A] For me I'm drawn to anything that's considered "dark". It's something that started with horror movies and literature, and has grown into a very diverse music preference. I try not to limit my exploration of new music by the genre it falls under, and because of that I've found some amazing artists I may not have otherwise.

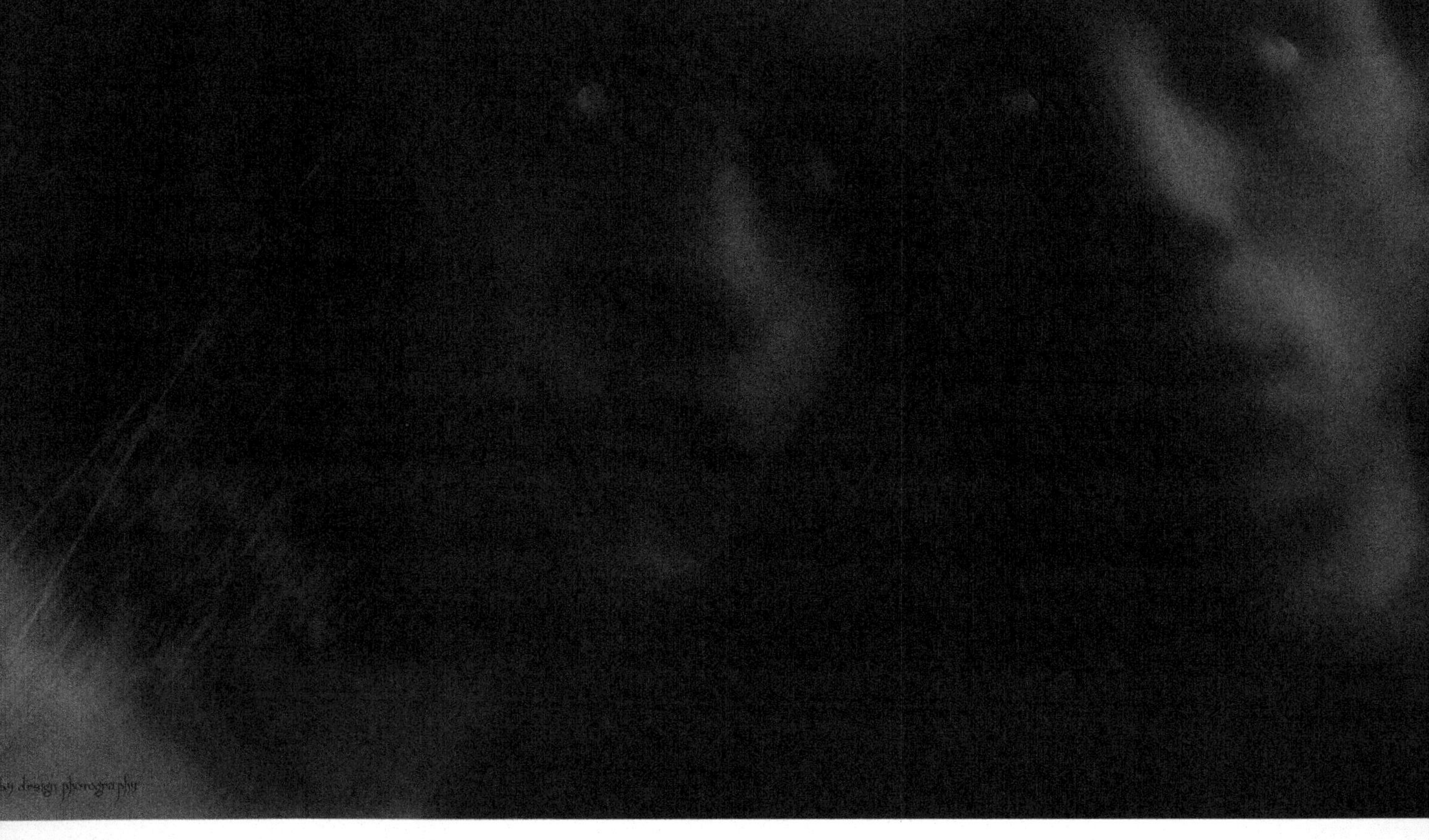

[G] I am still a 1980's and early 1990's Goth, through and through. While the Goth scene has certainly morphed and evolved with time, I'm still madly in love with spirit of it all. Drum machines and reverb, fog machines and dyed black hair, Halloween mixed with high art, the digital age mixed with the medieval and a solid dose of futurism. Good times.
Of course, I grew up in Yogaville, a community that celebrates "Unity in Diversity." From a very young age, I have been exposed to a wide variety of cultures, styles, beliefs and expressions. They have all influenced me in one-way or another, and I have musical roots in everything from psychedelic rock to Kirtan to reggae to hip-hop to world beat. Nonetheless, out of all of these influences, Gothic, Post-Punk, Neo-Medieval and classic Industrial hold my heart!

As for areas yet to explore, prepare yourself, because I'm about to geek out. I'm a huge fan of old video games, and I've spent the last year collecting and converting classic consoles and computers into modern synths. So far I've collected at least one Atari 2600, Atari 400, Commodore 64, NES, SNES, Sega Master System, Sega Genesis, Gameboy and Gameboy Advance, and I've modded nearly all of them for pro sound and MIDI control. It makes me teary eyed, it's so beautiful. *grins*. If all goes well, either I, or Angel and I will be composing and performing chip tunes in late 2015 or early 2016.

[ZB] *That... just sounds amazing... I cannot wait to see how that turns out! Make sure you have a Colecovision in there! And now for the favored and sometimes dreaded question! What's next for Gopal Metro and Angel?*

[G] There are a many things high on our list. First and foremost, is taking care of our family. This is followed closely by developing Gild the Mourn.

I also volunteer and work at Tinkersmiths, central Virginia's largest and most active makerspace, where I develop websites and teach Arduino and microcontroller basics.

Angel is quite tech savvy and creative, as well, so we are building many of the instruments, set pieces and controllers/props for Gild the Mourn's live show at Tinkersmiths. As Kai gets older, I fully expect that we will be spending more and more time there, as we gear up for a full-scale Gild the Mourn tour.

To stay posted on our progress and to receive notice on all of our latest releases, sign up for our mailing list on gildthemourn.com, follow us on Facebook at facebook.com/gildthmourn, facebook.com/angelmetro and facebook.com/gopalmetro, and follow us on Bandcamp at gildthemourn.bandcamp.com!

Zombie, thank you again for the interview, it is always a pleasure!

[A] Thank you, Zombie!

[ZB] *I mean it sincerely my friends when I say that the honor is ours. Readers please check out the following websites for more!*

Website - http://gildthemourn.com
Music - http://gildthemourn.bandcamp.com
Enquiries and Patronage Contact - gildthemourn@gmail.com
Band Facebook - http://www.facebook.com/gildthmourn
Angel's Facebook - http://www.facebook.com/angelmetr0
Gopal's Facebook - http://www.facebook.com/gopal.metro

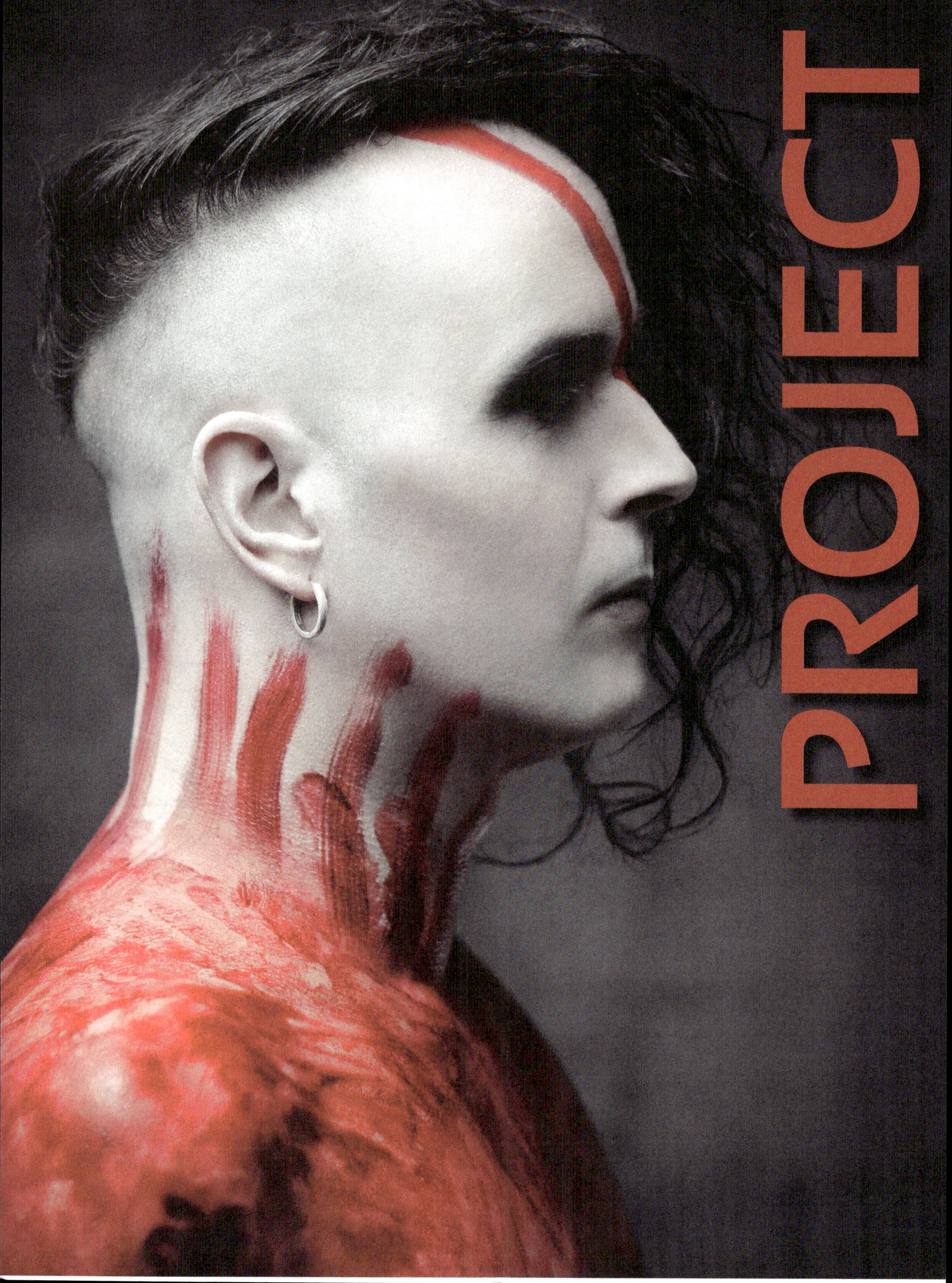
PROJECT

PITCHFORK

By Sonnett57

[Carpe Nocturne] *What was it that attracted you to the Industrial and Dark-Electro underground scene?*

[Peter Spilles]   My life lead me into this direction and the people I met in the scene made me feel sure about my decision.

[CN] *What prompted you to start creating the music?*

[PS] It was an urge beyond control.

[CN] *Do you recall your feelings the first time you played live on that stage in Hamburg?*

[PS] We were frightened as hell, but after the first applause in the completely sold out club we knew that we wouldn't and couldn't ever stop.

[CN] *Who has inspired you musically?*

[PS] Lots of artists who managed to create fantastic art beside the mainstream.

[CN] *Do you still DJ?*

[PS] Yes, I do from time to time.

[CN] *Other than Santa Hates You and IMATEM, are there any other side projects the band is involved in?*

[PS] You forgot JANSEN SPILLES. Nothing more in this very moment.

[CN] *The Project Pitchfork videos are all very visually stimulating. Do you design the storylines and direct them yourselves?*

[PS] Yes, I manage to do quite satisfying No-Budget video clips. Thank you.

[CN] *A number of the songs you have written are historically motivated. If you could live in a time from the past, what era would it be and why?*

[PS] I wouldn't because I feel here and now the best.

[CN] *How do you feel about the amount of independent labels, releases and genres that are out there today as opposed to the smaller number that were around in the 90's?*

[PS] I feel comfortable about it.

[CN] *One of the things I truly appreciate about your band is the fact that you create what you want, and perform how you want. I believe it has been said to "Expect anything from Project Pitchfork". Have you faced ridicule through the years for not conforming to a particular style?*

[PS] Not in person. Of course. But why do you think this might be the case with one of the things you truly appreciate about my band?

[CN] *On your newest release Blood. The word blood is used in every song title. What is the concept of the story you are telling with this?*

[PS] It is about life, the aspect of liquidity and its necessity to transport informations, oxygen and waste.

[CN]   *What can we expect from Project Pitchfork in the near future?*

[PS] As I sit metaphorically beside the never ending source of inspiration, you can expect lots of phenomenous compositions and spectacular activities.

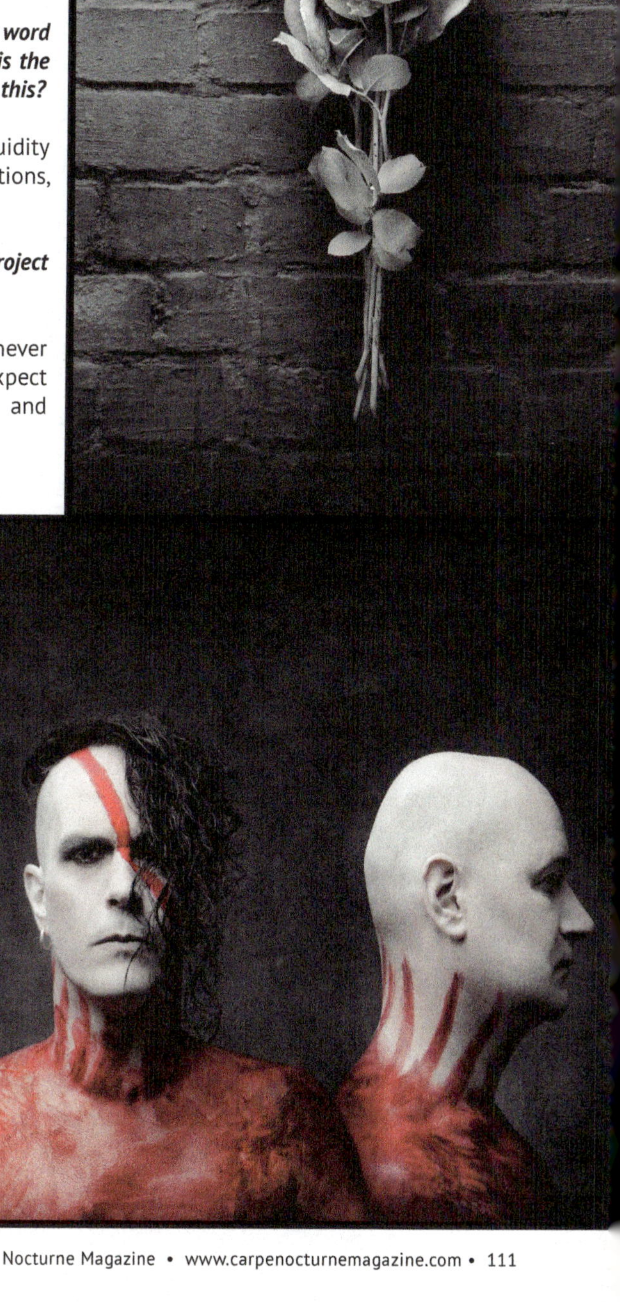

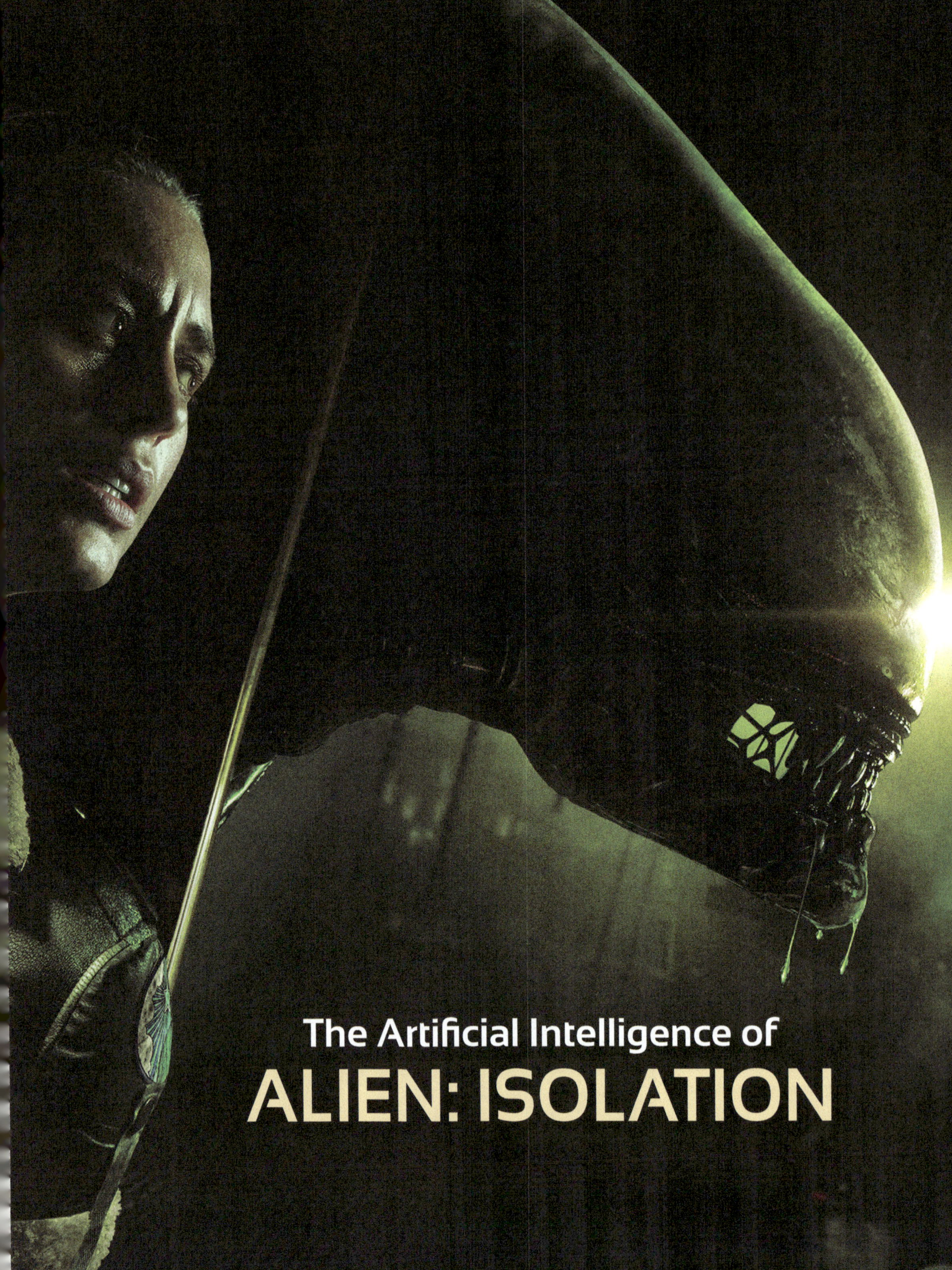

The Artificial Intelligence of
ALIEN: ISOLATION

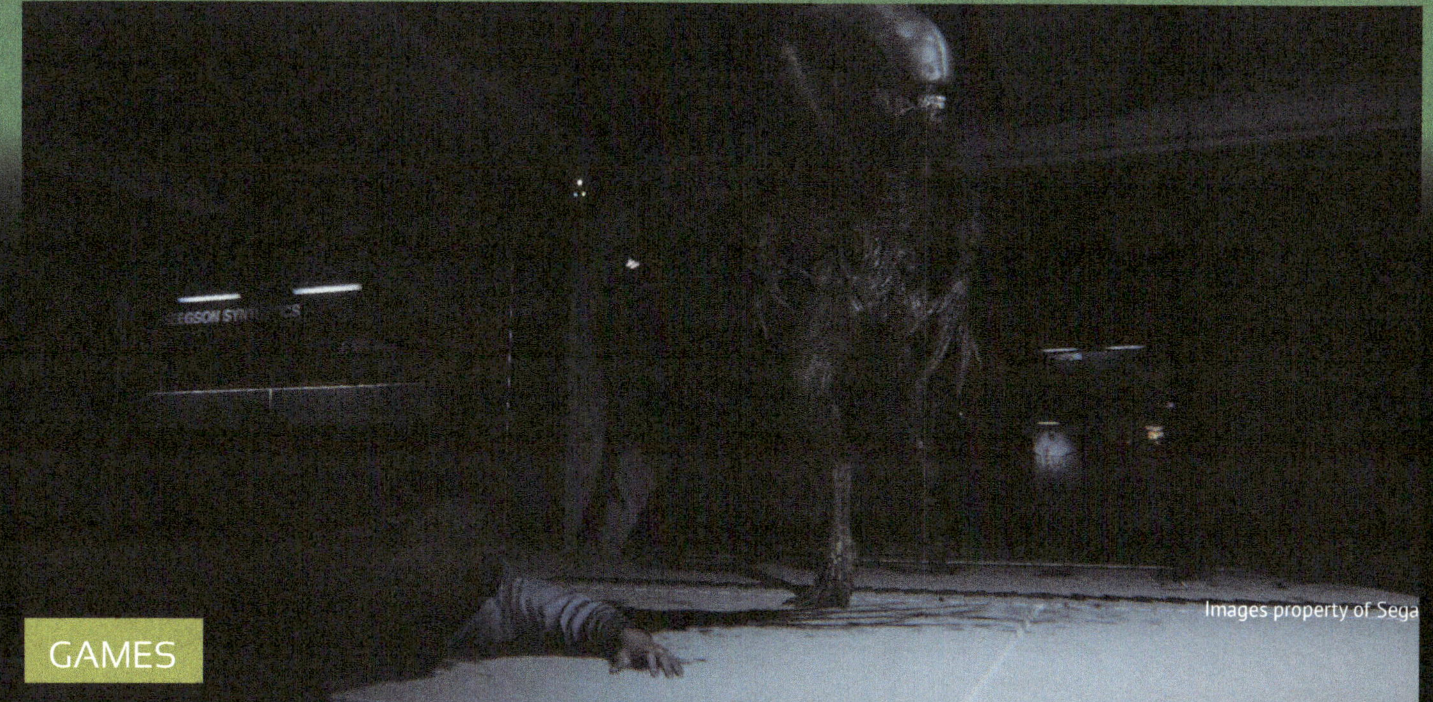

Images property of Sega

By Annabella Rios

I've been waiting a long time for a proper sequel to *Alien*. By proper I don't mean to say that *Aliens* wasn't a great movie, it was, but I was always disappointed that there wasn't a return to form after that initial tonal shift from alone-in-the-dark-terror to testoster-one-fueled-pulse-rifle-badassery. Thanks to *Alien: Isolation* I wait no longer.

Until now, almost every video game iteration of the Alien franchise has been a first-person action shooter - a festival of nearly limitless ammo and badly rendered and programmed xenomorphs that get torn apart like paper. This is the tried and true formula of the video game industry, but as disappointed players of the widely panned *Aliens: Colonial Marines* can attest, it isn't a formula that has worked for this particular Sci-Fi series.

Production team Creative Assembly took *Alien: Isolation* a step further than past developers with unique mechanics for this game. Unique and admitedly risky. Gamers, console gamers especially, are used to having their ammo and their endless cannon fodder. Creative Assembly took away both and created a survival-horror experience for the ages. In this game, you only have one xenomorph enemy, and that enemy is invincible. It stalks you through the abandoned space station known as the Sevestapol, and any guns you are given don't exactly guarantee your safety when fired. Most of the time the sound just attracts the xenomorph to you.

I haven't gotten very far into *Alien: Isolation*. Most of my time playing has been spent trying to unlearn years of FPS (first-person shooter) offensive tactics and bad habits; habits I learned even from the most sophisticated survival-horror games of the past. This game is about stealth and trying to keep a step ahead of your enemy. In this game, acting like Master Chief from *Halo* will get you killed.

Much of the difficulty of *Isolation* stems from the xenomorph's programming. It's behavior is nearly unpredictable and seems to learn from your actions, even your mistakes. I started off playing the game entirely in "crouch," knowing that running would make too much sound and alert the drone immediately, and that standing would make me too easy to spot. However, five levels into this game the xenomorph has become wise to my act. It actively searches under tables and tries to sniff the lockers I'm hiding in. If I don't hold my breath and press myself against the back of the locker in time, the drone will rip the door open and get me. Once the xenomorph finds you there is no fighting back. It's instant death.

Nowadays I'm trying out different tactics. Diversion seems to work when executed properly, but it comes with a considerable amount of nail biting. The game allows you to craft noise-makers you can throw to attract the drone. If you plan properly enough, you can use the time it's taking to inspect the device to escape the area or get to your next objective. If you don't have the noise-makers on hand you can always bang your wrench against any hard surface, although it is more dangerous since you have less time to find cover. A more morally questionable tactic is to use other human survivors of the Sevastpol as bait. Sometimes you can find them about trying to survive on their own and if you have the xenomorph fresh on your trail it becomes very convenient to use the humans as a way to break the drone's line of sight.

All of this, along with the instantly recognizable motion-detector from the film are just some of the things the player can use to try and survive *Alien: Isolation*. The drone is constantly in pursuit though, and there are very few scripted moments you can count on for predictability. It often shows up without warning, dropping down from ceiling vents or simply pulling you up into them after making the mistake of walking under its dripping saliva.

This game of cat and mouse is a battle of wits amid fear and terror. *Alien: Isolation* is one of the most enjoyable survival-horror games I've played in a long time, not only because it's terrifying but because it is smart. It is because the game is smart that it is able to be scary. I'm not just running from a group of pixels on rails. The xenomorph is like another player with a mind of it's own - feline and confident and relentless. Keep this in mind if you decide to pick the game and try it for yourself.

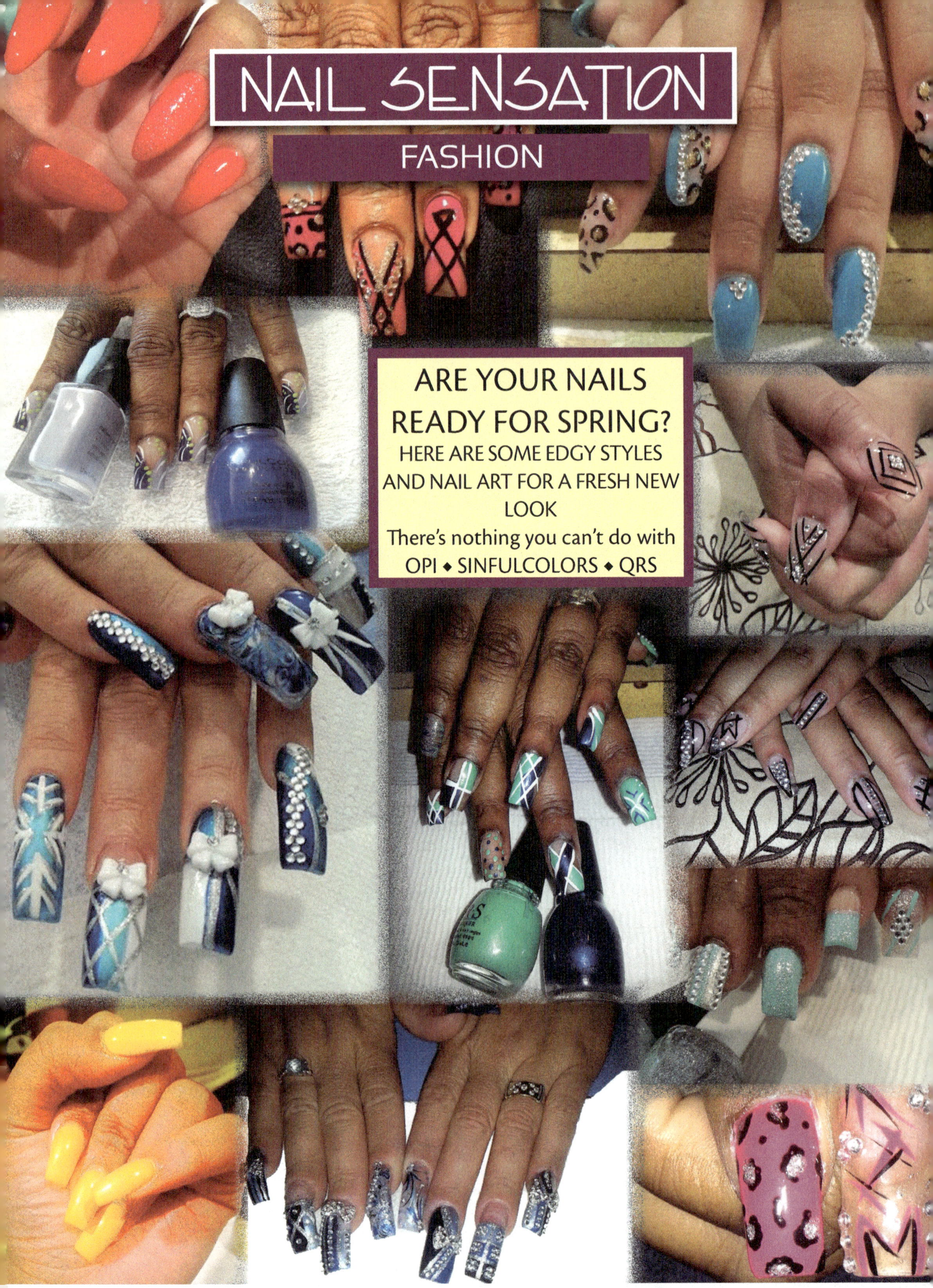
NAIL SENSATION
FASHION

ARE YOUR NAILS
READY FOR SPRING?
HERE ARE SOME EDGY STYLES
AND NAIL ART FOR A FRESH NEW
LOOK
There's nothing you can't do with
OPI ◆ SINFULCOLORS ◆ QRS

TEMPORARY FOIL TATTOOS

By Kathleen Sharkey

I am sure that anyone who glances around the internet has seen pictures like these: lithesome beautiful bodies with sun kissed tans and beautiful delicate foil tattoos in attractive places. I wanted to know more about these pretty little foil covered images, not because I am a sun kissed goddess but rather for costuming purposes.

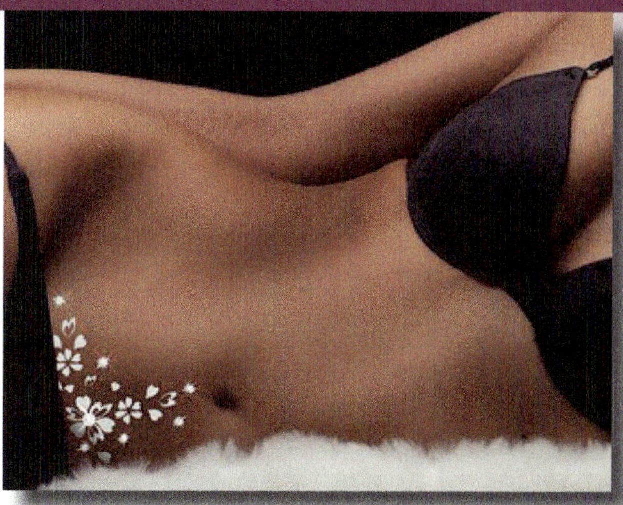

I began my search on Etsy and the range of possibilities was amazing. Unfortunately due to a billing flub I had to go elsewhere and wound up finding some foil tattoos at a local discount store.

These are very similar to ones I have seen on Etsy though the ones on Etsy tend to be a bit more complex.

So how could one use these in costuming, and in Science Fiction costuming in particular? My imagination ran wild when I saw these remembering broken wooden doll costumes, AI costumes and various other things I would have given an arm and a leg for metallic additions that I would not have to keep reapplying makeup to. Not only can these beautiful items be used as their creators originally planned, as beautiful temporary tattoos, but they can be metal leads to neuro implants. Some of the more decorous can be used as AI circuits imaginatively designed as necklaces. Breakpoints on hands and feet at wrist and ankle where the metal underneath is showing through, it only needs the imagination of the user.

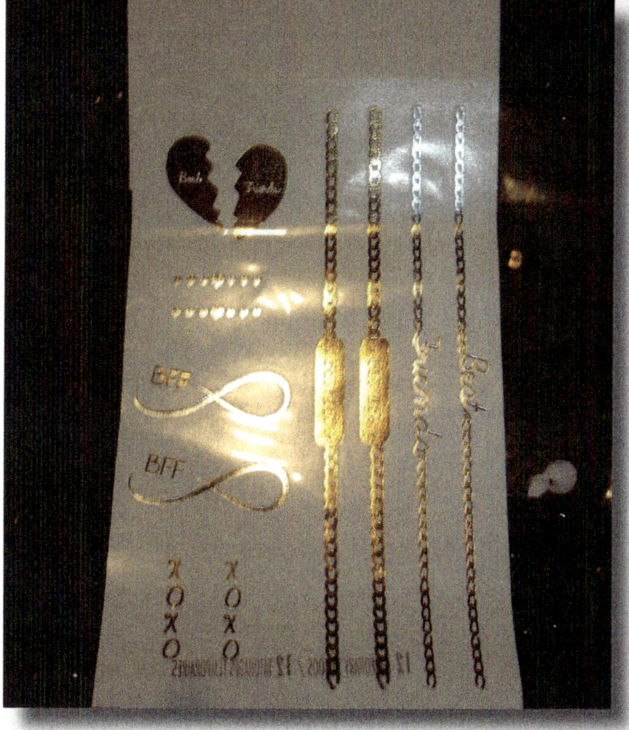

But wait here is the great part, the ease with which they go on. Ok many of us who might have used fake tattoos are aware, easy is not necessarily in the nature of temporary tattoos. It seems the more intricate the design the more delicate one needs to be. This is still the case. Since these little pieces of temporary body art are even more intricate then the .50 cent tattoos out of the vending machines you should definitely read the instructions carefully.

I respect those of you who will say, I prefer to paint my intricacies upon my cosplay self. I am all for talent and ingenuity. I merely offer these beautiful little ideas up to those of us who have awesome ideas but might not be quite so creatively talented. Here is hoping that this might help with some glorious costumes in the future. If it does send pictures to kathy@carpenocturne.net and we can share your awesome ideas with the rest of our readers.

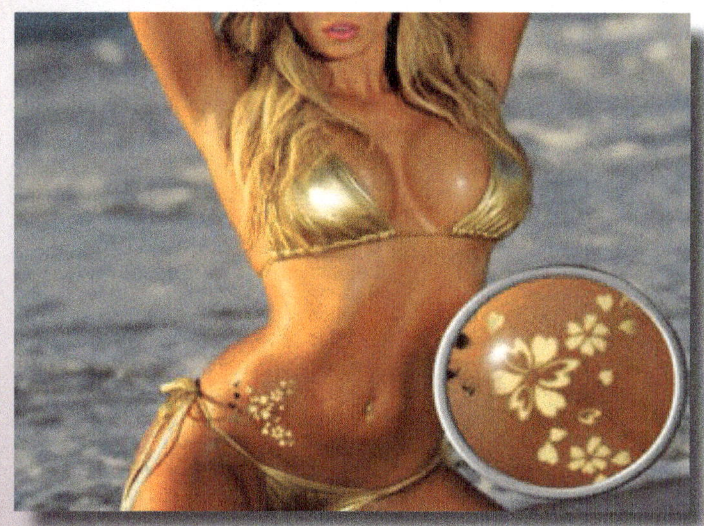

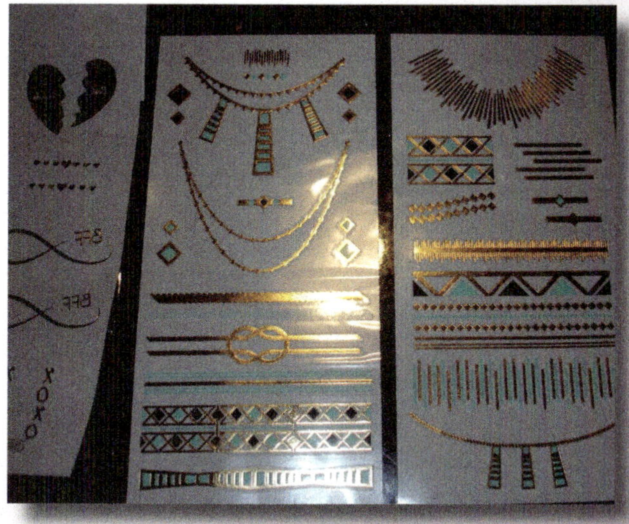

COSMIC HIPS...

By Zahara

Belly Dance Fusion draws inspiration from many sources, and the world of science fiction is no exception. When taking a cue from the sci-fi realm, belly dancers find inspiration in soundtracks, costuming, and character concepts. [To the right] is a picture of our troupe's interpretation of Dr. Who's stone-faced and deadly Weeping Angels.

While creating the piece, I felt inspired by their icy demeanor and absolute destruction. We tend to think of angels as "watching over us" and protecting our nurseries, gardens and graveyards. The concept that they are watching in order to kill us... that's a unique and terrifying twist. I thought it would be interesting if the angels were more enticing and ethereal in their movements (actually luring in their audience), then reverting to the statuesque murderers when it was too late for anyone to escape. Blending pieces of music that included snippets from "The Time of Angels" on the Dr. Who Soundtrack further tied our performance into the original source.

But does an audience of sci-fi novices respond well to these types of performances? We found that even if some viewers are unfamiliar with the Weeping Angel storyline, if the piece is entertaining through interesting costuming, solid dancing technique and excellent stage presence, viewers will respond well to the piece. The notion that an audience isn't going to "get it" shouldn't stop a belly dancer from drawing inspiration from the sci-fi well. But a belly dancer should always know her audience, and present these unique fusion pieces when appropriate. Listed below are two more performances where the dancer drew on a concept and created a unique belly dance performance.

One of the first sci-fi belly dance pieces I saw was Asharah's "Xenomorph" performance from Belly Horror in October 2009. She also performed this piece at Gothla US in 2010, which can be seen here (https://www.youtube.com/watch?v=AmHUqcXiGd4).

[Carpe Nocturne] *What inspired you to create the Xenomorph piece? Was it the Alien character, or HR Giger's art in general?*

[Asharah] The idea for "Xenomorph" sprang forth from a conversation a friend of mine and I were having over coffee. I remember saying, "I'm not sure what I want to do for Belly Horror," and then we began talking, and I said, "I want to do a Giger piece,". From there we started talking, and I narrowed it down to not only the Alien, but the mother Xenomorph. I've been a fan of Giger's work for as long as I've known about it (so since at least early high school, maybe even Junior High), and it was an aesthetic I hadn't explored with my dancing yet. The dance definitely began as a general idea, and then I narrowed it down. For a while, I wasn't sure what music to use, but then I remembered that I had always wanted to perform to Autechre's "Second Bad Vilbel," and thought it would be a great aesthetic match. Having a performance idea before having the music is quite unusual for me; usually, I start with the music, and then create the performance around it. My later Belly Horror performance in 2011, "Persephone Fallen," also began with a concept, for which I selected the music after creating the idea.

[CN] *How long did it take to create the costuming? What was the most intricate of that process?*

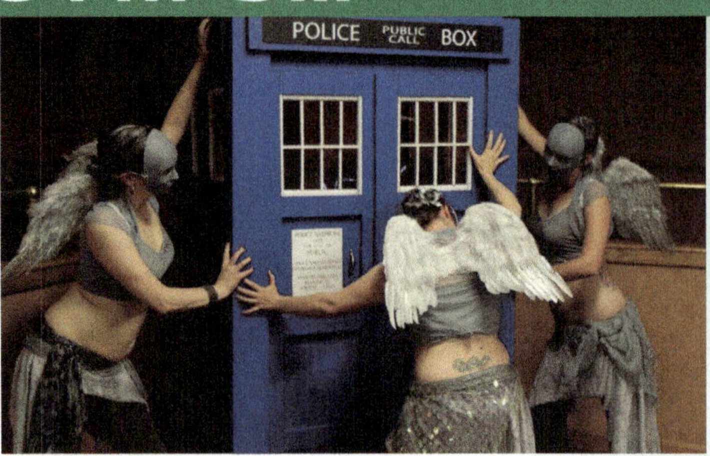

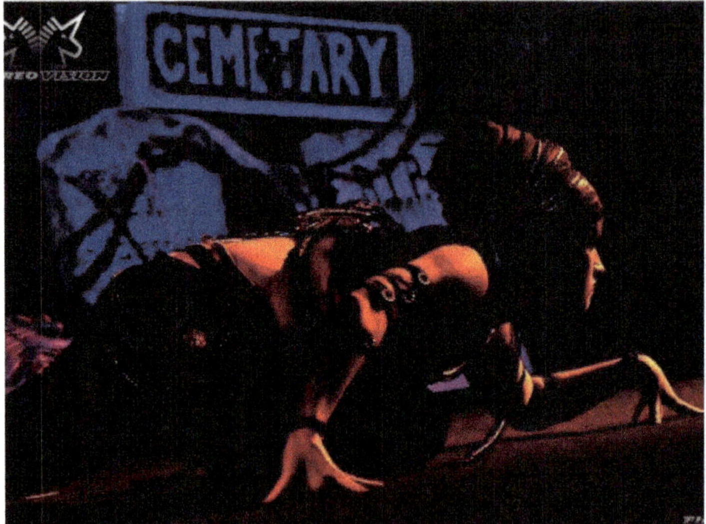

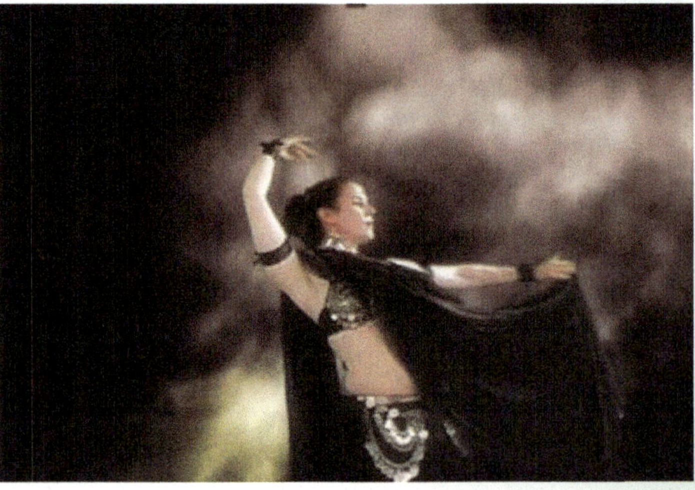

[A] I admit that for me, costuming is always a bit of an afterthought. I usually have the dance and theme idea well before the costume is ever made. This one was tricky, because it needed a specific costume. I wanted it lightweight, without restricting my movement, because I knew I wanted to do lots of floorwork and crawling. First, I researched Giger's original "Alien", looking at his drawings and painting, then looking at images from the "Alien" films. Then I sketched some designs (I always do preliminary costume sketches before sewing),

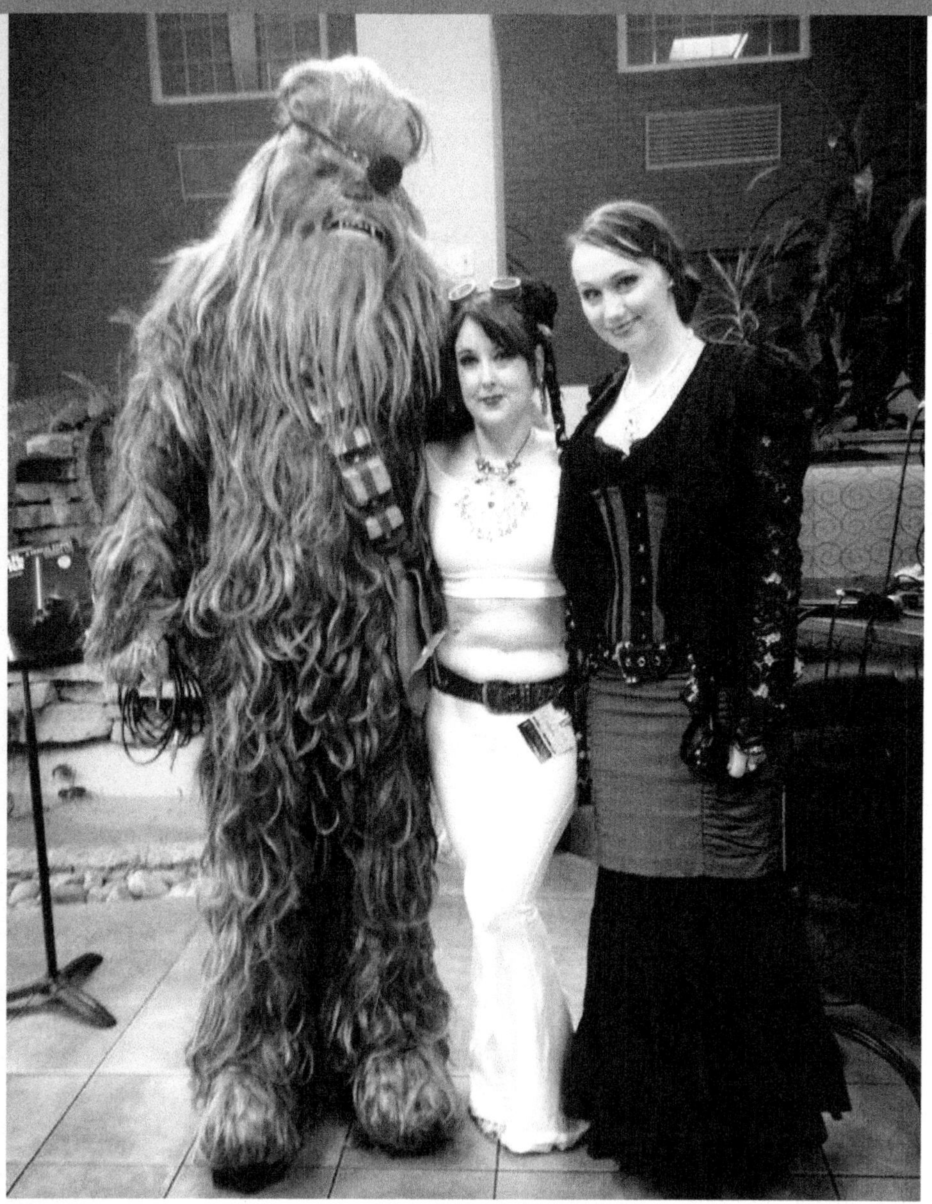

to the Steampunk Empire Symposium in Cincinnati, OH last year. She danced with her partner, Jon "The Wookiee Cellist" Silpayamanan, as the duet Secondhand that year.

[CN] *What aspects of Princess Leia did you incorporate into your piece?*

[Celeste] In this case, the bulk of the aspects that I incorporated in my performance were via costuming (see response to 4 for more on this). In terms of movements, I already have a movement in my repertoire that I dub "Help me, Obi-Wan", and I definitely incorporated it in. Outside of that, I tried to emulate how I would think Princess Leia would move. To me, she has an elegance and regard-bearing about her. Having a Wookiee cellist with me helped, too.

[CN] *Where have you performed this piece?*

[C] I performed this piece at the Steampunk Empire Symposium in Cincinnati last year. I did another version of Princess Leia at Gencon, this time with the slave Leia costume with steampunk accessories and a bit more covering than what true slave Leia would have.

[CN] *What was the audience's response at each location?*

[C] For the Steampunk Empire Symposium, the audience was more interested in the Wookiee Cellist, but they responded well to my Princess Leia, as well. For a portion of our set, I was just essentially the Wookiee's MC, so they didn't quite know what to make of me… and then I started dancing and they thought that it was cool. For the Gencon performance, it was the usual good response to a dancer.

and then sough out the fabric and materials. I would say that it took a month of actual making, because I wasn't even living in my own house at the time (I had just separated from my husband and was couch-surfing). I'd say the most intricate part of the costume was the top, because it laces up the back and has lots of crinoline tubing attached to it.

[CN] *What were you trying to portray in this particular performance? Was it strictly a character piece, and how did the audience react?*

[A] I was just beginning to go through my divorce, and in that, I was accepting how angry I was with how I had been living my life. The Xenomorph character allowed me to embody a character who was protecting and claiming her space, just as she does in the "Alien" films, and as I needed to do with my own life. At the original Belly Horror performance, I was ble to have a very theatrical lighting, and the stage then became my lair. It is a bit of an extension of my Tribal Fest 9 performance, "Grist," but in a more literal character sense. "Grist" is acknowledging my anger; "Xenomorph" is acting on it.

Honestly, I can't remember specifically how the audience reacted… I'm assuming they liked it!

For more information about Asharah and her dancing, visit her at www.asharah.com and www.bdpaladin.com

Celeste (Indianapolis, IN) portrayed a steampunk Princess Leia when she came

[CN] What do you feel was the most important aspect of your piece (costuming, prop use, etc.)?

[C] Definitely the most important aspect was the costuming. For SES, I went for a more of an inspiration than downright cosplay, and I think that it worked well. I went for the white color scheme and the shapes. The costume itself is a cross between the archetypal Princess Leia white outfit and the Padme one with a crop top.

Visit Celeste's website at http:// celestebellydance.com for more information about her performances and workshops. Jon Silpayamanan can be found at http:// boldcellist.com, which includes his many projects and upcoming performances.

SCI-FI FASHION ON THE RUNWAY

By Kathleen Sharkey

Fashion has always been a fascinating creative display, art to be worn. Line, shape, color, they blend together to display an artist's individual concept in three dimensions blended with movement, flow and presence. Whether it be sharp angles and dark colors or gentle curves and pale pastels, fashion, like all art, can be left open to interpretation. On the runway in 2014, however, there were definitely some designers who were greatly inspired by Science Fiction. Since this was our theme for this issue I wanted to share some of the beautiful designs of the 2014 runway with you.

Rodarte

Flowing dresses fit for Star Wars princesses with draping sleeves and crystal accents in beautiful pale colors. Jackets flown in from outer space with open shoulder sleeves, angular lines and raucous vibrant colors studded with bright glitter. Even the more earthy designs in browns and greys pay homage to the sometimes medieval fashion of science fiction. Created by Rodarte designers Laura & Kate Mulleavy. When interviewed by Style (Style.com) the designers stated that these designs were an homage to childhood and the hyper visualization childhood can create in our memories, which includes, beauty, color and design.

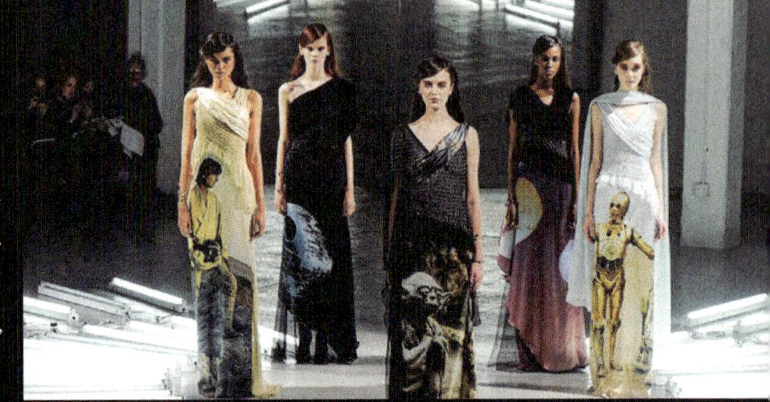

Gareth Pugh

Like white space satyrs, these models were embraced by stunning white or silver designs ranging from almost an almost Audrey Hepburn-esque homage, to aluminum foil chic, to snow queen. The variety of lines and design, over the simplistic encompassed leg, displayed an amazing diversity of fashion pieces. Even though the dichromatic display seemed simple the artistic elements were far from such, displaying gentle playful curves in one design and sharp angles in another.

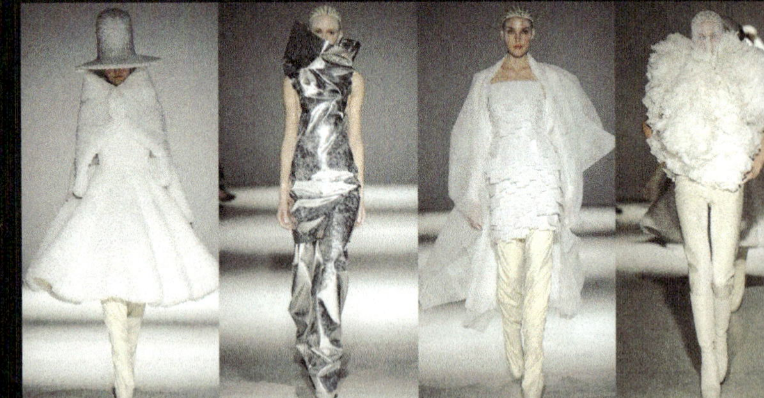

Sadie Williams

The collection created by Sadie Williams for the 2014 runway bespoke Dune royalty to my mind. These neoprene dresses of armor could have just stepped off of the royal courier ship while still maintaining a modest gown line. These designs capture, in sparkling sharp colors and angular strident lines, futuristic ladies in waiting and revolutionary sword wielding Grande Dames ready to rush into laser battles.

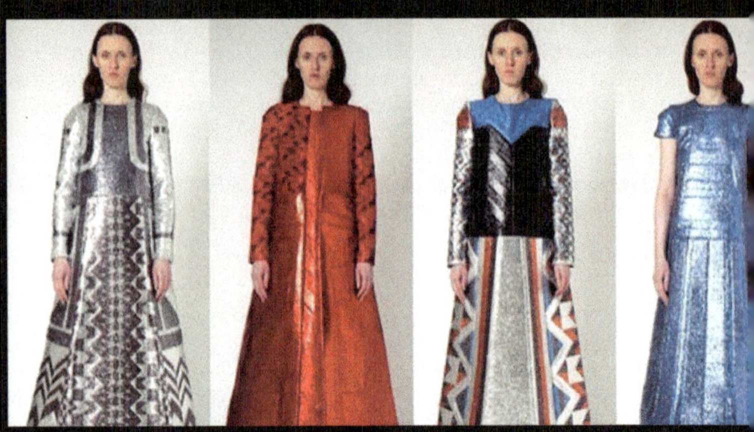

Two-Thousand and Fourteen

Jean Paul Gaultier

In 2014 Jean Paul Gaultier decided to bring a distinct British flavor to science fiction fashion in 2014. The raucous British flag design on most of the pieces makes for a playful display. It is in the colors, materials and complete package that one harkens to Dr. Who, or Alice Lost in a futuristic Wonderland. Gaultier never stops with his beautiful fabric performances. In his 2014 productions he included "normal" models, kids, beautiful silver haired models and even some gloriously plus sized models. Definitely a designer who breaks the mold at every turn. Plus, heck, his models actually look like they are having fun on the runway.

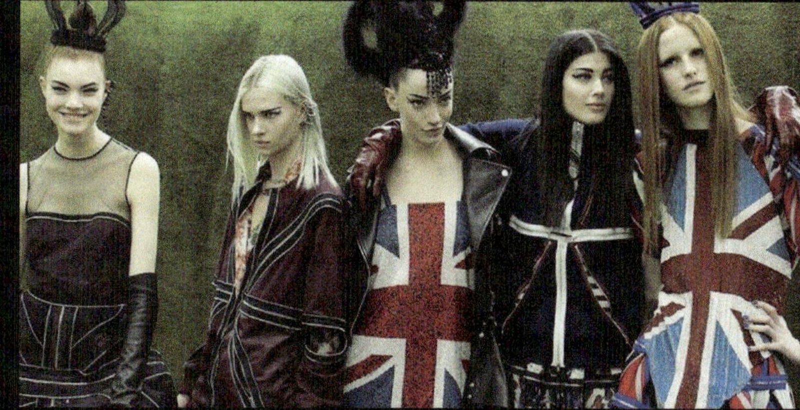

Balmain

Balmain's 2014 designs brought my mind to the beauty of "Firefly". I know the sporty safari-esque colors don't really appear to be very science fiction on the surface but when one remembers the designs of the space westerns these designs could easily blend into the costumes for strong female leads. Though muted the colors are allowed to stand out by the use of design and line. No color can over-power the next due to pleat or fold. Elegant design beauty with earthy tones and fun quirky inspiration.

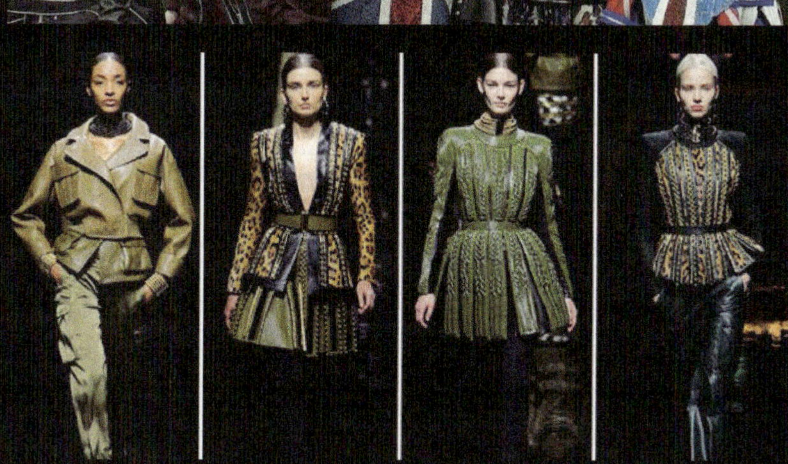

David Koma

When I saw these designs my first thought was to wonder if someone had fallen in love with the color and design of the Dr. Who Tardis as much as I had. The sapphire blues used in Koma's designs are the perfect blue color. If one looks closer at the beautiful blue gown on the end you can see that it even has pockets, larger on the inside then the outside. Other than the Dr. Who possibilities I could even see the women of Battle Star Galactica, out of uniform of course, walking down the pre-apocalyptic Earthen streets in these lovely designs.

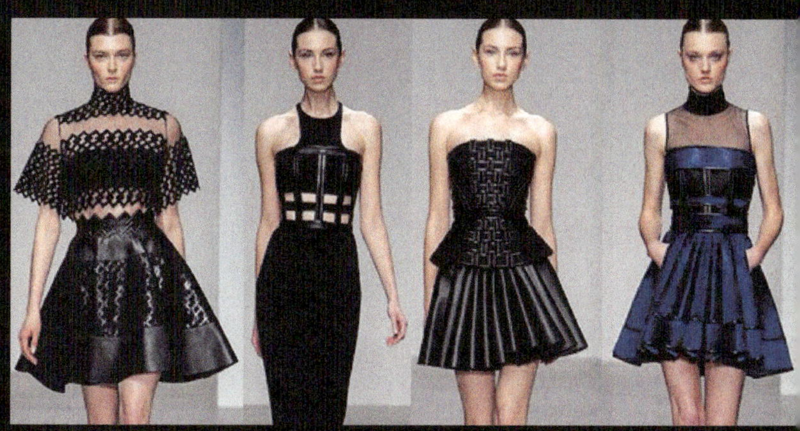

The above designs are only a small few of the Science Fiction designs 2014 brought to light. It seems that fashion has finally caught up with the design expectations of the 30's. But heck this is the year we are supposed to have hover boards right? Right? Cause I want to put my order in right now.

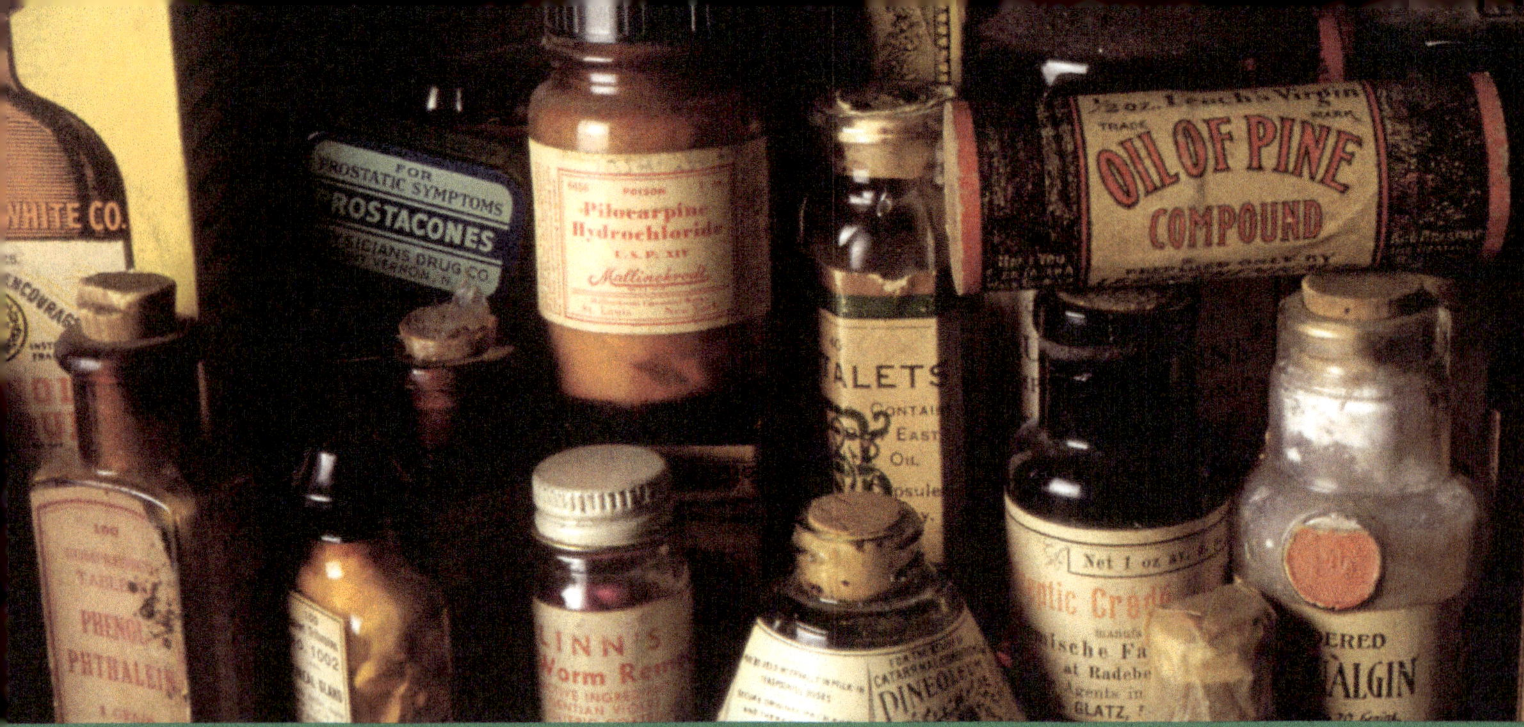

FROM THE ALCHEMIST'S CLOSET:
Seasonal Allergies

HEALTH

By Michael Jack and XXX Zombieboy XXX

From holistic guru XXX Zombieboy XXX and Registered Pharmacist Michael Jack, we present two different approaches to treat common ailments. In this Issue's installment, we tackle the misery that is seasonal allergies. Let us begin with Michael Jack and the Pharmaceutical approach.

Michael:

When walking into a drug store, it is easy to be overwhelmed by the amount of products that claim to treat seasonal allergies. There are nasal sprays, pills, eye drops, who knows what else, that forms a dizzying display of choices and uncertainties. What's best for you? I find it varies from person to person, but there are generalities I can make and proven successes that form the basis of my recommendations. In this installment, I will tackle the three main areas of allergy relief...nasal sprays, allergy pills, and eye drops.

I think one of the most underutilized form of allergy control is nasal sprays. I like them because they act more locally in the sinuses, and are absorbed less throughout the body. There are a lot of choices, and soon you will be bombarded by ads from Flonase and Rhinocort, which both recently went over the counter. These are both good products and work well, but they are steroids, and I don't recommend them for long term use due to side-effects. My choice for a very long time has been Nasalcrom. It works differently than other nasal sprays, and actually prevents allergy outbreaks as well as treats acute symptoms. No other spray can claim that. Nasalcrom is

also safe for people who suffer from high blood pressure, diabetes, depression, and has less side effects. It is my clear choice in this area.

There are a slew of over the counter pills in any given pharmacy to treat symptoms of allergies. Many carry the same active ingredients, claim the same things, but are just packaged differently under different trade names. I think the big three are Claritin, Allegra, and Zyrtec. All three are non-drowsy, available in once daily or twelve hour dosing, and give you the option of buying the D version to combat congestion. I really think they are all good products. I am a long time allergy sufferer, and Zyrtec works best for me, and for the majority of the customers I've consulted. Like I said, everyone is different, and if you are a Claritin or Allegra fan, stick with it. I do recommend the twelve hour tablets over the twenty four hours ones because it gives better control of the symptoms, and are less drying. Again, Zyrtec-D is my choice if, like me, you often feel like your head is going to explode from the pressure. Just be careful with this product, because it can exacerbate a number of health problems, and I recommend checking with your local pharmacist first before using it.

Finally, there is the problem of itchy and puffy eye hell. Any of the above products will help in this area, but sometimes you need immediate relief...eye drops. My go to in this area is Naphcon A. It's been around for a long time, tends to be a little pricey, and stings when going in. It's worth it, because this product is effective. Naphcon A delivers the relief allergy sufferers long for. If you are looking for something cheaper or a little different, go with one of the many generics containing Ketotifen. It's twice daily dosing makes it convenient, although I've found the drops don't exactly last twelve hours like they claim. It's a trade off. I find I have better control using the four time a day Naphcon A, but that's just me. Allergies are an ogre, and I'm bringing the best arsenal of products available to combat it.

Now let us take a look at a more naturalistic and holistic approach to Hay Fever.

XXX ZOMBIEBOY XXX:

Growing up in Tallahasee, FL which is one of the hay fever capitols of the world I am very familiar with this ailment and have resorted to many different means of relief. Michael has brought up a number of good points and some may be reflected here again. To begin, I think it important to understand what an allergy is.

An allergy is basically an aggressive immune response in the body. It can be triggered by many different things. Such allergy causing variable may include foods, touching a substance dermal (skin) or inhaling such things as spores, pollen, animal dander, dust, mold and fungus. So to defeat the symptoms or prevent the problem, we must look to increase the bodies efficiency at fighting them or get our body's reactions to "chill out".

Allergies can also be caused by weak immunity, weak adrenal or weak digestive functions.

Let us discuss prevention as this is often better than a cure right? A common theme you will find in my posts is basic nutrition. In this scenario, we must look to increase immunity and body function. To help prevent hay fever and it's messy symptoms, be sure you are eating a lot of dark greens, yellow and orange vegetables, and any foods with high Vitamin D content. Taking an extra vitamin D tablet a day is a good suggestion to improving immunity. There are a number of other foods that can be added to your diet that help fight hay fever.

Garlic
Onions
Horseradish
Cayenne
Bamboo Shoots
Cabbage
Beets (particularly the tops)
Carrots
Ginger

It is also important to note that if you are suffering from hay fever, there are some things to avoid. At least while hay fever is an issue. You should avoid eating a lot of citrus, dairy, red meat, sugar and wheat. You should also avoid high doses of alcohol, caffeine, and believe it or not bananas. Smoking can also deaden the cilia in the throat that help us get rid of airborne hay fever causes.

To improve digestive health and immunity there are also many supplements and vitamins that one can take. For digestive health,

an increase in probiotics is suggested. Good Belly is one example. Flaxseed intake should also be increased. Getting high doses of Omega 3's will also help your overall health and can be found in wild salmon and fish oil supplements amongst other foods.

There are many multivitamins out there on the market. Buy organic brands if possible as your body will absorb them better. Be sure you are getting the following daily!

> *Vitamin C* – this amount can be different for everyone. It is important to remember that too much can actually give you the runs! So watch out!
> *Vitamin A* – 25,000 IUs daily
> *Vitamin E* – 400 - 500 IUs daily
> *Vitamin D3* – 600 IUs daily (Over 71 take 800). Note* Getting good sunlight actually increases your Vitamin D intake!
> *Zinc* – 30 mg daily.
>   Note: Zinc is an excellent immunity builder!

Now let us discuss some herbs. Again I want to stress that higher quality and organic is worth the extra money. What you may not know is that low quality brands, though containing the herbs legally, you may actually wind up urinating a lot of it out. The same goes for vitamins. Talk about "pissing your money away!" So try to spend the extra $5 or so! There are a number of herbs that act as antihistamines in very much the same way as say Benadryl. Dong Quai and Stinging Nettle have been used for centuries for this purpose. Milk Thistle also reduces allergic reaction and fights histaminic reactions in the body. Ginkgo Biloba is a wonderful herb that not only works as an anti-inflammatory but also increases blood flow to the brain, which is why it is often referred to as a "smart herb". So if you have a cold or are having hay fever symptoms and have to still go into work, this is one to pick up!

There are also some things you can do to help relieve they symptoms. A "Netty" pot filled with saline is a time honored and useful folk remedy that works. There is a new nasal product out there that actually uses hot pepper. This may sound insane but (like many other insane things) I tried it and though I ran around the room for a minute it worked! Hot foot baths and a cold cloth on the forehead can help relieve the symptoms. There is even the option of acupuncture. It is also important to be getting the necessary rest one needs otherwise your immune system suffers. Studies have shown that bee pollen can decrease allergies to certain plants.

Be Well!

XXX Z XXX

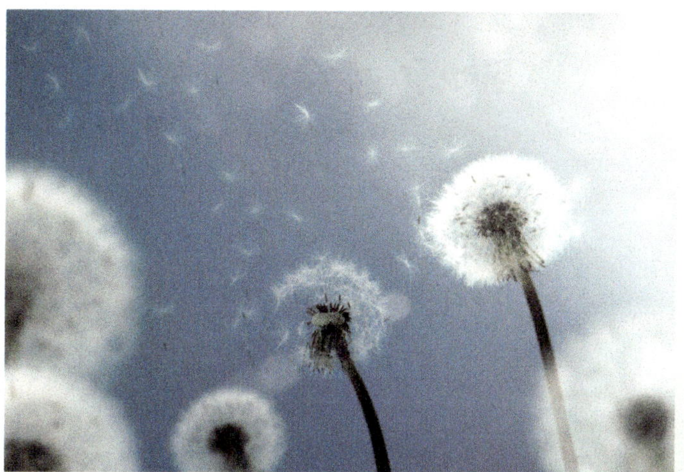

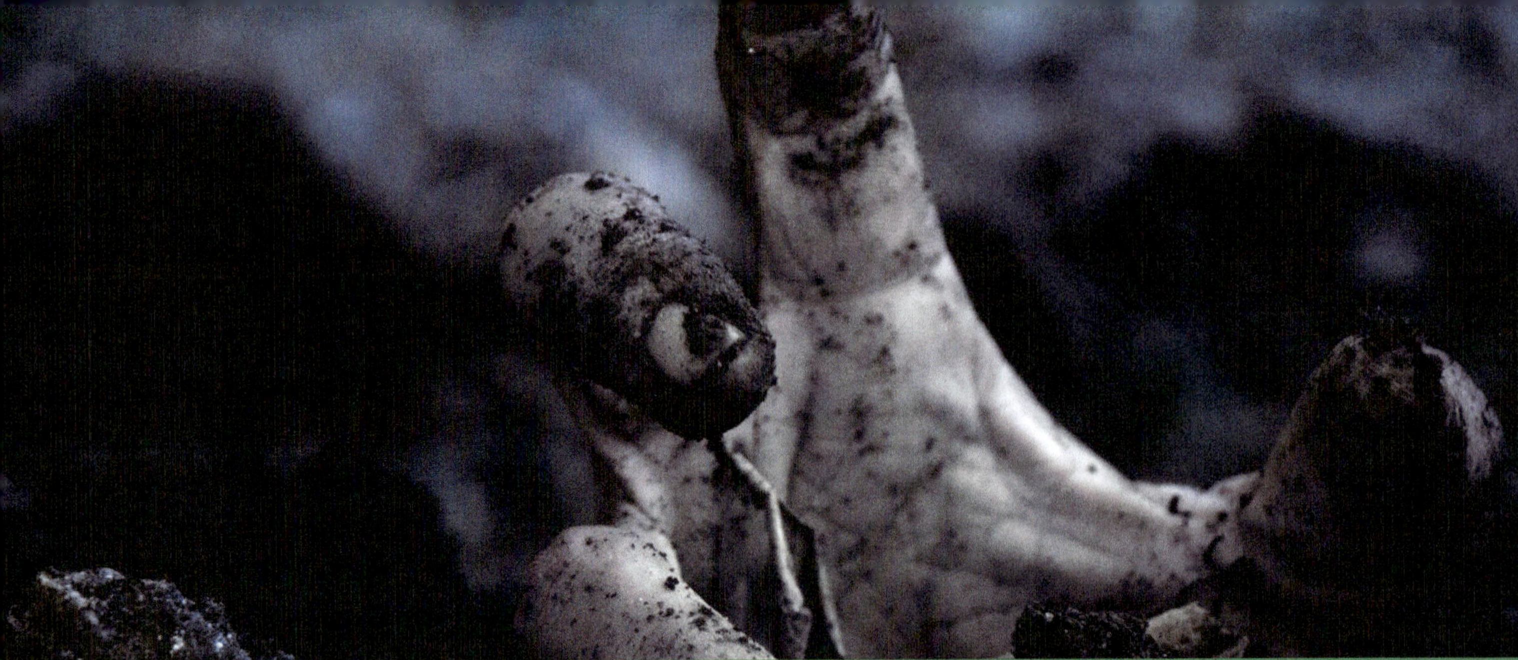

HOW NOT TO GET EATEN:
Surviving the Zombiepockylypse!

By XXX Zombieboy XXX

Welcome to your lifeline for the dead rising! We here at Carpe Nocturne don't want to see our readers get eaten. And whom better to answer the call than a Zombie! So each issue moving forward I will provide you with tips and helpful guidelines to keep you alive in modern times and to keep you from getting eaten in the future! Most of these will have a specific theme but I thought I would begin with some eclectic tips on how to survive what I refer to as the Zombiepockyclypse!

Step One: DON'T PANIC!

This is possibly the greatest tip in survival under any circumstances. It is imperative that you maintain a calm and sound mind. Panic will cause you to act stupidly and without proper thought which will either get you killed by the dead or by your own party of survivors! Remember The Hitchhiker's Guide to the Galaxy and DON'T PANIC!

Step Two: Stay clean!

This is one of the first things taught in basic survival. It is important to maintain cleanliness for health. It also improves state of mind and keeps them from smelling you as easily (assuming they can smell).

Step Three: Food and water.

Zombies are not the only ones that need to eat. You can actually go for quite some time with minimum food. Without water however you cannot go for long at all. Particularly under stress and exertion. Water procuring is something a whole article can (and will) be

written on. For now I think it is just important to stress that staying hydrated is incredibly important. Food is also important of course, because you will begin to get weak before long without it. Again, more attention will be brought to this later.

Step Four: Weapons!

Now we come to some fun stuff. Weapons are a huge element in your survival. And they will get their own article eventually as well. For now here are some important things to think about. You are one of the lucky ones with a gun! Good for you! Now, do you know how to shoot it? Do you know how to clean it? Do you know how to procure ammunition or reload your own rounds? If your answer to any of these things is no then, well... you will at best take out six or so zombies before you run dry and become one. Having a big gun will feel good in this world. Until it runs out or you find out you are a lousy shot. Discipline, learning, safety, cleaning and care for your gun are vital or you just got yourself a great big phallic symbol that will make a great club till you get torn apart. More on guns to come! For now just understand that you need to know your weapon and your abilities with it. And make those abilities stronger. Also, have some form of melee weapon back up. A bat, a lead pipe, a candlestick (the makers of CLUE did not pay me to write this) and anything heavy and dull that can break a skull apart. And before you go reaching for a Samurai sword, make sure once again you know how to use it! Bladed weapons are awesome if you know how to use them. If not you are going to look mighty foolish when it gets stuck in the rips or muscles of a zombie! My main point here: Know your weapon and be damned good with it. If you don't then stick to clubs and bats. You will live longer.

Step Five: Supplies.

You would be surprised with just how far you can get in any survival situation with these three items; a knife, a fire source and a light source. I am seldom if ever without all of these everywhere I go. And I mean everywhere. A small jackknife, a lighter and a small LED flashlight. Have them on you at all times.

thing new. Use your instincts and tune into that part of yourself that knows how to climb a mountain or hunt or fight. We all have it. You just need to wake it up!

Step Nine: FIGHT!

You are going to have to. Better start learning now. Fighting zombies you must remember two things. One, they don't really fight back. That's the good part. Two, the bad part is they don't feel pain. It will be great to know how to break bones and cause pain when you fight other human's but in a battle hand to hand with zombies, it is far batter to know styles such as Judo, Aikido and Jujitsu. Learn to throw them off of you rather than trying to knock them out. You won't get far with that.

Step Ten: Have fun!

This may sound silly, but think about all the other steps I have told

---

"Stick matches. Plain old fashioned stick matches. You never know when you might need them." - Escape from L.A.

Step Six: People.

People are more dangerous than zombies. In the original outbreak there will be riots and panic. A mob mentality that is lethal. Rioters will act as there is no law (and they will be right) thus bringing violence. Those panicking bring the stupid and stupid gets people killed (see #1). It is important to be wary of people during the outbreak. After the dead have risen you will have even more to fear from people. Why? Because the living now are the ones tough enough to survive. And they may have done so through means that are somewhat unsavory. There will be those that thrive on violence. Those who use the situation to their own profit. And those that are opportunistic enough to create a powerhouse for themselves. There will also be roving groups that survive in numbers. Be very careful and cautious of other survivors when it all goes down. I cannot stress how much more dangerous people will be when the dead rise.

Step Seven: Sleep.

You will begin to lose your mind slowly but surely after the third day of no rest. It is important that you still be able to sleep. Having a buddy can help if you sleep in shifts. If however you are alone, try to find a place where you are both hidden and secure. It would also help if you are out of direct wind so that your scent is not easy to catch. A tree may be opportune if you can steady yourself and maintain a good hiding place.

Step Eight: Be creative.

You are going to have to think outside of the box a thousand times a day when all the we know (internet, cell phones, GPS, authority, law) change and disappear! Don't be afraid to be creative and try some-

you. It is important to maintain a healthy body and mind. Whenever and wherever you can unwind, let off steam and have a good time, do not feel guilty about doing so nor let anyone tell you it is not appropriate. As Tallahassee said in Zombieland, "Gotta enjoy the little things!"

This is only the beginning. Keep calm, don't panic and have fun!

XXX ZOMBIEBOY XXX

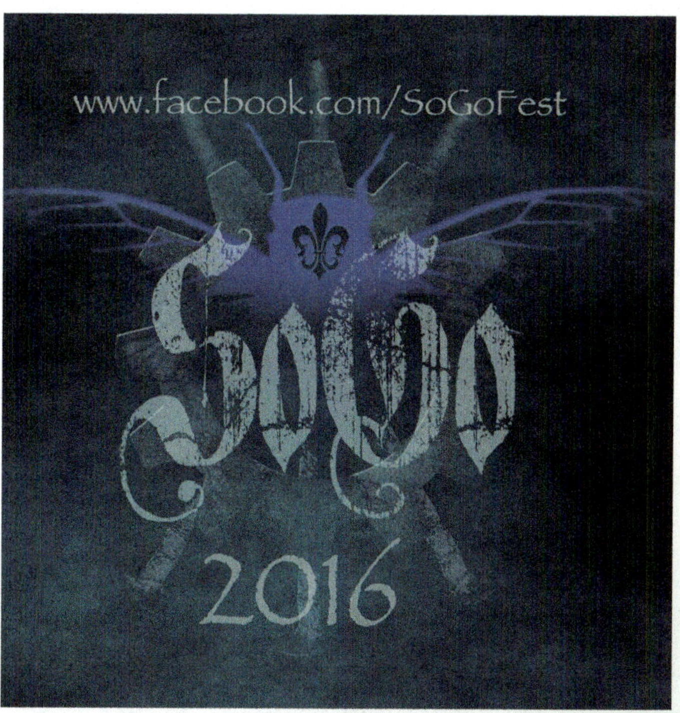

DEARLY DEPARTED

Two memorable musicians to celebrate in April

By Chirality

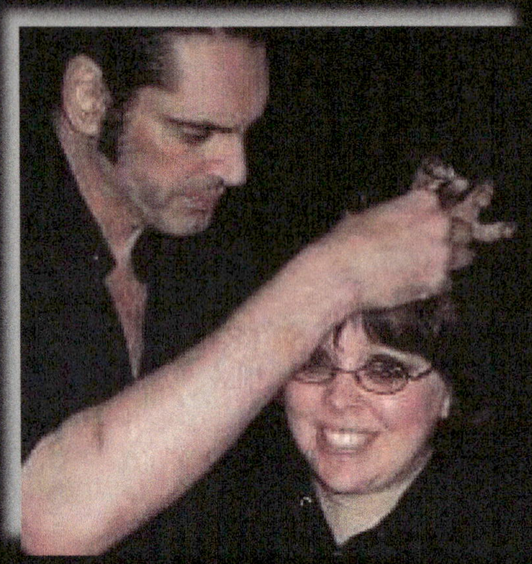

Type O Negative – RIP Peter Steele

April 14, 2010: A day that is burned forever into my memory. It was a day as memorable as when I first heard Black No. 1, and Christian Woman. Peter Steele was the larger than life playboy lead singer of Carnivore, Fallout, and Type O Negative. As far as I am concerned, they put gothic metal on the map. He was 6'6 with that gorgeous mane of ebony hair and those green eyes. Yes, I am partial. It changed my taste in music. Peter, Johnny, Kenny and Josh: The four dicks from Brooklyn.

It was 2007 and I went to see Type O at the Troc in Philadelphia. I waited with my roommate until 2:30am for them to come out after the show so I could meet Peter. He finally came out and said to me as he walked up "Hi, I'm Peter." All I could mutter was, "I'm shaking!" I then asked to take a picture, to which he mentioned me having a lumpy head… bit my head with his teeth, and the picture was of me with a goofy smile and him hovering over my head. I still love that picture no matter how silly.

When I got the news that Peter had passed I was devastated. Everyone knew I would be devastated. Their shows were larger than life. Peter would come out and heckle the audience. The audience would chant "YOU SUCK!" Type O album is worth owning, and if you have not listened to Type O Negative, then get moving!

Peter passed from an aortic aneurysm, April 14th 2010 at the age of 48. When he passed away, Type O Negative did as well.

Peter is the God of torment. Dark and beautiful torment. His deep, luscious voice rolling over every lyric. He is terribly missed.

RIP Peter Thomas Ratajczyk 1962-2010

Kurt Cobain

Do I even need to get into Kurt and Nirvana? Metal or not, Goth or not, you cannot deny their influence on music. They literally killed the 80's metal scene in one swoop. I for one loved (and still love) my hair metal, but when I saw Nirvana and "Smells like Teen Spirit," I knew I was watching history. I am very happy my 18 year old brother can also appreciate his music. Nothing has come since for people to stand up and take notice. I for one still question the suicide.

Soaked in Bleach will be released this year, and is a movie focusing on Tom Grant, the private investigator Courtney Love hired when her husband disappeared back in 1994.

When I was 14, I had come home from school like any normal day. I went to the computer when my mom came in telling me my dad heard something awful on the news. Kurt Cobain shot himself. I ran to the TV, and there was Kurt Loder on MTV news. I cried. I was fourteen. I knew nothing of life, other than it sucked. I was awkward, I was in a terrible religion, and I was being bullied like nothing. I always wore flannels, combat boots…. I didn't care what they said. I epitomized the 90's grunge, and I hate life fashion. That night my phone rang to my friend, not believing it… "YOU'RE LYING!" she wailed. She called me later breaking down. We were all lost teenagers with nowhere to go, and Kurt was our outlet. I wore black the entire week. I was tormented. I still have a special place for Nirvana and Kurt. I have always been somewhat of a tormented soul, and back then, there were not many tormented souls. Sure, there was metal, but I couldn't identify with the harder metal. I did, however, identify with someone who was both soft and gruff. Grunge was raw, growling, and dirty. That's why I loved it.

Twenty one years. Twenty one years. Who knows what could have been. We will never know. All I know is I still get a soft ache when I see those blue eyes and listen to that painful wail of his.

RIP Kurt Donald Cobain 1967-1994.

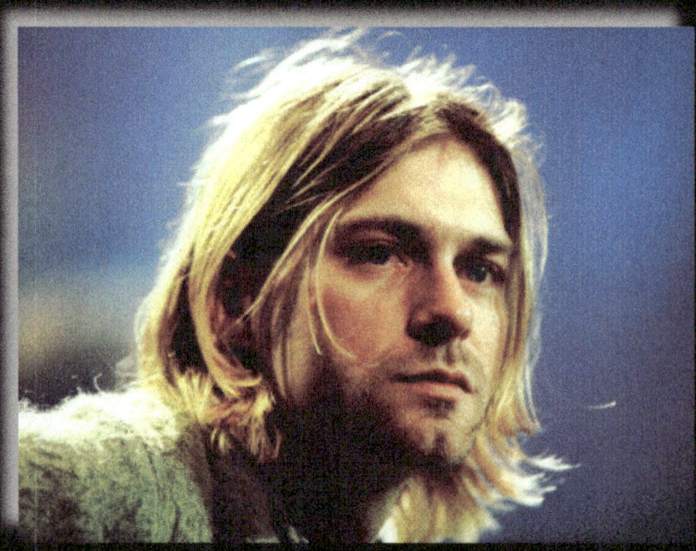

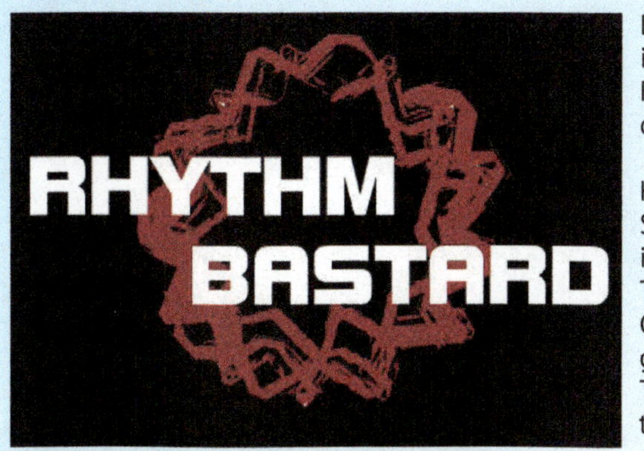

MUSICAN SPOTLIGHT

Eric DiGiovanni, a.k.a. Rhythm Bastard is an independent Nerdcore Punk musician who has been playing since 2008. His first album, "Dino Hunter MD: The Sound Track" came out in 2013 and is a collection of songs done for a web series he did with some college friends called "Dino Hunter MD", about an anesthesiologist that fights dinosaurs.

Rhythm Bastard has played several conventions throughout 2014 and 2015. Usually doing at least 5 conventions a year, this artist works a regular 9 to 5. Although he's not able to drop everything and tour, he loves playing shows at cons, which he sees as taking a little vacation, even it's for a weekend; and one where he usually sees some guests he wants to meet. Admittedly, his music is all over the place; going from punk to garage rock to blues, and about just about everything, from video games to comics to Magic The Gathering.

Rhythm Bastard got his start as a musician playing the trumpet as part of the school band in seventh grade, and continues on to the marching band for his alma mater, Stony Brook. He's always been big into the video games which Harmonix makes, as they are a company made up entirely of musicians. In 2005, they came out with a game called Guitar Hero for the Playstation 2 where you play rock songs on a plastic guitar controller. When the sequel came out a year later, his Dad suggested he take up the real thing, and he's been teaching himself guitar ever since. Learning his craft through self-teaching, Rhythm Bastard goes off tabs from the internet, and utilizes the video game Rocksmith, which is great for learning covers and warming up.

He started playing open mic nights at Stony Brook University having been inspired by favorite bands such as; The Dead Kennedys, The Aquabats!, Green Day, and Janelle Monae. He goes on to say that he really enjoys The Aquabats! "They're thing is that they're a rock band of super heroes who fight bad guys on stage and their sound changes album to album from ska-punk to surf rock to synth pop. I'm also a huge fan of the Dead Kennedys who work so well together as a band, and who's lyrics are (unfortunately) still relevant as they were back in the 70's and 80's."

Growing up in the late-90's early 2000's Rhythm Bastard's preferred music background has always been pop-punk. It's simple enough to where he can manage singing and playing guitar effectively. He does stray a lot to other genres, such as folk, metal, even dropping a couple rap songs, but he always finds himself going back to rock.

Having met many of the artists whose music inspires him, he speaks about his favorites. He says, "I saw Green Day live around the time 21st Century Breakdown came out. Their show went on for THREE STRAIGHT HOURS and not once could you see them dip in energy. I also saw Andrew WK live, and I don't there was a single second where I wasn't in a mosh pit. Plus Andrew is such a funny, upbeat guy that it's impossible to not leave with a smile on your face."

Some new, emerging artists Rhythm Bastard mentioned that readers can watch for is one he actually worked with, S.S. Hanami, a rock band from Melbourne, FL that fashions themselves after the J-Rock Visual Kei genre that use the koto in a lot of their songs. He also thinks it's time Janelle Monae and Walk the Moon had Top 40 hits.

On the topic of 'Status Quo Radio' he explains that it's a concept album originally inspired by the video game Team Fortress 2. With each character having radically different playing styles, which Rhythm Bastard tried to convert into different types of music. From there, it morphed into its own thing with its own mythology, and the videogame became more of a framework of a story about revenge and trying to find your way again.

While he'd like to have nice equipment, so far he's been able to get some seriously good music going with cheap instruments. He does carry a box of audio equipment to all his shows, because he's played enough cons that didn't have the right parts, and he believes in always being prepared.

Rhythm Bastard explains how he chose his name in two answers. The Kayfabe Reason: "Back in 1964, some friends and I from High School, formed a band called The Brawlers after our school's football team, the Bayside Brawlers. We thought is a funny idea to name ourselves after our positions in the band, so as I was the vocalist and rhythm guitar player, I was Rhythm Brawler.

We played at a party some friends were holding for graduation, and right in the middle of the set, his neighbor comes and says "TURN THAT SHIT, YOU FUCKING BASTARDS!" and we've been The Bastards up until 1968, where the rest of my band mates got mauled to death on a live broadcast."

The Real Reason: "In 2008, I started a blog called RB Experiment, short for Rock Band (another Harmonix game) Experiment where I'd learn the songs from Rock Band on the guitar. Eventually I changed that, since I'd be doing my own thing. I settled on Rhythm Bastard since I wanted to keep the initials RB and was reading the comic Transmetropolitian at the time, where the main character, journalist Spider Jerusalem, refers to himself as a bastard frequently. I've thought about changing it to Rhythm Brawler, but people really respond to Bastard, so it stays."

Website: http://rhythmbastard.co.nr/
Facebook Page: https://www.facebook.com/RhythmBastard

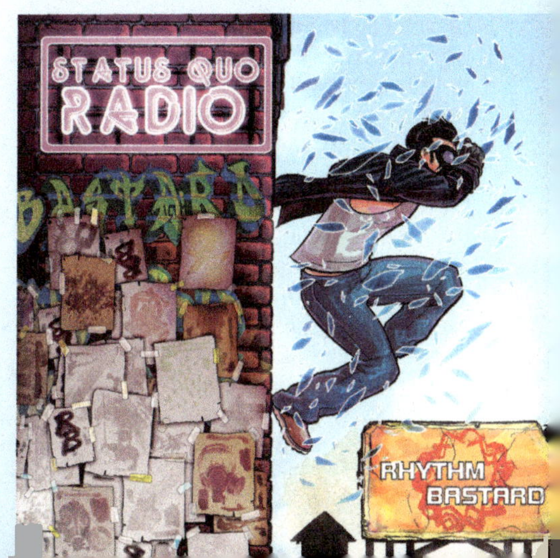

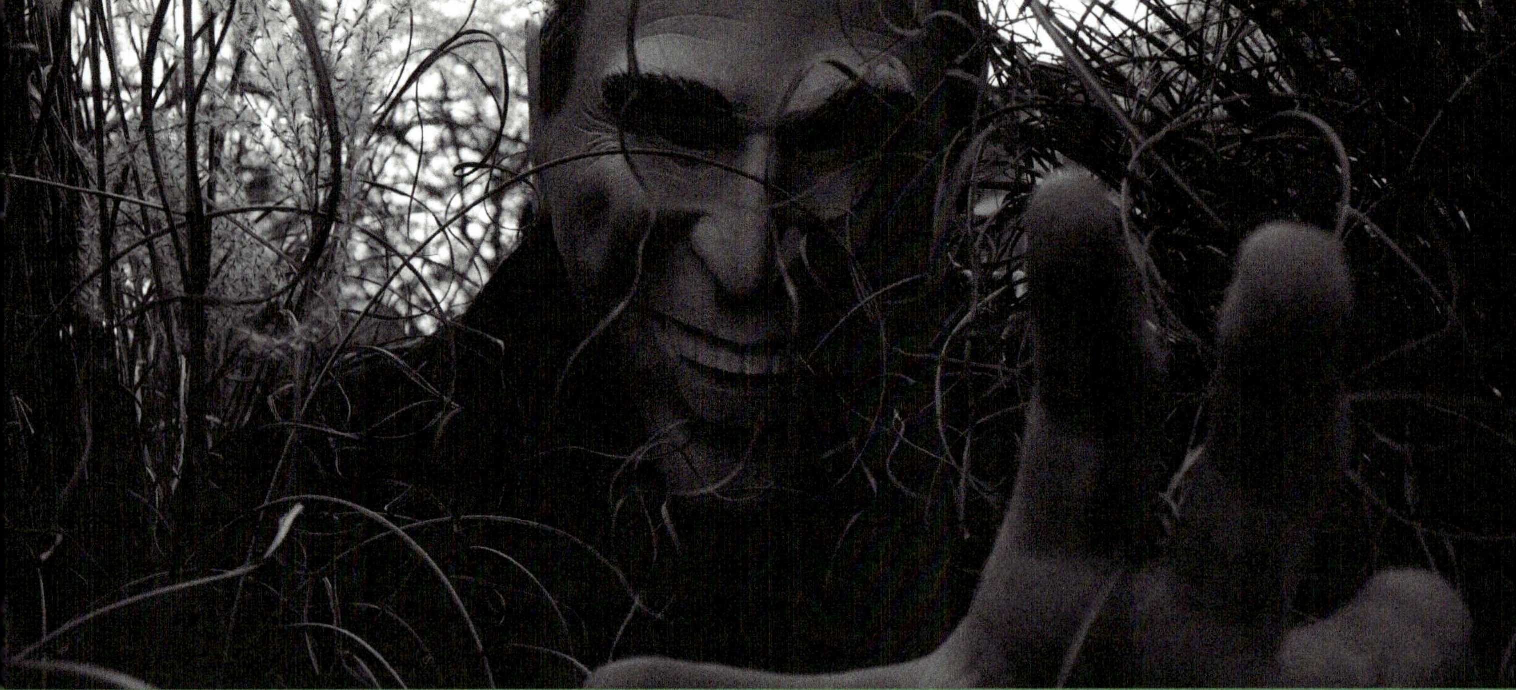

A PRIMER FOR ACTING IN LOW-BUDGET HORROR MOVIES

By River Gareth

"I'm shooting a horror movie. Do you want to be in it?" asks your buddy, Edgar Filmmaker, over a beer and a basket of chicken wings. You'd love to—fake blood and bendy knives turn you on—but the extent of your acting experience is lying to your parents about skipping school to write poetry in a graveyard.

What do you do? Put down the chicken wing (the camera really does add 10 pounds) and say "yes." Acting is a unique thrill you don't want to miss. It is the ultimate mind game. Think about it this way, when you act you are manipulating your brain/body into reacting to imaginary circumstances as if they were real. There are volumes written about the best way to make that happen, but here is a streamlined approach for acting in your first horror flick.

Let's say Edgar Filmmaker gives you a script with the following scenario and asks you to play Vicky: Vicky Victim and Temporary Todd arrive at a remote cabin in the woods for a romantic weekend. The happy couple unpacks and then heads outside to spend the remaining hour of daylight exploring the woods around the cabin. They find a creek and a playful water fight ensues. The sky starts to darken and the couple walks back to the cabin to change into dry clothes. Todd takes off his wet shirt and Vicky notices a hickey on his neck. She confronts him about it, and they get into a heated argument. Vicky accuses Todd of sleeping with Easy Emily. Todd storms out of the cabin. Vicky curls up on the couch with a paperback novel to wait for Todd. An hour goes by and Todd hasn't returned. It's pitch dark outside. Vicky is alone in the cabin, stranded in the middle of the woods. Vicky hears something strange outside and turns on all of the lights. She opens the front door and calls out to Todd. A window crashes at the back of the cabin. She turns around to find Serial Cyril standing in the middle of the living room with a knife. He lunges toward her. Vicky runs into the woods, and Cyril pursues her.

Most of the work an actor does is before the shoot. Start by carefully reading the script and answering these questions from Vicky's perspective: Who am I? Where am I? When is it? What am I doing? Why am I doing it? Use any clues you can pick out of the script about the type of person you are and your relationships with other people. Be as specific as you can and use your imagination to elaborate on the facts in the script. For example, the script is clear that you and Todd are a couple, and you elaborate on that simple fact by making the choice that you have been a couple for two years, you met at the Crüxshadows booth at Dragon*Con, you kissed him while you were drunk and dressed like slave Princess Leia, your first real date was at the Italian restaurant down the street from your apartment and he ordered the eggplant parmesan, the first time you made love was on a futon in his messy bedroom, and on and on. All of these details will add color to your relationship with Todd that will show up on screen.

Once you have the facts down, it's time to prepare yourself emotionally. Start by attaching feelings to the facts. What was your first kiss with Todd like? Close your eyes, picture the moment, and feel the sensation like you are remembering that kiss. What did he smell like? What was the texture of the back of his neck on your fingertips? How did your body respond? Were you worried that your breath smelled like cheap rum? Go through this process for the facts in your background that are most relevant to the circumstances in the script.

Be sure to develop background for every person and situation mentioned in the script. If you accuse Todd of sleeping with Emily, you need to prepare who she is and how you feel about her. How does it feel to think of Todd and Emily together? Are you jealous? Angry? Hurt?

With this background as your foundation, now it's time to prime your emotional pump for the panic and fear associated with being hunted in the dark woods by Cyril and his big shiny knife. The trick here is to combine a real, personal emotional trigger with the imaginary circumstances of the script. Close your eyes and pull up all of your fears of death, every potential that would go unfulfilled if you died in the woods. Imagine running between the trees and through the brush, doing everything you can to protect yourself and your future. Work with bringing these emotions up until the mere thought of Cyril's knife puts you on edge.

The stakes are already life or death in a horror movie such as this one, but you may want to consider raising the stakes even higher. For example, you could make the choice that you're pregnant and Todd is the father. You never disclose this fact, because it isn't written into the script, but it will add fuel to both your argument with Todd and your will to survive. You aren't just running to save your own life; you're also running to save the life of your unborn child.

The next step is memorizing your lines. Write your lines, word for word, on a separate sheet of paper and memorize them by rote. Don't pre-plan how you are going to deliver the lines, just memorize the actual words. You can say them aloud fast and flat or write them out by hand over and over again. Do whatever you need to do to get them in your head. You should know your lines so well that you can deliver them without thinking.

Okay, fast-forward. You're standing in the cabin's bathroom looking at the hickey on Todd's neck and Edgar Filmmaker yells, "ACTION." You feel nervous, your head is swimming, and you're questioning whether this acting thing was a good idea. Don't panic (not until you're getting chased through the woods, anyway). Make it your intention to slip into your character. Let go of all of your homework and just be Vicky, trusting that all of the factual and emotional background you created for her is alive inside you. Your choices will affect how she talks and how she moves, without you, the actor, having to think about it.

Now, connect with the other actor. Shift your focus from yourself to the actor playing Todd. Take him in—the look in his eye, the tension in his jaw, the way he is crossing his arms. His behavior will impact how you feel.

His defensiveness may make you angrier or it may make you want to comfort him. Work off his behavior and let it instinctually affect your reactions and how you deliver your lines.

All you have to do now is work truthfully moment to moment. Be sure not to push. "Pushing" or "overacting" are terms actors use to mean acting beyond where you are emotionally. For example, if you yell and scream at Todd because you, the actor, thinks that you should, but you aren't feeling anger in your gut, then it will sound forced and unnatural. Fake crying is another great example. Pretending to have emotions that you aren't actually experiencing doesn't come across well and your audience will know. When you see bad acting in films or on television, pushing is usually the culprit. Yeah, so don't do that.

Finally, after the shoot it is important to pull yourself out of the emotional muck. Sing the zip-a-dee-doo-dah song, think of fuzzy black kittens, call a loved one, do something to leave your character behind and rejoin your real life. Vicky will always be with you on some level, but don't get stuck in the darkness you dredged up to fuel the character.

While bad acting is one of the hallmarks of low-budget horror films (and can sometimes add entertainment value), the film will be scarier if the acting is good. The more believable the acting, the more realistic the nightmare will seem to the audience. The audience will fall into the imaginary circumstances of the film and experience your fear. That's your gift as an actor—you allow the audience to get lost in the present moment and, for a short time, trade all of the fear in their own lives for your fear on screen. You offer people relief and that is worth the effort. And, who knows, rock this one and maybe you'll get to be the next big Scream Queen.

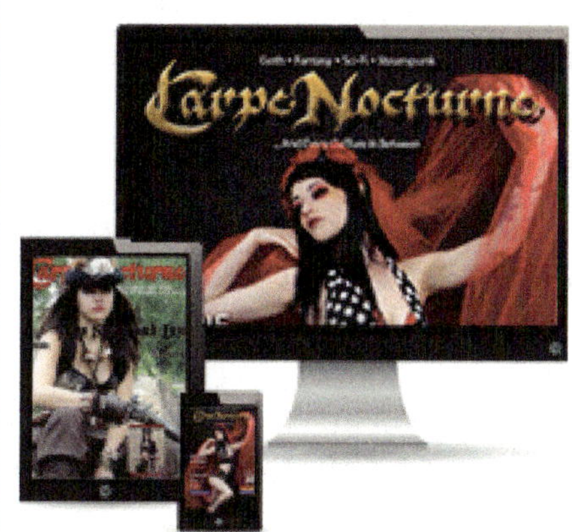

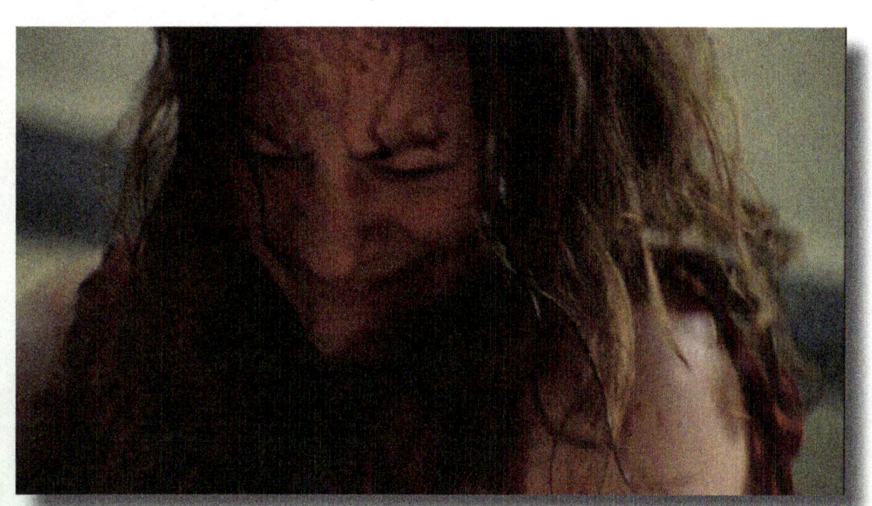

BLOODY MARVELOUS

By XXX Zombieboy XXX

Greetings and Salutations! As a lover of strange and exotic foods I, Zombie, shall write a little blurb for you in each issue of Carpe Nocturne regarding either a new Bloody Mary recipe, a bizarre cocktail, a strange food find, or perhaps all of the above!

The following can be altered or adjusted per personal taste but this is how you drink like a Zombie! And it just might make you one!

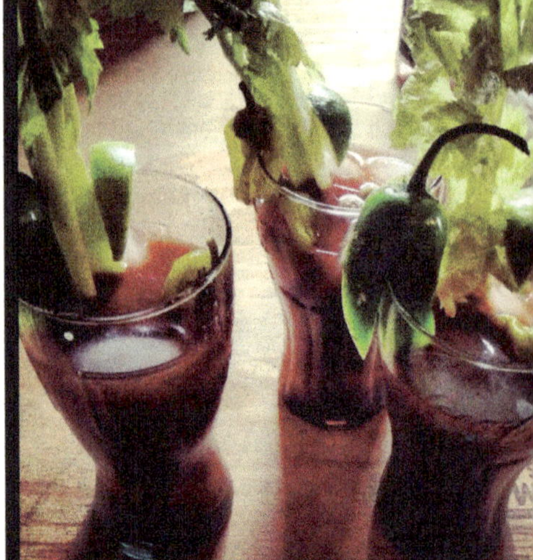

XXX ZOMBIEBOY'S SPICY MARYANNE XXX

• Light candles to honor the Aztec gods that invented tequila. I usually use Saint Candles available at most grocery stores. Use your own per taste.

• Procure a tall glass or even better a mason jar.

• Add two shots of Scorpion Mescal. Other brands I recommend for this are El Jimador, Don Julio, Black Death or any Mescal. Anejo is preferable.

• Begin grilling or frying foods to eat with this. Take the shot you just poured. Then refill the glass/jar. Continue!

• Add 1 shot of pickle juice.

• Add 1 shot of olive juice.

• Add three-six shots of Louisiana Hot Sauce.

• Add six shakes of Worcestershire Sauce.

• Add a tea spoon of horseradish.

• Stir vigorously with celery. Not with a spoon.

• Add pepper (about six shakes)

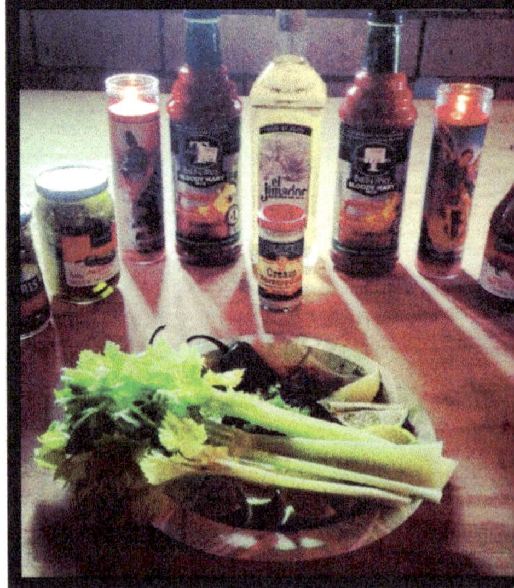

• Squeeze two slices of lemon and two slices of lime.

• Add three olives, one jalapeno and stir again.

• Pour in Mr. T's Bold and Spicy Bloody Mary Mix (The market is thick with many wonderful brands of mix. This is just my go to. Spicy V8 works well also).

• Stir once more.

• Add ice if preferred but only after all of the mixing is done.

• Garnish with sliced jalapeno, three olives, spice green beans, lime, spicy pickle, celery stick and bacon if on hand.

Note: for even greater flavor, add bacon to tequila/mazcal a week or more before using

• It is also nice to rim the glass with either sea salt or Cajun seasoning!

• Toast to the ancient Aztecs and to your own blood and then enjoy with the food you began preparing and some good friends. As a southern boy I can tell you this fiery concoction goes really well with a crawfish broil, a seafood get together, raw oysters and a great grilled steak! It is also a meal in itself!

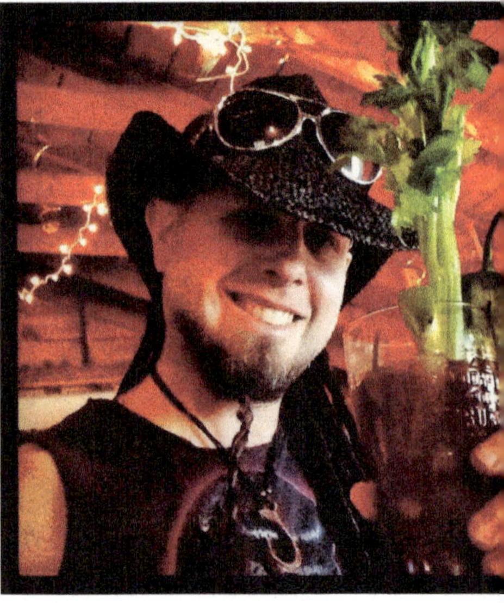

ENLIGHTENED TERROR:

A look at the best horror stories the Sci-Fi genre has to offer.

By Annabella Rios

My college literature professor used to say, "Horror is not a genre. Horror is an emotion." What he meant was that a literary genre deals with a story's subject matter, and that horror was the emotion authors hoped to invoke in their audiences as a result. Few genres have the potential to invoke fear as efficiently as science-fiction does. Writers have been fascinated with the potential social and existential consequences of scientific discovery since the beginning of the Enlightenment and the Age of Reason itself. For centuries we have been warned against unethical experimentation, reckless discovery, and separation from our spiritual selves. Plenty of shallow stories have attempted to create cheap and forgettable thrills from these themes for a quick wad of Hollywood cash. Here are the stories that actually endure, the masterworks of Sci-Fi-based fear.

Frankenstein: or, The Modern Prometheus

Don't let anyone tell you otherwise: Science-fiction was invented by a teenage girl. Although 19-year-old Mary Wollstonecraft Shelley had proto-predecessors in the forms of William Shakespeare, Jonathan Swift and even the philosophers of ancient Greece, she catapulted the gothic horror novel out of the supernatural and romanticized, paving the way for the modern science-fiction story.

Frankenstein deals primarily with the theme of man playing the role of God in creation. Victor Frankenstein learns harsh lessons as his reanimated creature is not the image of beauty and perfection he imagined it to be. The Creature has a will of it's own, and asserts his own personhood and right to a happy livelihood. To achieve this end, Frankenstein's monster will destroy everything Victor holds dear. The Creature rejects his creator, just as Victor had rejected his own, and both characters experience tremendous despair as a consequence.

Shelley inspired about a million film adaptations and a billion more stories dealing with similar themes. The concept of the "mad scientist" still persists in popular science-fiction, and any story dealing with the consequences of scientific experimentation has much to credit Mary Shelley with in it's success. Remember Frankenstein any time you encounter a zombie outbreak, or genetically manipulated monstrosities.

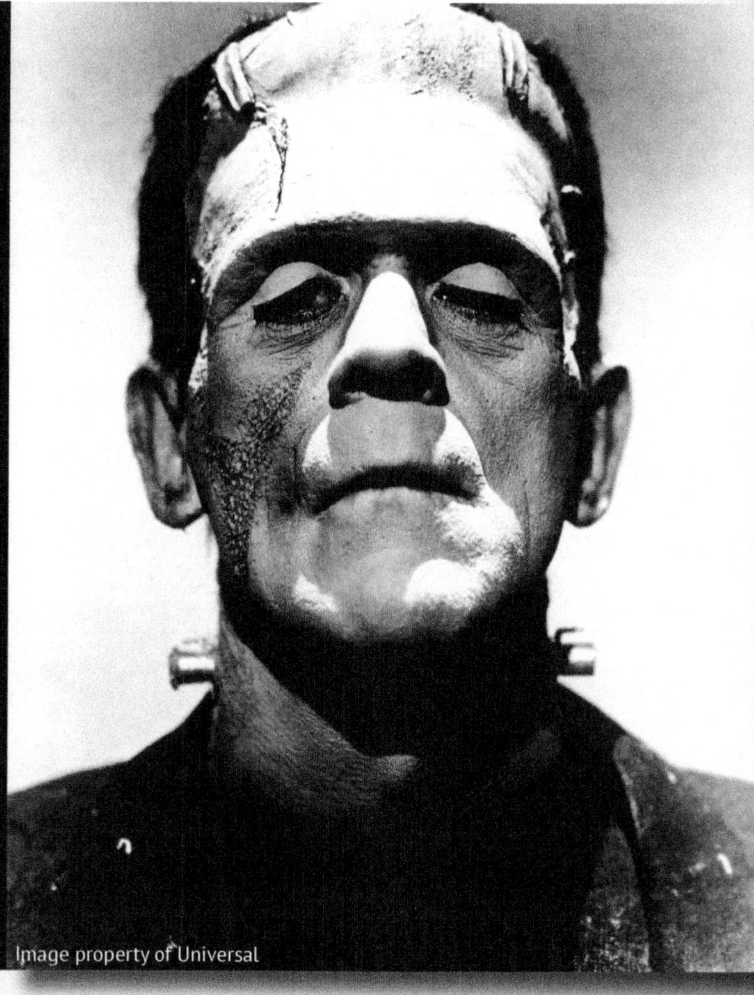

Image property of Universal

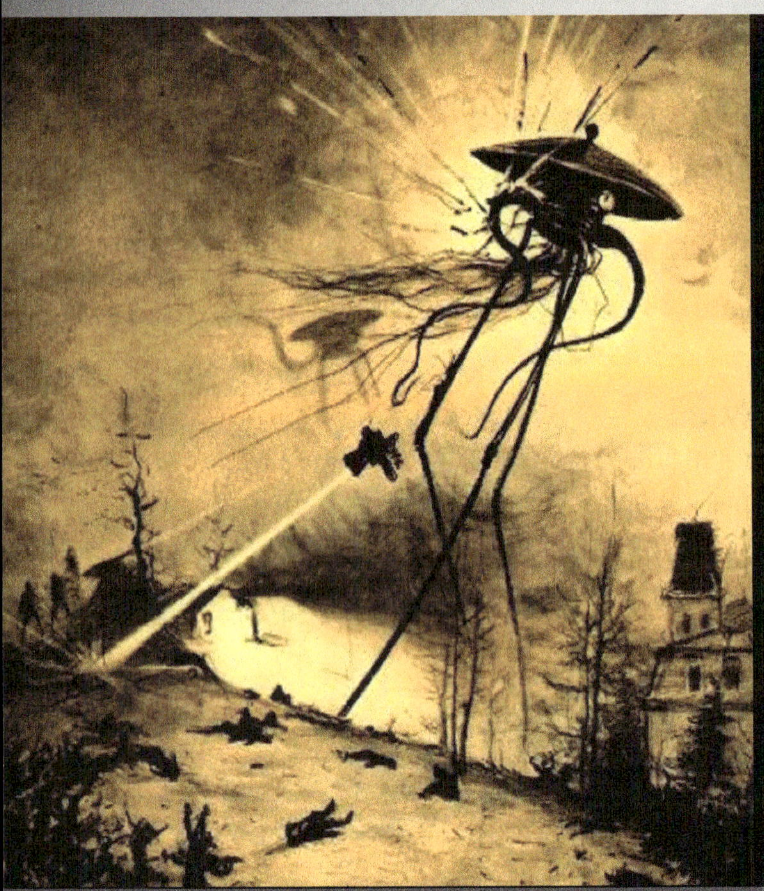

The War of the Worlds

H.G. Wells' alien invasion story may not seem to most people as a definitive Sci-Fi/Horror story, but that may be because we have become desensitized to the concept of the alien threat as a whole. For the past century since its initial publication, The War of the Worlds has served as a fictional vehicle for the various war-time insecurities that have plagued humanity's hearts in the modern era.

No adaptation of this story has illustrated this better than Orson Welles' 1938 radio broadcast of 1938. Presented as a series of simulated news bulletins, this particular adaptation incited mass panic in a mid-western American audience already reeling with the very real possibility of the Munich Crisis actually reaching their doors. Having missed the previously broadcasted disclaimers of the broadcast being fictional, listeners were convinced an invasion was actually happening.

The 1953 film adaptation of The War of the Worlds reflects it's radio-broadcasted predecessor in that it contains an overt undercurrent of Cold War-era trepidation and uncertainty. And although Steven Spielberg's 2005 remake has more of a disaster-film feel, there are a few noteworthy gems that truly do tap into the terror one might feel upon being harvested by merciless invaders. As a species we have come to repeatedly explore the possibility of our complete eradication in our art, and the feelings inspired by it will continue well into the next one-hundred or so years.

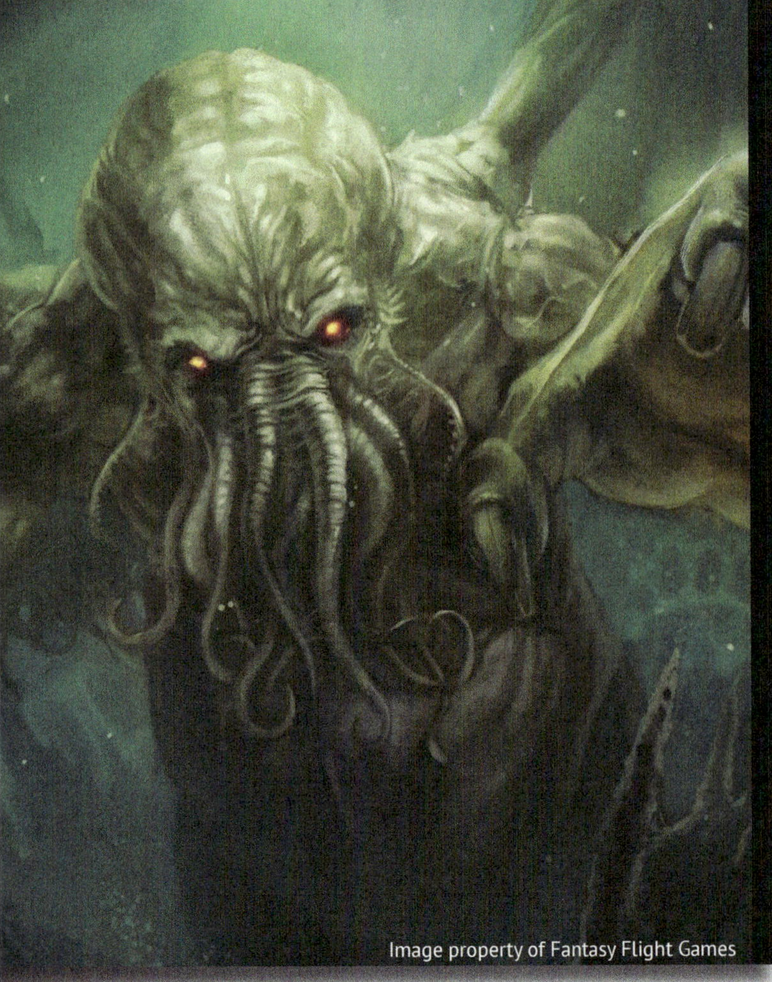

H.P. Lovecraft's Cthulhu Mythos

Some would argue that true horror comes from the realization of your own insignificance. There's something to be said about the existential crisis as a theme in literature. After all, the majority of humanity's cultural achievements stem from the very question of, "Why are we here?" To realize that the Universe doesn't have a reason, nor does it care to give you one flies in the face of everything human beings have ever thought of or accomplished in an attempt to bring meaning to our own existence. Concrete evidence of such a cruel reality might cause people to literally lose their minds. H.P. Lovecraft was all about making his readers go a little crazy.

A majority of his stories are part of a shared fictional universe; one where a pantheon of "Great Old Ones" from space slumber in wait to reclaim the Earth they once ruled. The civilizations built by these deities defy any convention for logical human thought or experience, and actually gazing upon these archaeological wonders often drives Lovecraft's characters into insanity they can never recover from.

Unfortunately, there are not many direct film adaptations of Lovecraft's stories. Many writers, directors and artists take inspiration from the Cthulhu mythos, especially in terms of creature and monster design. Any horror movie you've ever seen with some dreadful, tentacled mass owes it's concept mostly to Lovecraftian lore. It's a shame most of these works tend to go for either a comedic or action-oriented tone as opposed to an attempt at true horror, but here's hoping for a future where film audiences can finally experience existential terror.

Image property of Fantasy Flight Games

I Am Legend

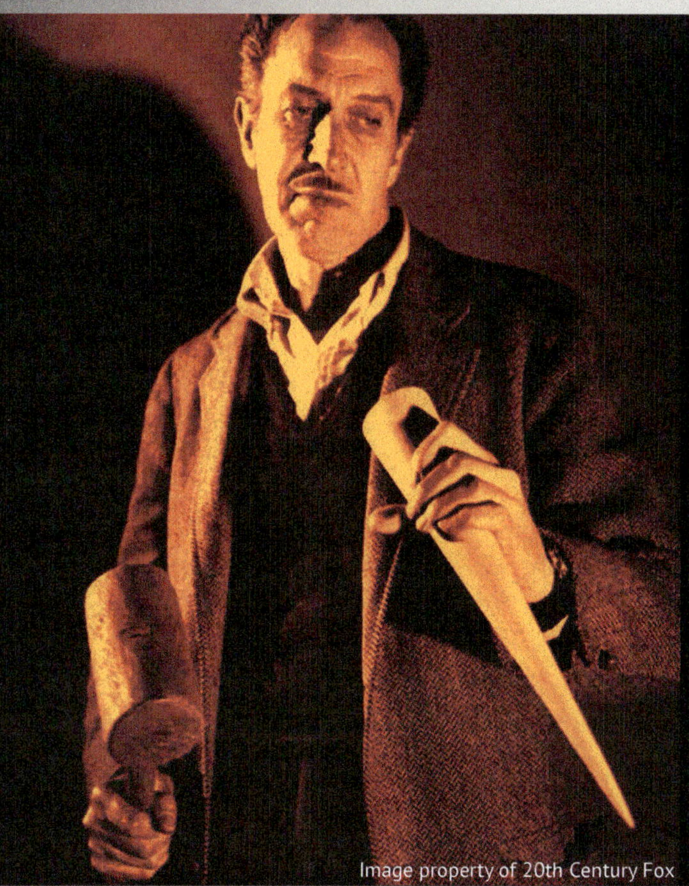
Image property of 20th Century Fox

Richard Matheson's 1954 novel pretty much gave birth to the zombie genre as we know it today, as it is the origin for the vampirism/zombification-due-to-disease trope, but the true horror behind I Am Legend lies not with the vampiric-horde that serves as the novel's primary antagonist but with the overlying theme of true isolation and desperation. Robert Neville drives himself nearly mad as the last surviving member of the human race. As inherently social creatures, human beings strive to avoid dying alone and in the dark, and as such, I Am Legend touches upon our most basic and primal fears.

There is also the idea of humanity becoming obsolete as a species, and for a reason you might not expect. I Am Legend achieves a unique revelation for the reader that I don't wish to spoil for the unaware. Of the three film adaptations, only the 1964 Vincent Price-classic The Last Man On Earth attempts to remain true to the novel's original ending. Charlton Heston and Will Smith, unfortunately, fall into the trap of starring in typical zombie outbreak movies which lack the depth of the novel they took inspiration from.

Alien

I would almost go out of my way to say that Alien is the definitive Sci-Fi/Horror experience, and the best horror story on this list. Ridley Scott managed to present not only a genre-defining narrative of predator vs. prey, but also change the way horror movies were filmed up until today. Alien is a perfect example of how to do a horror movie the right way, and although many horror films today neglect to emulate Alien's example, there is something to do be said about Scott's technique of making the audience fear what they do not actually see.

The film is an inherently psychological experience, and it shows in the monster designs by the late H.R. Giger. By referencing sexual organs in the biomechanical designs of the various creatures, Giger was able to invoke the subconscious human fear of sexual assault and violation in addition to the more overt fears that come from being hunted by an unknown foe.

Ridley Scott's film spawned several sequels, a prequel, as well as books, comics and video game crossovers with the contemporary Predator franchise. Unfortunately, none of Alien's sequels were quite able to match the profound tone of the first film, often opting for an action-movie feeling over horror. It goes to show successful Alien was at invoking the emotion of fear; 20th Century Fox has spent the past thirty-six years since it's release helping it's audiences feel more in control of such a terrifying and helpless situation.

Image property of 20th Century Fox

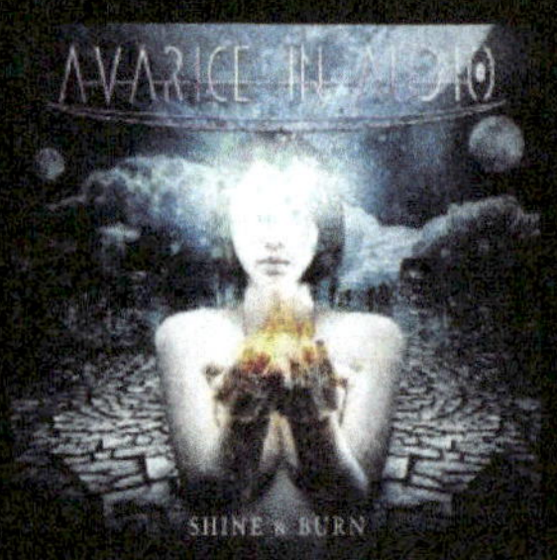

AVARICE IN AUDIO
Shine & Burn

By Asylum Attendant

The angelic, operatic vocals of Jade Pegg collide with the aggressive growls of Gerry Hawkins to create dark synthpop that will leave you in a trance. Avarice in Audio's Shine & Burn glows like the ethereal night sky, then burns like wildfire.

The lead single "Frostbite" is conceptual in both lyrics and instrumentation. Frosty synths dance among beautiful descriptions of tundra winds and glaciers. Jade's amazing vocal range is almost hypnotic strewn against the pulsing beats. "China White" has a clear traditional Asian influence, and the prominent screams of Gerry are reminiscent of Daniel Graves from Aesthetic Perfection.

The duo team up on the songs "Lacklustre" and "The Cassandra Complex", blending their contrasting vocals into haunting EDM soundscapes. Jade's glass shattering siren calls cannot be duplicated.

"Behind Your Mask" opens with what sound like Gregorian chants and is a switch into slower electronica. The track is a collaboration with electronic rock band MiXE1, featuring a moodier, more atmospheric feel. The swift "Bleed as One" rolls into a distorted vocal dupstep breakdown that blurs genre lines.

The lyrical complexity of Shine & Burn propels the listener on an electronic odyssey of transcendence. Before you take a listen, make sure you know your way back to reality.

JUNKSISTA
High Voltage Confessions

By Asylum Attendant

Simultaneously making me dance and laugh out loud, Junksista's newest album, entitled High Voltage Confessions, is jam packed with dirty punch lines, groovy guitars, imaginative synths and sultry spoken vocals. Panties are optional.

The big fat bass of the opening track, "Get a Grip," displays the raunchy lyrics and cool dance beats that Junksista is known for. Funky guitar riffs and the soulful vocals of Jane Badler on "Live a Little" reveal the diversity of the tracks on High Voltage Confessions. The unexpected synth addition in the bridge keeps the sound freshly retro.

"I Hate You" is a vindictive song with fast, driving synths. Junksista's humor comes out strong as lyrical revenge comes in the form of hiding a TV remote. "Sex on a Stick" is about irresistible polar opposites. It's sexy, but in a gentle, almost sweet way. Dark, heavy synths and double meaning lyrics about feeding the cat...that's "True Love" for you.

What can be said about the hip hop track "P.I.T.T." (Punch In The Twat)? It's certainly the most hardcore song on the album, and the fan vocal participation is ironic considering the snooty fun vibe of the track. Songs like "Confide" and "Happiness" demonstrate the deeper, more emotional side of Junksista. And then there's "Panties" to remind everyone through lesbian crushes and Iron Maiden shirts that this band doesn't take itself too seriously.

All in all, High Voltage Confessions is fiercely silly, and will have you boldly confessing your sexual desires on the dirty dance floor.

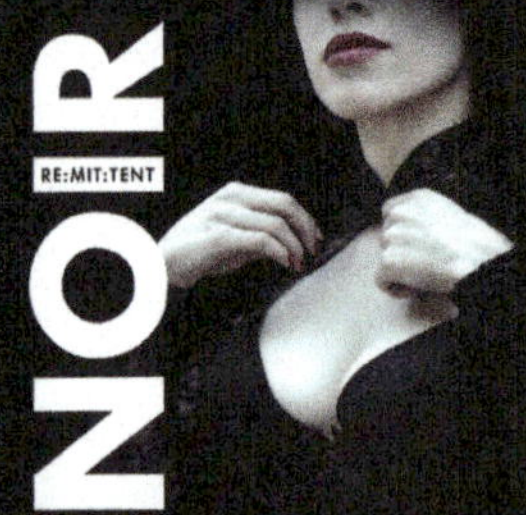

NOIR
Remittent

By Asylum Attendant

Remittent, the new album from the dark electronic project NOIR, is chock full of danceable remixes of songs from the group's 2013 release, Darkly Near. Lots of genres are covered, from ambient to EBM to industrial. The album is certainly not repetitive with electronic acts such as Assemblage 23, Ego Likeness and more adding their touch to NOIR's decadent tracks. There's even a ManMadeMan remix of NOIR's cover of The Cure classic, "A Forest".

NOIR features Athan Maroulis of the industrial group Spahn Ranch and the dark cabaret band Black Tape for a Blue Girl. The sound of the project is both futuristic and retro, similar to a silent black and white film come to life with moody soundscapes. Athan uses his extensive musical expertise to create melancholic electronica that captures his enticing vocals. Athan's inclusion of his love of New York City and jazz and blues music is the perfect touch to his gothic synthpop.

The eclectic essence of NOIR is not lost on Remittent. The rapid Anti-Mechanism remix of "Timephase" throws Athan's brooding vocals alongside a club ready industrial beat. The dark ambience of the Metrognome vs. Falcotronik remix of "The Voyeurs" has a sound similar to Aphex Twin.

Throughout the album, listeners can dance like Rivetheads, meditate into a trance state or transport themselves into a large city at nighttime. The album could be a soundtrack to The Twilight Zone television series or any number of mysterious silent films from the past or future. All in all, Remittent leaves one longing for a foggy night atop a Manhattan high-rise with a stiff drink in hand.

MANKIND IS OBSOLETE Mobius Loop

by Michael Jack

One of the things I love about Mankind is Obsolete is you can never be quite sure what you are going to get when you listen to one of their albums. There is so much variety in their music, drifting between Rock, Metal, Punk, Pop, Industrial, and many different combinations of the aforementioned genres. MKIO can punch you in the face with power chords and scratchy vocals, or sing you a lullaby about hopelessness and despair, accompanied by only a piano. "Mobius Loop," the band's third full length CD, maintained the tradition of not fitting into one single genre. What amazes me about Mankind is Obsolete, is they do everything well. There is not a single song on "Mobius Loop," no matter how different it is, that I do not like or downright love.

The CD begins with the heavier synth song "On Fire Again," and it is one of my favorite tracks on the album. This song is slightly more Rock than Pop, and very upbeat. The second song, "Lock and Key," mixes up their sound completely, and throws you straight back into the 80's Punk era. This song is fast, drum heavy, and gritty. Now I feel like I am starting to experience the eclectic style that is MKIO. The third track is by far my favorite on the entire CD, and in my opinion, one of the best songs the band has written to date. It is titled "Lucifer's Song." It's a slow driving rock song with an aggressive chorus, and set in to an overall haunting tone. Love is the word I would best use to describe it. Even my nine year old son walks around the house singing, "Too long in silence."

There are many songs that stand out on "Mobius Loop." "Shadow Man," is definitely more Electro-Industrial, and fantastic. "Garden of Eden" reminds me of something I might hear on a Siouxsie record. "Empty" closes out the album, and it is one of those great melancholy slow songs I love from Mankind is Obsolete. Overall, "Mobius Loop" is a great CD. If you have liked anything by MKIO in the past,

you will certainly find at least several songs you enjoy on this album. My guess is you will be like me, and love the whole thing.

FRACTURED FAIRYTALES
Egregore

by Michael Jack

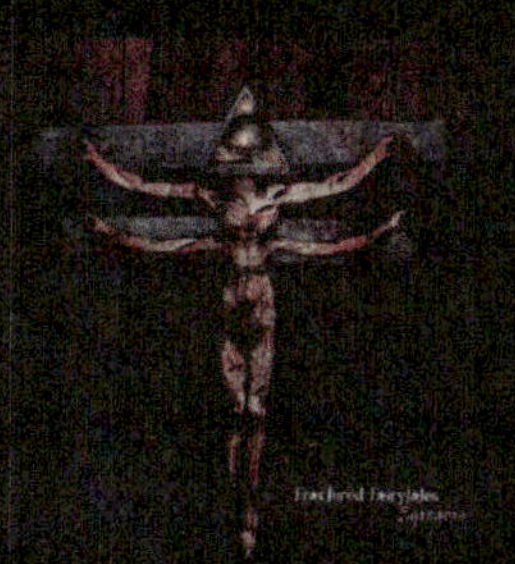

There are many bands that claim to be Industrial-Metal, but few capture the sound so completely and so perfectly as Fractured Fairytales. Their new release, "Egregore," is the band's third full-length CD, and a masterful addition to a growing discography aimed at smashing your senses. This CD is more than just death metal on steroids. It assaults with you with ripping vocals over a barrage of double bass drums, then switches to the more melodic fused with haunting synths. If I could describe "Egregore" simply, it would be what you might expect if Pantera, Rob Zombie, and Trent Reznor ever collaborated on an album.

From the first track, "Placebo Salvation," Egregore hooks you in. The song begins with a simple organ, adds industrial beats, and then escalates to all out warfare. This tempo is continued throughout the CD, until the final track, "No Time for Time," throws you into the dirt and buries you. This final song reminds me of the time I was locked in a psychotic amusement park, or was that just the nightmare brought on by "Egregore?" For me, the best tracks on the album are "Dear Human" and "Trickery," but I'm sure everyone will find their own favorites. With thirteen songs, there is an assortment of apocalyptic fun to choose from. The other track that really stood out to me on "Egregore" was "Dark Prayer for a Dying Dream," because it is for the most instrumental. To describe the song you only need to look back at the title. It's appropriately named.

Fractured Fairytales is not your typical doom driven, guitar-blasting, in your face metal acts. They can do that, and they prove it on their single "Null and Void," but there is so much more depth and complexity to their music. Just listen to the industrial sounds. It is amazing how well it is fused with the drums and guitars, that it almost becomes one complete sound. I love the horror themed synths. When they play, generally the music slows, and it gives the listener a second to catch their breath... if they aren't holding it. The vocals are amazing, and vary between guttural chaos and nightmarish bliss. If you have not heard Fractured Fairytales before, I highly suggest you do. My guess is it won't be long before you are buying "Egregore."

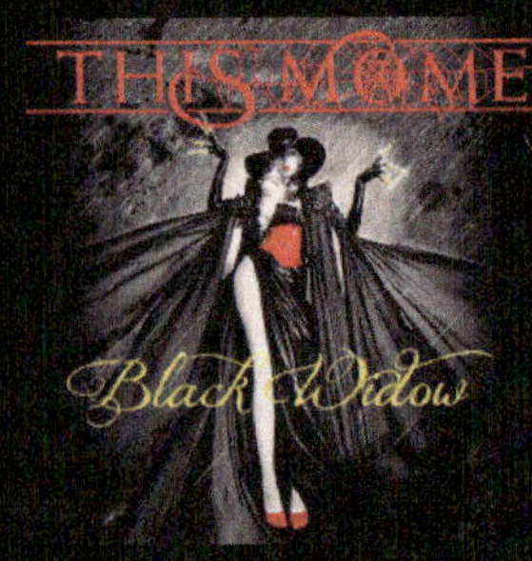

IN THIS MOMENT
Black Widow

by Michael Jack

In This Moment is back, and they have unleashed their new CD "Black Widow" on the masses. This CD is more in your face than anything they have previously recorded. The songs hit hard with strong sexual tones and lyrics geared towards female empowerment. For the skeptics who think women can't front Metal bands, Maria Brink is proof they can. The first track after the intro, "Sex Metal Barbie," speaks out to the naysayers, the critics, and everyone who has tried to discredit her talent and image. This song sets the tone for the entire CD.

"Black Widow" comes across as more than a straight forward Metal album. I would almost label it experimental Metal, as the band fuses funk into songs like "Bloody Creature Poster Girl," "Dirty Pretty," and "Big Bad Wolf." The latter song, with the addition of Maria rapping, reminds me of the classic song, "Epic" by Faith No More, but way more intense. It is one of the best tracks on the entire album, and the band's second single. Their first single, "Sick Like Me," is exactly what you would expect from In This Moment… powerful driven verses followed by melodic choruses. It just works for them.

This CD is not without those amazing power ballads we have come to expect from In This Moment. They do it better than any Metal band out there today, in my opinion. The first slowed tempo song we are introduced to on "Black Widow" is actually a duet with Shinedown's Brent Smith. The song is called "Sexual Hallucination," and let me tell you…I can only hope this pair teams up again. Brent and Maria blend perfectly together, and hold your complete attention. You have to listen even if you don't want to. It's that captivating. "The Fighter" is another great ballad on "Black Widow," but my favorite is the last song on the CD. Running at a length of just over six and a half minutes, "Out of Hell" is very down tempo. Maria, accompanied by only a piano, delivers the most heart-wrenching, depressing story in a song I have heard in a while. It's sadly beautiful.

Overall, I love this CD. "Black Widow" not only gave me what I would expect from In This Moment, but everything I didn't as well. I like how they were not afraid to play with their sound, and it worked. There was a natural progression to this album, and accompanied with several short intros, gave me a definite feeling I was taking a journey. That journey began with the "Sex Metal Barbie," and in the end, led me "Out of Hell." It might be difficult for In This Moment to top "Black Widow," but I am sure looking forward to them trying. For now, I'll just enjoy this masterpiece they have put together.

SENTINEL OF ETERNITY
Sentinel of Eternity

by Michael Jack

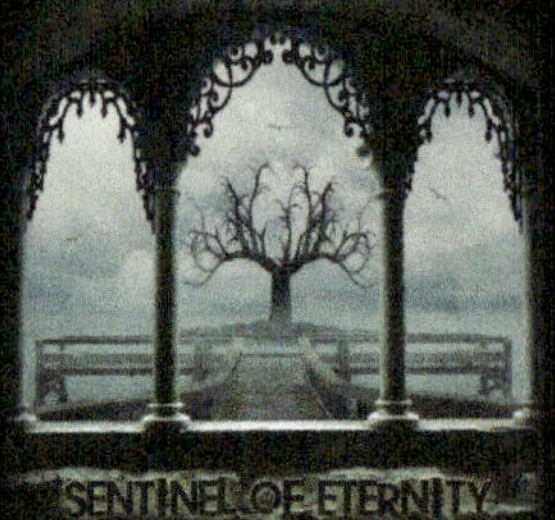

The self-titled debut album by Sentinel of Eternity is a masterful creation of audible imagery from composer Stephane Marty. With dance-able beats, darker themes, and pure electronic sounds, this CD is certain to become a favorite among club goers everywhere. Add the intelligent and mesmerizing vocals of Braindance frontman Sebastian Elliot, and the visual creativity and vocals of French artist Salandre, Sentinel of Eternity becomes a CD rich in depth and layered with emotion.

For me, Sentinel of Eternity is truly a tale of two albums in one. The first half of the CD gives off the aforementioned dance club vibe. It begins with the electronic instrumental song "Cyberia," follows it with club-esque "Surrender," where you are first introduced to the powerful voice of Sebastian Elliot, and then goes into the project's first release, "Mandragore." This track is arguably the best song on the entire CD, and combines the voices of Sebastian and Salandre, woven against a black shroud of dance floor intrigue. "Desire," the next track on the CD, is the only song on Sentinel of Eternity that features only the voice of Salandre. With spoken verses and melodic choruses, this track easily slides into my second favorite on the album. "Monolith," another great instrumental club track, rounds out for me what I consider to be the first half of the album.

Beginning with the song "The Exchange," the tempo is slowed, and the self-titled album begins to take on a more atmospheric soundscape. There are still those aggressive beats, but natural sounds are introduced, organs tend to take over the pure synthetic sounds, and the emotions sway from necessary movement to haunting darkness. I think the two best songs on the second half of this CD are "The Sentinel" and "Something in the Wind." "The Sentinel" is an amazing blend of tribal beats and eerie cathedral music that breaks into EBM half way through. I love it. "Something in the Wind" is the most down tempo song on the CD, feels a little more ethereal, and Sebastian's vocals really shine in his unique dramatic delivery.

Sentinel of Eternity is one of the best new projects I have had the pleasure of listening to in a long time. Stephane Marty is brilliant, and I can not wait to see the evolution of his talents. This album should be spun in Goth and Industrial clubs everywhere, and I will be shocked if it isn't.

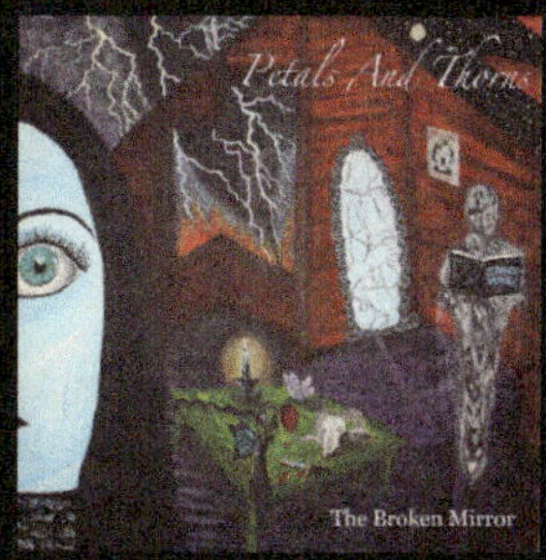

PETALS AND THORNS
The Broken Mirror

by Michael Jack

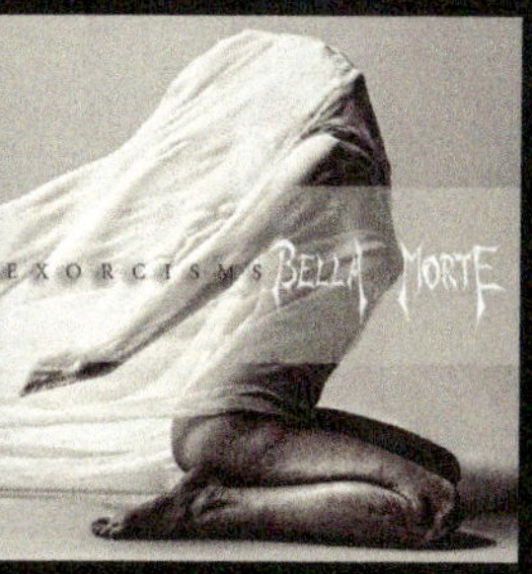

BELLA MORTE
"Exorcisms"

by Sergio Manghina

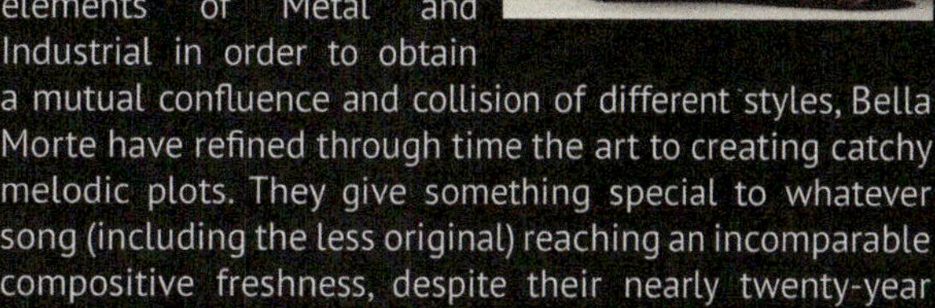

"The Broken Mirror" is the debut album from Cleveland based duo Petals and Thorns. The CD is eight tracks of metal meets chilling ambiance, with just a touch of Goth-Cabaret thrown in. The closest I can compare Petals and Thorns to is Darling Violetta meets Sirenia, although some might disagree. This album was self-produced, self-promoted, and shines brightly at times. I listen to a lot of bands and a lot of CDs, and my assessment of Petals and Thorns is they have the potential to be a major player in the underground scene.

Musically, I loved "The Broken Mirror." Johnny Thorns does an amazing job of blending aggressive guitars with haunting pianos, and tying both together with irregular drum beats. The atmosphere created by this CD is eerie, sinister, and tension building. "The Broken Mirror" would make an incredible soundtrack for a horror movie, or at the very least, the perfect accompaniment to your next Halloween party. This album builds a dark ambiance that is easy to get lost in.

The vocals, for me, gave me mixed feelings. Mia Petals has a good voice, and at times, raises the hair on the back of your neck with haunting ethereal vocals. The song "Lift the Veil" is a good example of this. There are other times when she pushes too hard to do something special with her voice, particularly when sustaining her higher range for longs periods of time. It just doesn't work for me, and at times, comes off a bit campy. The song "Endless Abandon" is this way for me. I think Mia has the potential to be every bit as good as Karin of Collide, for her style is similar. She just needs to let her natural voice shine.

Overall, I like "The Broken Mirror," and the more I listened, the more I liked it. The CD definitely grows on you. The song "Method to the Madness" deserves immediately play in clubs and radio stations everywhere. I would love to see the song "This Wilting Rose" redone with slightly different vocals, because it can be phenomenal, and is the track that would put this band on the map. If I could fast forward a few years, I am willing to bet I am reviewing Petals and Thorns' third full-length CD and absolutely loving it. Mia and Johnny have talent, and they are only scratching the surface of what they can do.

Crossing borders from Darkwave to Synthpop to Death Rock, also incorporating elements of Metal and Industrial in order to obtain a mutual confluence and collision of different styles, Bella Morte have refined through time the art to creating catchy melodic plots. They give something special to whatever song (including the less original) reaching an incomparable compositive freshness, despite their nearly twenty-year career.

This new album represents a further step to an accomplished dimension of goth-tinged synthpop, sometimes more ballad-oriented and with a notable retrieval of a certain '80s dark allure.

The opening title track, is seducing and solemn like an anthem, with moderate metal guitars and great synths, while their cover of Depeche Mode's "Never Let Me Down Again" is dazzling.. This is a great start for this work which continues with a formidable sequence of tunes. The interlocutory ballad "As Fire" is in fact the prologue to a superb poker of aces, songs that perfectly blend together melancholy, passion and strength such as "Watching The Sky", "Water Through Sand", "Reflections", "The Dark", connecting the dots between powerful intros and melodies characterized by a brilliant harmonic sense.

After the intense acustic sound of "Tired" the heavy guitars of "A quiet place to die" push the gas pedal closer to the floor, toward a more classic hard rock territory, bridgehead to the final track, "Entwined", the most shadowy and evocative piece in the bunch, showing a great performance of the charismatc leader Andy Deane, dominant voice on an album mostly made up of relevant vocal parts.as well as impeccable arrangements.
Exorcisms is, with no doubt, one of the brighter products originated from the current Goth scene.

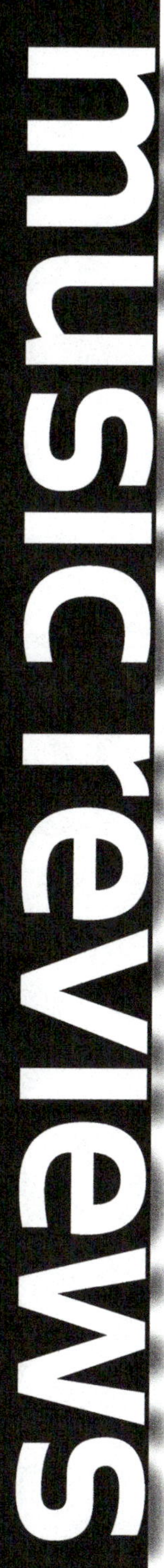

Aliens: Inhuman Condition
Author/Illustrator: Sam Kieth
Publisher: Dark Horse Comics
Released: April 2013

by Mark Hickman

Inhuman Conditions is a graphic novella set within the expanded universe of the Aliens franchise. Personally, I have mixed feelings about this book. On one hand, I enjoyed the overall story but on the other, I wasn't a very big fan of the art.

I found that the art was the weakest aspect of the work. I'm not a fan of the artist style utilized by Kieth, and it can often look rather silly. Specifically, whenever a person smiles, it looks off-putting and unrealistic. Additionally, I wasn't a fan of the illustrator's decision to leave eyes off the androids in this series. However, the aliens themselves were far more engaging from an artist's standpoint.

Alternatively, the story we are given in Inhuman Condition is an interesting one. I enjoyed the heady themes, especially the exploration of the concept that humanity has become a more savage species than the aliens. Inhuman Condition approaches this concept by pointing out that unlike humans, the aliens don't turn on one another. I also enjoyed the idea that perhaps the main character may have gone insane due to her past traumatic experiences with the aliens. The only plot hole that I would have liked to see explored further would have been information on how she survived for so long.

In closing, Inhuman Condition is more the kind of comic that would appeal to serious fans of the Aliens franchise. It's not the best graphic novel I've ever read, but it's certainly not the worst.

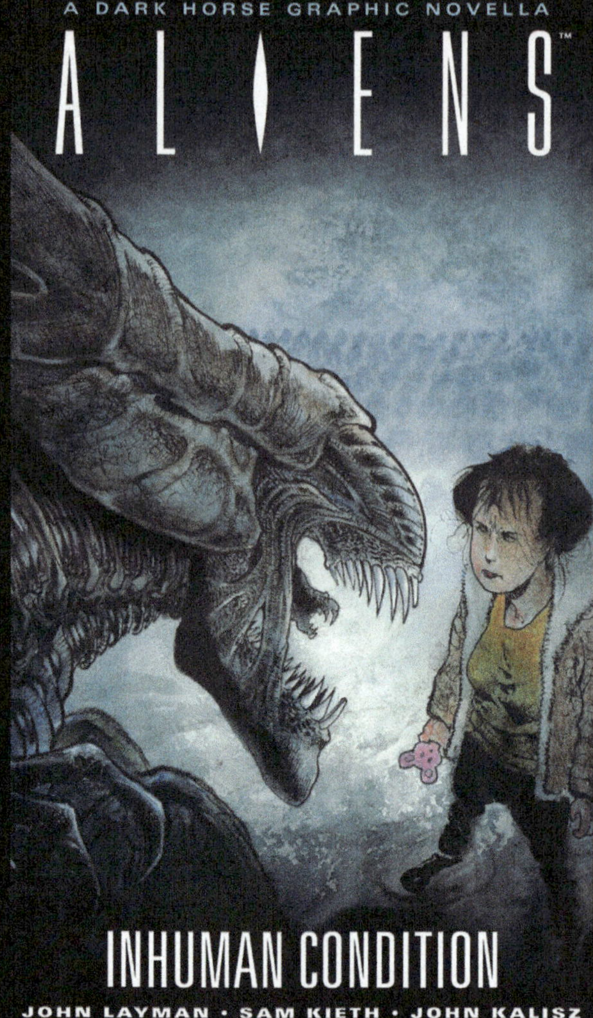

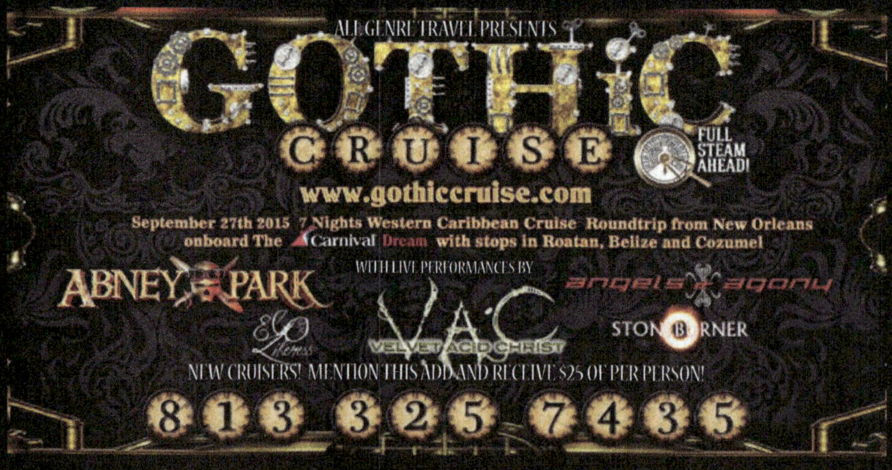

The Crow: The Beauty of the Original, the Misery of the Sequels

by LinnieSarah Helpern (@linnieloowho)

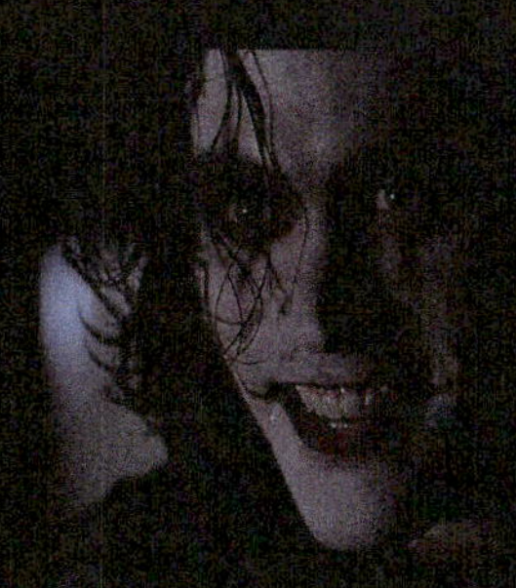

If you're of a certain age, and lived a certain lifestyle (specifically born in the early in the early 80s and maybe fancied yourself a bit of a goth kid), there is a decent chance that Alex Proyas' The Crow (1994) means just about everything to you. Proyas did a gorgeous job bringing James O'Barr's comic series of supernatural revenge to the screen, but as you likely know, The Crow has come to symbolize something so much more to fans. The death of actor Brandon Lee, son of martial arts legend Bruce Lee, due to an on-set accident has come to set The Crow apart as a film that exists as much as a eulogy as it is a reminder of all that Brandon Lee could have been.

More than a film anchored by a beautiful performance from Lee, and a fabulous supporting cast including Tony Todd and Michael Wincott, The Crow is a reminder of a time when gothic culture, and the supernatural, were so much more the norm. We can look back at the original Crow film as a time capsule of an era when alternative culture was more widely accepted that it is even now. Regardless of the mythos, The Crow would have, and still has, scores of dedicated fans that loved it for its style, its theme, and its star. Yet, when Lee died on set, The Crow became part of Hollywood mythology, and as the studio system can't help itself from doing, it began clamoring for sequels to a phenomenon that could never (and would never) be re-created.

The Crow: City of Angels came just two years later, with an entirely new character out for revenge, and an entirely new "Crow." The mythology of the original stories was kept, but Brandon Lee was replaced with Vincent Perez, who may have had some of the physicality of Lee but absolutely none of his charisma. City of Angels was atrocious, from beginning to end. A cast of villains including Iggy Pop and an unrecognizable Thomas Jane (who dies while servicing himself in a peep show booth), turned this sequel into more of an unintentional comedy than a supernatural horror film. Even the story anchoring the film is ridiculous, as Perez's Ashe Corven is seeking revenge for the death of his son and himself when his son ran toward gunshots to investigate instead of away from them and got them both killed. Every minute of this film is torture, but there was at least the promise future sequels to The Crow couldn't get much worse.

Boy, was that a mistaken assumption. More on that later though.

Next came The Crow: Salvation in 2000, starring Eric Mabius as Alex Corvis, aka Crow #3. I just assumed Mabius would be the worst possible casting choice for a role like this, given his extensive background in Hallmark movies and Ugly Betty. But Salvation turned out to be the least offensive of the Crow sequels. If you had completely removed the Crow mythology from the story and started it from scratch as its own film, it might not have been terrible. Salvation had a fabulous cast of horror veterans and soon-to-be stars, including Dale Midkiff (Pet Sematary), Walton Goggins (Justified), Fred Ward (Tremors), and William Atherton (the asshole in every 80s movie you love). The story was solid and interesting, and you get to watch Kirsten Dunst get her mouth sewn shut. If you're anything like me, that's a huge plus. The Crow: Salvation is still an entirely unnecessary sequel to a borderline perfect film, but it is by leaps and bounds the ONLY one you should watch if you feel the morbid desire to watch one of these movies.

And then it became clear they saved the worst for last. The Crow: Wicked Prayer starred Edward Furlong as Jimmy Cuervo (it hurts)/The Crow and... Tara Reid. And uh, Tito Ortiz. I don't even know where to begin with how hilariously awful this final (HOPEFULLY) Crow sequel is, that I suppose I will just start with the plot. Based LOOSELY in Aztec mythology, Jimmy Cuervo is in love with a Mexican girl, but a Satanist gang leader played by David Boreanaz and named Luc Crash (seriously, I'm getting a migraine) isn't down with that for some inexplicable reason, so he and his girlfriend Lola, played by a typically confused Tara Reid, kill Cuervo and his girlfriend so Luc can be the devil? Within twenty minutes, I had NO idea what was going on, Danny Trejo showed up with a shotgun, Dennis Hopper came out of nowhere talking like Tupac, and Macy Gray was cast... to make Tara Reid look focused and grounded I suppose? It all felt awkward and tremendously offensive and Furlong as The Crow looked more like Helena Bonham Carter as Mrs. Lovett in Sweeney Todd. All I can do is suggest that if one of your friends says they want to watch The Crow: Wicked Prayer, you gather your things, leave the house, and start looking for a new friend immediately.

There has been word buzzing for years that a reboot to the original The Crow is in development, but with every step forward that makes, it seems to take two backwards. So we can all only hope that it remains where it belongs: in development purgatory, next to the Gremlins reboot and the Suspiria remake.

CLOCKWORK KNOTWORK

DANIEL O'RYAN AKA. DR. O., TONYA DEN NORSE AND LEON CECILI MARTINE.

First, let me introduce myself. I am Daniel O'Ryan, currently known as Dr. O. I was born in Kilkenny, Ireland in the late 1400s, not quite sure of the exact date. I was very young then. I grew up around a lot of music and a warm house. My father would take me to the pub with him when I was a young boy and it was there that I learn to play many different instruments. Winds, strings and percussions were my favorites. However, one day a set of bagpipes were brought into town and the owner took me under his wing and I learned them very quickly. A couple years later, there was a package waiting for me at the pub. I opened it and there was my own set of pipes! A gift from the man I learned from. By this time, I was around 13 years old and decided to travel all over my country. I had many fine adventures over the next few decades.

In 1535, I landed in Liverpool, England to see the Island of Britain. I ran across some other traveling musicians just outside of Oxford. We met in an abandon field where once a great battle took place. We hit it off so well that we decided to take the music into town. I said, "This is some great Craic!" and thus we called the band, The CRAIC Show!

We performed all over Britain and gained much popularity! OK, this is where it gets a bit weird and I'll give you the short version. The year was 1541 and we were going to perform in a new town. When out of the blue, marauders came and attacked! Most everyone was killed and my whole band slaughtered. In the aftermath, I sat alone in shock when I was approached by a group of men in robes. They called themselves 'The Immortals' and they bestowed on me the gift of extremely long life. I then spent the next 340 years studying Horology, (the study of time). On the winter Solstice of 1881, I went back in time to the night before the CRAIC Show was attacked. I appeared as a spirit to my band and told them of the coming horror. They heeded my warning and met up with the Immortals the next day and they were also given the gift of long life. They then had to live out the 340 years in a parallel reality. We were then reunited in 1881 near Oxford England on the same night I had gone back in time.

It was the clockwork of the universe and the knotwork of the stars that brought The CRAIC Show of old back together. Therefore, we shall henceforth, be known as Clockwork Knotwork. We shall play the music of the New Era, that of Elysium and bring about peace to the world. Our music is of never ending origins, it is of the Deep Magic. When one listens to it, they gain a better quality of life, immortality in small doses.

As we approach the turn of the century, in this steam powered, industrial age at the close of the1800s, we have lived these many years mostly undercover. Helping other musicians play the magical music of the soul. The kind of music that moves you in waves of goodness and pleasure. We felt that in this new age, we could come out and let everyone know exactly who we are! Hence this interview! We've lived through centuries of music and love them all! So at any given Clockwork Knotwork show, you will hear music dating from the Renaissance, through the Age of Enlightenment, into the Modern Age. And having dabbled in time-travel here and there, we also borrow from ages yet to come.

In closing, we would love to offer up our latest creation, "Elixir Mandragora" it is an original musical tale meant to be heard in its entirety. Follow the story of a young Irish immigrant who finds himself in New Orleans in the year 1903. He meets the store keep of a Curio shop, who is also the "Keeper" of both a mandrake root and an ancient recipe for the all healing, Elixir Mandragora, the Tea of Legend & Lore. Experience the transformation as this lowly immigrant becomes the nationwide sensation known as, "The Apothecary!" But everything comes with a price, while healing them all, can he save himself from what is to come? We are elated and excited to present this work to the world! Cheers!

Get the music and more at www.ClockworkKnotwork.com

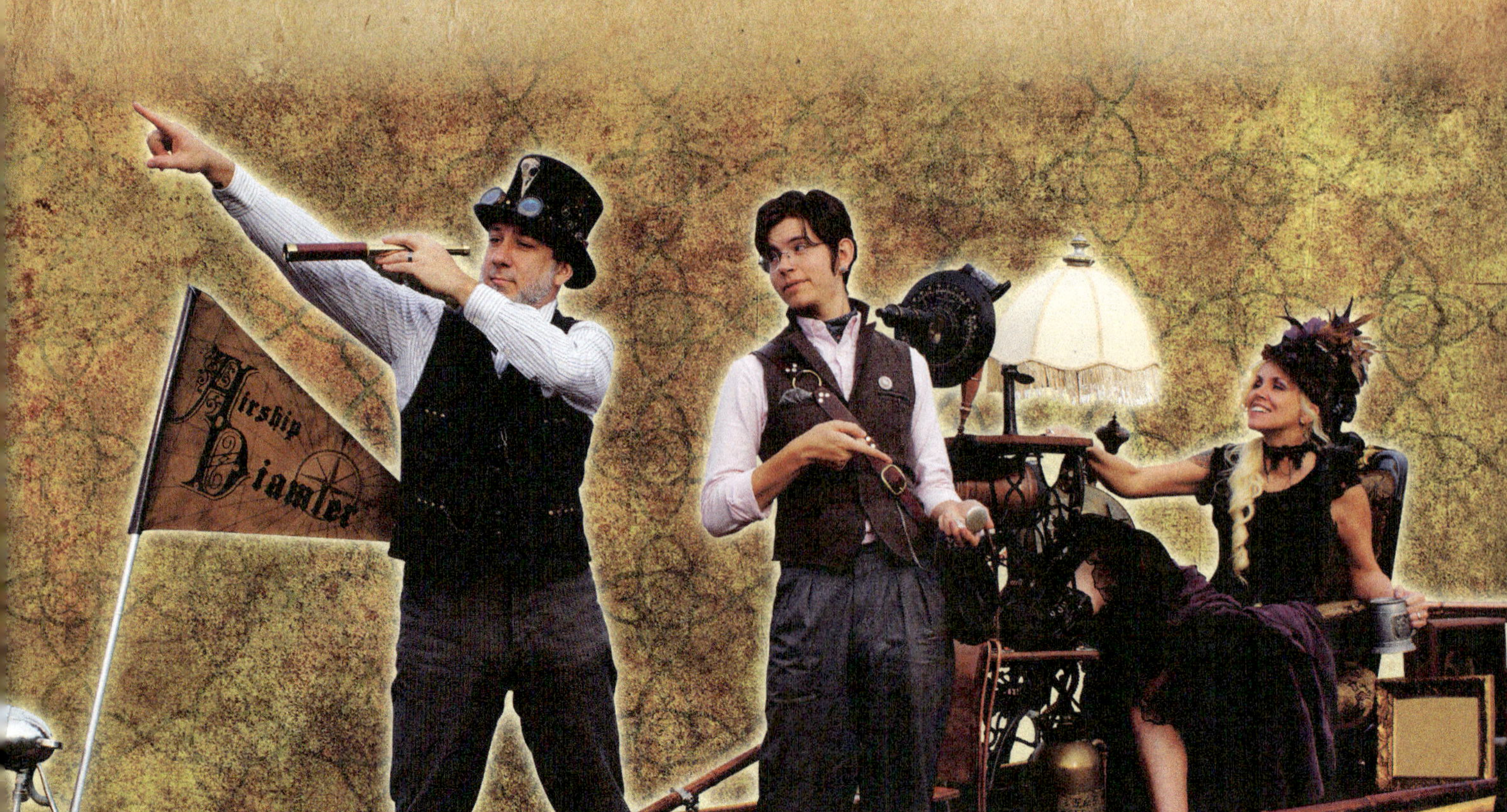

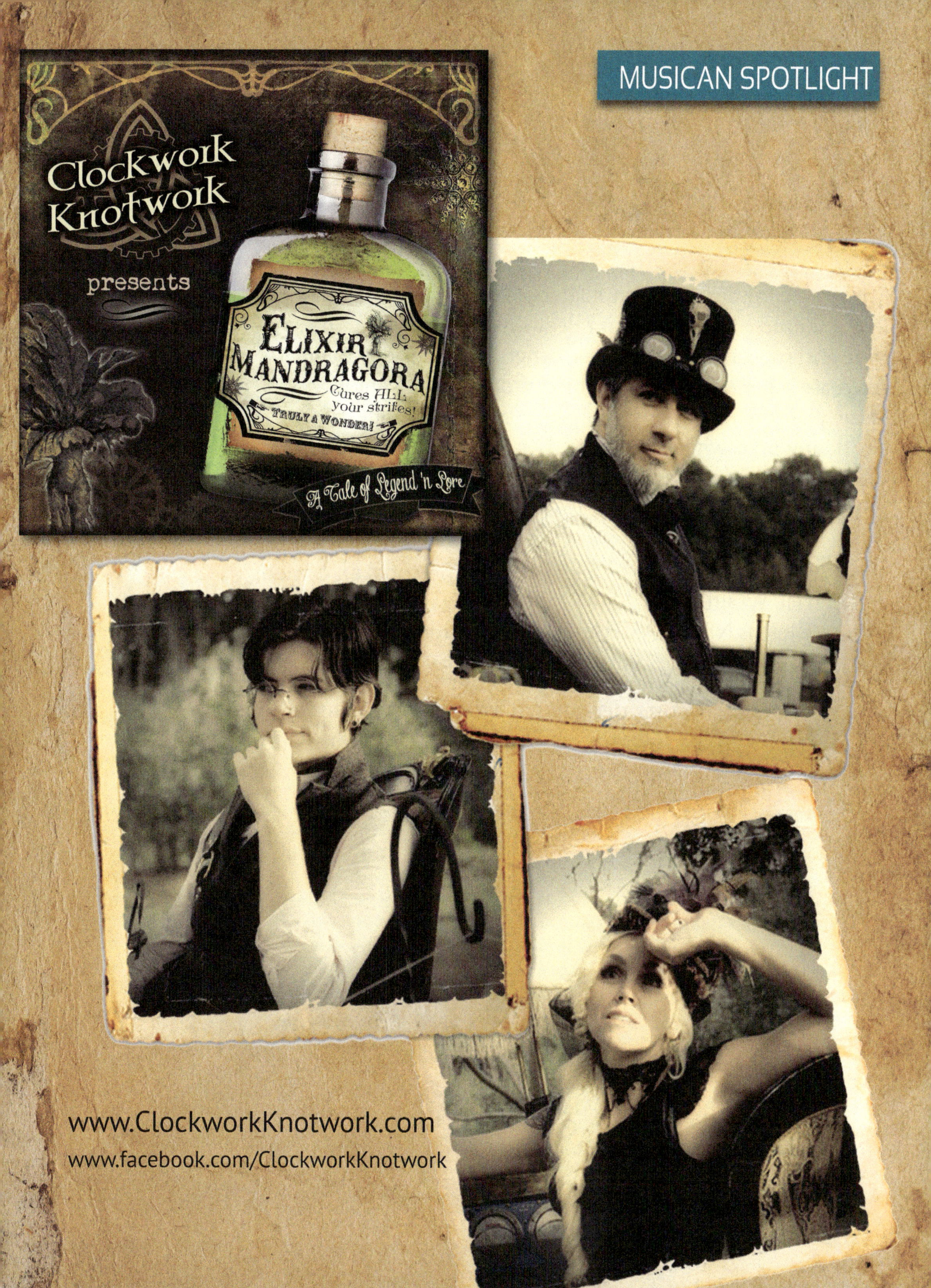
MUSICAN SPOTLIGHT
Clockwork Knotwork
presents
ELIXIR MANDRAGORA
Cures ALL your strifes!
TRULY A WONDER!
A Tale of Legend 'n Lore
www.ClockworkKnotwork.com
www.facebook.com/ClockworkKnotwork

SPOTLIGHT FEATURE

There are a lot of truly talented people out there, especially in our culture. Some use this talent simply for passing the time and personal growth, while others develop their talent to create services, works and objects for others to enjoy. Some post their creations on their website and never try to sell their works, while others use their talents to supplement or create their income. Carpe Nocturne Magazine admires, respects, and supports YOUR TALENT!

Whether you are creating to sell or only for personal enjoyment, LET THE WORLD SEE WHAT YOU'VE GOT! There is NEVER A CHARGE to be Spotlighted or Featured!

The feature within Carpe Nocturne Magazine spotlights artists, designers, photographers, crafters and others with a creative side.

Does your work relate to the subject matter of this publication. Whether you do what you do for self-enjoyment or to sell your craft, we support you.

Contact: art@CarpeNocturneMagazine.com
Subject Line: Spotlight Feature

ARTIST • CRAFTER • DESIGNER • MUSICIAN • PHOTOGRAPHER